Vol. 2

By Aya Kanno

HAMBURG // LONDON // LOS ANGELES // TOKYO

Soul Rescue Volume 2
Created by Aya Kanno

Translation - Christine Schilling
English Adaptation - Meadow Jones
Retouch and Lettering - Star Print Brokers
Production Artist - Courtney Geter
Graphic Designer - John Lo

Editor - Katherine Schilling
Digital Imaging Manager - Chris Buford
Pre-Production Supervisor - Erika Terriquez
Art Director - Anne Marie Horne
Production Manager - Elisabeth Brizzi
Managing Editor - Vy Nguyen
VP of Production - Ron Klamert
Editor-in-Chief - Rob Tokar
Publisher - Mike Kiley
President and C.O.O. - John Parker
C.E.O. and Chief Creative Officer - Stuart Levy

A **TOKYOPOP** Manga

TOKYOPOP and are trademarks or registered trademarks of TOKYOPOP Inc.

TOKYOPOP Inc.
5900 Wilshire Blvd. Suite 2000
Los Angeles, CA 90036

E-mail: info@TOKYOPOP.com
Come visit us online at www.TOKYOPOP.com

SOUL RESCUE by Aya Kanno © 2001 Aya Kanno All rights reserved. First published in Japan in 2002 by HAKUSENSHA, INC., Tokyo English language translation rights in the United States of America and Canada arranged with HAKUSENSHA, INC., Tokyo through Tuttle-Mori Agency Inc., Tokyo English text copyright © 2007 TOKYOPOP Inc.

ISBN: 978-1-59816-673-6

First TOKYOPOP printing: April 2007
10 9 8 7 6 5 4 3 2 1
Printed in the USA

Soul Rescue

Aya Kanno

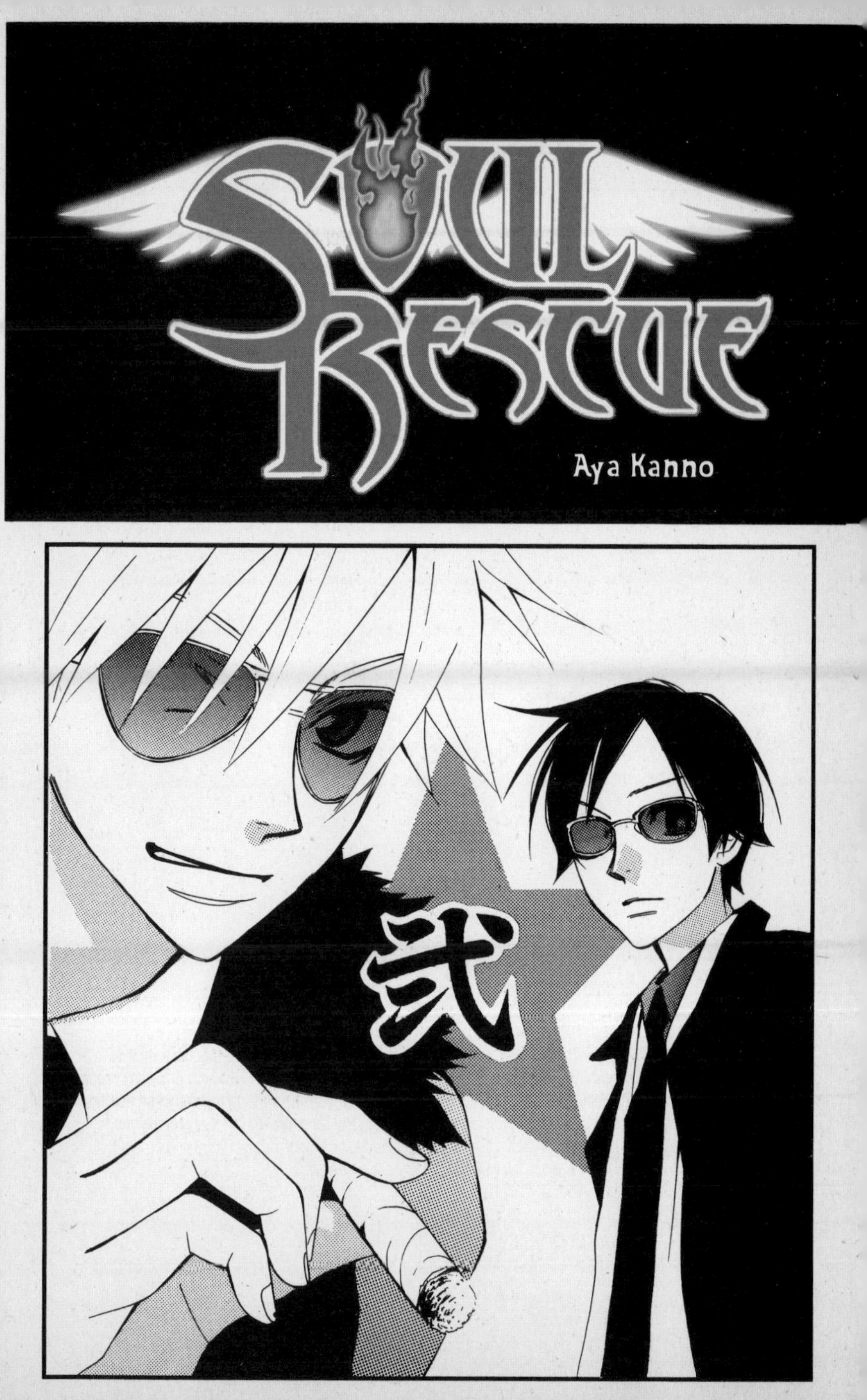
弐

Table of Contents

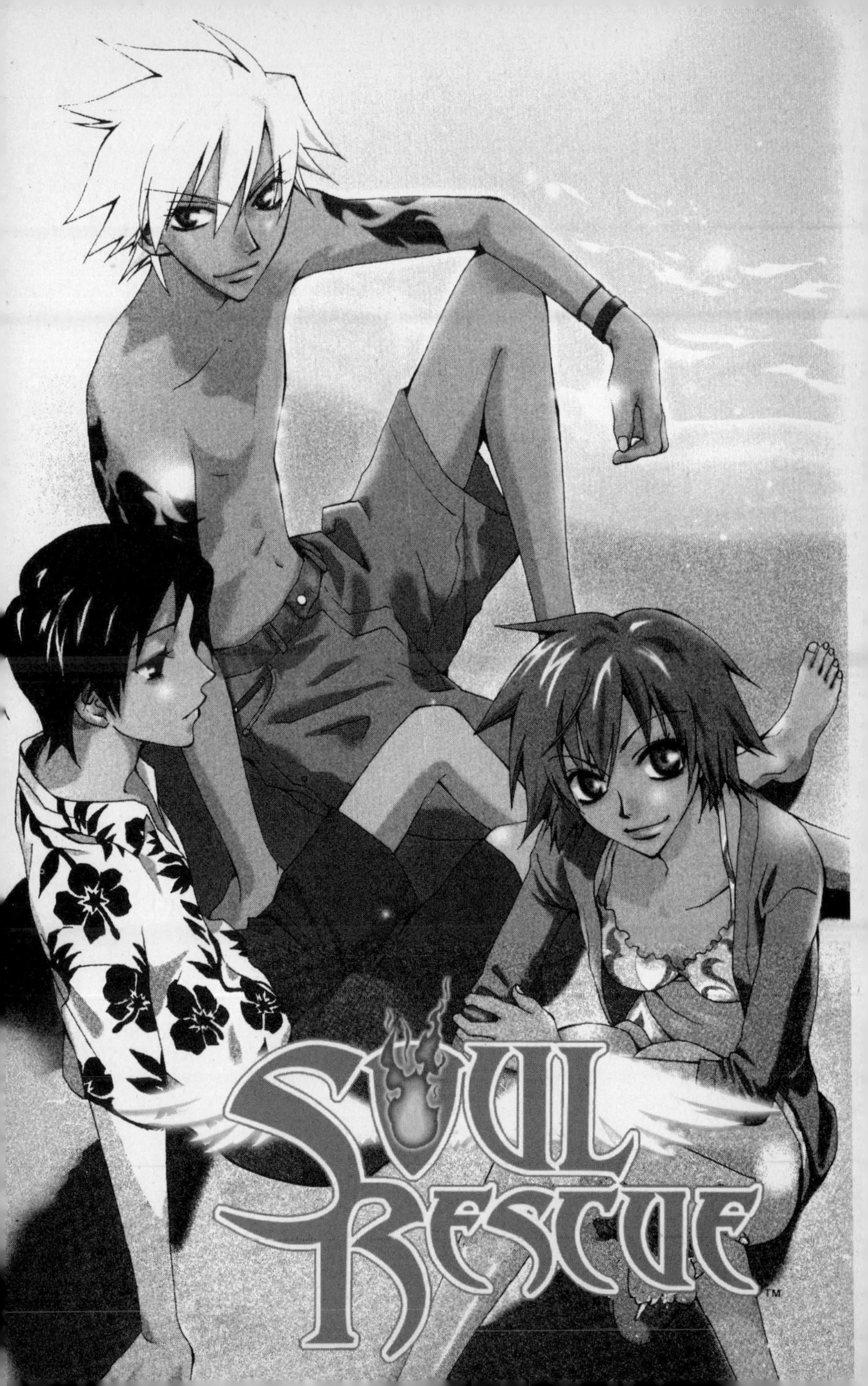
SOUL RESCUE™

SR

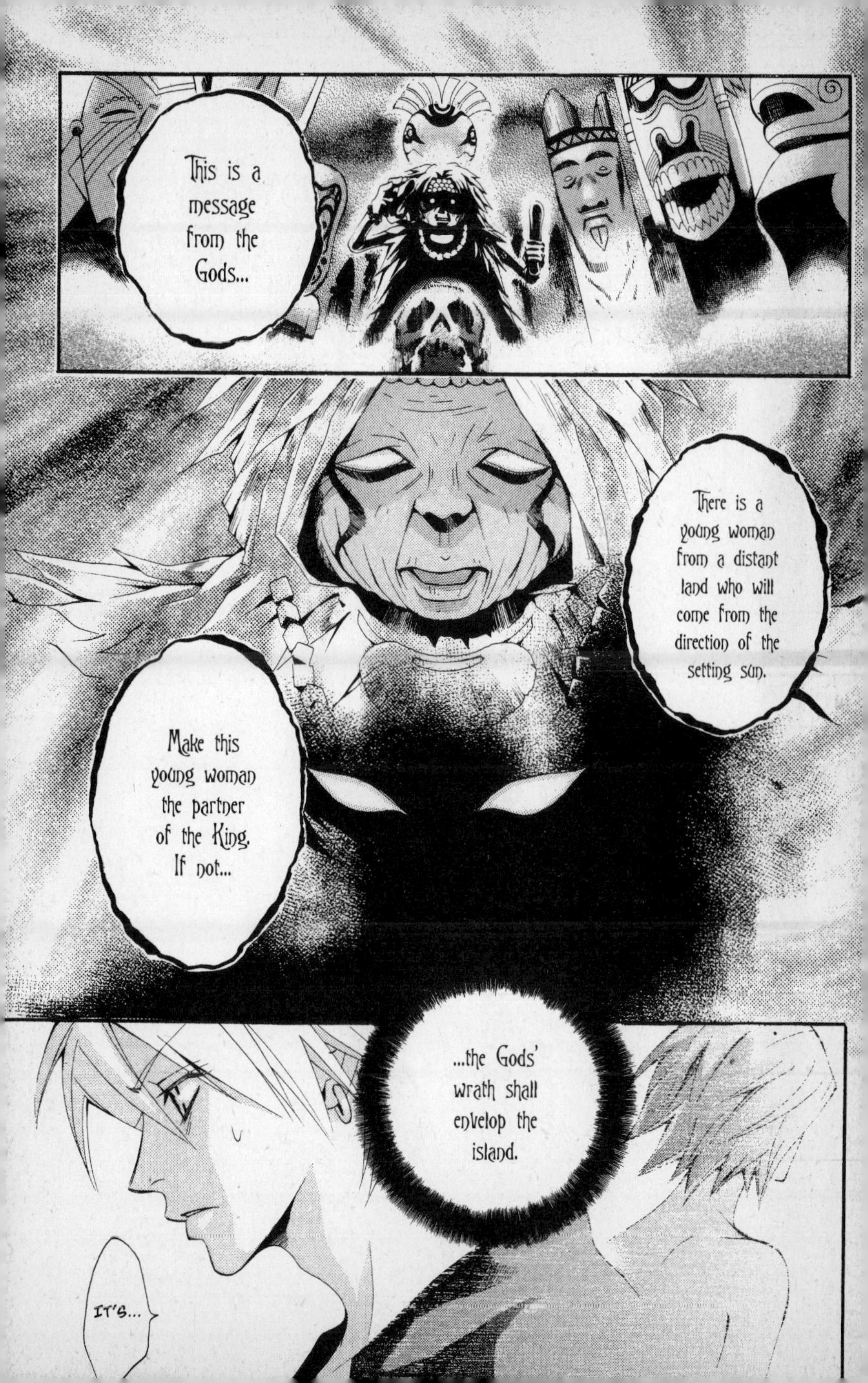
This is a message from the Gods...
There is a young woman from a distant land who will come from the direction of the setting sun.
Make this young woman the partner of the King. If not...
...the Gods' wrath shall envelop the island.
IT'S...

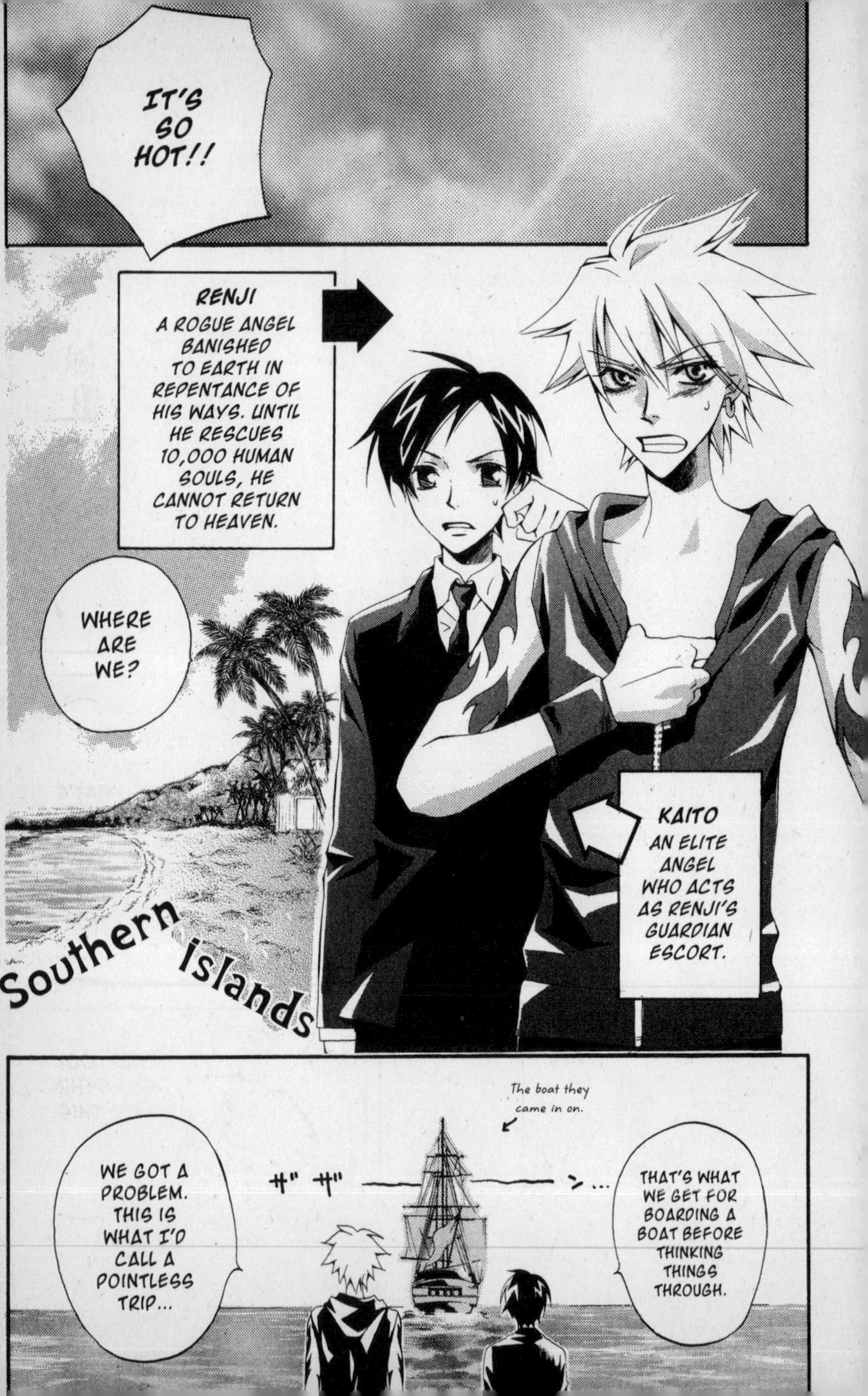

IT'S SO HOT!!
RENJI
A ROGUE ANGEL BANISHED TO EARTH IN REPENTANCE OF HIS WAYS. UNTIL HE RESCUES 10,000 HUMAN SOULS, HE CANNOT RETURN TO HEAVEN.
KAITO
AN ELITE ANGEL WHO ACTS AS RENJI'S GUARDIAN ESCORT.
WHERE ARE WE?
Southern Islands
THAT'S WHAT WE GET FOR BOARDING A BOAT BEFORE THINKING THINGS THROUGH.
The boat they came in on.
ザ ザ
WE GOT A PROBLEM. THIS IS WHAT I'D CALL A POINTLESS TRIP...

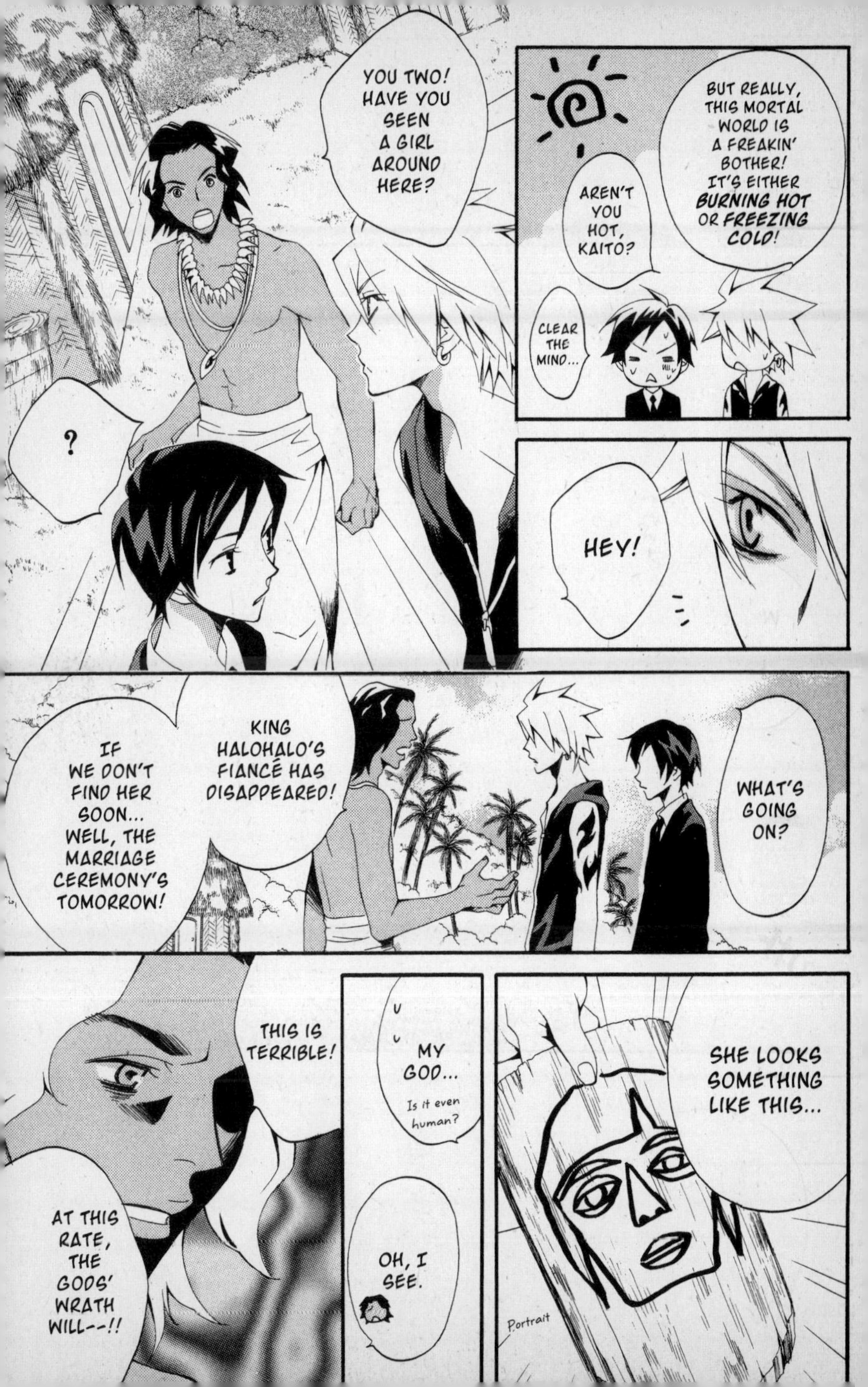
BUT REALLY, THIS MORTAL WORLD IS A FREAKIN' BOTHER! IT'S EITHER BURNING HOT OR FREEZING COLD!
AREN'T YOU HOT, KAITO?
CLEAR THE MIND...
HEY!
YOU TWO! HAVE YOU SEEN A GIRL AROUND HERE?
?
WHAT'S GOING ON?
KING HALOHALO'S FIANCÉ HAS DISAPPEARED!
IF WE DON'T FIND HER SOON... WELL, THE MARRIAGE CEREMONY'S TOMORROW!
SHE LOOKS SOMETHING LIKE THIS...
Portrait
MY GOD...
Is it even human?
OH, I SEE.
THIS IS TERRIBLE!
AT THIS RATE, THE GODS' WRATH WILL--!!

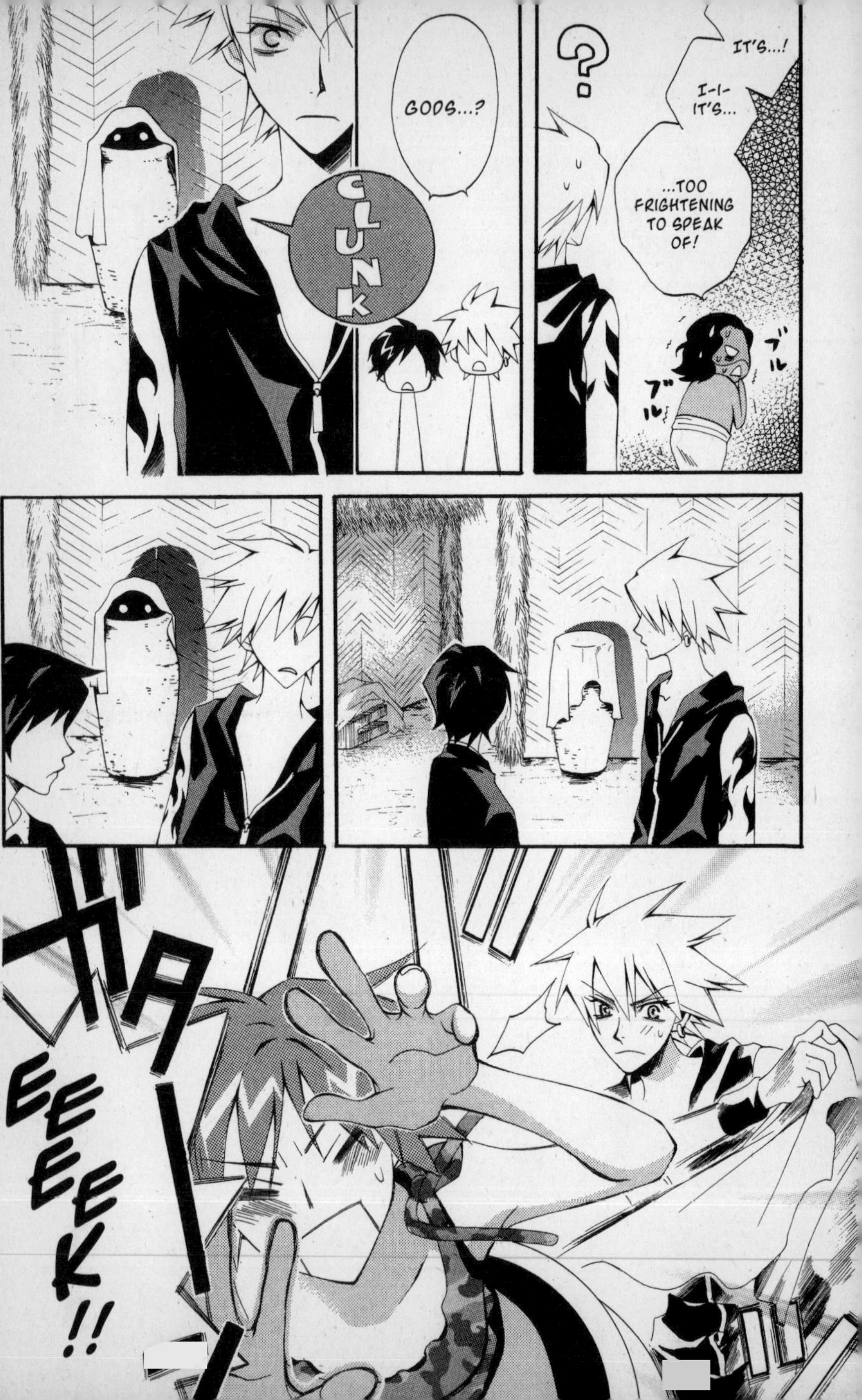
?
IT'S...!
I-I-IT'S...
...TOO FRIGHTENING TO SPEAK OF!
ブル
ブル
GODS...?
CLUNK
HYA—EEEEK!!

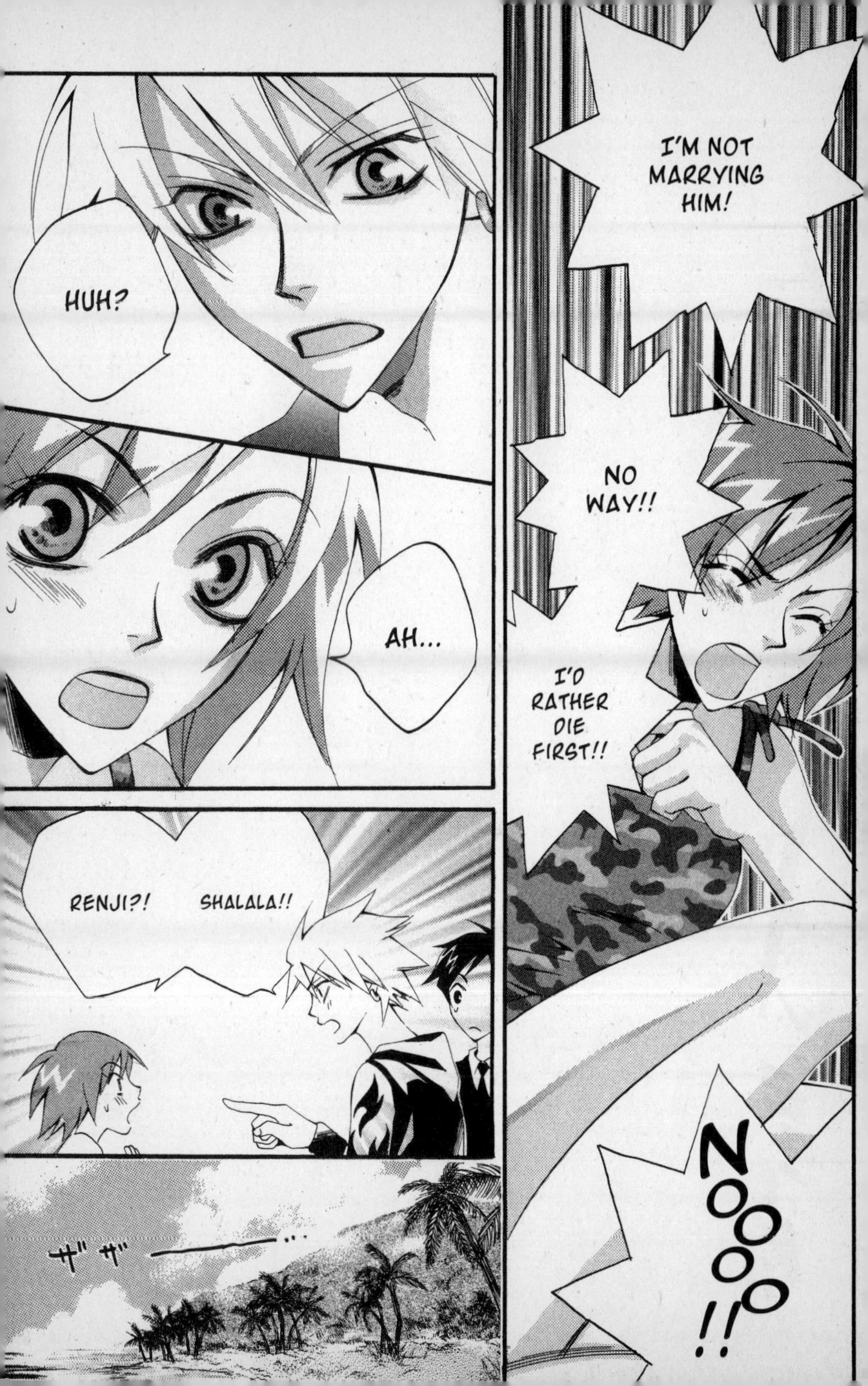
I'M NOT MARRYING HIM!
NO WAY!!
I'D RATHER DIE FIRST!!
NOOOO!!
HUH?
AH...
RENJI?! SHALALA!!
ザザ——…

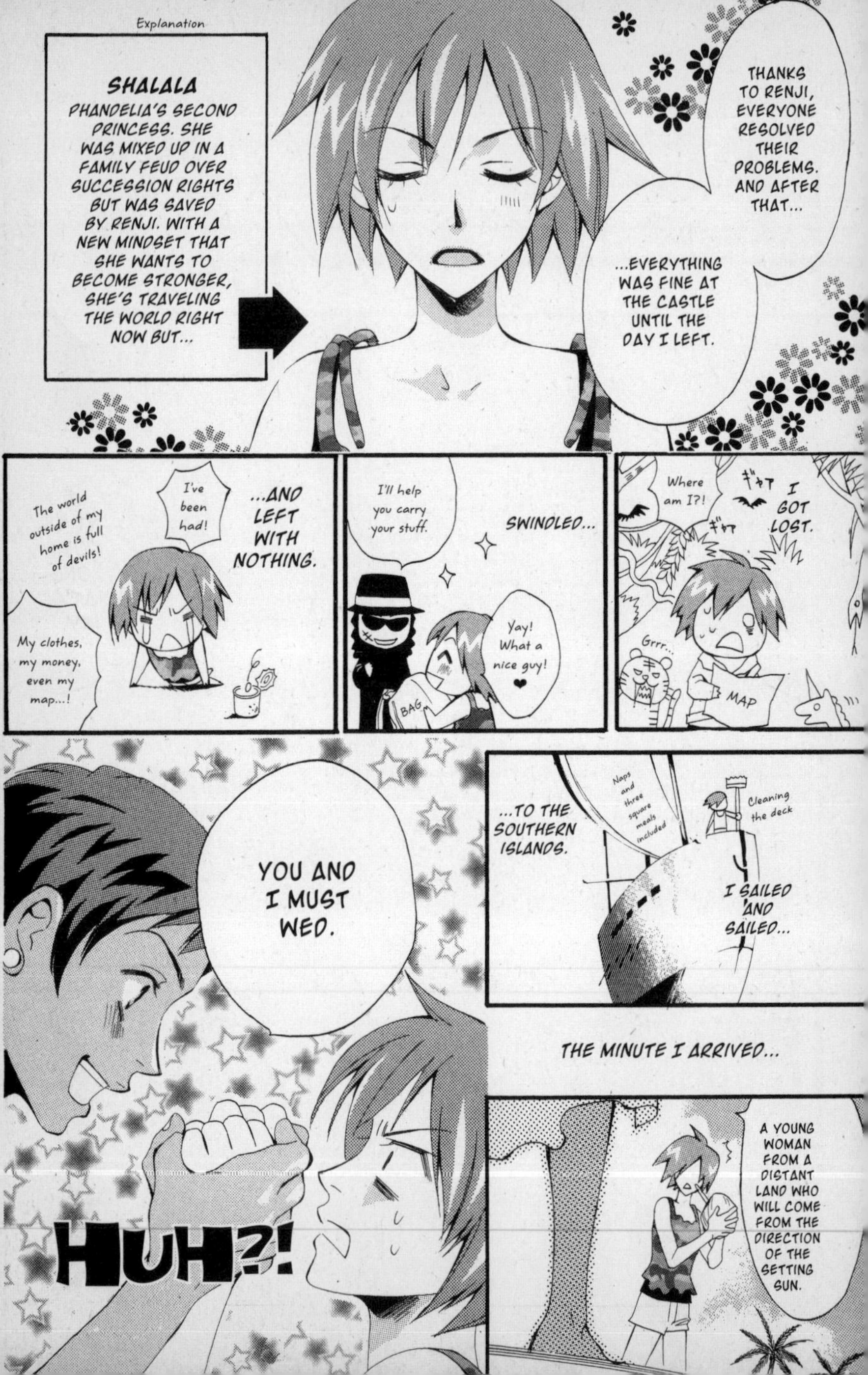
THANKS TO RENJI, EVERYONE RESOLVED THEIR PROBLEMS. AND AFTER THAT...
...EVERYTHING WAS FINE AT THE CASTLE UNTIL THE DAY I LEFT.
Explanation
SHALALA
PHANDELIA'S SECOND PRINCESS. SHE WAS MIXED UP IN A FAMILY FEUD OVER SUCCESSION RIGHTS BUT WAS SAVED BY RENJI. WITH A NEW MINDSET THAT SHE WANTS TO BECOME STRONGER, SHE'S TRAVELING THE WORLD RIGHT NOW BUT...
Where am I?!
I GOT LOST.
Grrr...
MAP
I'll help you carry your stuff.
SWINDLED...
Yay! What a nice guy!
BAG
...AND LEFT WITH NOTHING.
I've been had!
The world outside of my home is full of devils!
My clothes, my money, even my map...!
Cleaning the deck
Naps and three square meals included
I SAILED AND SAILED...
...TO THE SOUTHERN ISLANDS.
THE MINUTE I ARRIVED...
A YOUNG WOMAN FROM A DISTANT LAND WHO WILL COME FROM THE DIRECTION OF THE SETTING SUN.
YOU AND I MUST WED.
HUH?!

SR

I'm happy to see you all again!! This is Kanno and this is the second volume of Soul Rescue! The second volume! Wee!! This is all thanks to my readers. Thank you!!

For this chapter about Shalala's reappearance, I used images of the Bahamas and the like for the background to make for an overall southern island feeling. Though I think I ended up drawing it like it was a resort or something. Even though in reality, I'm sitting here in this tiny apartment downtown sweating at my desk...and it's summer! Summer!! But it's okay. As long as I can go to a rock concert. I'm happy if I can have my live performances... Spring, Summer, Fall, and Winter = Plenty of shows!

Aaah...but where I really want to go is the tropics.

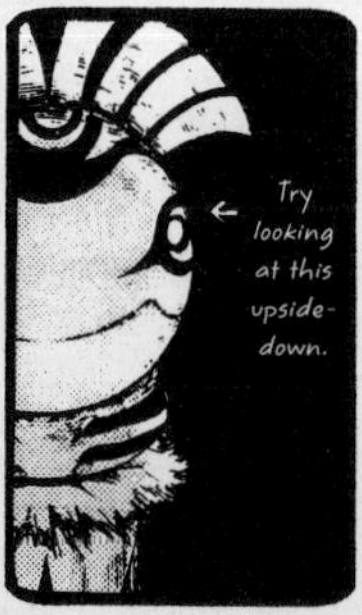
← Try looking at this upside-down.

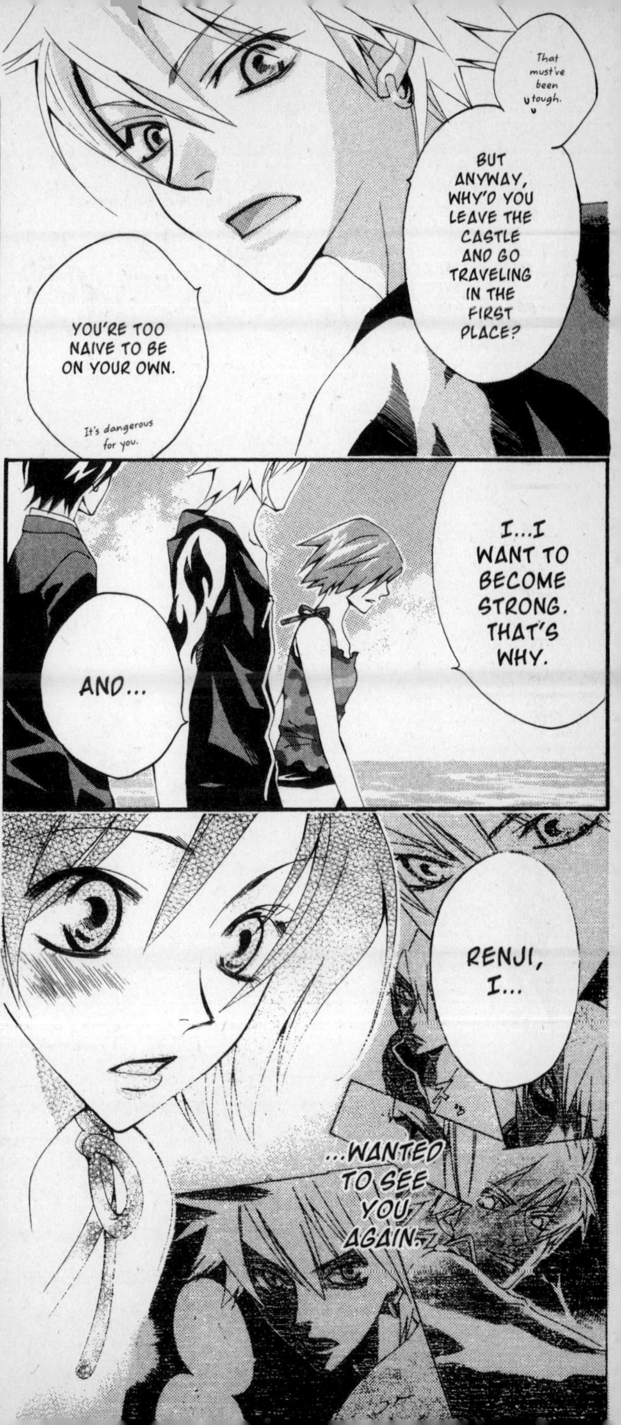
That must've been tough.
BUT ANYWAY, WHY'D YOU LEAVE THE CASTLE AND GO TRAVELING IN THE FIRST PLACE?
YOU'RE TOO NAIVE TO BE ON YOUR OWN.
It's dangerous for you.
I...I WANT TO BECOME STRONG. THAT'S WHY.
AND...
RENJI, I...
...WANTED TO SEE YOU AGAIN.

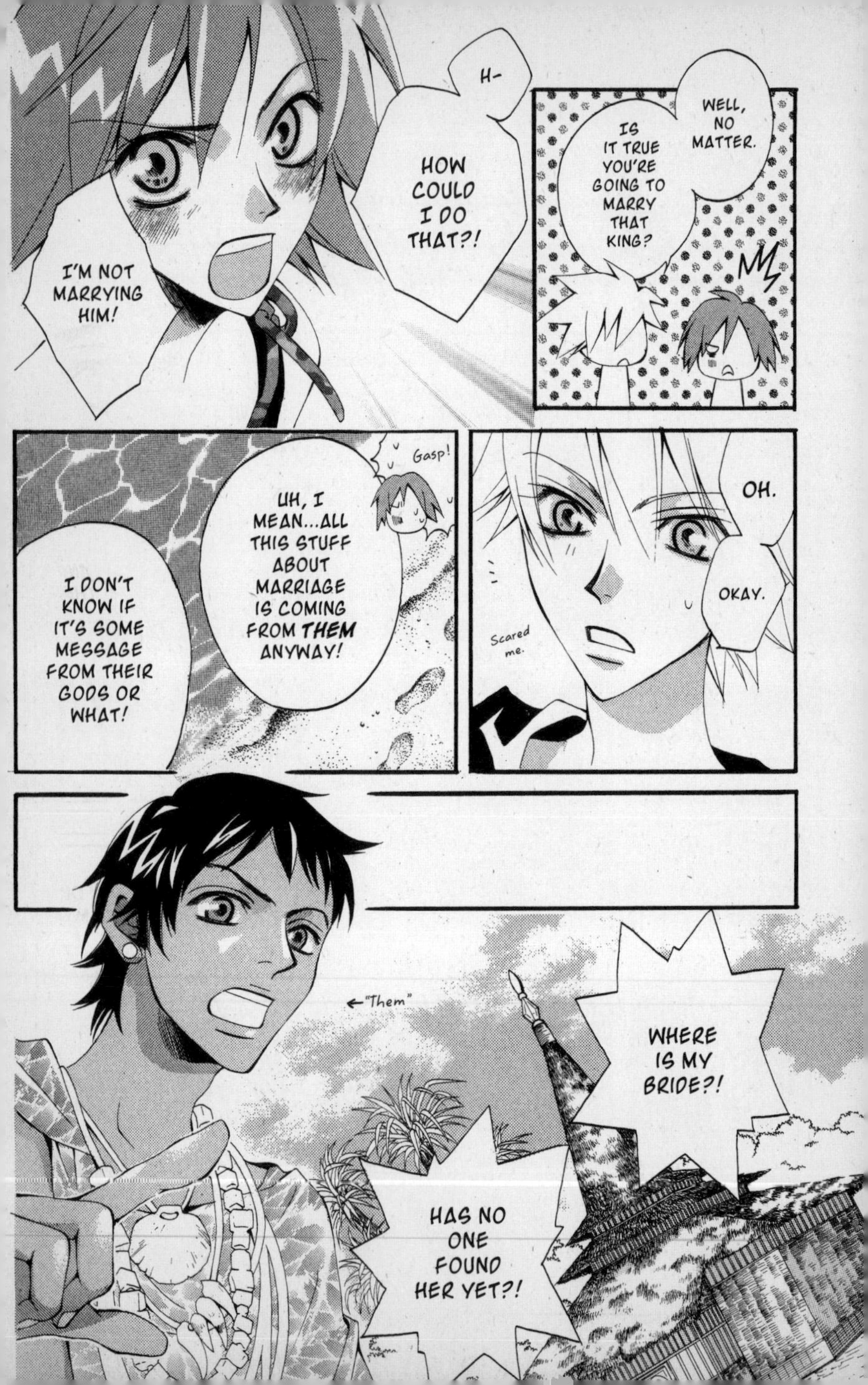
WELL, NO MATTER.
IS IT TRUE YOU'RE GOING TO MARRY THAT KING?
H-
HOW COULD I DO THAT?!
I'M NOT MARRYING HIM!
OH.
OKAY.
Scared me.
Gasp!
UH, I MEAN...ALL THIS STUFF ABOUT MARRIAGE IS COMING FROM **THEM** ANYWAY!
I DON'T KNOW IF IT'S SOME MESSAGE FROM THEIR GODS OR WHAT!
WHERE IS MY BRIDE?!
HAS NO ONE FOUND HER YET?!
←"Them"

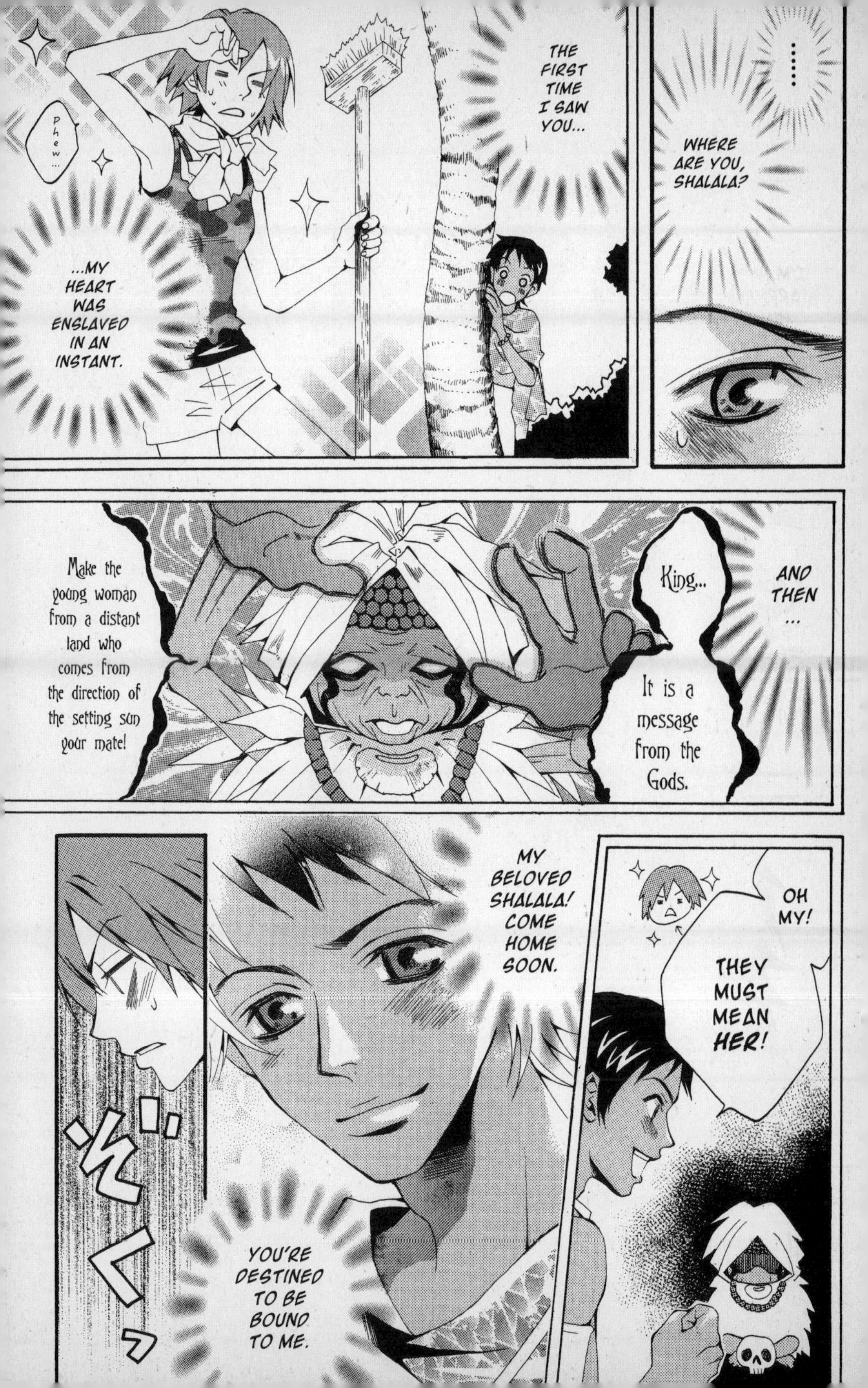
......
WHERE ARE YOU, SHALALA?
THE FIRST TIME I SAW YOU...
Phew...
...MY HEART WAS ENSLAVED IN AN INSTANT.
AND THEN...
King...
It is a message from the Gods.
Make the young woman from a distant land who comes from the direction of the setting sun your mate!
OH MY!
THEY MUST MEAN HER!
MY BELOVED SHALALA! COME HOME SOON.
YOU'RE DESTINED TO BE BOUND TO ME.

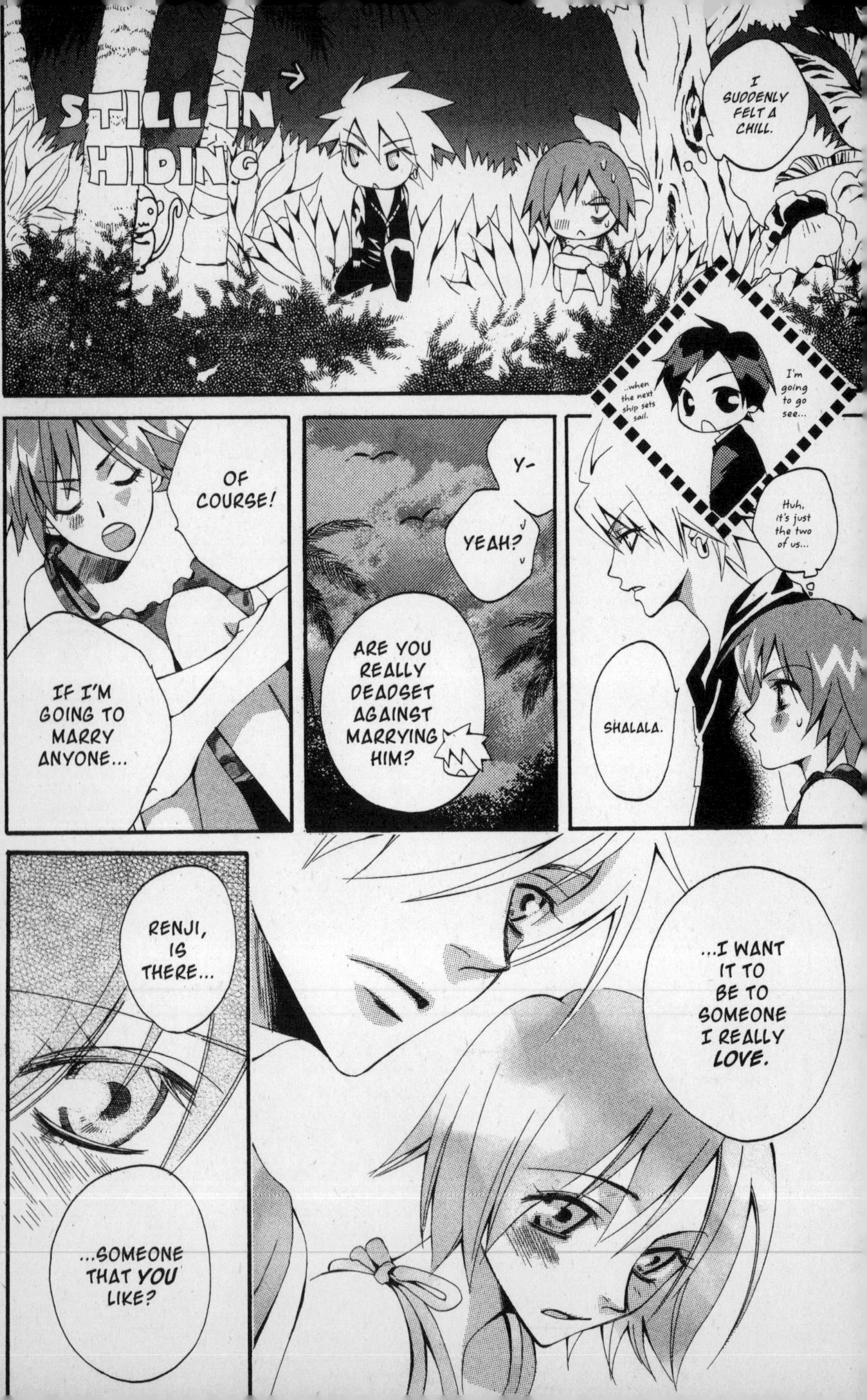
I SUDDENLY FELT A CHILL.
STILL IN HIDING
I'm going to go see...
...when the next ship sets sail.
Huh, it's just the two of us...
SHALALA.
Y-
YEAH?
ARE YOU REALLY DEADSET AGAINST MARRYING HIM?
OF COURSE!
IF I'M GOING TO MARRY ANYONE...
...I WANT IT TO BE TO SOMEONE I REALLY LOVE.
RENJI, IS THERE...
...SOMEONE THAT YOU LIKE?

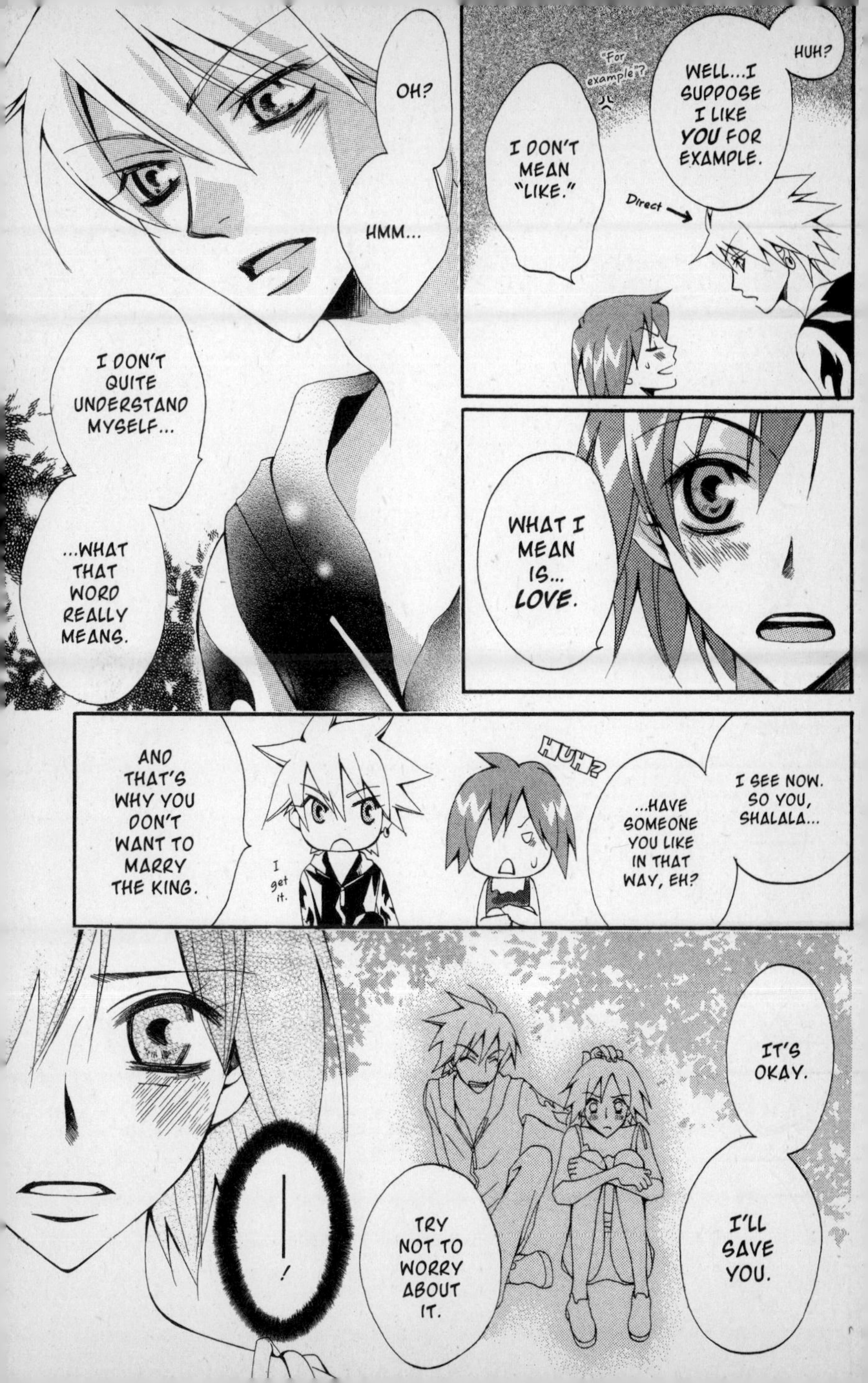
HUH?
WELL...I SUPPOSE I LIKE YOU FOR EXAMPLE.
Direct
"For example"?
I DON'T MEAN "LIKE."
WHAT I MEAN IS... LOVE.
OH?
HMM...
I DON'T QUITE UNDERSTAND MYSELF...
...WHAT THAT WORD REALLY MEANS.
I SEE NOW. SO YOU, SHALALA...
...HAVE SOMEONE YOU LIKE IN THAT WAY, EH?
HUH?
AND THAT'S WHY YOU DON'T WANT TO MARRY THE KING.
I get it.
IT'S OKAY.
I'LL SAVE YOU.
TRY NOT TO WORRY ABOUT IT.
!

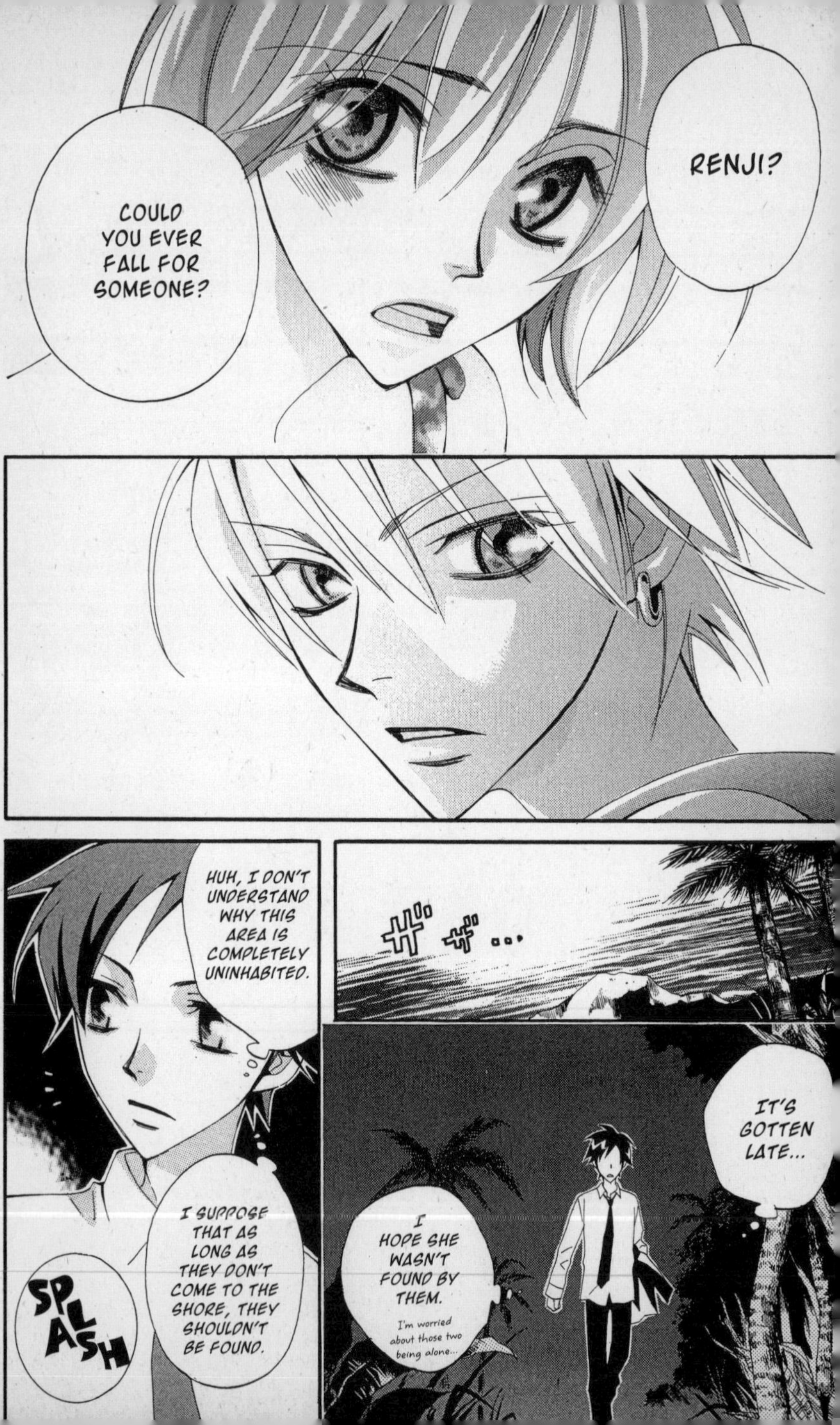
RENJI?
COULD YOU EVER FALL FOR SOMEONE?
ザザ...
IT'S GOTTEN LATE...
I HOPE SHE WASN'T FOUND BY THEM.
I'm worried about those two being alone...
HUH, I DON'T UNDERSTAND WHY THIS AREA IS COMPLETELY UNINHABITED.
I SUPPOSE THAT AS LONG AS THEY DON'T COME TO THE SHORE, THEY SHOULDN'T BE FOUND.
SPLASH

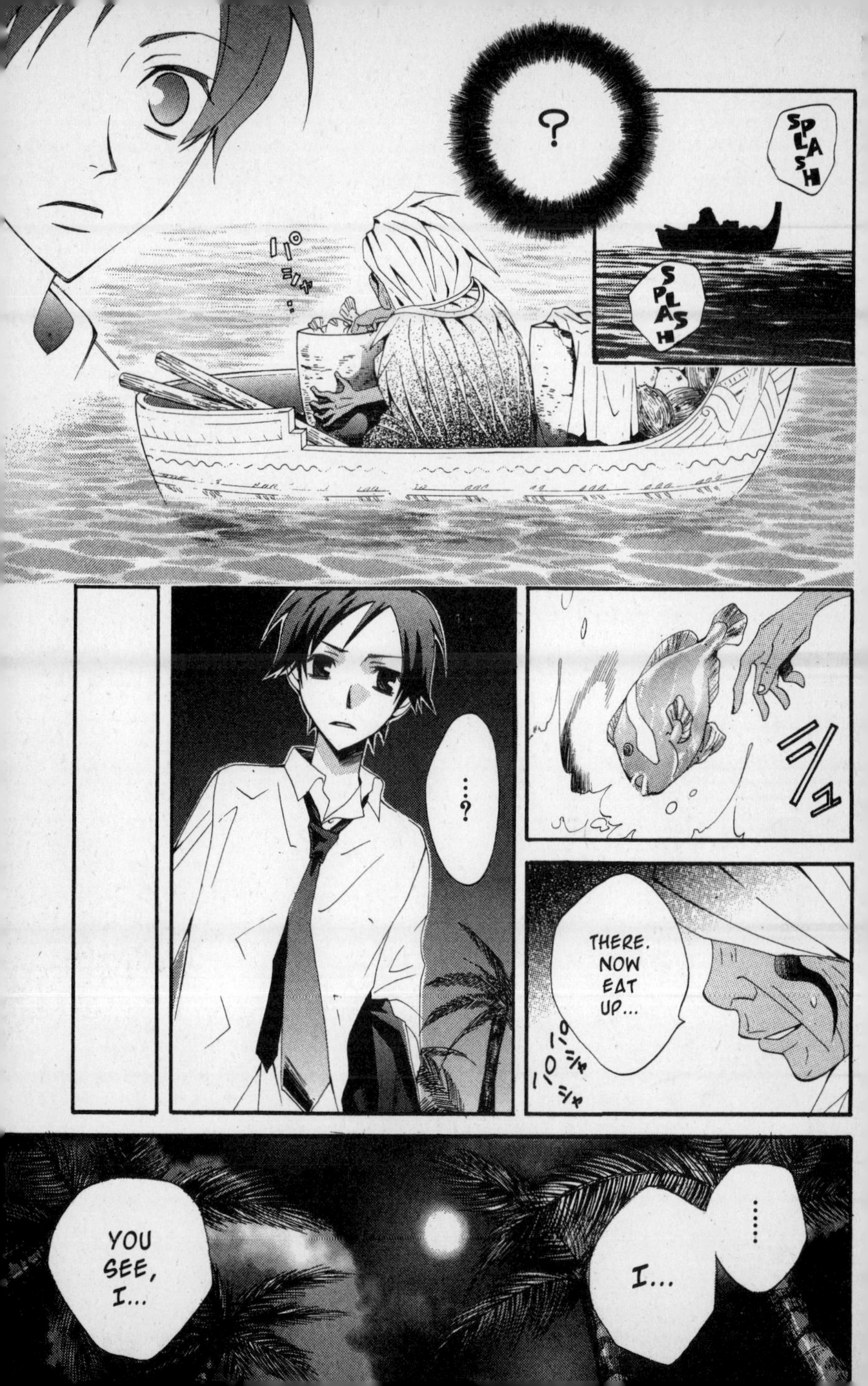
SPLASH
?
SPLASH
THERE. NOW EAT UP...
...?
......
I...
YOU SEE, I...

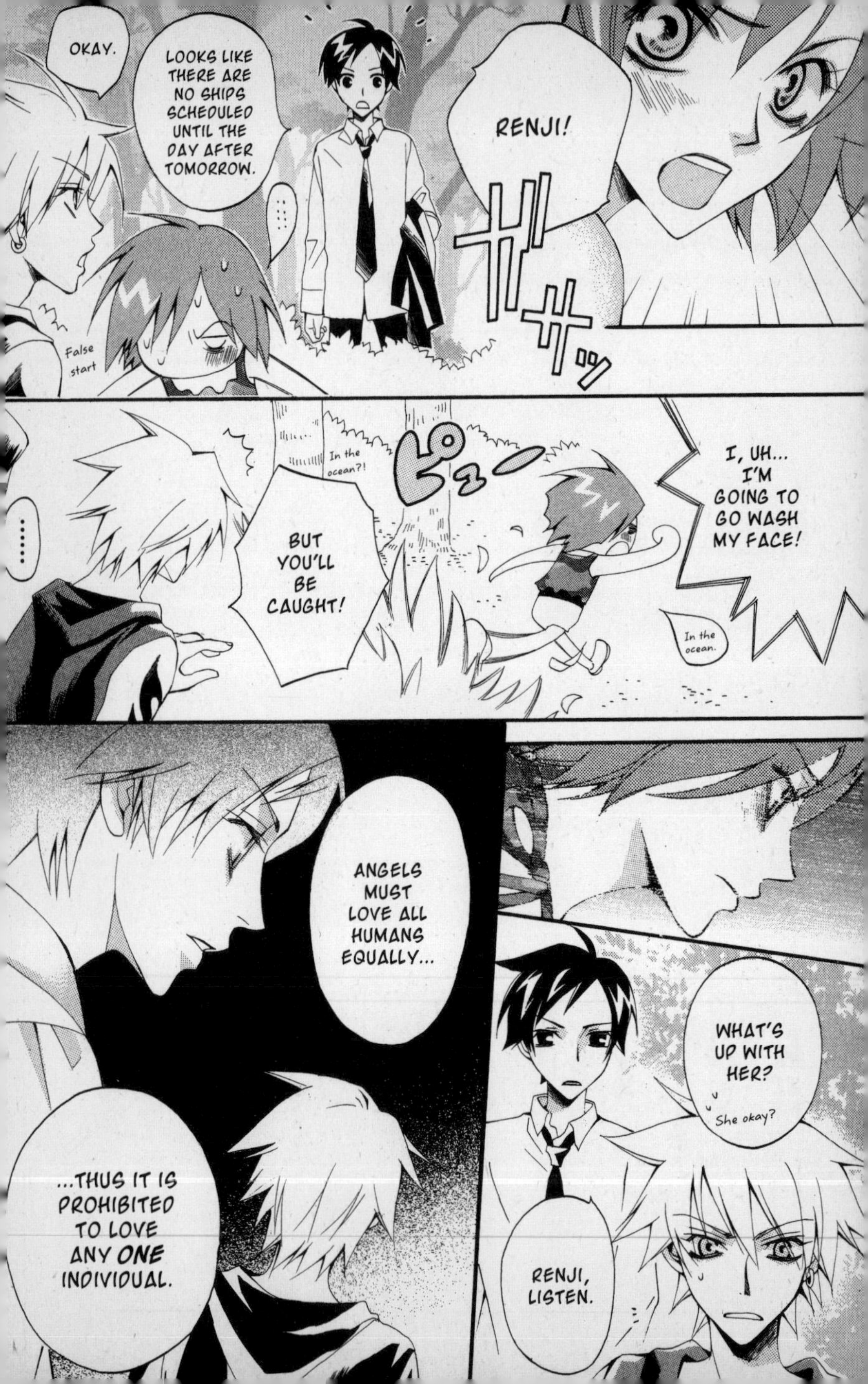
RENJI!
ガサッ
LOOKS LIKE THERE ARE NO SHIPS SCHEDULED UNTIL THE DAY AFTER TOMORROW.
OKAY.
False start
I, UH... I'M GOING TO GO WASH MY FACE!
In the ocean.
In the ocean?!
BUT YOU'LL BE CAUGHT!
......
WHAT'S UP WITH HER?
She okay?
RENJI, LISTEN.
ANGELS MUST LOVE ALL HUMANS EQUALLY...
...THUS IT IS PROHIBITED TO LOVE ANY ONE INDIVIDUAL.

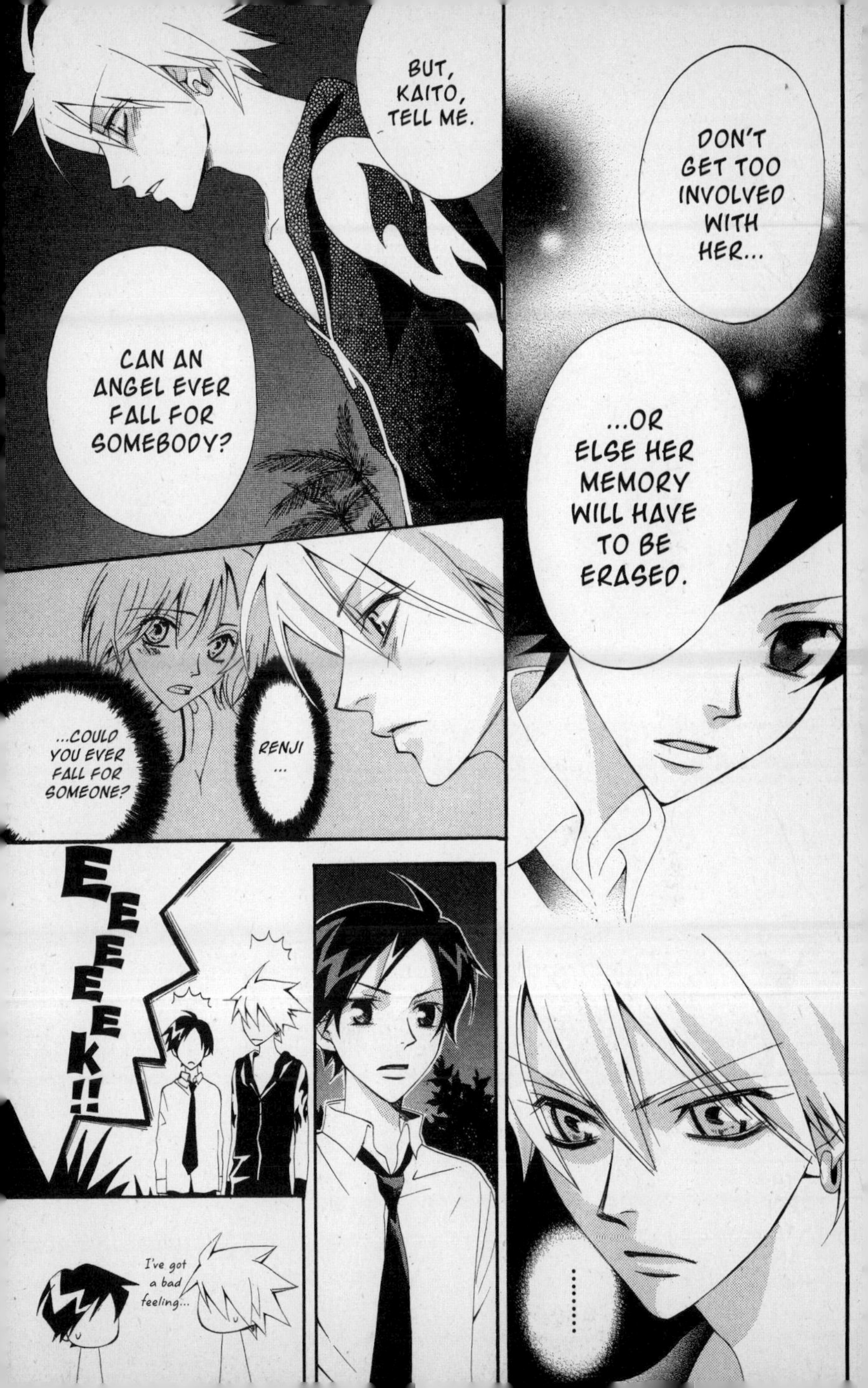
DON'T GET TOO INVOLVED WITH HER...
...OR ELSE HER MEMORY WILL HAVE TO BE ERASED.
BUT, KAITO, TELL ME.
CAN AN ANGEL EVER FALL FOR SOMEBODY?
RENJI ...
...COULD YOU EVER FALL FOR SOMEONE?
......
EEEEEK!!
I've got a bad feeling...

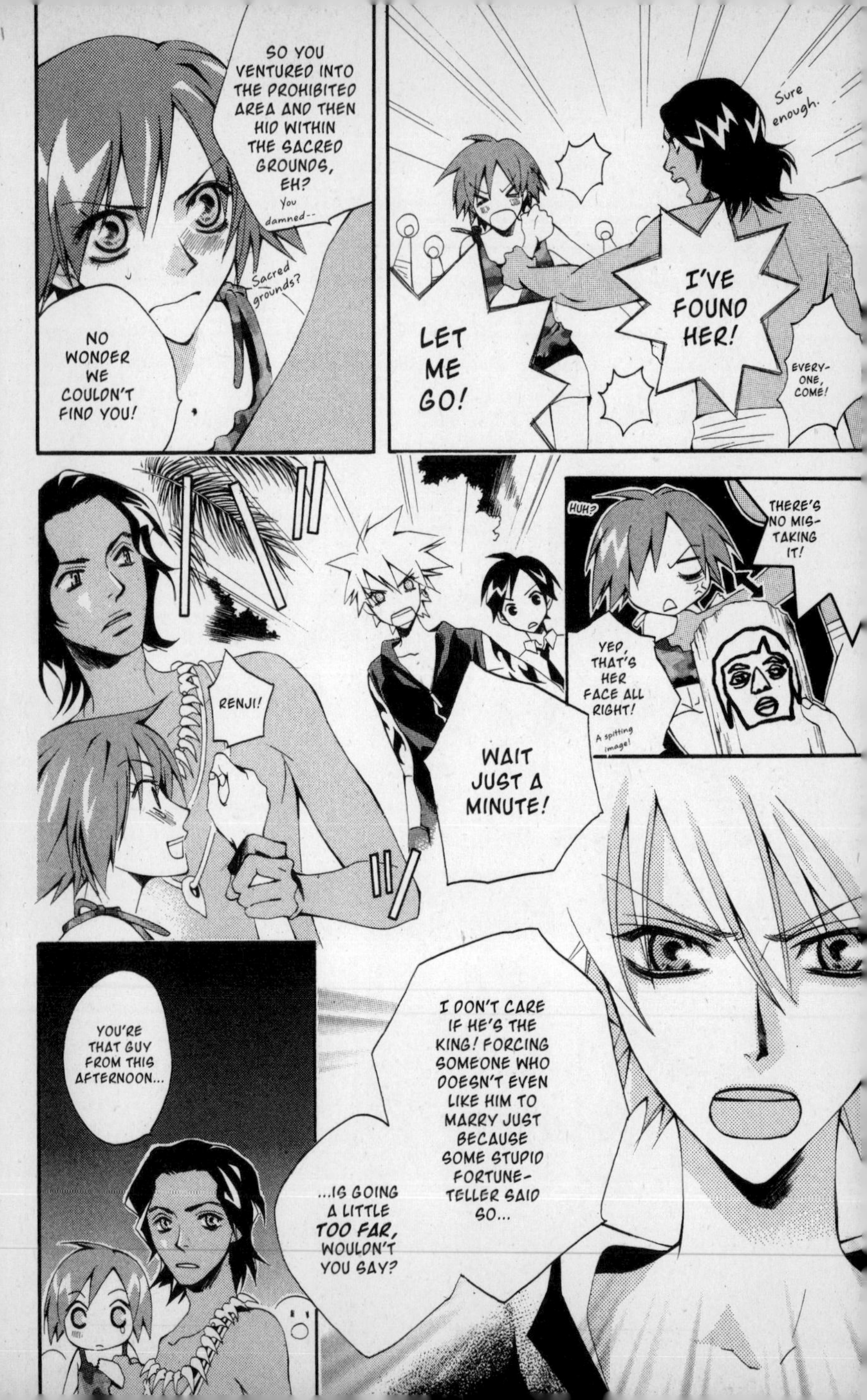

Sure enough.
I'VE FOUND HER!
EVERY-ONE, COME!
LET ME GO!
SO YOU VENTURED INTO THE PROHIBITED AREA AND THEN HID WITHIN THE SACRED GROUNDS, EH?
You damned--
Sacred grounds?
NO WONDER WE COULDN'T FIND YOU!
THERE'S NO MIS-TAKING IT!
HUH?
YEP, THAT'S HER FACE ALL RIGHT!
A spitting image!
WAIT JUST A MINUTE!
RENJI!
I DON'T CARE IF HE'S THE KING! FORCING SOMEONE WHO DOESN'T EVEN LIKE HIM TO MARRY JUST BECAUSE SOME STUPID FORTUNE-TELLER SAID SO...
...IS GOING A LITTLE TOO FAR, WOULDN'T YOU SAY?
YOU'RE THAT GUY FROM THIS AFTERNOON...

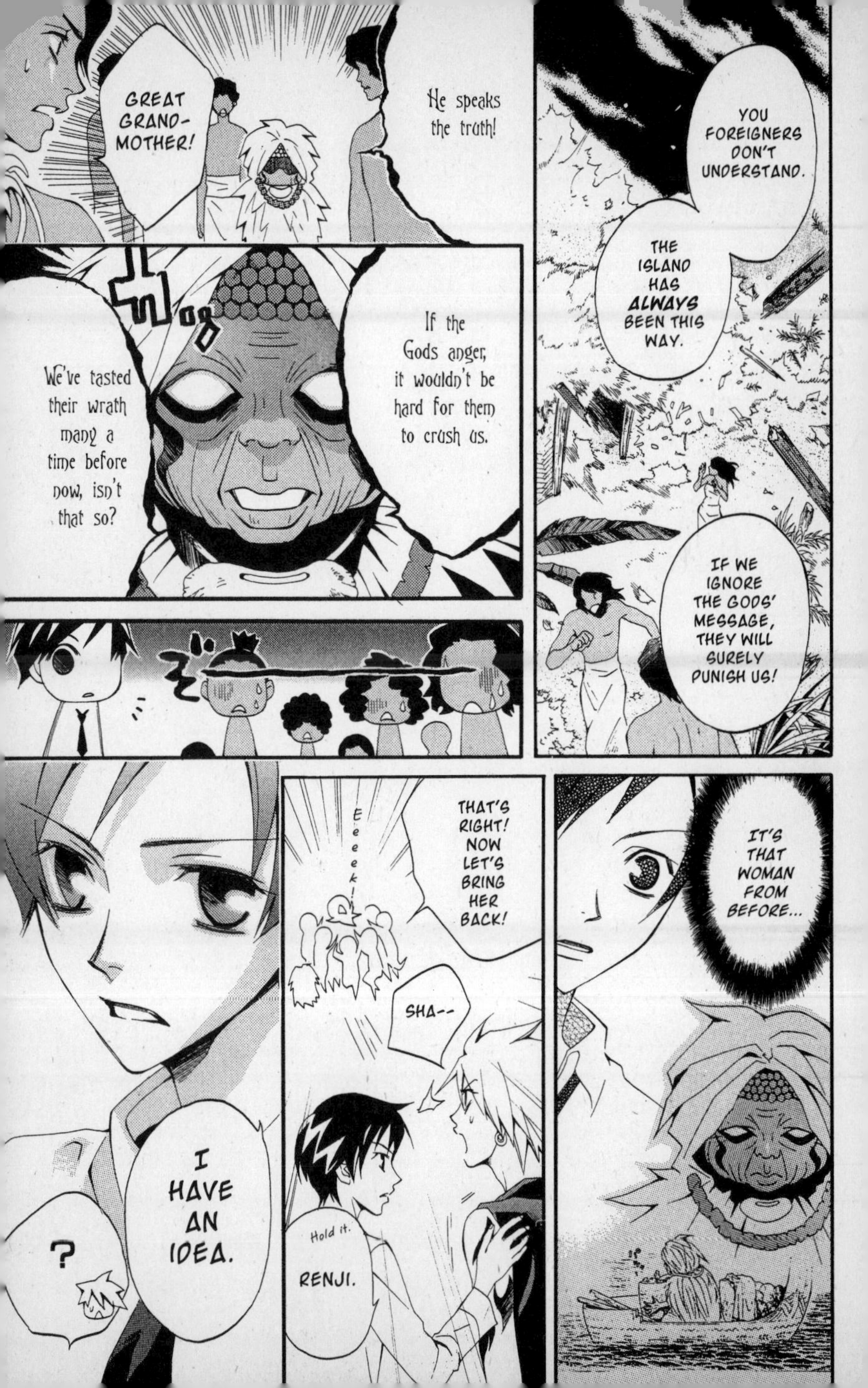

YOU FOREIGNERS DON'T UNDERSTAND.
THE ISLAND HAS **ALWAYS** BEEN THIS WAY.
IF WE IGNORE THE GODS' MESSAGE, THEY WILL SURELY PUNISH US!
He speaks the truth!
GREAT GRAND-MOTHER!
If the Gods anger, it wouldn't be hard for them to crush us.
We've tasted their wrath many a time before now, isn't that so?
IT'S THAT WOMAN FROM BEFORE...
THAT'S RIGHT! NOW LET'S BRING HER BACK!
Eeeeek!
SHA--
Hold it.
RENJI.
I HAVE AN IDEA.
?

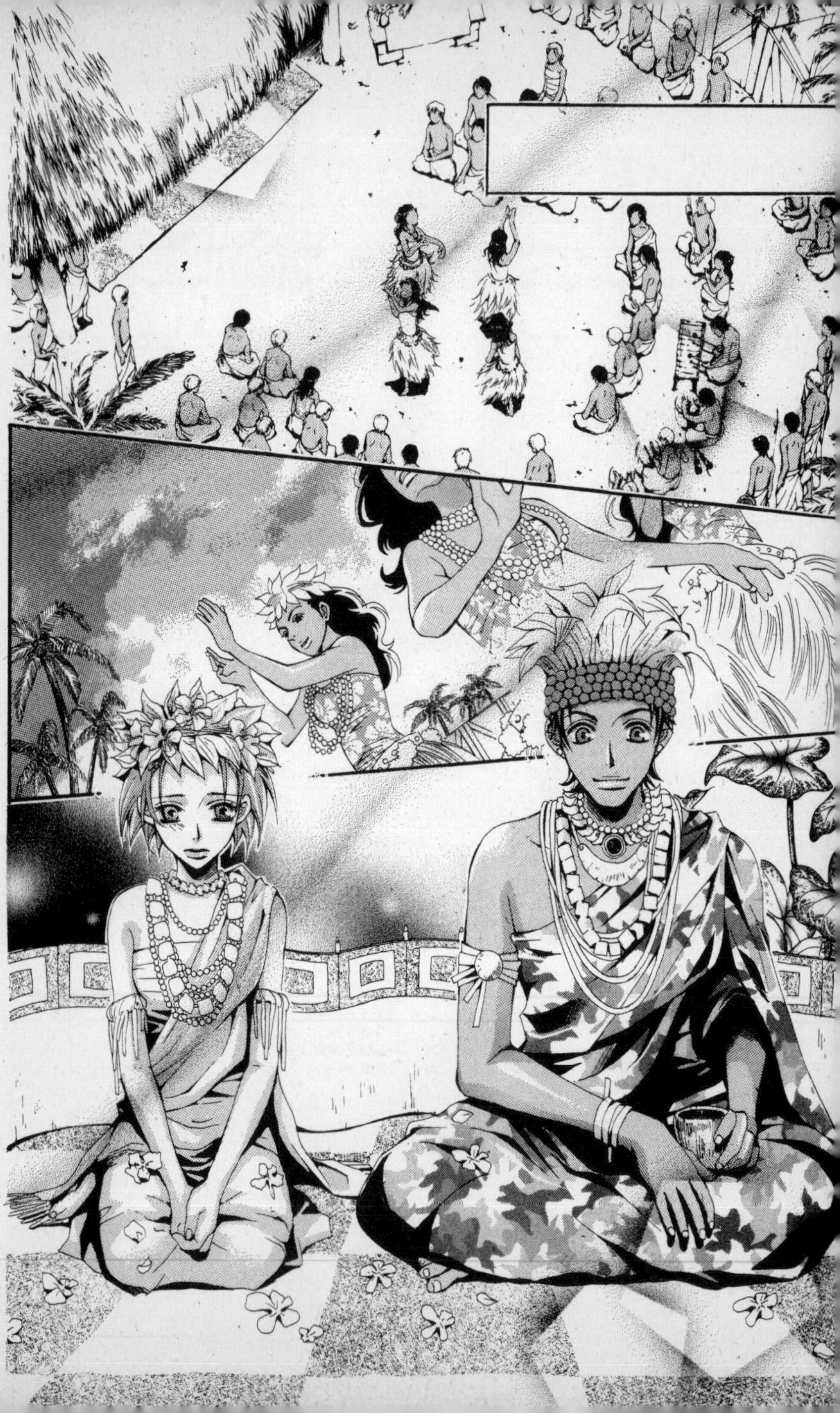

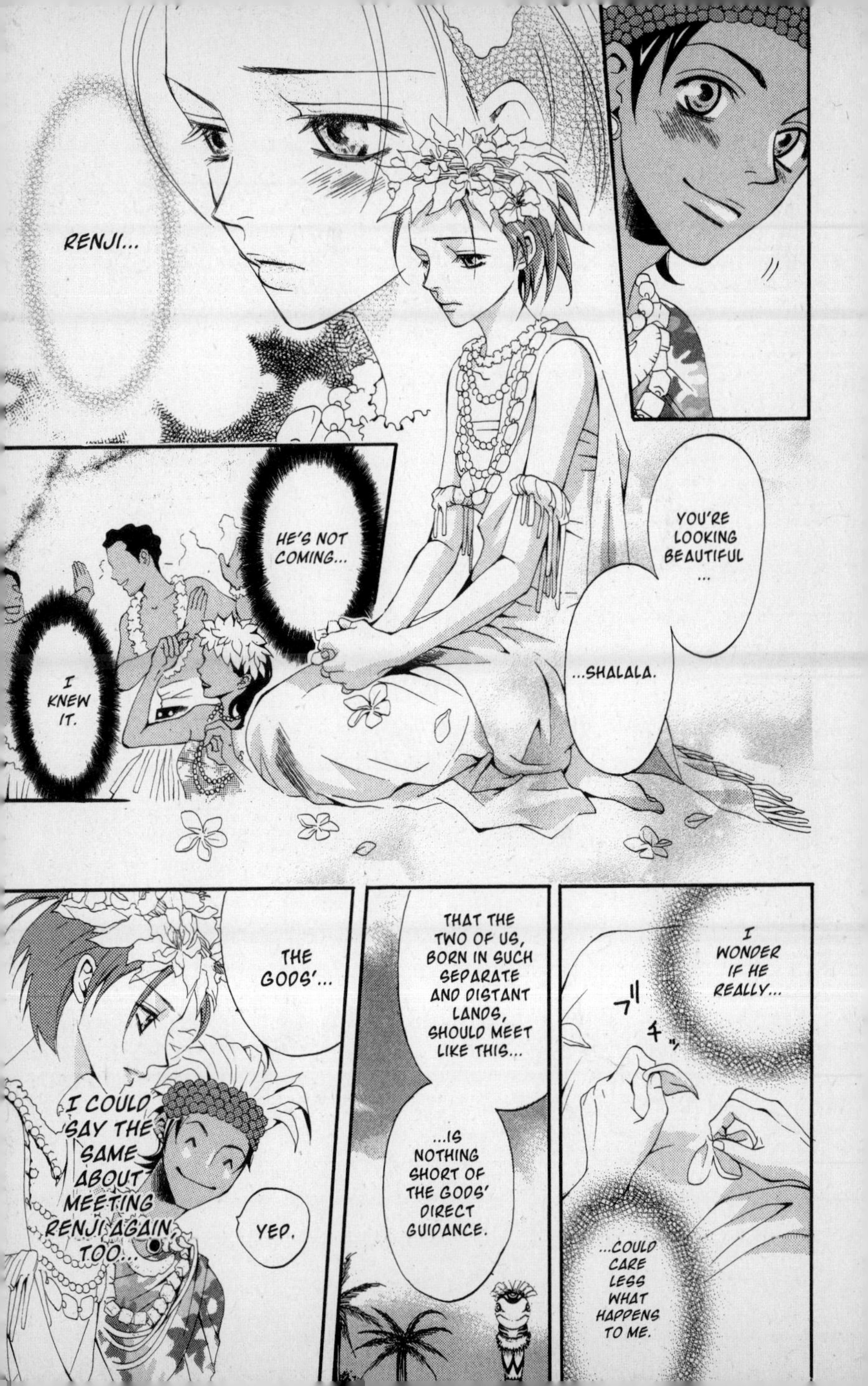
RENJI...
YOU'RE LOOKING BEAUTIFUL ...
...SHALALA.
HE'S NOT COMING...
I KNEW IT.
I WONDER IF HE REALLY...
ブリ
チッ
...COULD CARE LESS WHAT HAPPENS TO ME.
THAT THE TWO OF US, BORN IN SUCH SEPARATE AND DISTANT LANDS, SHOULD MEET LIKE THIS...
...IS NOTHING SHORT OF THE GODS' DIRECT GUIDANCE.
THE GODS'...
YEP.
I COULD SAY THE SAME ABOUT MEETING RENJI AGAIN, TOO...

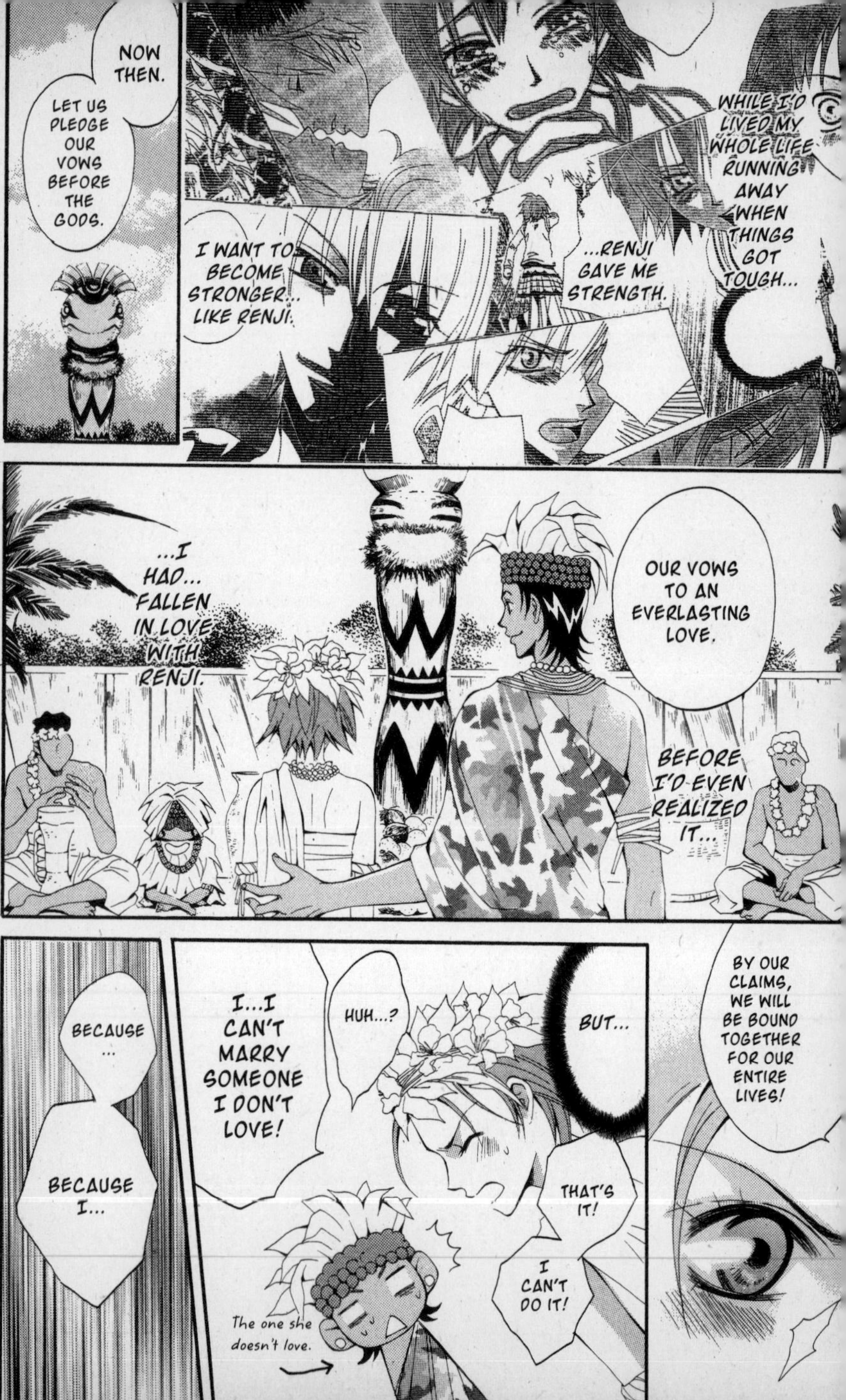
WHILE I'D LIVED MY WHOLE LIFE RUNNING AWAY WHEN THINGS GOT TOUGH...
...RENJI GAVE ME STRENGTH.
I WANT TO BECOME STRONGER... LIKE RENJI.
NOW THEN.
LET US PLEDGE OUR VOWS BEFORE THE GODS.
OUR VOWS TO AN EVERLASTING LOVE.
BEFORE I'D EVEN REALIZED IT...
...I HAD... FALLEN IN LOVE WITH RENJI.
BY OUR CLAIMS, WE WILL BE BOUND TOGETHER FOR OUR ENTIRE LIVES!
BUT...
HUH...?
I...I CAN'T MARRY SOMEONE I DON'T LOVE!
THAT'S IT!
I CAN'T DO IT!
The one she doesn't love.
BECAUSE...
BECAUSE I...

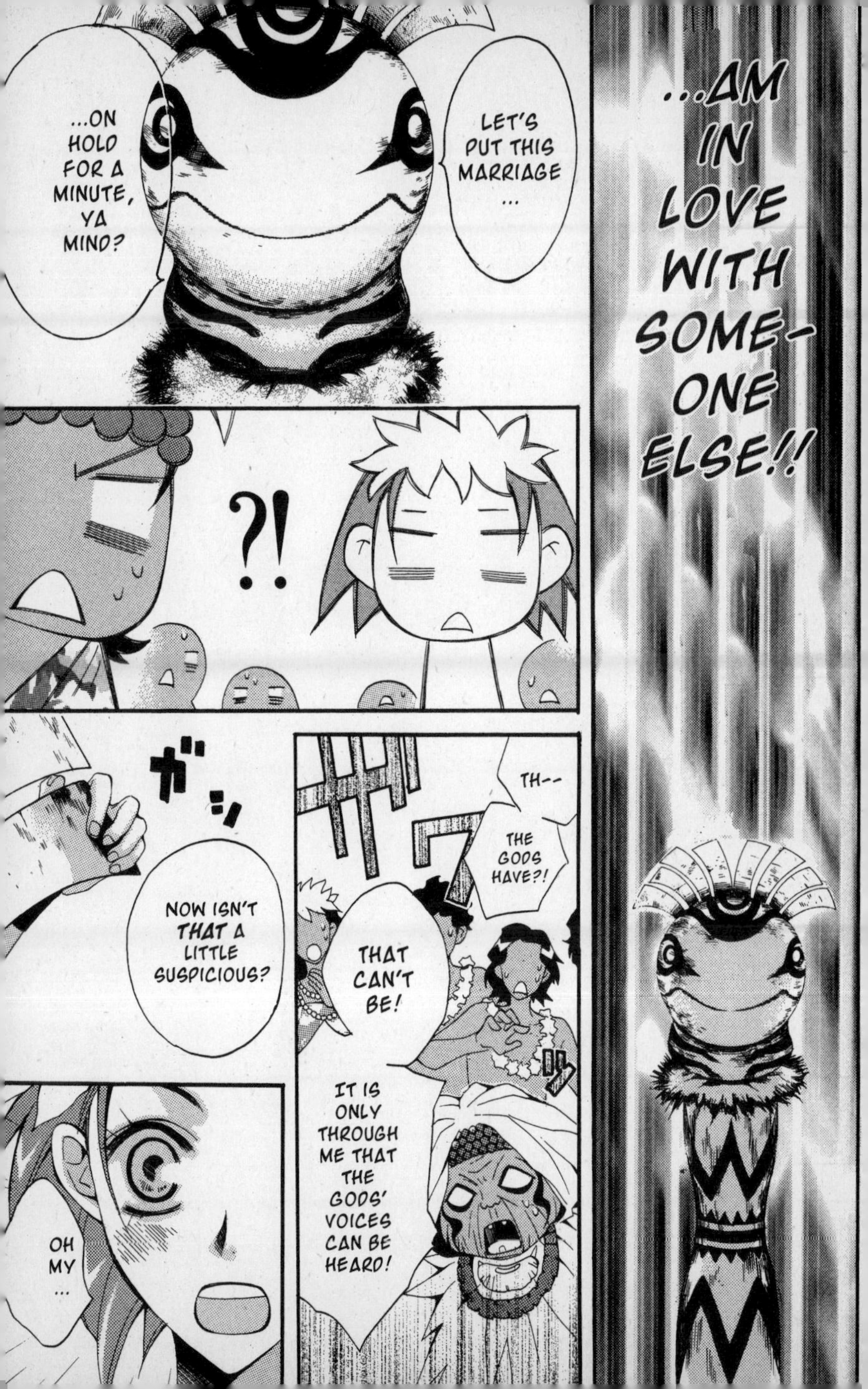
...AM IN LOVE WITH SOME-ONE ELSE!!
LET'S PUT THIS MARRIAGE ...
...ON HOLD FOR A MINUTE, YA MIND?
?!
TH--
THE GODS HAVE?!
THAT CAN'T BE!
ガッ
NOW ISN'T THAT A LITTLE SUSPICIOUS?
IT IS ONLY THROUGH ME THAT THE GODS' VOICES CAN BE HEARD!
OH MY ...

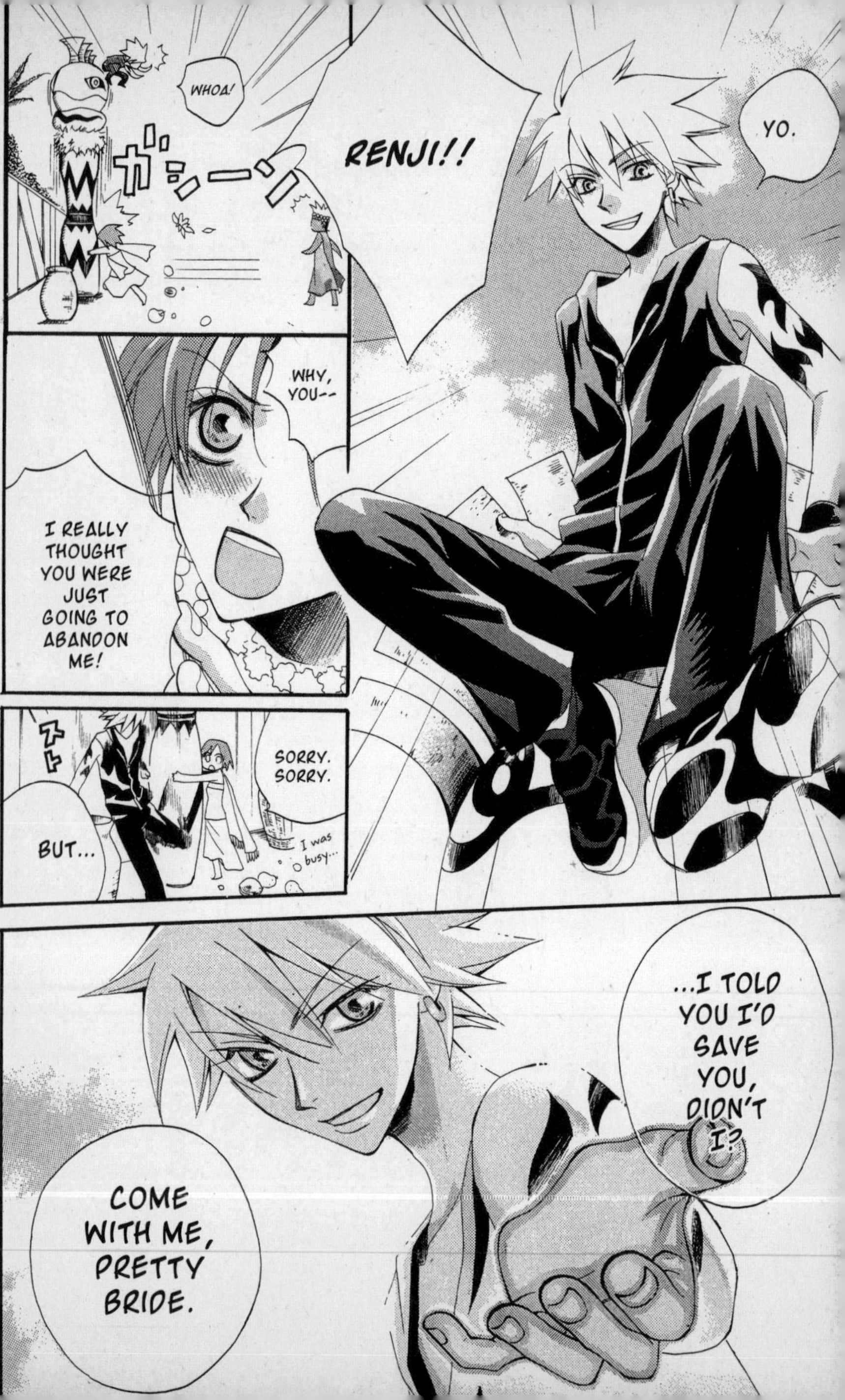
YO.
RENJI!!
WHOA!
WHY, YOU--
I REALLY THOUGHT YOU WERE JUST GOING TO ABANDON ME!
SORRY. SORRY.
I was busy...
BUT...
...I TOLD YOU I'D SAVE YOU, DIDN'T I?
COME WITH ME, PRETTY BRIDE.

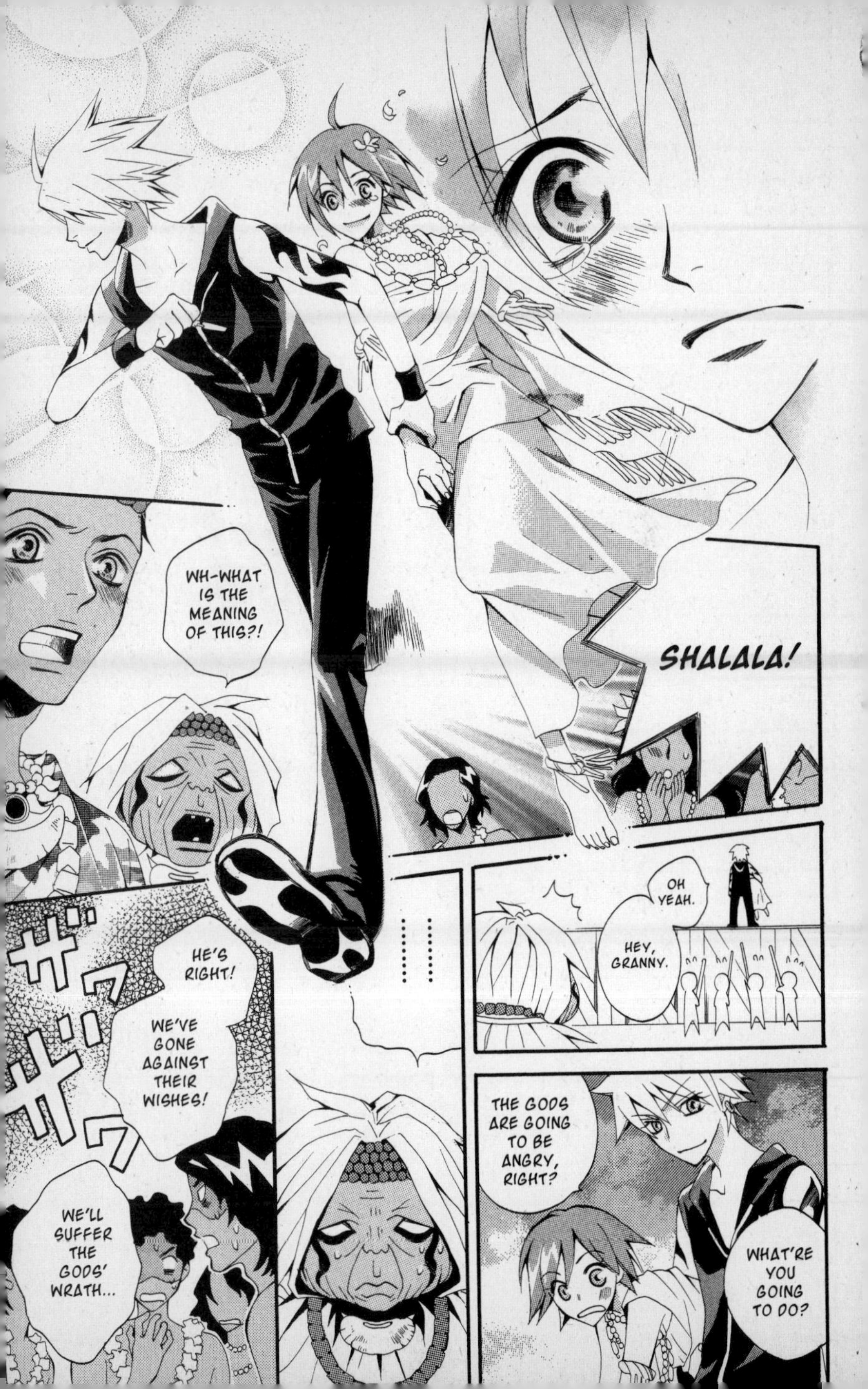
SHALALA!
WH-WHAT IS THE MEANING OF THIS?!
OH YEAH.
HEY, GRANNY.
THE GODS ARE GOING TO BE ANGRY, RIGHT?
WHAT'RE YOU GOING TO DO?
HE'S RIGHT!
WE'VE GONE AGAINST THEIR WISHES!
WE'LL SUFFER THE GODS' WRATH...

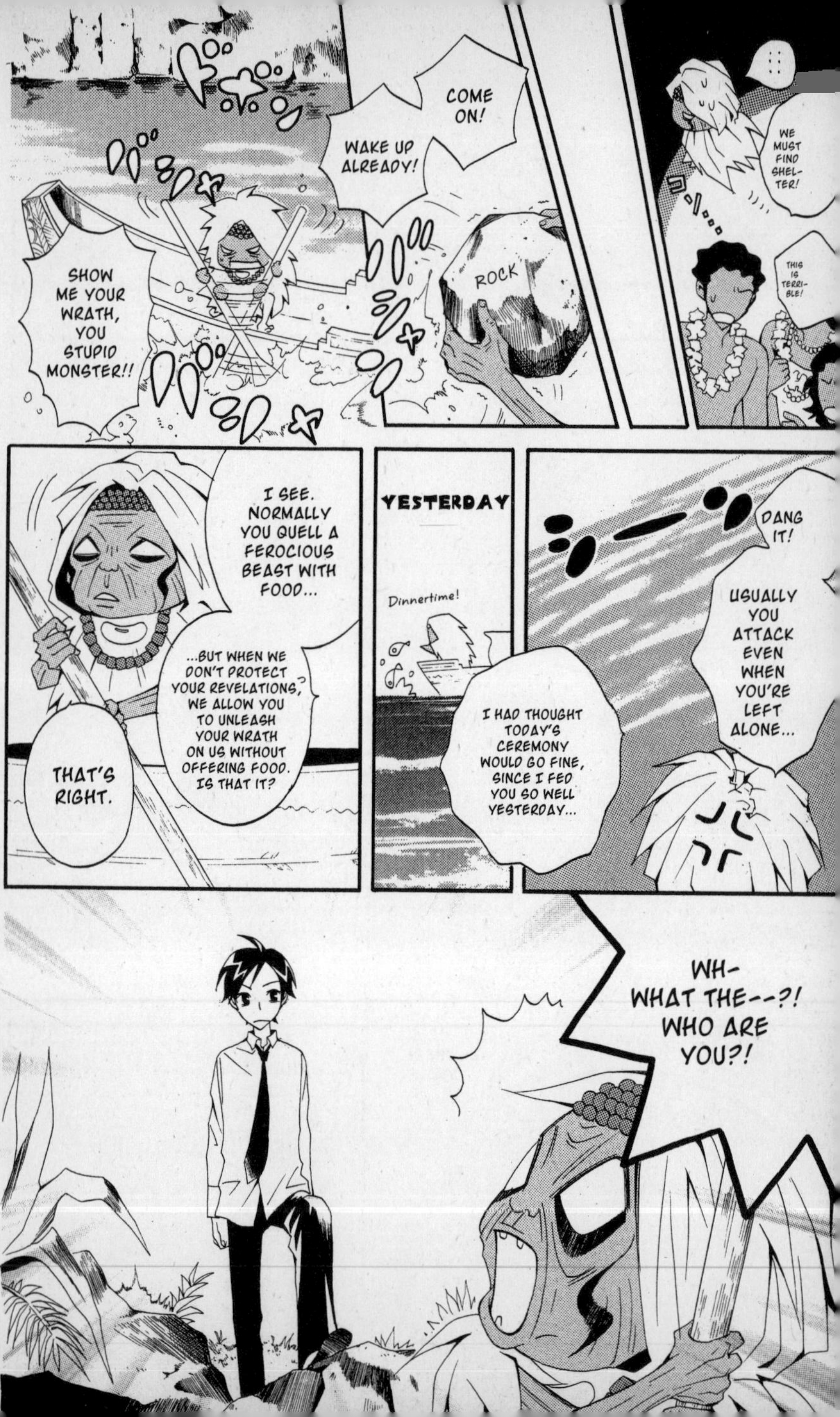
WE MUST FIND SHELTER!
THIS IS TERRIBLE!
COME ON!
WAKE UP ALREADY!
ROCK
SHOW ME YOUR WRATH, YOU STUPID MONSTER!!
DANG IT!
USUALLY YOU ATTACK EVEN WHEN YOU'RE LEFT ALONE...
I HAD THOUGHT TODAY'S CEREMONY WOULD GO FINE, SINCE I FED YOU SO WELL YESTERDAY...
YESTERDAY
Dinnertime!
I SEE. NORMALLY YOU QUELL A FEROCIOUS BEAST WITH FOOD...
...BUT WHEN WE DON'T PROTECT YOUR REVELATIONS, WE ALLOW YOU TO UNLEASH YOUR WRATH ON US WITHOUT OFFERING FOOD. IS THAT IT?
THAT'S RIGHT.
WH- WHAT THE--?! WHO ARE YOU?!

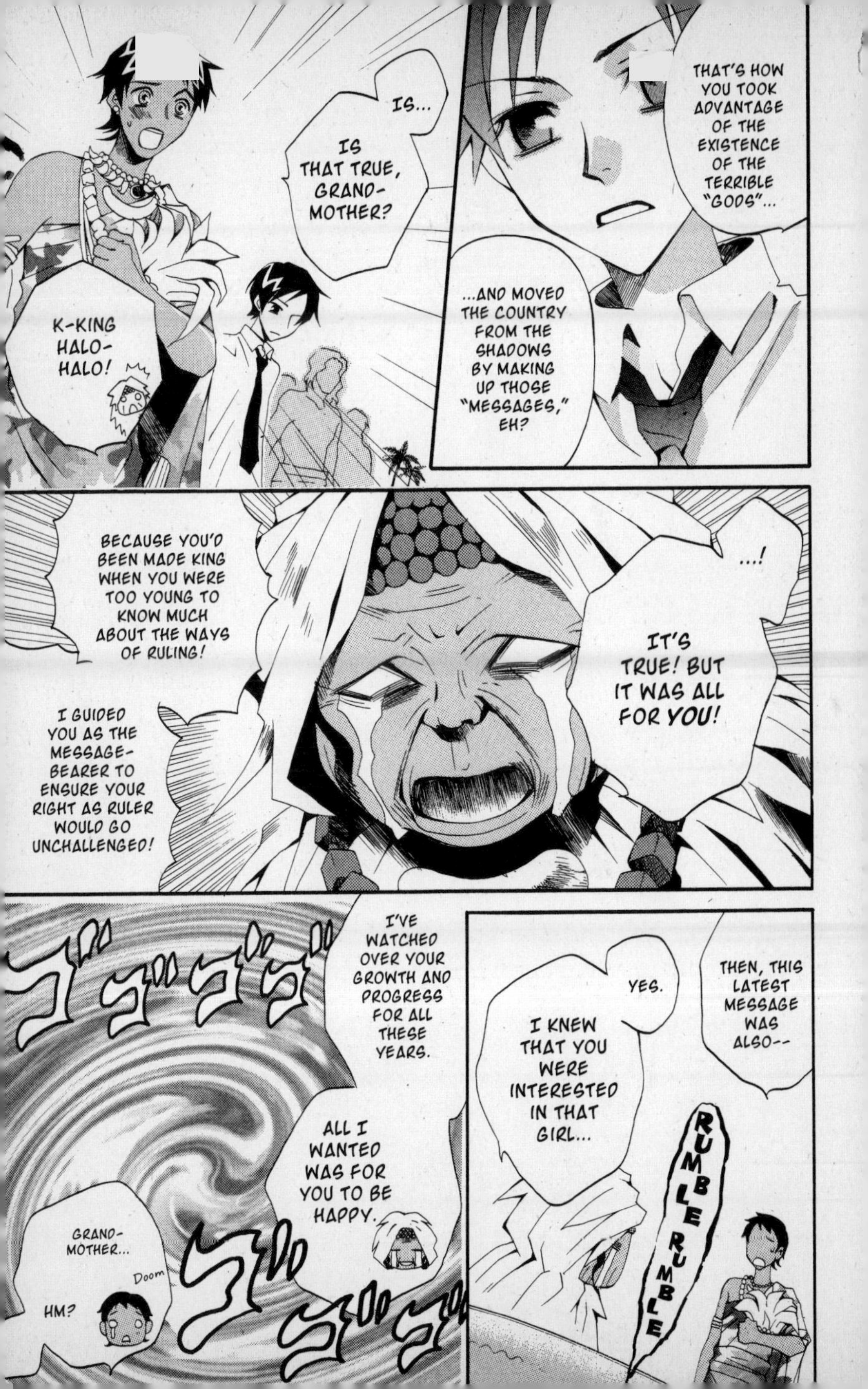
THAT'S HOW YOU TOOK ADVANTAGE OF THE EXISTENCE OF THE TERRIBLE "GODS"...
...AND MOVED THE COUNTRY FROM THE SHADOWS BY MAKING UP THOSE "MESSAGES," EH?
IS...
IS THAT TRUE, GRANDMOTHER?
K-KING HALO-HALO!
...!
IT'S TRUE! BUT IT WAS ALL FOR YOU!
BECAUSE YOU'D BEEN MADE KING WHEN YOU WERE TOO YOUNG TO KNOW MUCH ABOUT THE WAYS OF RULING!
I GUIDED YOU AS THE MESSAGE-BEARER TO ENSURE YOUR RIGHT AS RULER WOULD GO UNCHALLENGED!
THEN, THIS LATEST MESSAGE WAS ALSO--
YES.
I KNEW THAT YOU WERE INTERESTED IN THAT GIRL...
RUMBLE RUMBLE
I'VE WATCHED OVER YOUR GROWTH AND PROGRESS FOR ALL THESE YEARS.
ALL I WANTED WAS FOR YOU TO BE HAPPY.
GRANDMOTHER...
Doom
HM?

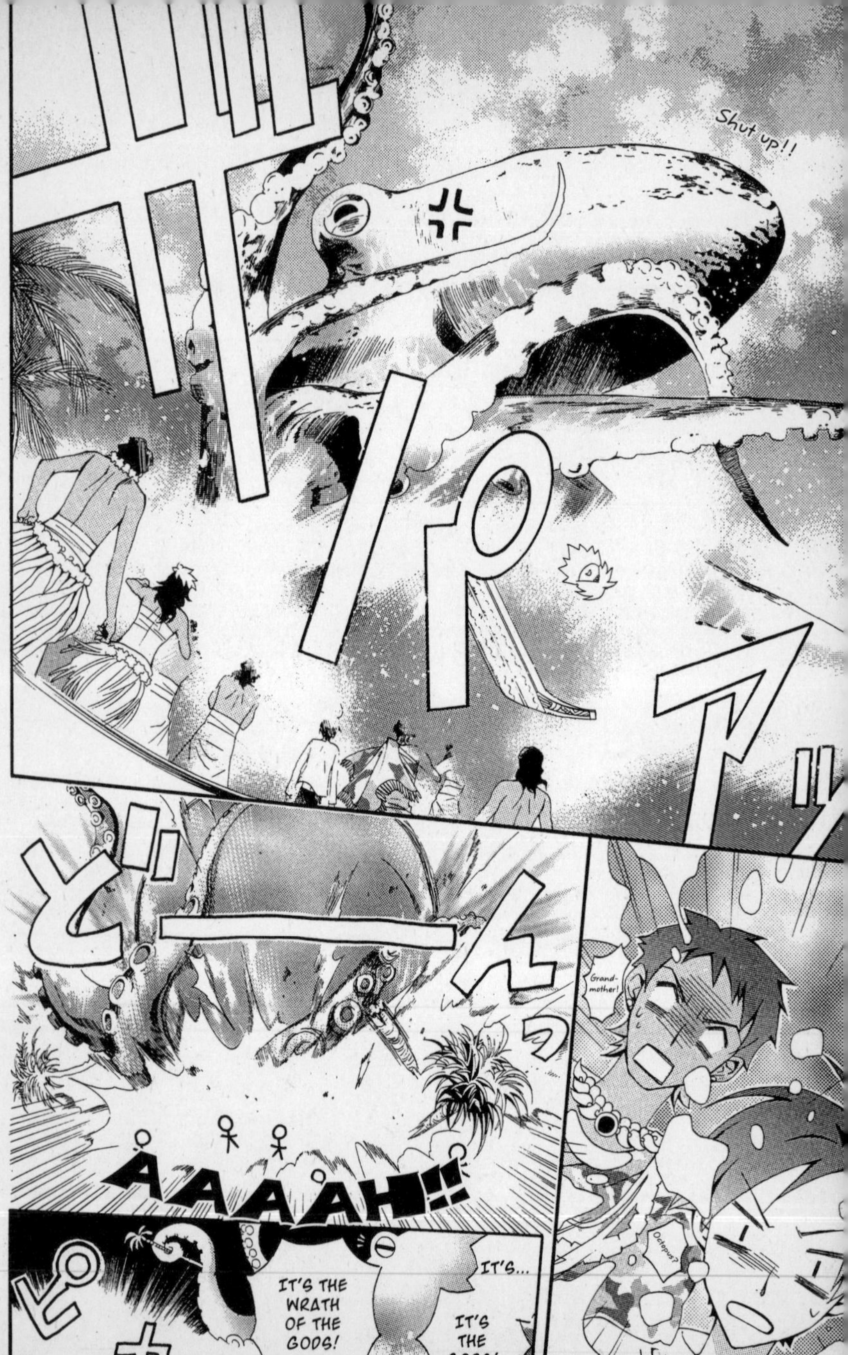
Shut up!!
Grand-mother!
Octopus?
AAAAAH!!
IT'S...
IT'S THE GODS!
IT'S THE WRATH OF THE GODS!

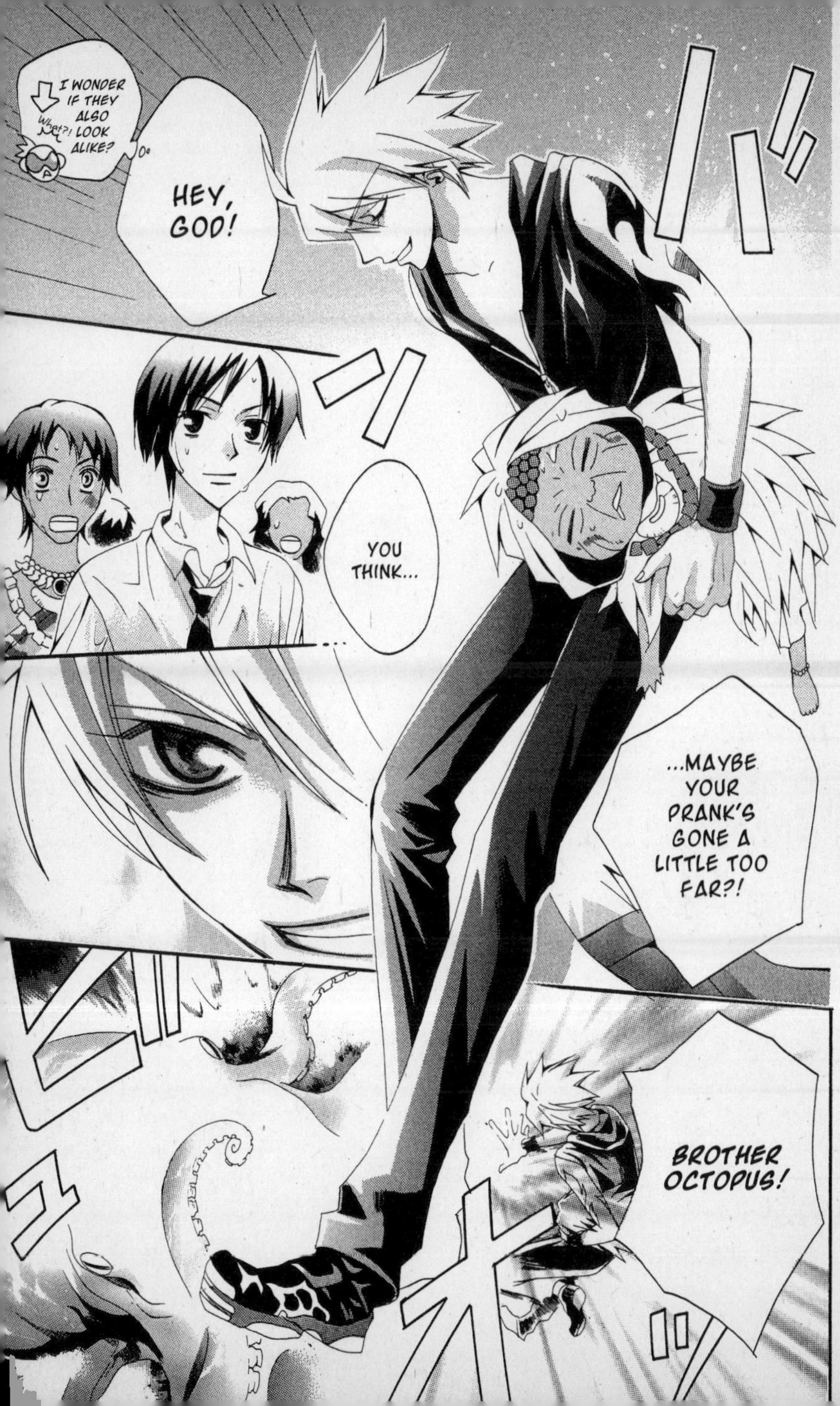
HEY, GOD!
I WONDER IF THEY ALSO LOOK ALIKE?
What?!
YOU THINK...
...MAYBE YOUR PRANK'S GONE A LITTLE TOO FAR?!
BROTHER OCTOPUS!

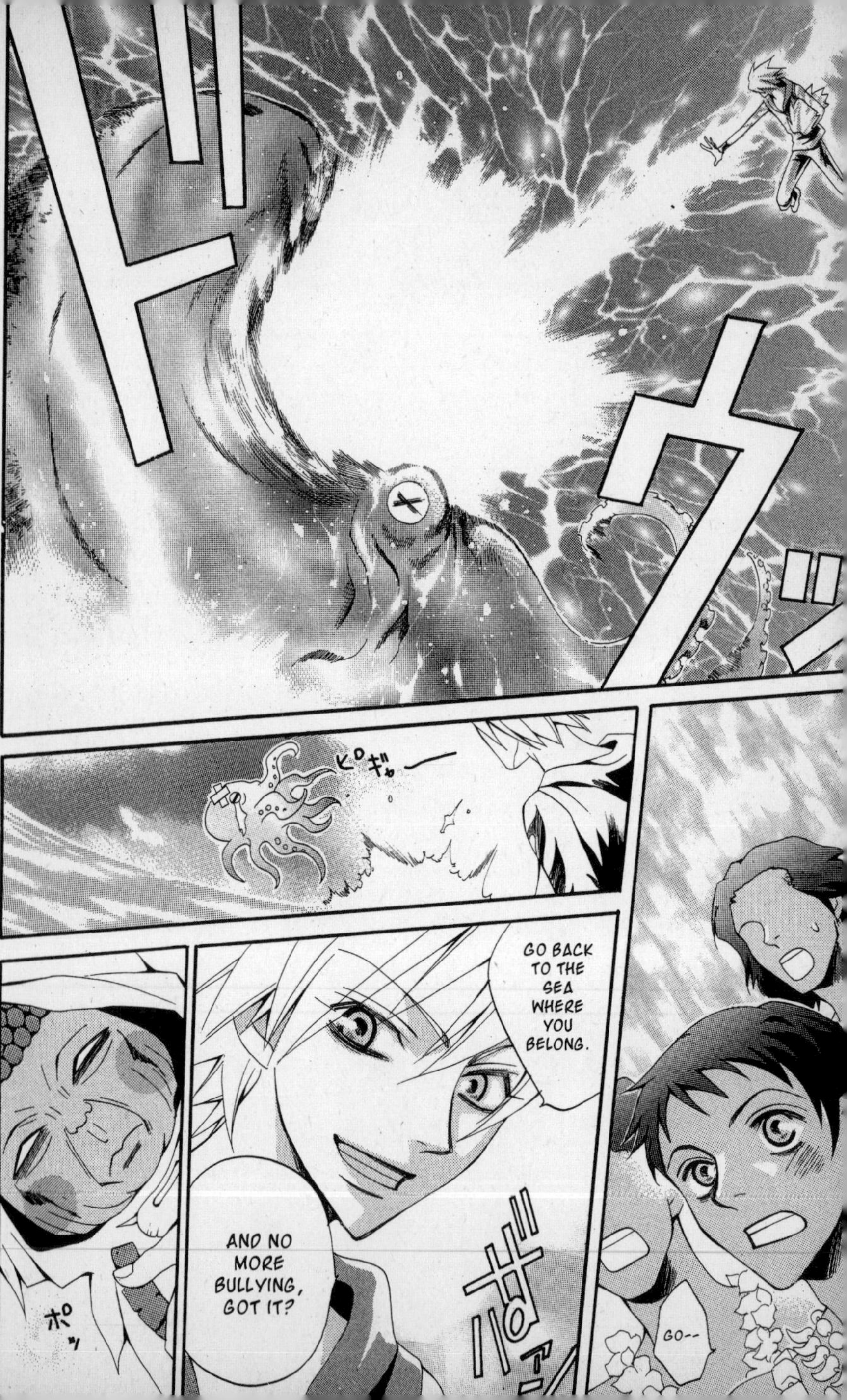
GO--
ピギャー
GO BACK TO THE SEA WHERE YOU BELONG.
AND NO MORE BULLYING, GOT IT?
ポッ

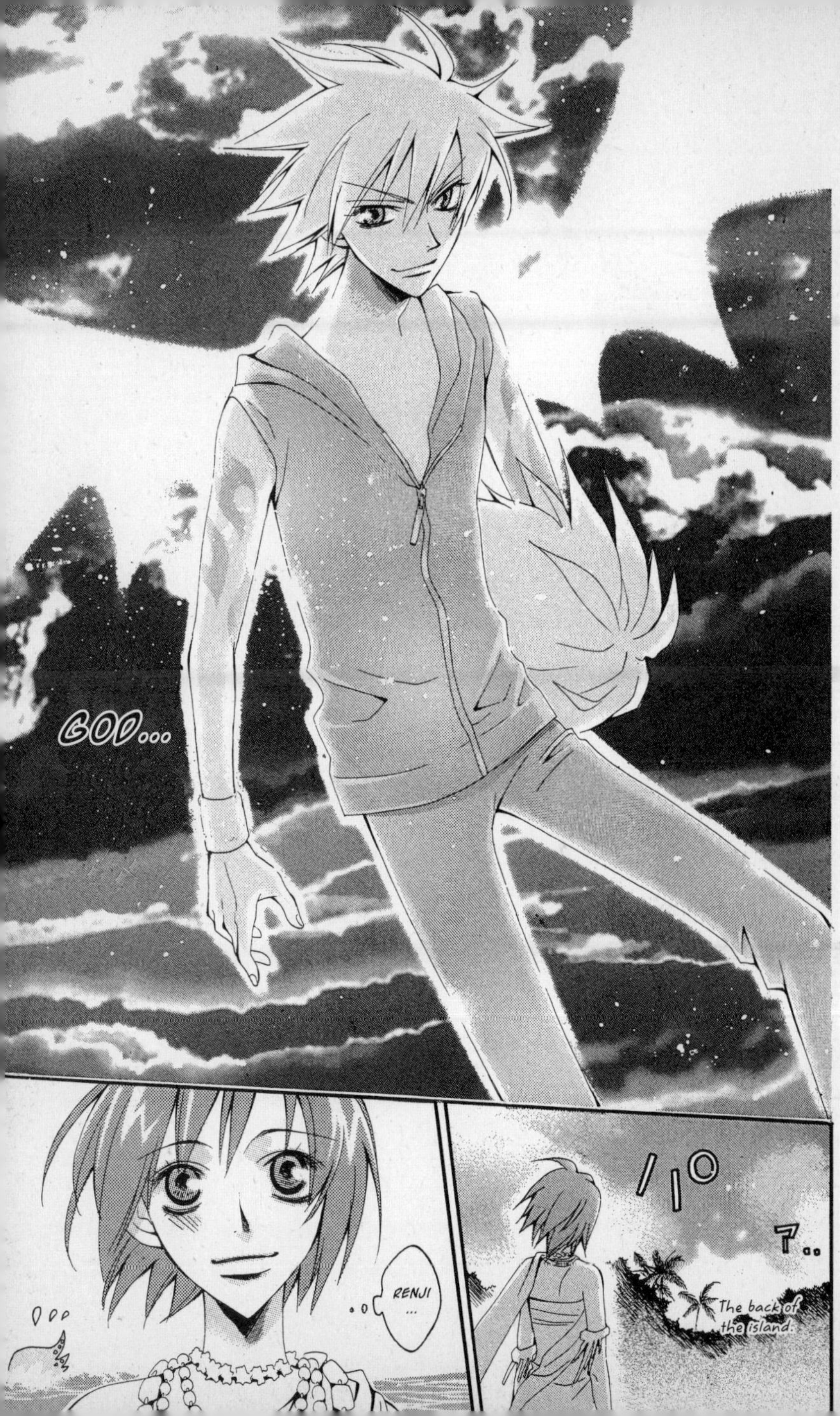
GOD...
The back of the island.
RENJI ...

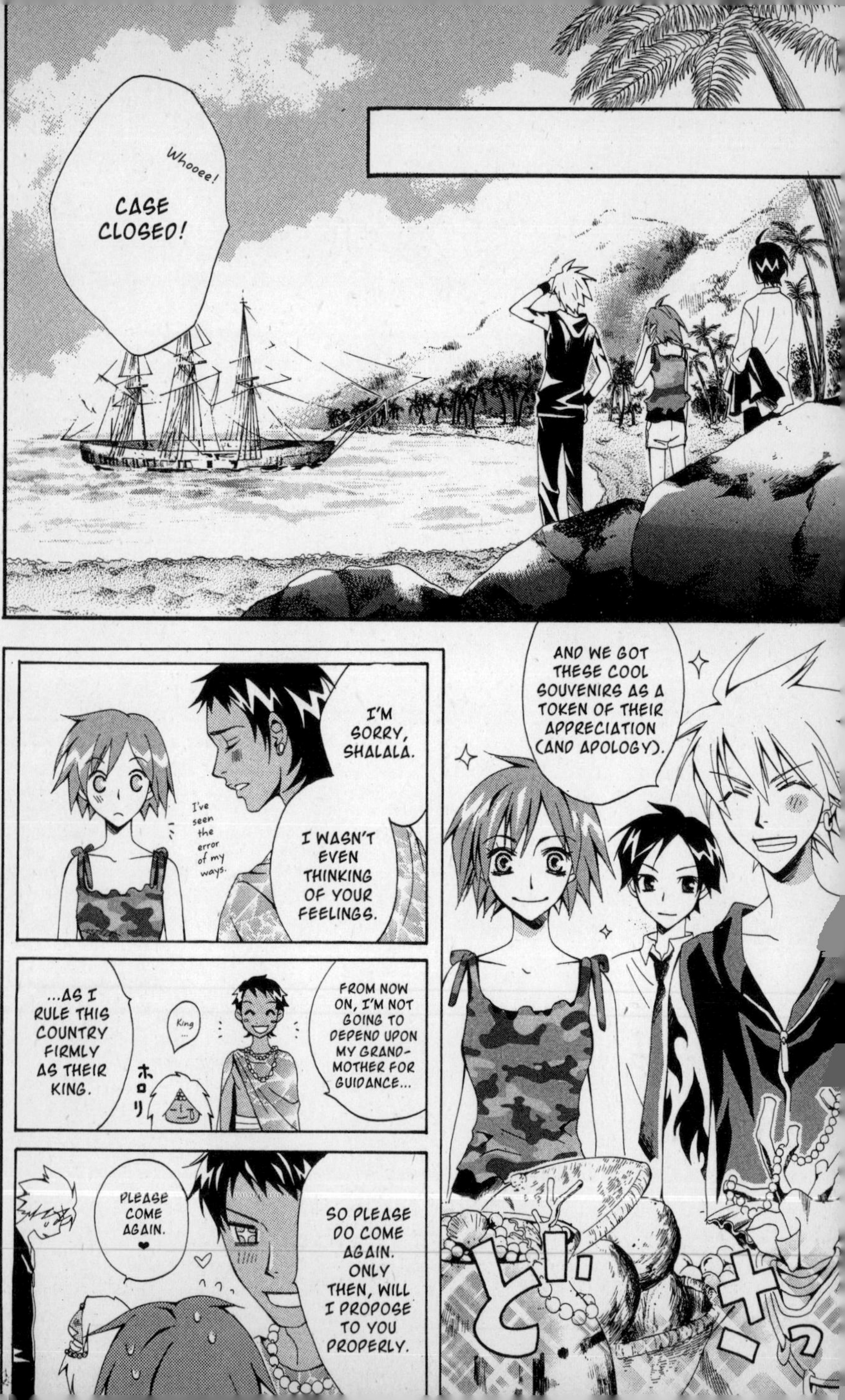
Whooee!
CASE CLOSED!
AND WE GOT THESE COOL SOUVENIRS AS A TOKEN OF THEIR APPRECIATION (AND APOLOGY).
I'M SORRY, SHALALA.
I WASN'T EVEN THINKING OF YOUR FEELINGS.
I've seen the error of my ways.
FROM NOW ON, I'M NOT GOING TO DEPEND UPON MY GRANDMOTHER FOR GUIDANCE...
King...
ホロリ
...AS I RULE THIS COUNTRY FIRMLY AS THEIR KING.
SO PLEASE DO COME AGAIN. ONLY THEN, WILL I PROPOSE TO YOU PROPERLY.
PLEASE COME AGAIN. ♥

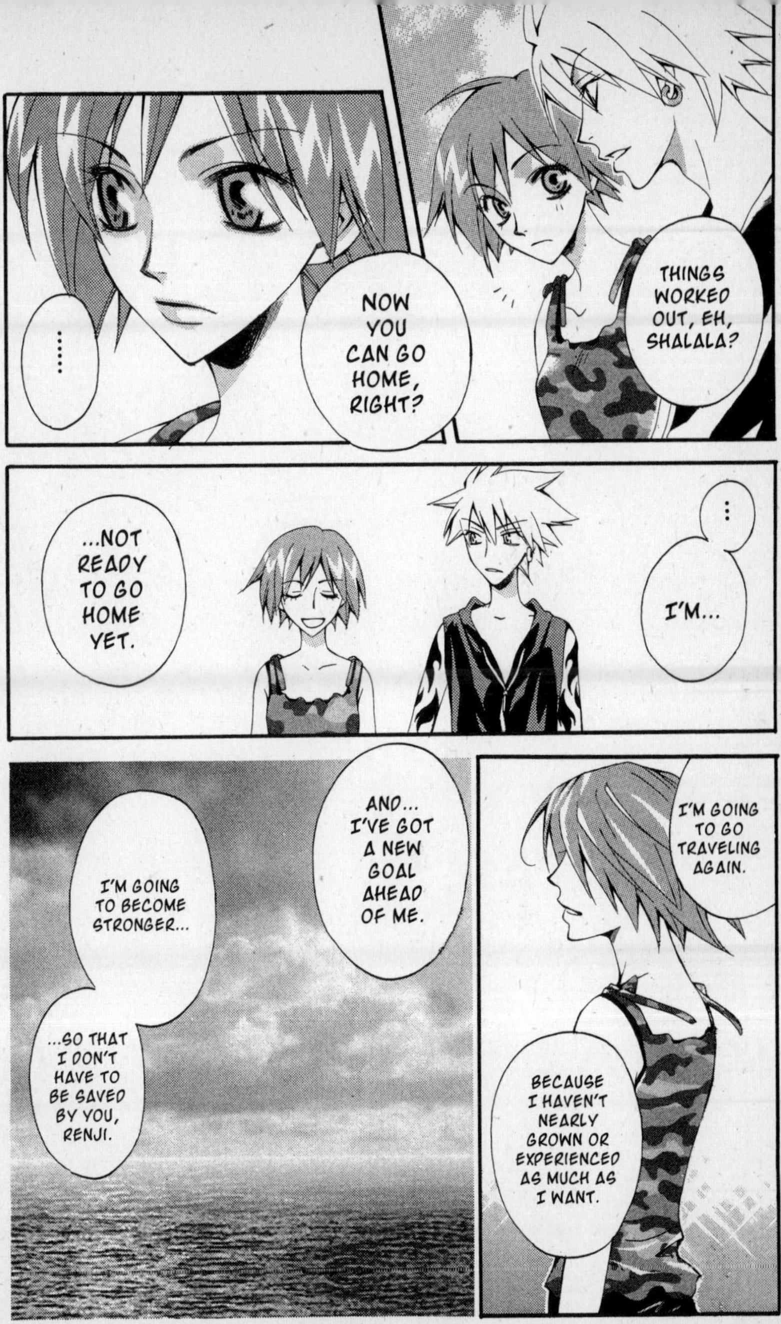
THINGS WORKED OUT, EH, SHALALA?
NOW YOU CAN GO HOME, RIGHT?
......
...
I'M...
...NOT READY TO GO HOME YET.
I'M GOING TO GO TRAVELING AGAIN.
BECAUSE I HAVEN'T NEARLY GROWN OR EXPERIENCED AS MUCH AS I WANT.
AND... I'VE GOT A NEW GOAL AHEAD OF ME.
I'M GOING TO BECOME STRONGER...
...SO THAT I DON'T HAVE TO BE SAVED BY YOU, RENJI.

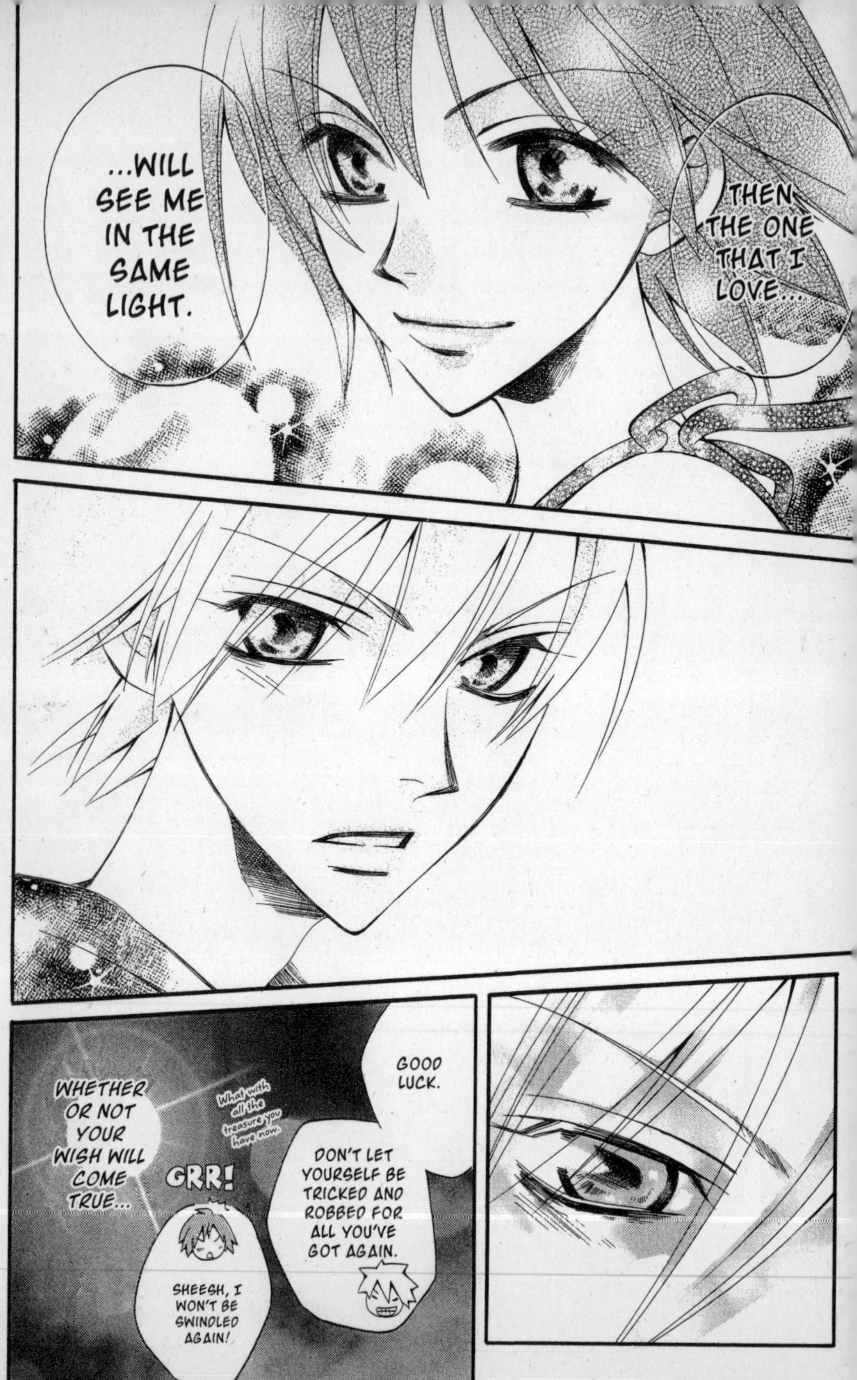
THEN THE ONE THAT I LOVE...
...WILL SEE ME IN THE SAME LIGHT.
GOOD LUCK.
DON'T LET YOURSELF BE TRICKED AND ROBBED FOR ALL YOU'VE GOT AGAIN.
What with all the treasure you have now.
WHETHER OR NOT YOUR WISH WILL COME TRUE...
GRR!
SHEESH, I WON'T BE SWINDLED AGAIN!

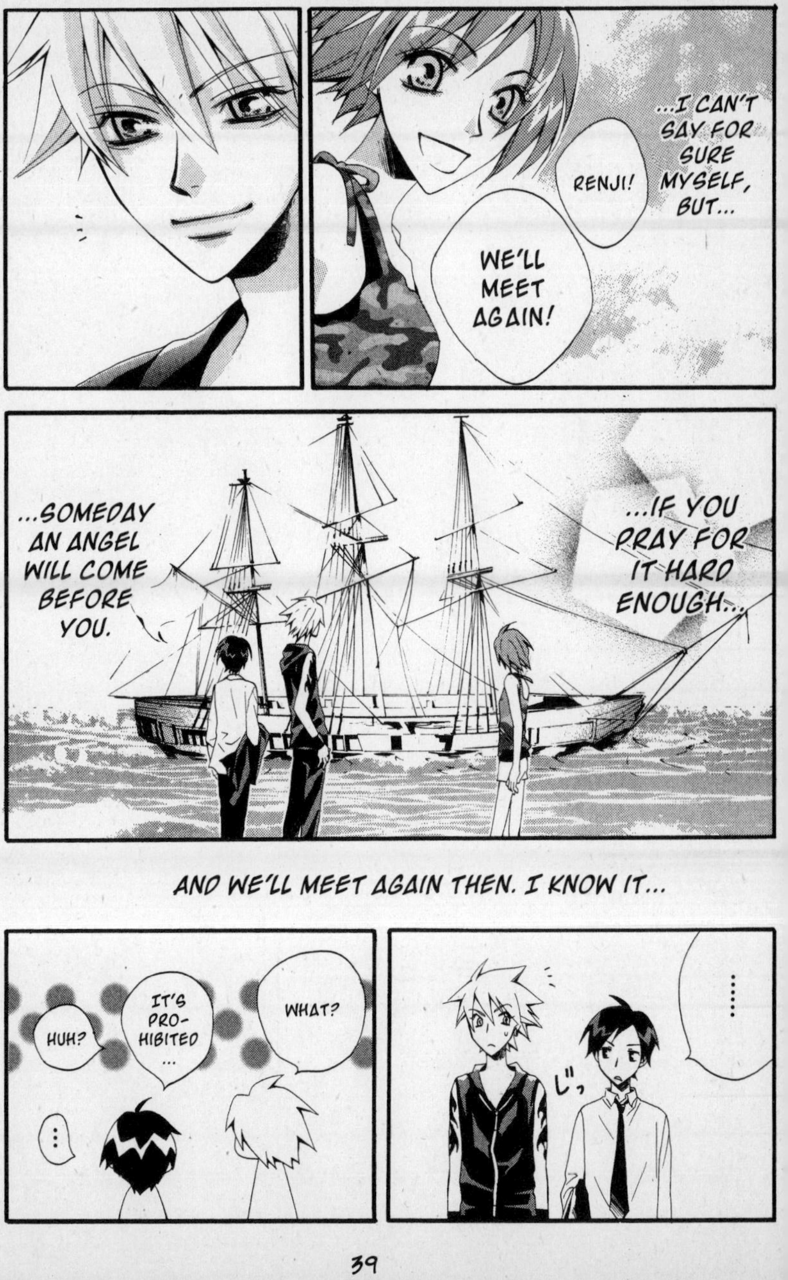
...I CAN'T SAY FOR SURE MYSELF, BUT...
RENJI!
WE'LL MEET AGAIN!
...IF YOU PRAY FOR IT HARD ENOUGH...
...SOMEDAY AN ANGEL WILL COME BEFORE YOU.
AND WE'LL MEET AGAIN THEN. I KNOW IT...
......
じっ
WHAT?
IT'S PRO-HIBITED...
HUH?
...

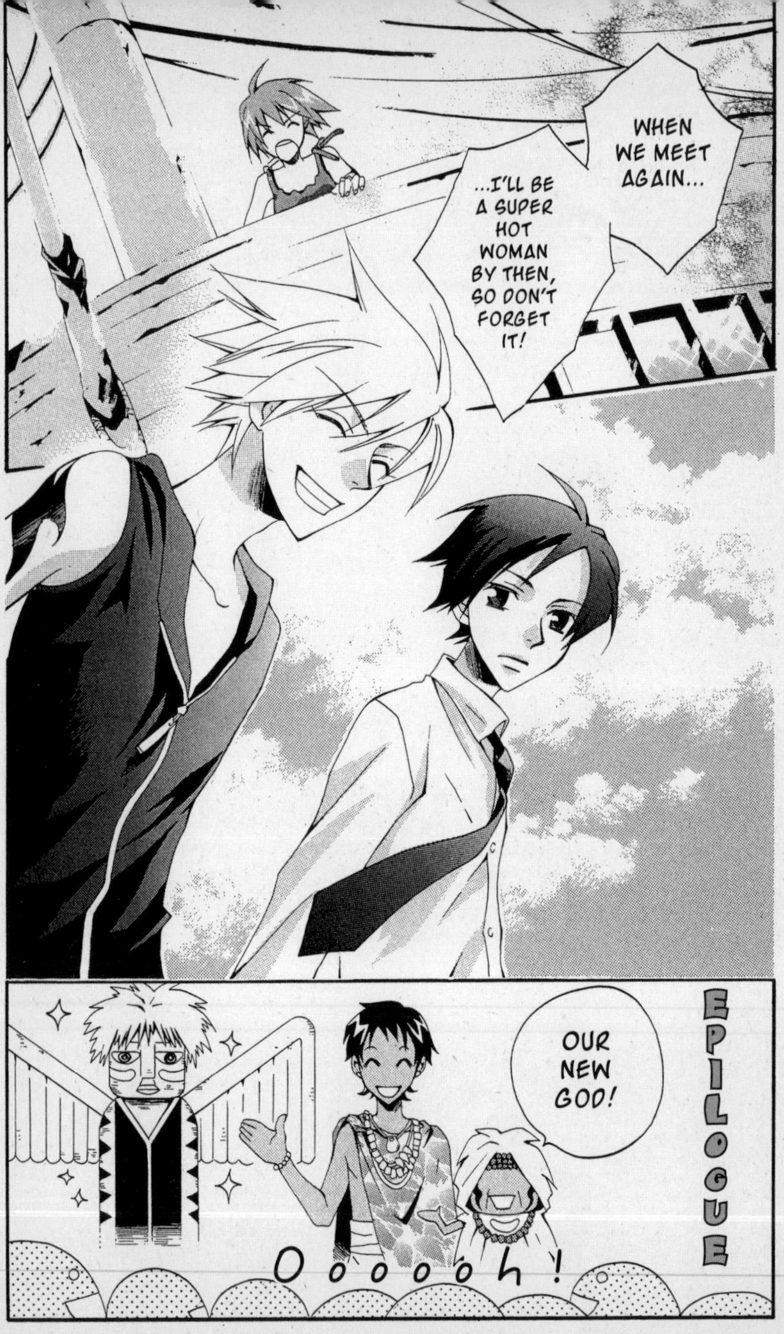
WHEN WE MEET AGAIN...
...I'LL BE A SUPER HOT WOMAN BY THEN, SO DON'T FORGET IT!
EPILOGUE
OUR NEW GOD!
Oooooh!

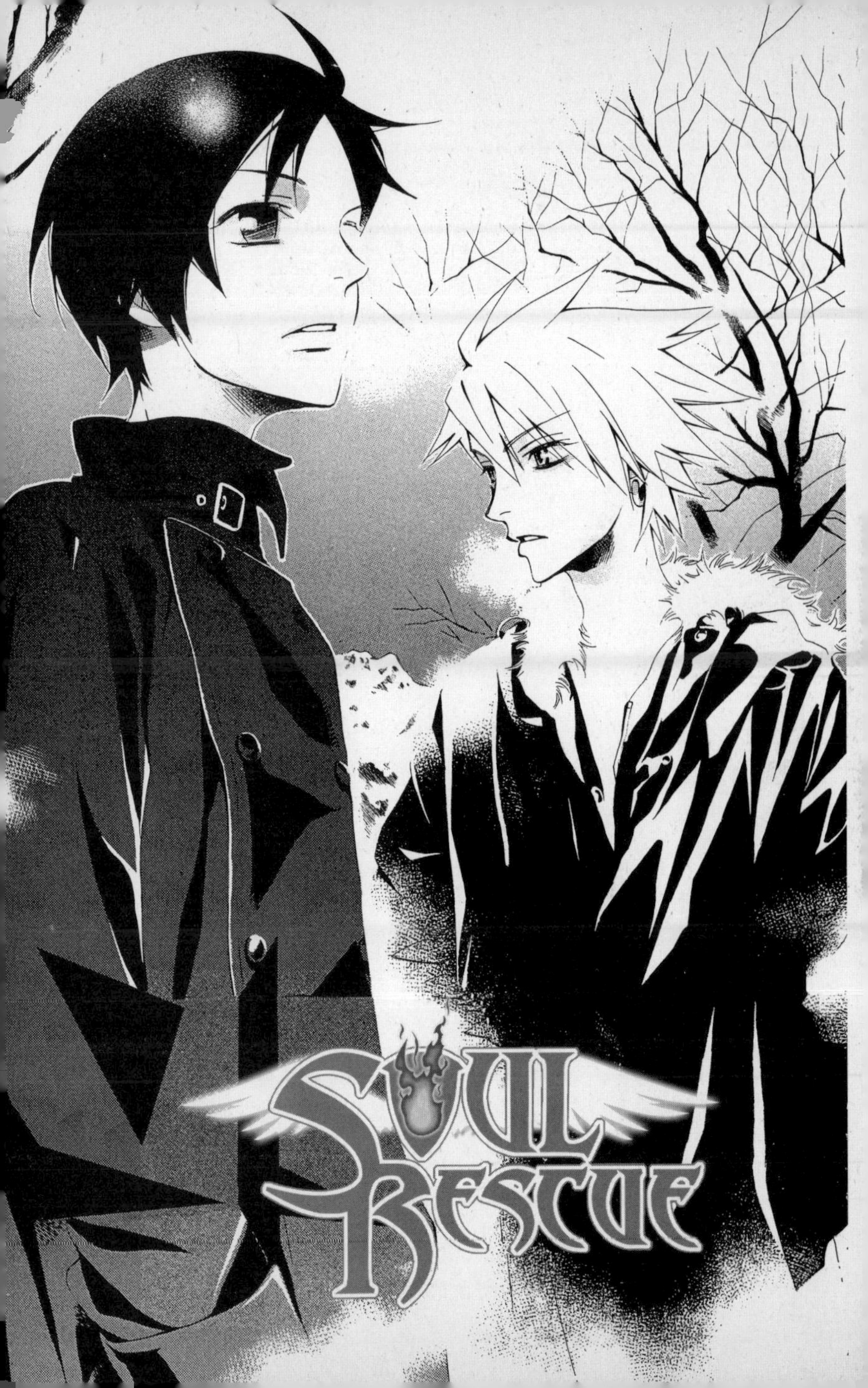
SOUL RESCUE

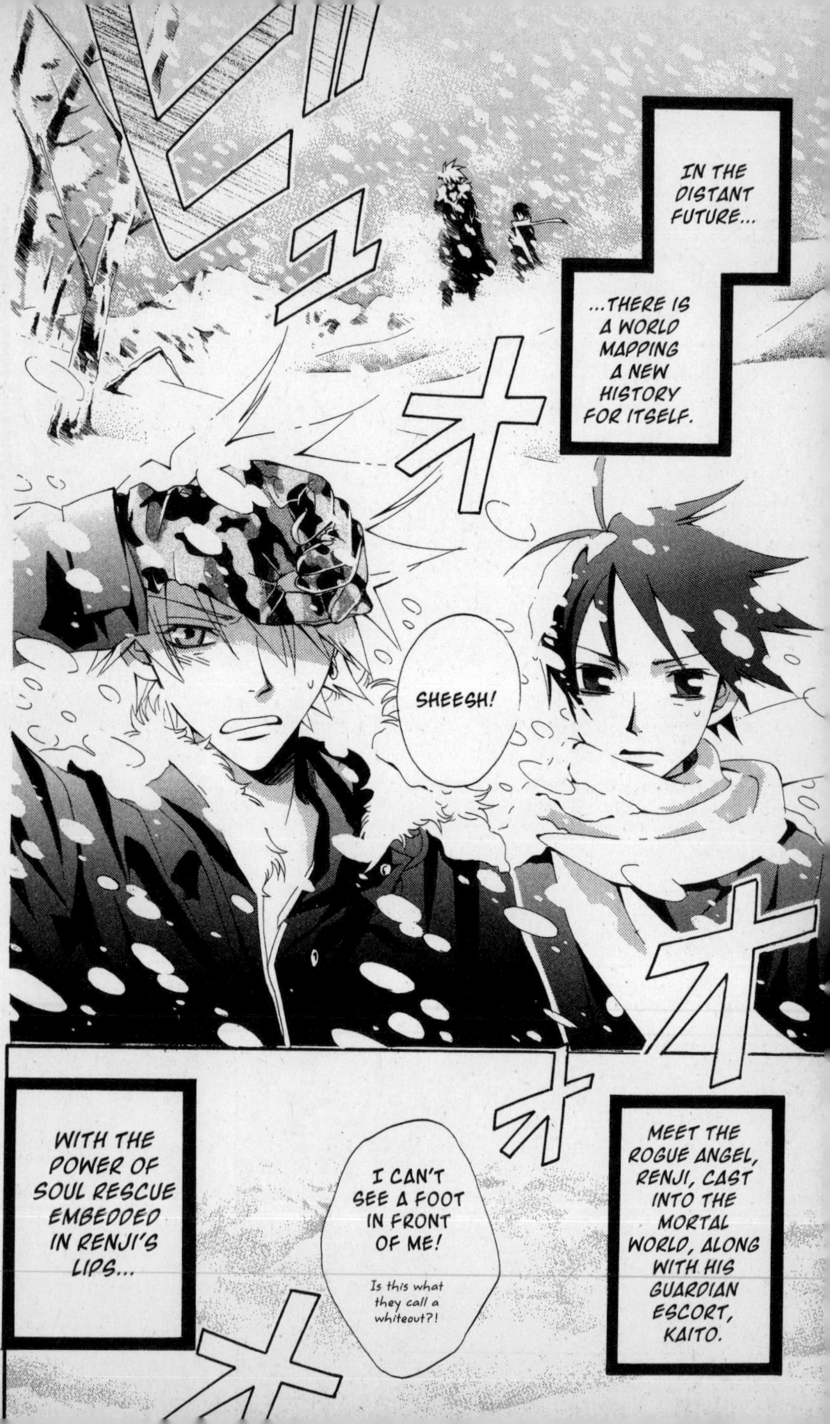
IN THE DISTANT FUTURE...
...THERE IS A WORLD MAPPING A NEW HISTORY FOR ITSELF.
SHEESH!
MEET THE ROGUE ANGEL, RENJI, CAST INTO THE MORTAL WORLD, ALONG WITH HIS GUARDIAN ESCORT, KAITO.
I CAN'T SEE A FOOT IN FRONT OF ME!
Is this what they call a whiteout?!
WITH THE POWER OF SOUL RESCUE EMBEDDED IN RENJI'S LIPS...

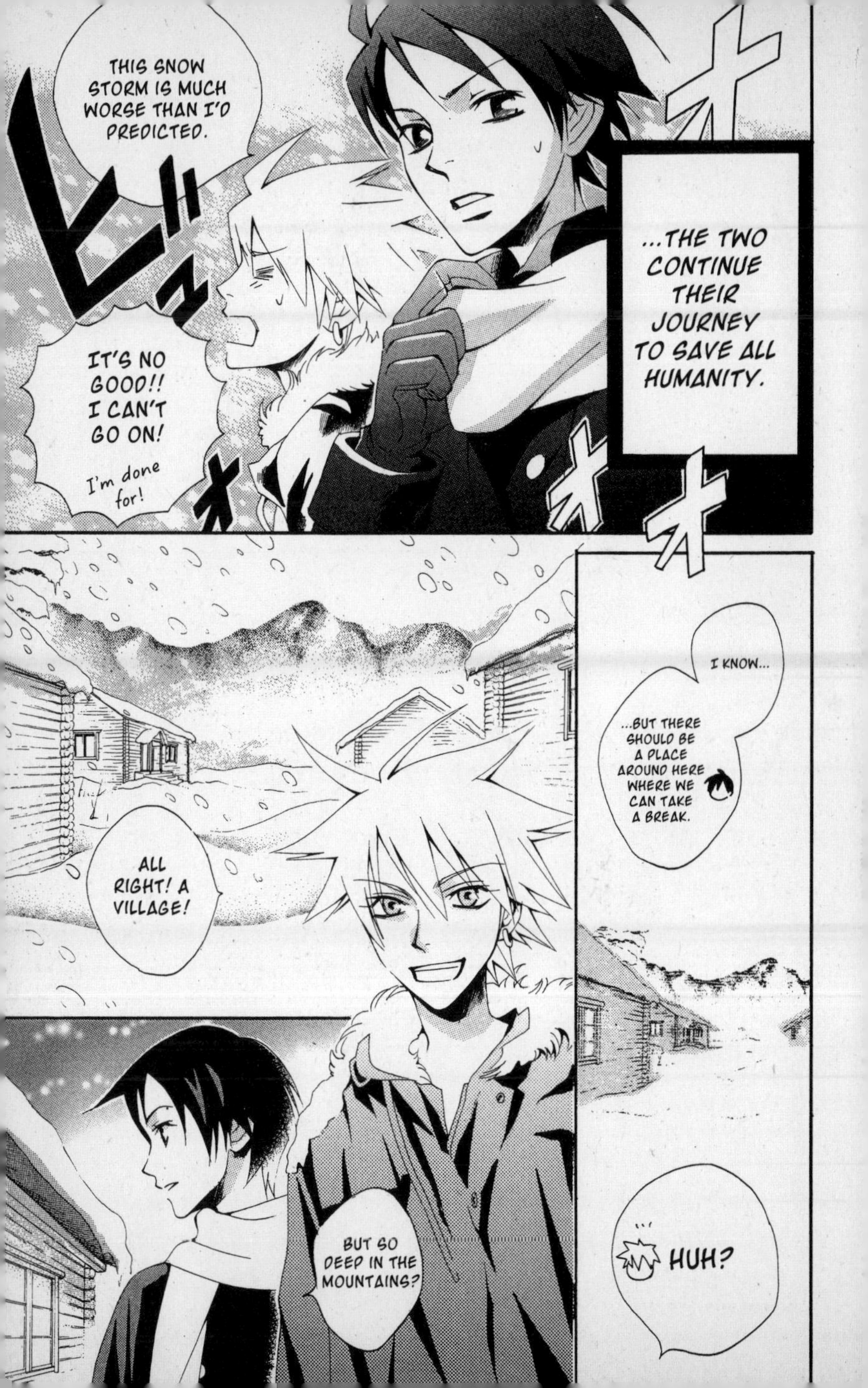
...THE TWO CONTINUE THEIR JOURNEY TO SAVE ALL HUMANITY.
THIS SNOW STORM IS MUCH WORSE THAN I'D PREDICTED.
IT'S NO GOOD!! I CAN'T GO ON!
I'm done for!
I KNOW...
...BUT THERE SHOULD BE A PLACE AROUND HERE WHERE WE CAN TAKE A BREAK.
HUH?
ALL RIGHT! A VILLAGE!
BUT SO DEEP IN THE MOUNTAINS?

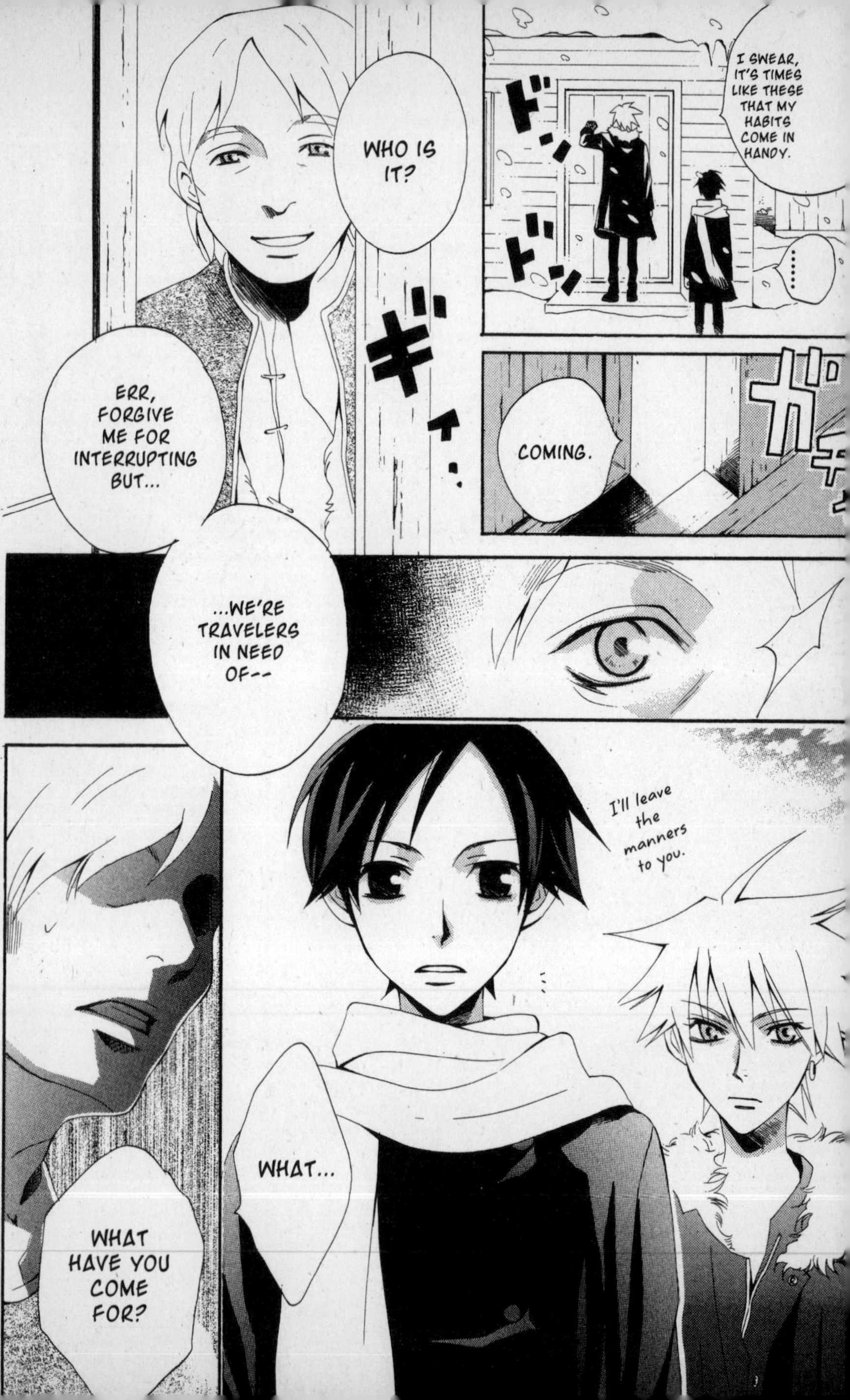
I SWEAR, IT'S TIMES LIKE THESE THAT MY HABITS COME IN HANDY.
......
ドン
ドン
COMING.
WHO IS IT?
ギィ...
ERR, FORGIVE ME FOR INTERRUPTING BUT...
...WE'RE TRAVELERS IN NEED OF--
I'll leave the manners to you.
WHAT...
WHAT HAVE YOU COME FOR?

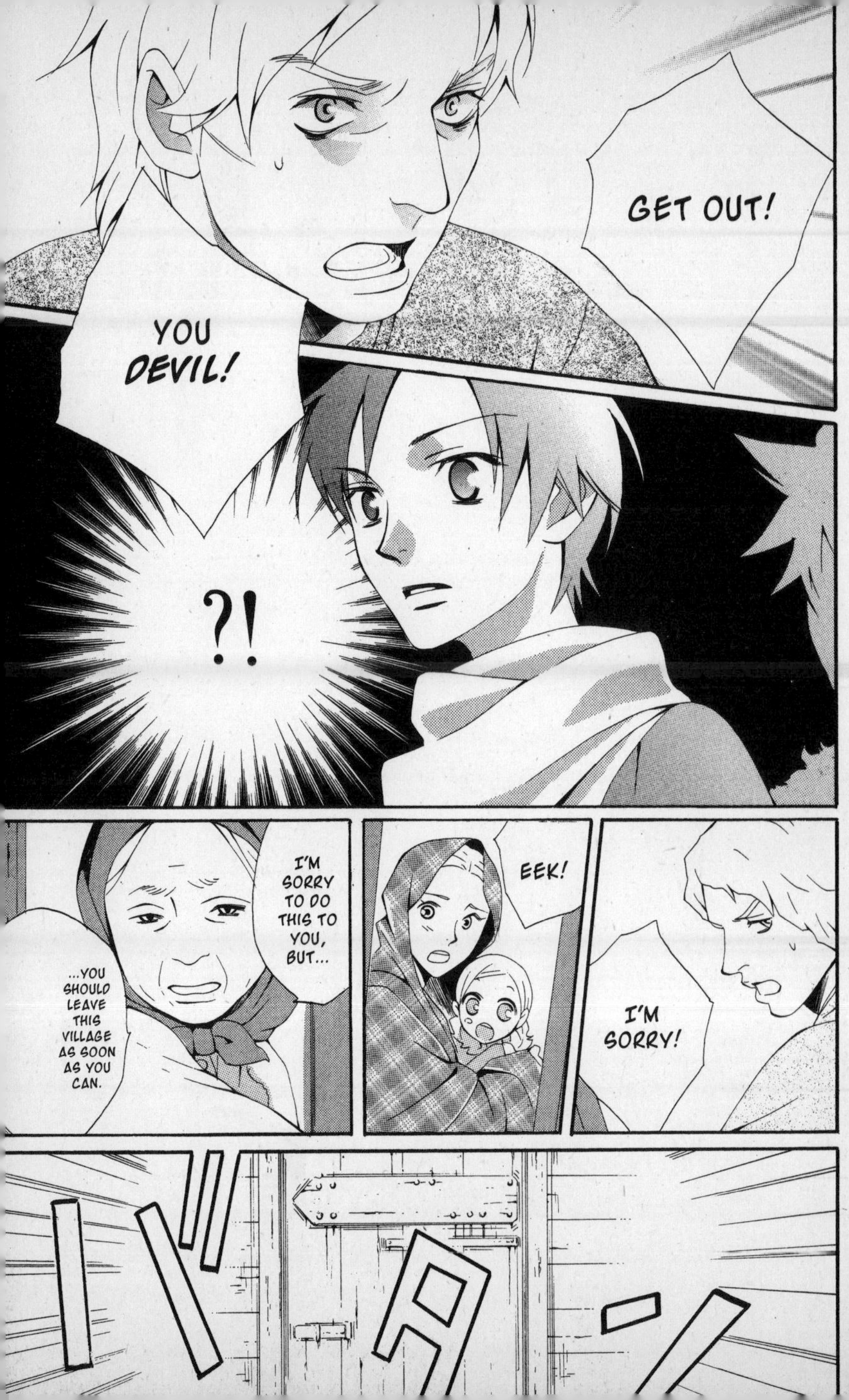
GET OUT!
YOU DEVIL!
?!
I'M SORRY!
EEK!
I'M SORRY TO DO THIS TO YOU, BUT...
...YOU SHOULD LEAVE THIS VILLAGE AS SOON AS YOU CAN.

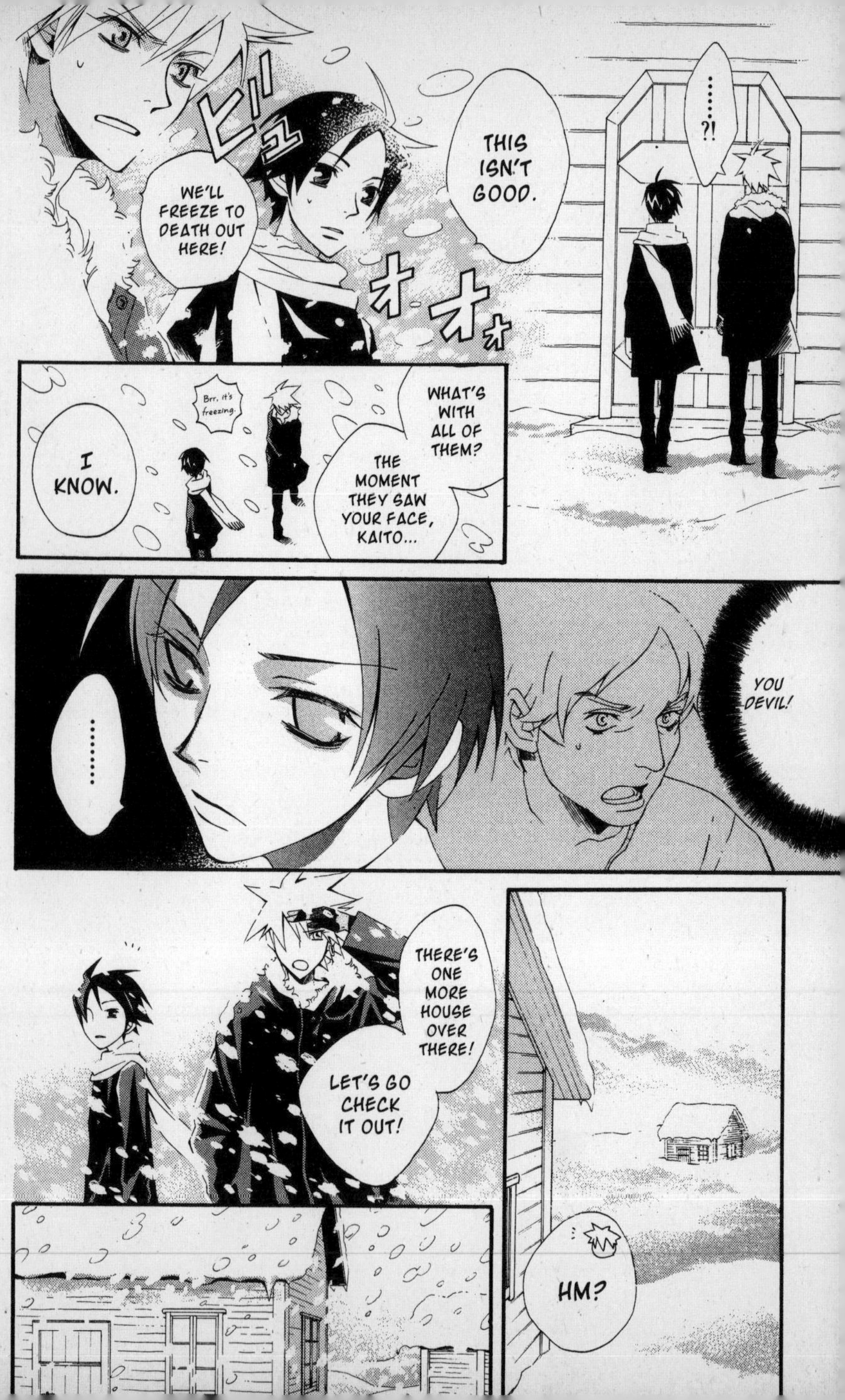
......?!
THIS ISN'T GOOD.
WE'LL FREEZE TO DEATH OUT HERE!
ヒュ
オオォ
WHAT'S WITH ALL OF THEM?
THE MOMENT THEY SAW YOUR FACE, KAITO...
Brr, it's freezing.
I KNOW.
YOU DEVIL!
....
HM?
THERE'S ONE MORE HOUSE OVER THERE!
LET'S GO CHECK IT OUT!

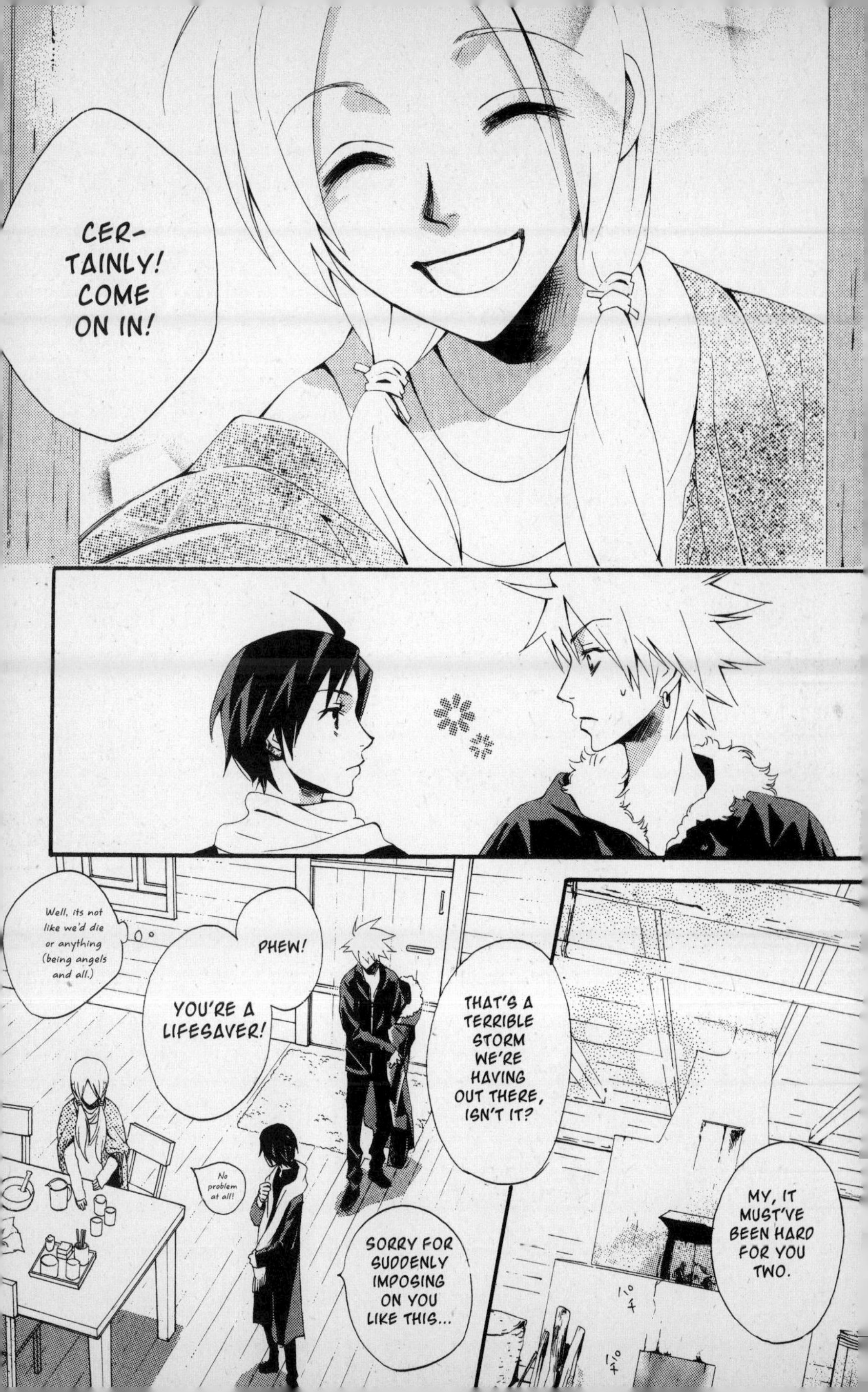
CER-TAINLY! COME ON IN!
MY, IT MUST'VE BEEN HARD FOR YOU TWO.
THAT'S A TERRIBLE STORM WE'RE HAVING OUT THERE, ISN'T IT?
PHEW!
YOU'RE A LIFESAVER!
Well, its not like we'd die or anything (being angels and all.)
SORRY FOR SUDDENLY IMPOSING ON YOU LIKE THIS...
No problem at all!

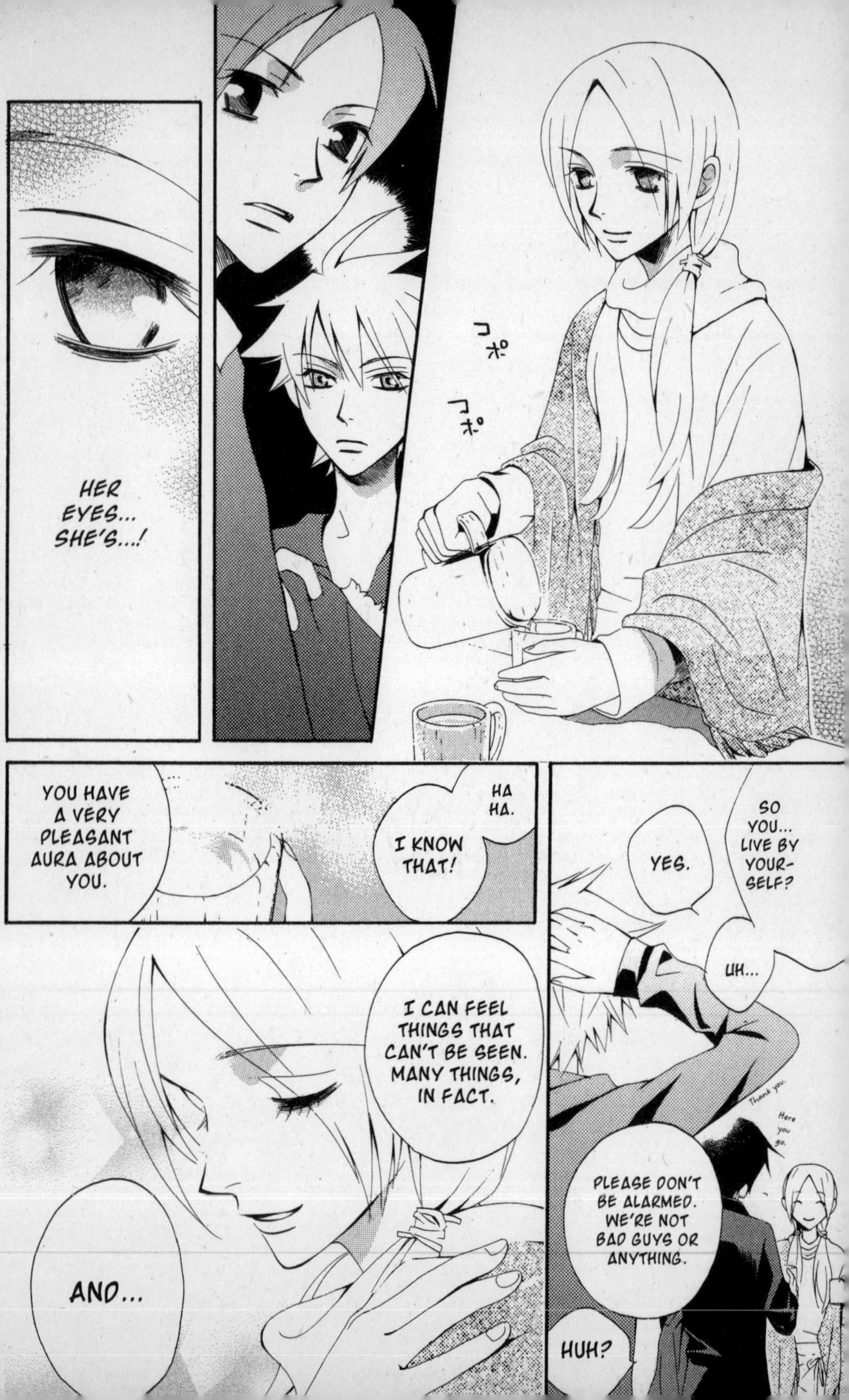
コポ
コポ
HER EYES... SHE'S...!
SO YOU... LIVE BY YOUR-SELF?
YES.
UH...
Here you go.
Thank you.
PLEASE DON'T BE ALARMED. WE'RE NOT BAD GUYS OR ANYTHING.
HUH?
HA HA.
I KNOW THAT!
YOU HAVE A VERY PLEASANT AURA ABOUT YOU.
I CAN FEEL THINGS THAT CAN'T BE SEEN. MANY THINGS, IN FACT.
AND...

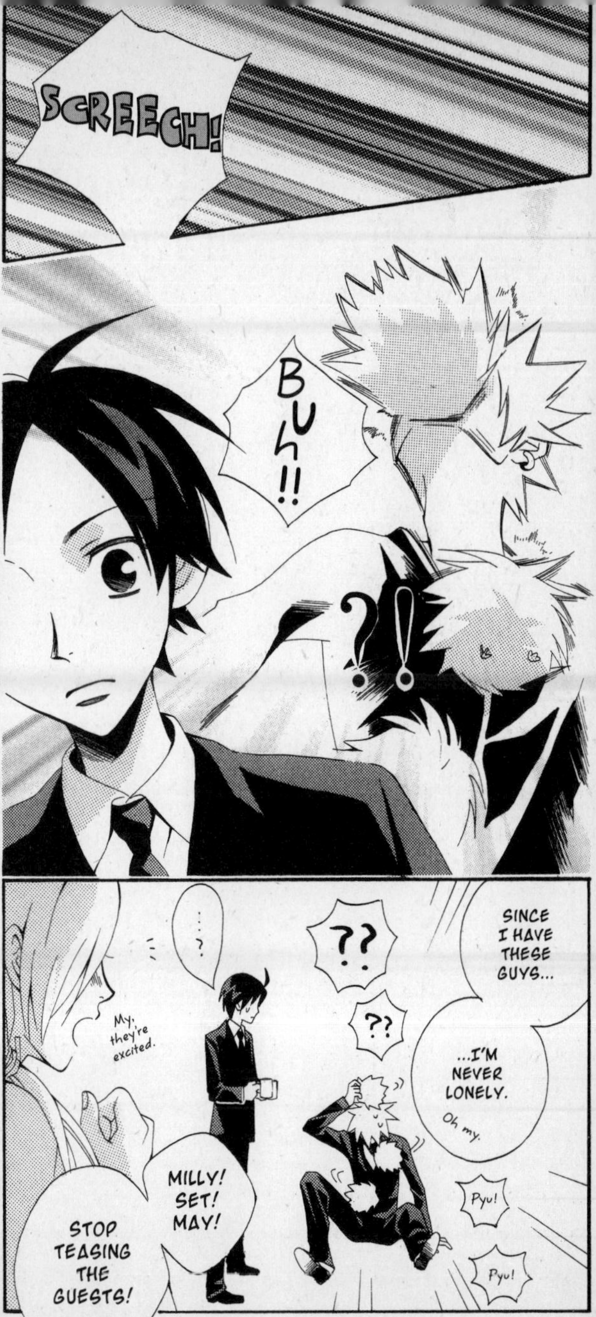
SCREECH!
BUん!!
?!
SINCE I HAVE THESE GUYS...
...I'M NEVER LONELY.
Oh my.
??
??
Pyu!
Pyu!
...?
My, they're excited.
MILLY! SET! MAY!
STOP TEASING THE GUESTS!

SR

I'm actually very bad at handling the cold! I have a downright hypersensitivity to the cold. I like winter. I think it's the landscape and the quality of the air that I like the best. There's something about the dreary atmosphere to it all that's just so great. Maybe because I was born in winter? Oh, speaking of birthdays, in many letters I've been asked the question, "When are Renji and Kaito's birthdays, and how old are they?" Since they're angels, they don't have birthdays. But since they used to be human, in their previous existence, they must've had them then. As for their age, they're around a couple of thousand of years old. After all, they exist in a very different dimension from humans.

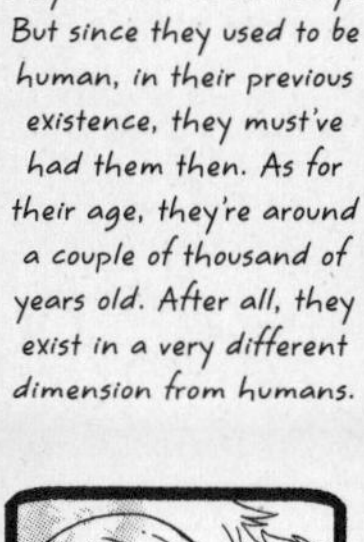

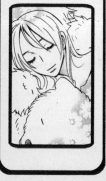

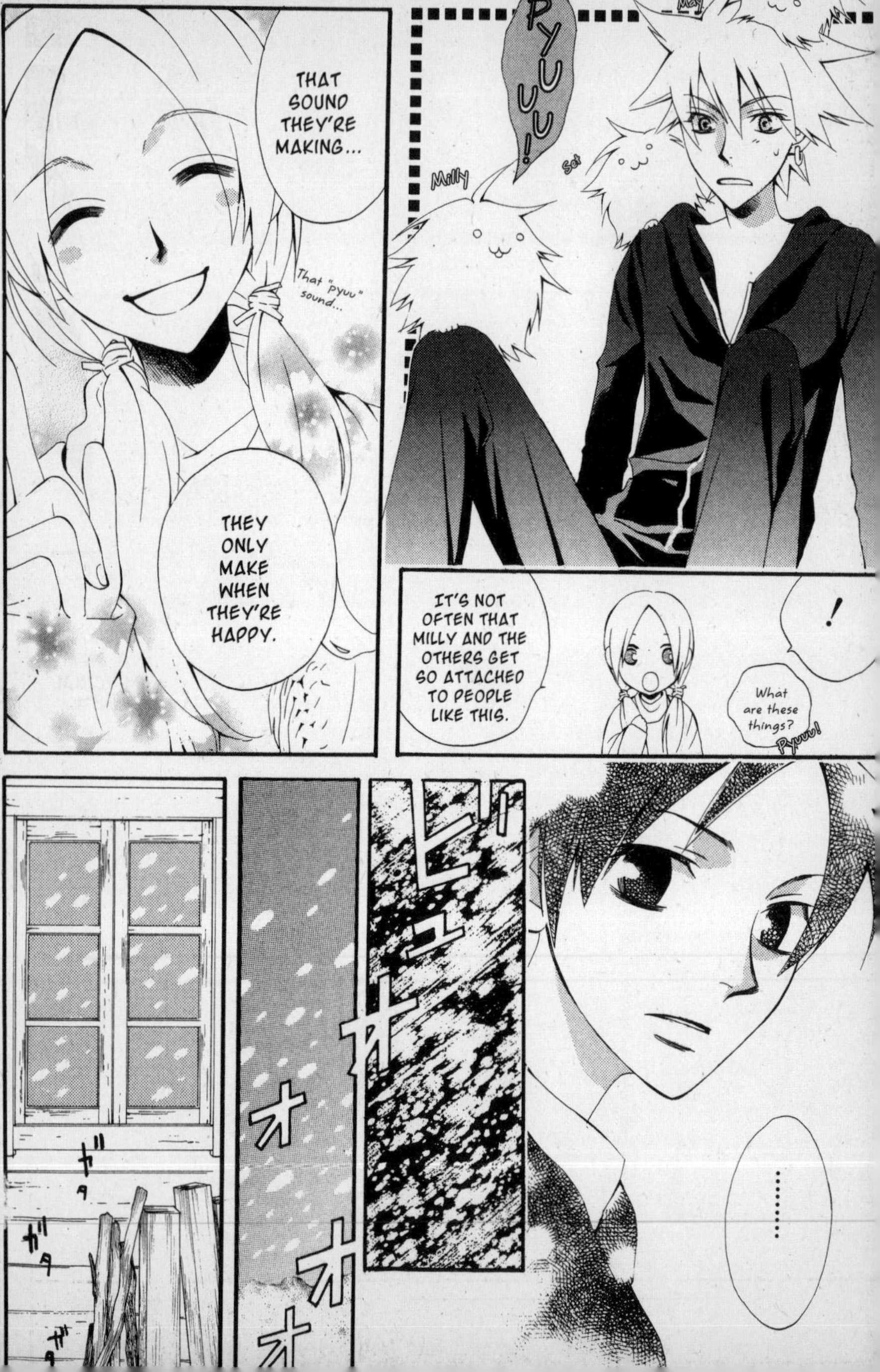
May
PYUUUU!
Sat
Milly
!
What are these things?
Pyuuu!
IT'S NOT OFTEN THAT MILLY AND THE OTHERS GET SO ATTACHED TO PEOPLE LIKE THIS.
THAT SOUND THEY'RE MAKING...
That "pyuu" sound...
THEY ONLY MAKE WHEN THEY'RE HAPPY.
......
ビュオオオオ
ガタガタガタ

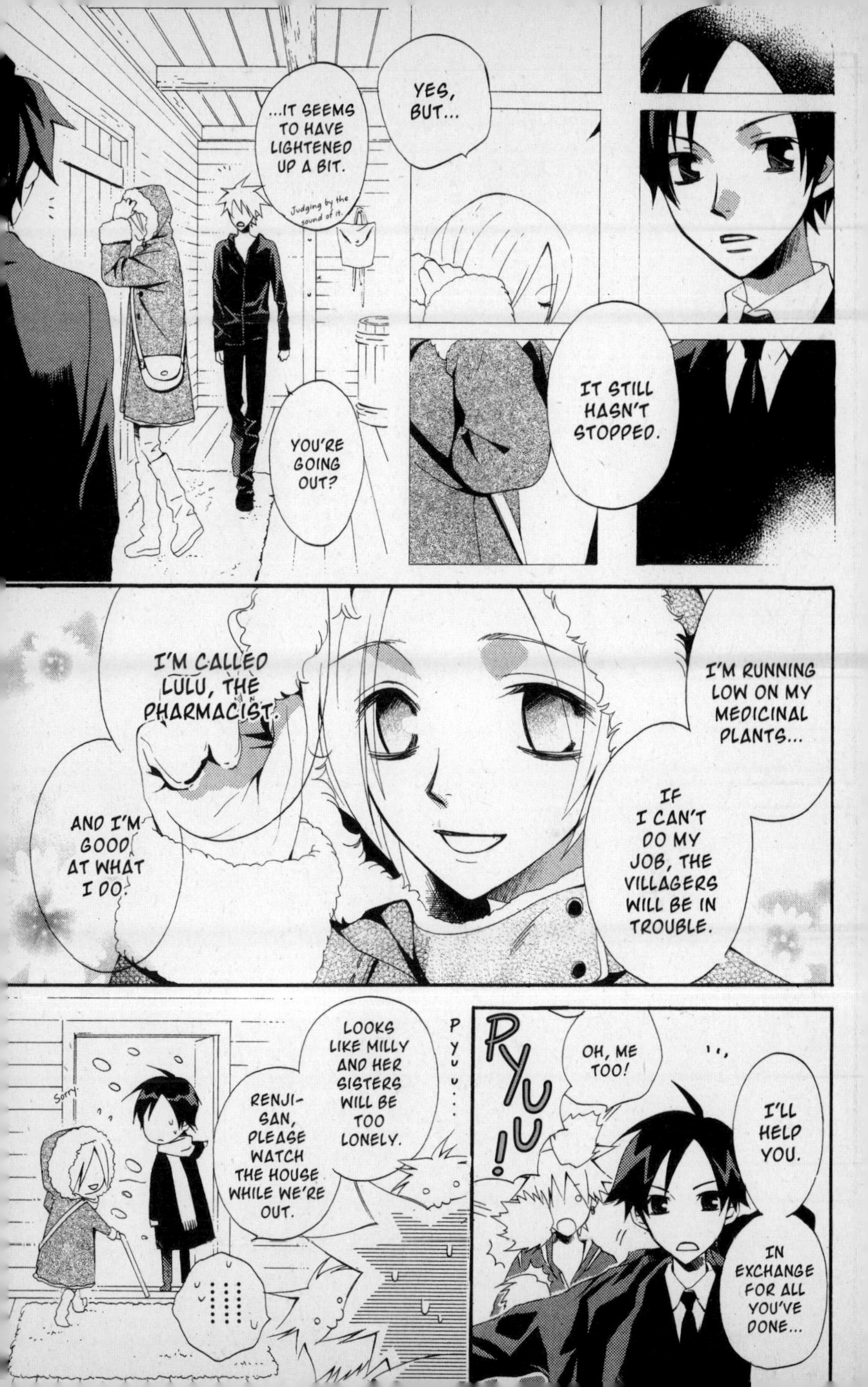
IT STILL HASN'T STOPPED.
YES, BUT...
...IT SEEMS TO HAVE LIGHTENED UP A BIT.
Judging by the sound of it.
YOU'RE GOING OUT?
I'M RUNNING LOW ON MY MEDICINAL PLANTS...
IF I CAN'T DO MY JOB, THE VILLAGERS WILL BE IN TROUBLE.
I'M CALLED LULU, THE PHARMACIST.
AND I'M GOOD AT WHAT I DO.
I'LL HELP YOU.
IN EXCHANGE FOR ALL YOU'VE DONE...
OH, ME TOO!
PYUU!
Pyuu...
LOOKS LIKE MILLY AND HER SISTERS WILL BE TOO LONELY.
RENJI-SAN, PLEASE WATCH THE HOUSE WHILE WE'RE OUT.
Sorry.

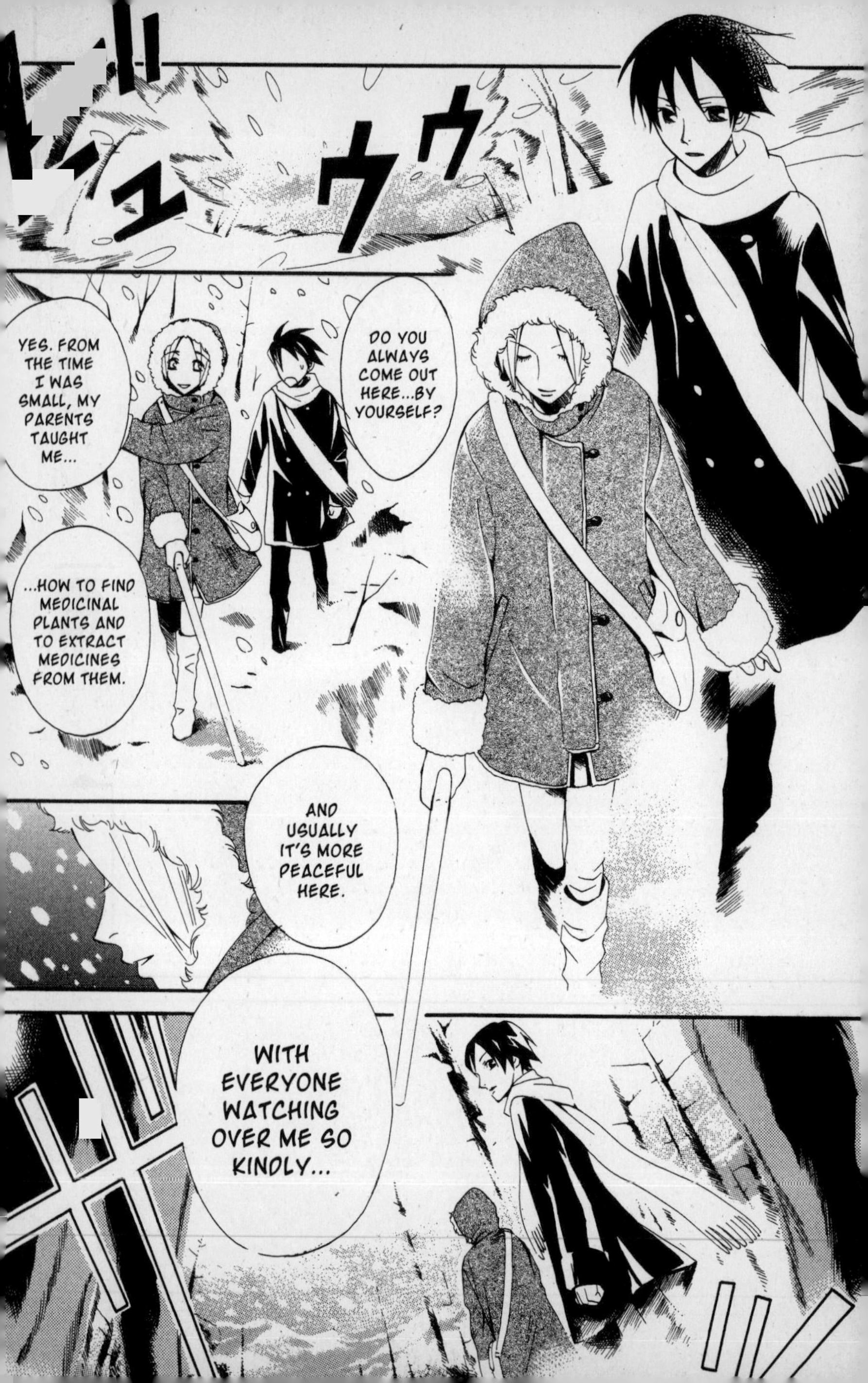
ュウウ
DO YOU ALWAYS COME OUT HERE...BY YOURSELF?
YES. FROM THE TIME I WAS SMALL, MY PARENTS TAUGHT ME...
...HOW TO FIND MEDICINAL PLANTS AND TO EXTRACT MEDICINES FROM THEM.
AND USUALLY IT'S MORE PEACEFUL HERE.
WITH EVERYONE WATCHING OVER ME SO KINDLY...

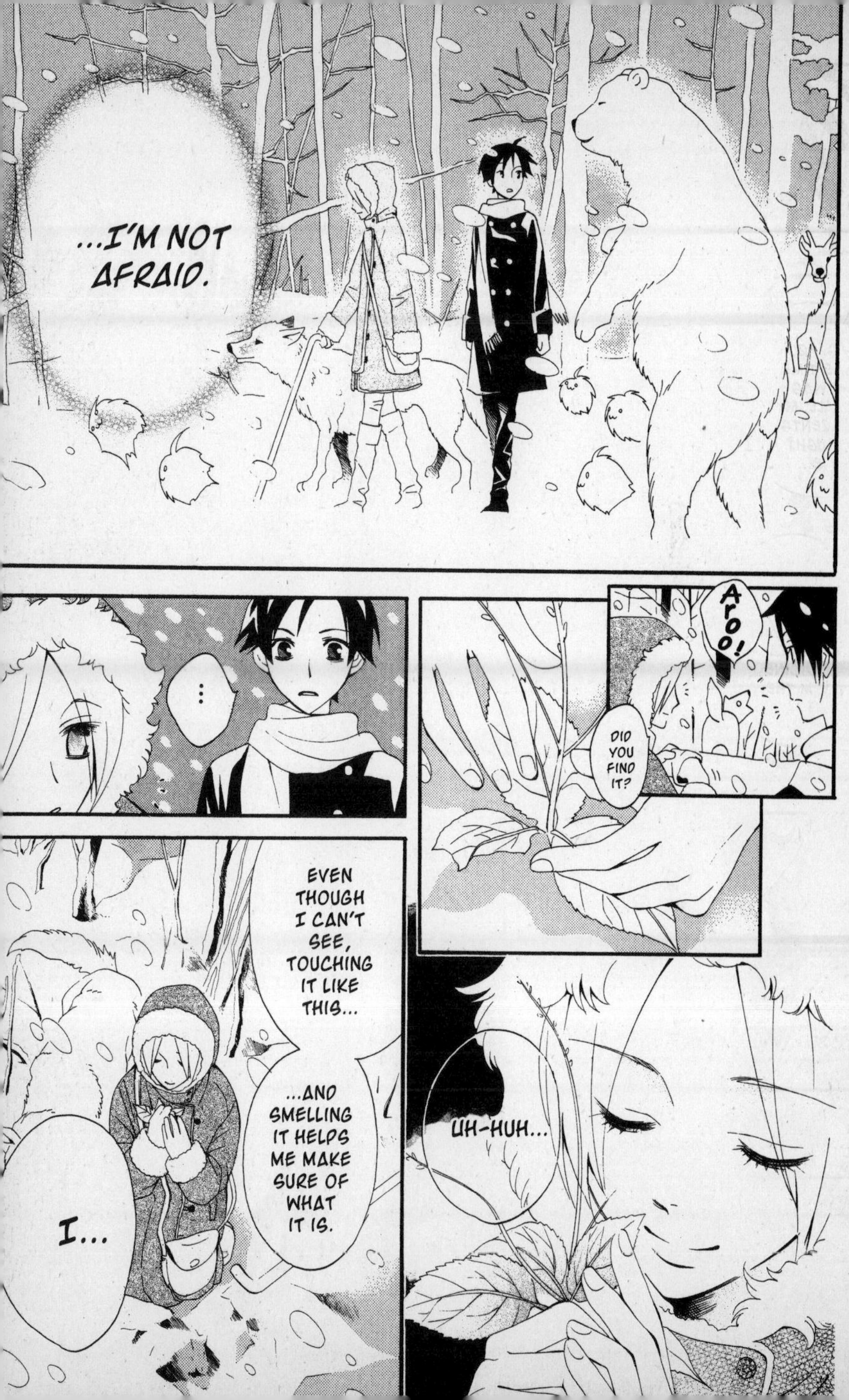
...I'M NOT AFRAID.
Aroo!
DID YOU FIND IT?
UH-HUH...
...
EVEN THOUGH I CAN'T SEE, TOUCHING IT LIKE THIS...
...AND SMELLING IT HELPS ME MAKE SURE OF WHAT IT IS.
I...

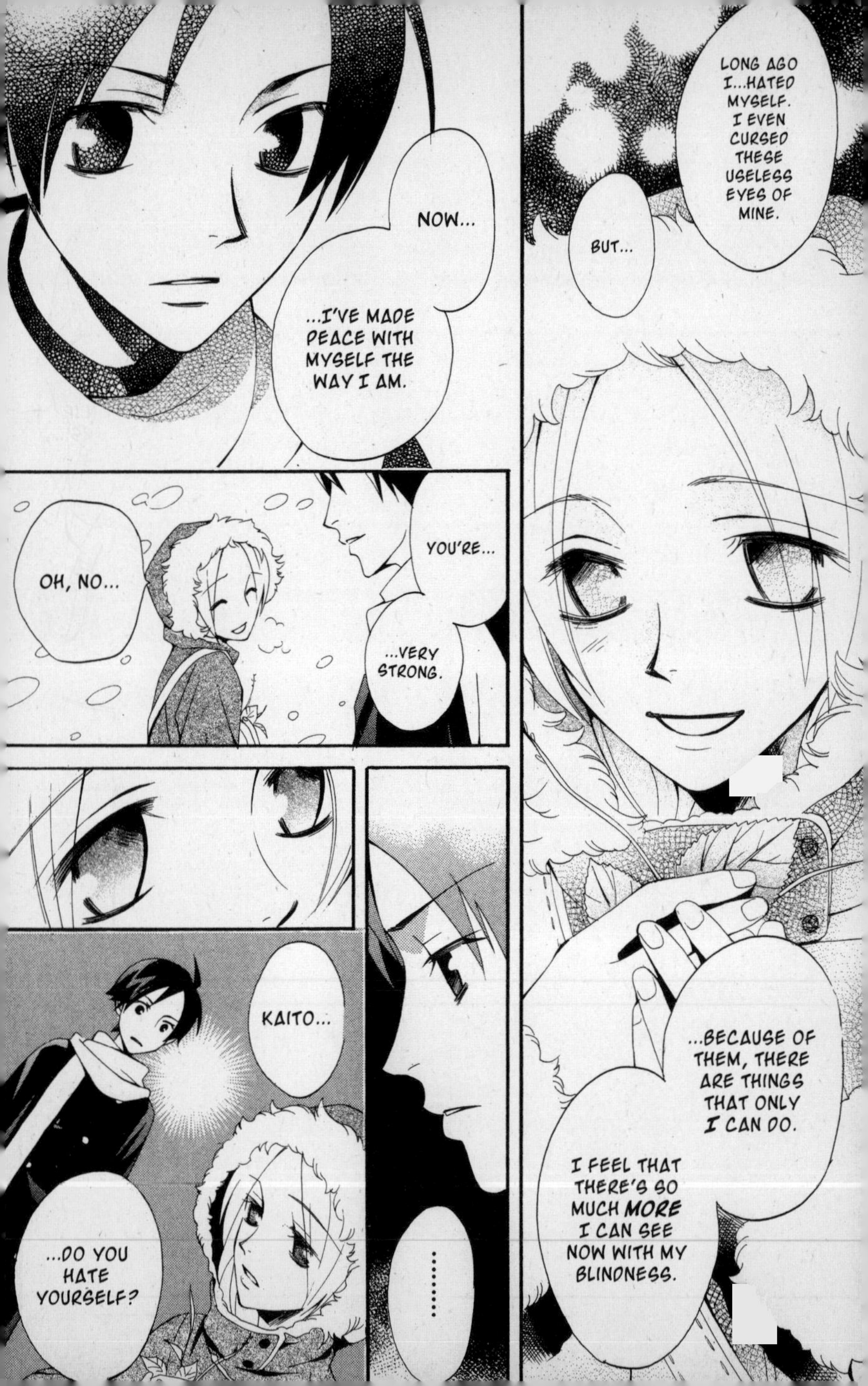
LONG AGO I...HATED MYSELF. I EVEN CURSED THESE USELESS EYES OF MINE.
BUT...
...BECAUSE OF THEM, THERE ARE THINGS THAT ONLY *I* CAN DO.
I FEEL THAT THERE'S SO MUCH *MORE* I CAN SEE NOW WITH MY BLINDNESS.
NOW...
...I'VE MADE PEACE WITH MYSELF THE WAY I AM.
YOU'RE...
...VERY STRONG.
OH, NO...
......
KAITO...
...DO YOU HATE YOURSELF?

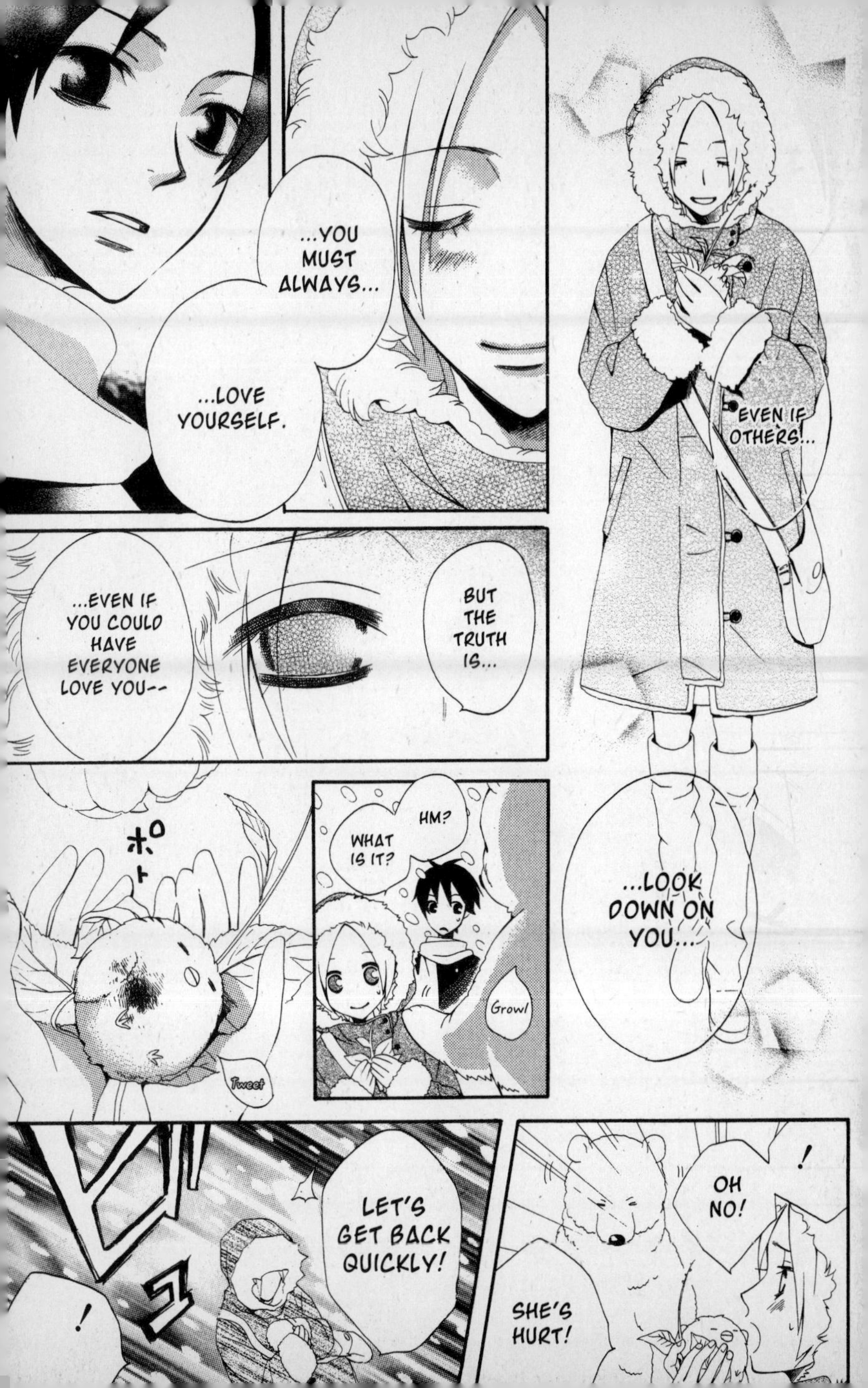
EVEN IF OTHERS!...
...LOOK DOWN ON YOU...
...YOU MUST ALWAYS...
...LOVE YOURSELF.
BUT THE TRUTH IS...
...EVEN IF YOU COULD HAVE EVERYONE LOVE YOU--
HM?
WHAT IS IT?
Growl
ポト
Tweet
!
OH NO!
SHE'S HURT!
LET'S GET BACK QUICKLY!
!

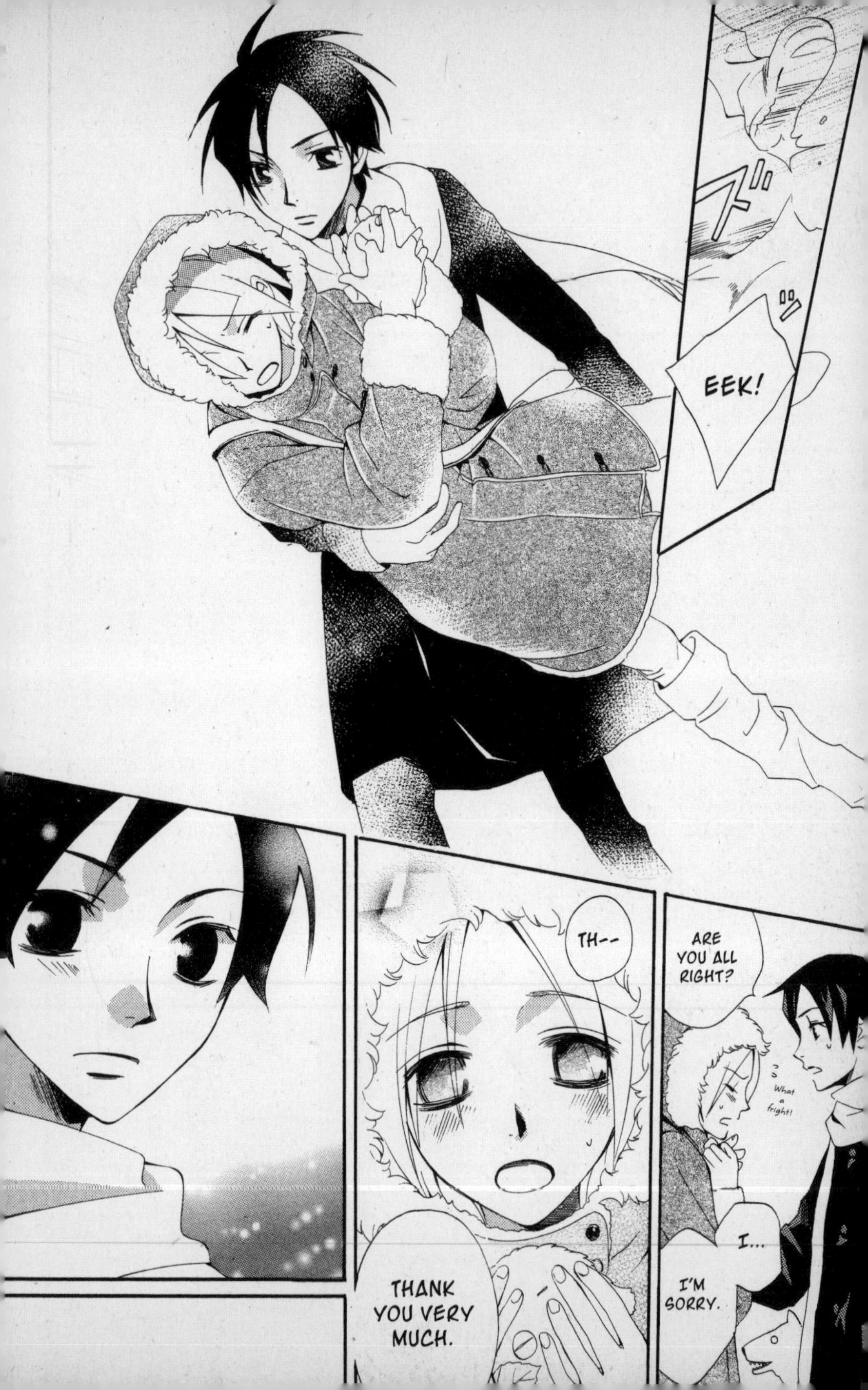
EEK!
ARE YOU ALL RIGHT?
What a fright!
I...
I'M SORRY.
TH--
THANK YOU VERY MUCH.

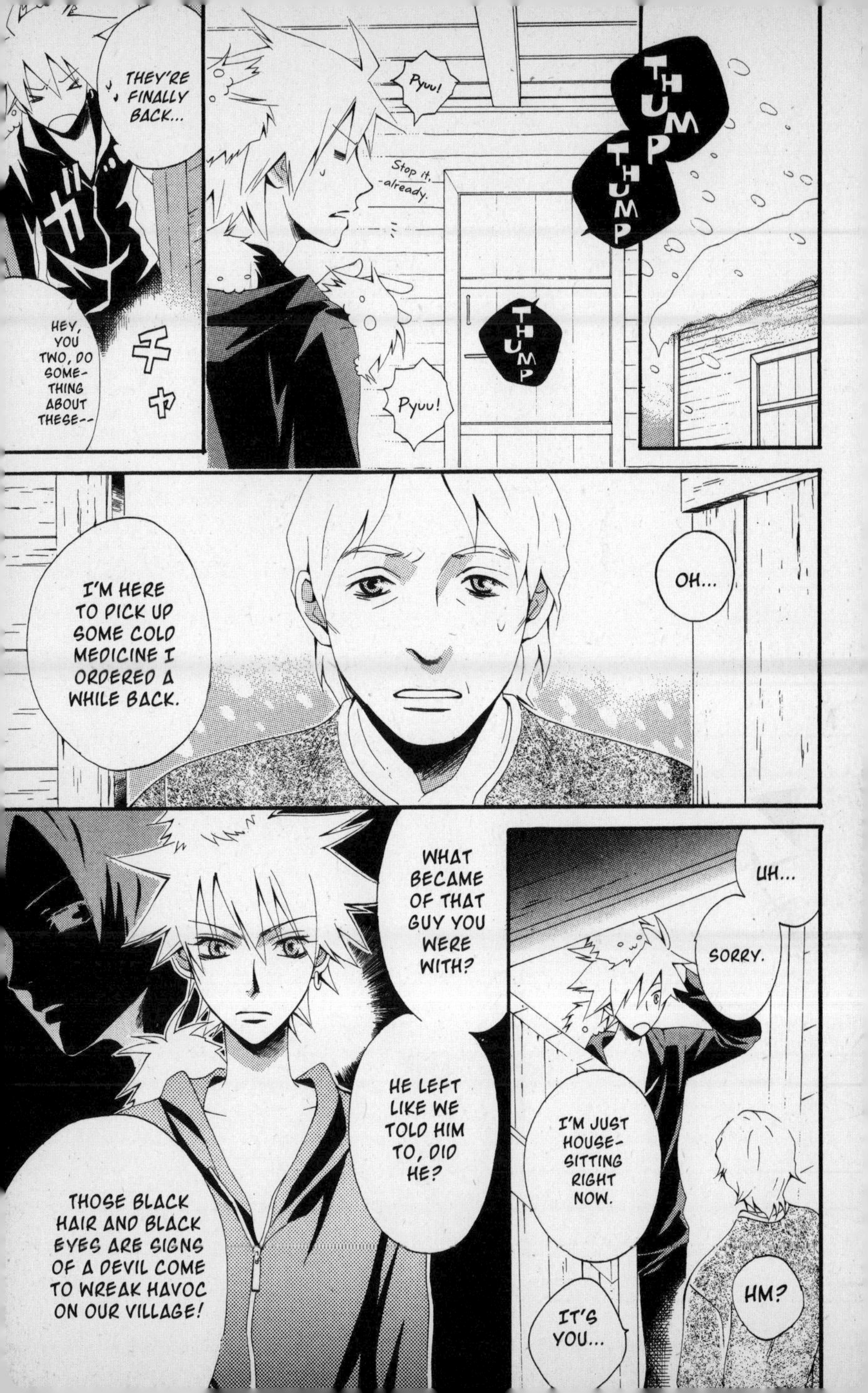
THUMP THUMP
THUMP
Pyuu!
Stop it, already.
Pyuu!
THEY'RE FINALLY BACK...
ガチャ
HEY, YOU TWO, DO SOME-THING ABOUT THESE--
OH...
I'M HERE TO PICK UP SOME COLD MEDICINE I ORDERED A WHILE BACK.
UH...
SORRY.
I'M JUST HOUSE-SITTING RIGHT NOW.
HM?
IT'S YOU...
WHAT BECAME OF THAT GUY YOU WERE WITH?
HE LEFT LIKE WE TOLD HIM TO, DID HE?
THOSE BLACK HAIR AND BLACK EYES ARE SIGNS OF A DEVIL COME TO WREAK HAVOC ON OUR VILLAGE!

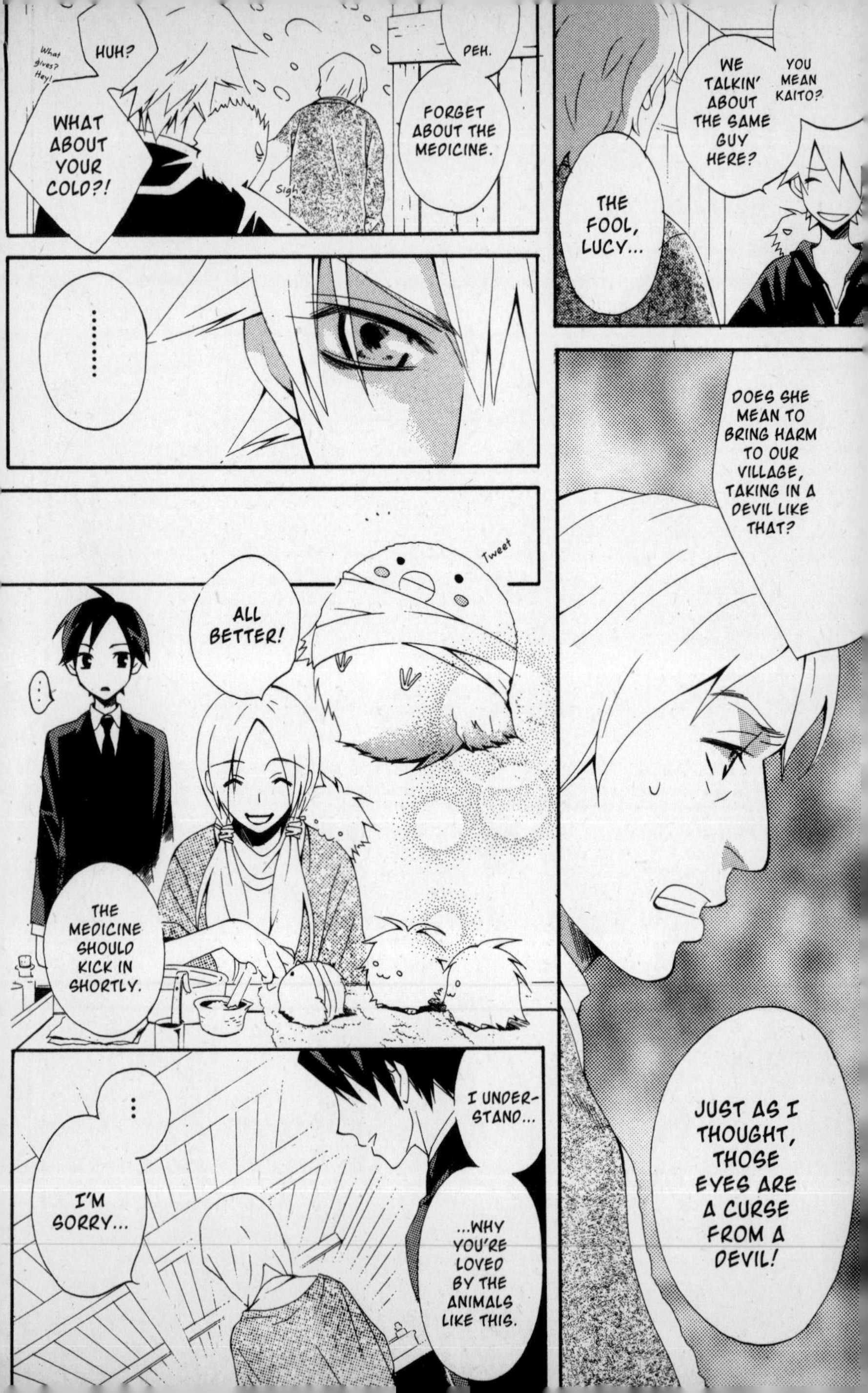
WE TALKIN' ABOUT THE SAME GUY HERE?
YOU MEAN KAITO?
THE FOOL, LUCY...
DOES SHE MEAN TO BRING HARM TO OUR VILLAGE, TAKING IN A DEVIL LIKE THAT?
JUST AS I THOUGHT, THOSE EYES ARE A CURSE FROM A DEVIL!
PEH.
FORGET ABOUT THE MEDICINE.
Sigh
HUH?
What gives? Hey!
WHAT ABOUT YOUR COLD?!
......
...
Tweet
ALL BETTER!
...
THE MEDICINE SHOULD KICK IN SHORTLY.
I UNDER-STAND...
...WHY YOU'RE LOVED BY THE ANIMALS LIKE THIS.
...
I'M SORRY...

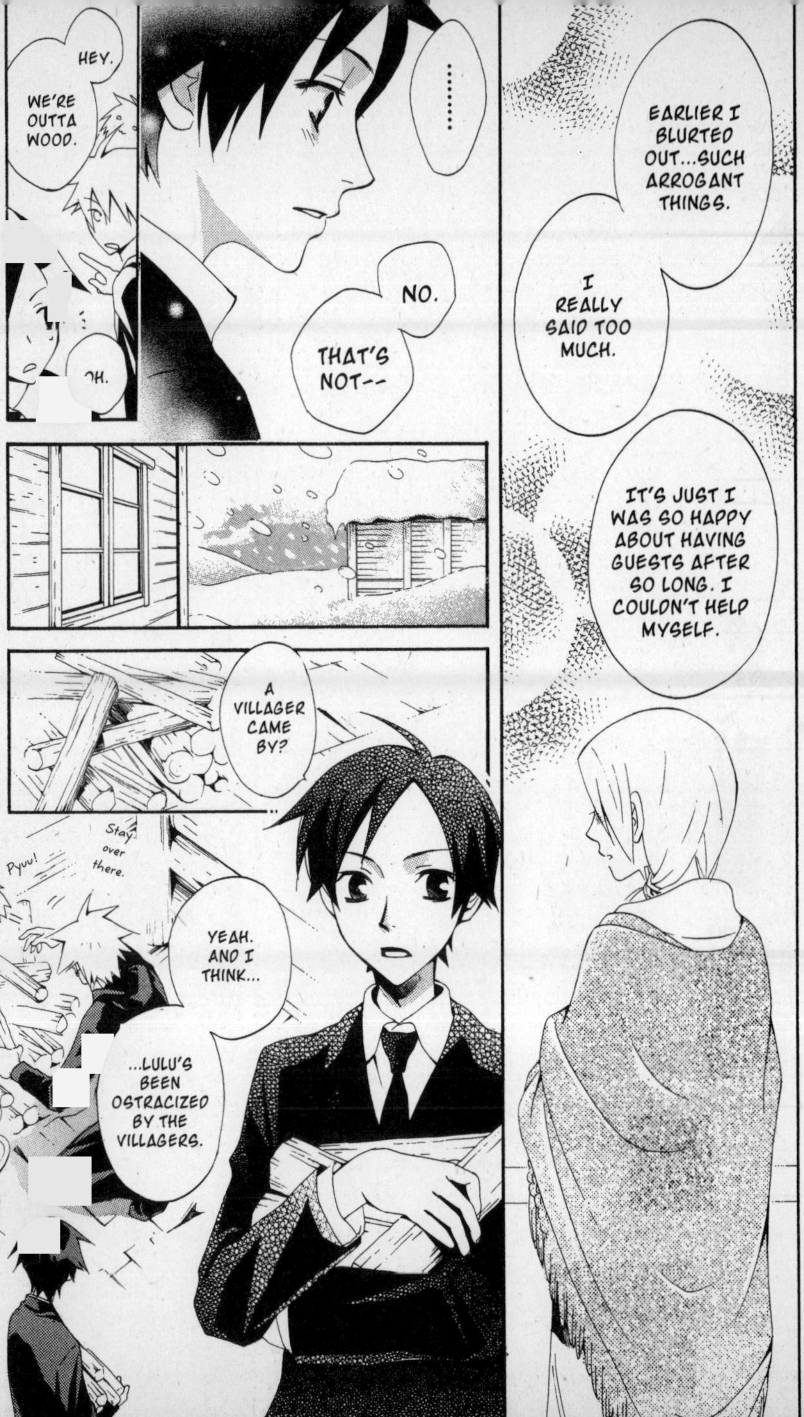
EARLIER I BLURTED OUT...SUCH ARROGANT THINGS.
I REALLY SAID TOO MUCH.
IT'S JUST I WAS SO HAPPY ABOUT HAVING GUESTS AFTER SO LONG. I COULDN'T HELP MYSELF.
......
NO.
THAT'S NOT--
HEY.
WE'RE OUTTA WOOD.
A VILLAGER CAME BY?
YEAH. AND I THINK...
...LULU'S BEEN OSTRACIZED BY THE VILLAGERS.
Stay over there.
Pyuu!

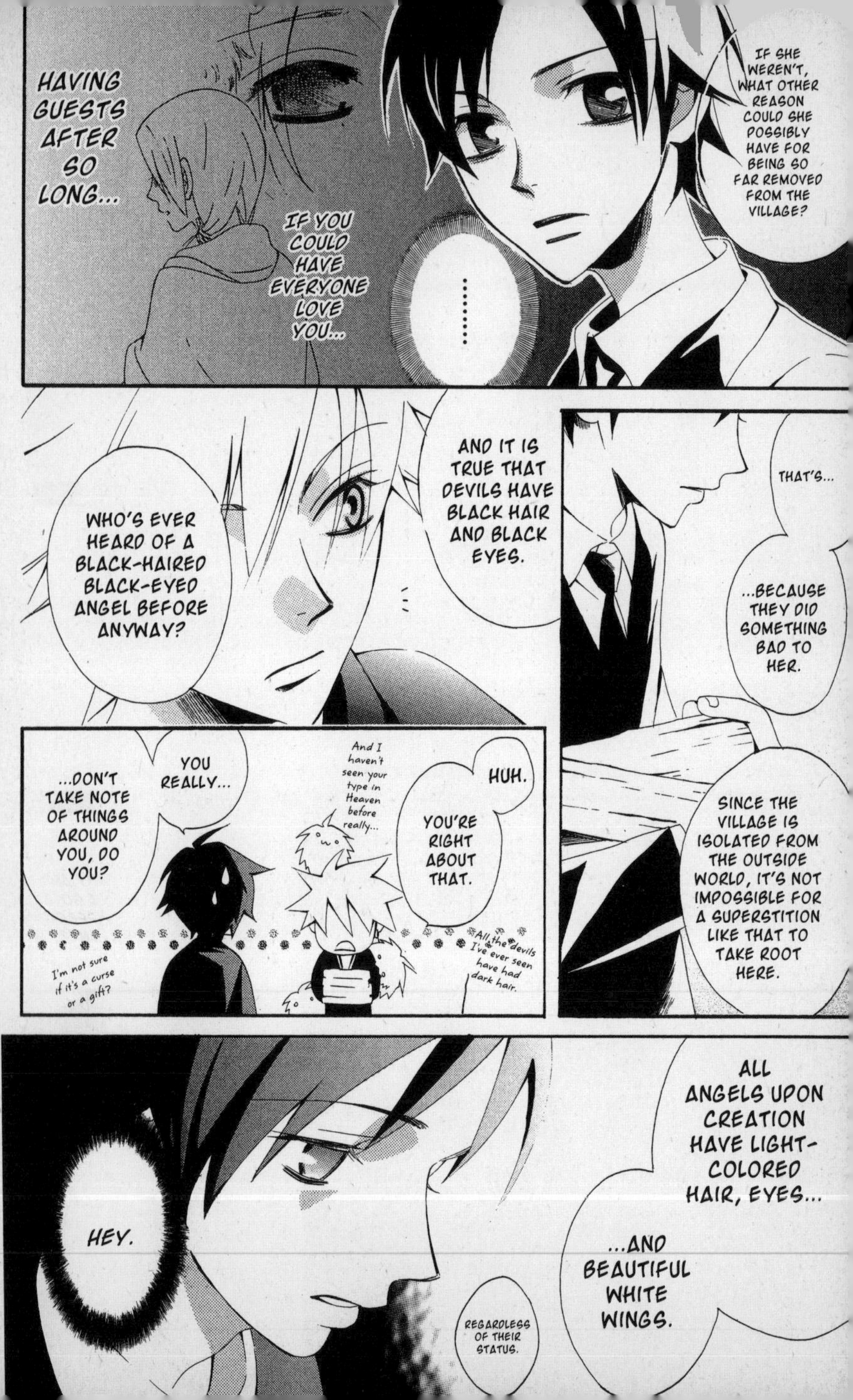
IF SHE WEREN'T, WHAT OTHER REASON COULD SHE POSSIBLY HAVE FOR BEING SO FAR REMOVED FROM THE VILLAGE?
......
IF YOU COULD HAVE EVERYONE LOVE YOU...
HAVING GUESTS AFTER SO LONG...
THAT'S...
...BECAUSE THEY DID SOMETHING BAD TO HER.
SINCE THE VILLAGE IS ISOLATED FROM THE OUTSIDE WORLD, IT'S NOT IMPOSSIBLE FOR A SUPERSTITION LIKE THAT TO TAKE ROOT HERE.
AND IT IS TRUE THAT DEVILS HAVE BLACK HAIR AND BLACK EYES.
WHO'S EVER HEARD OF A BLACK-HAIRED BLACK-EYED ANGEL BEFORE ANYWAY?
All the devils I've ever seen have had dark hair.
HUH.
YOU'RE RIGHT ABOUT THAT.
And I haven't seen your type in Heaven before really...
YOU REALLY...
...DON'T TAKE NOTE OF THINGS AROUND YOU, DO YOU?
I'm not sure if it's a curse or a gift?
ALL ANGELS UPON CREATION HAVE LIGHT-COLORED HAIR, EYES...
...AND BEAUTIFUL WHITE WINGS.
REGARDLESS OF THEIR STATUS.
HEY.

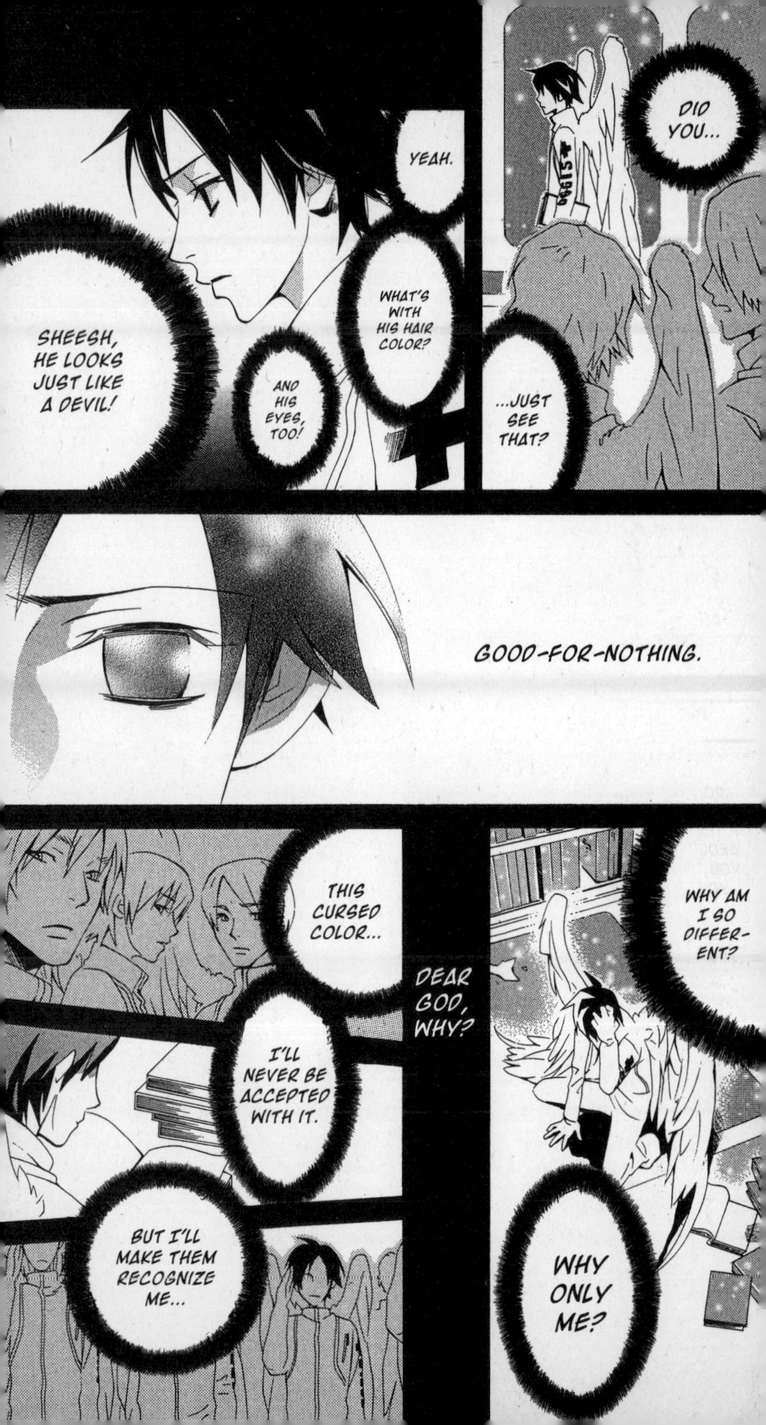
DID YOU...
...JUST SEE THAT?
YEAH.
WHAT'S WITH HIS HAIR COLOR?
AND HIS EYES, TOO!
SHEESH, HE LOOKS JUST LIKE A DEVIL!
GOOD-FOR-NOTHING.
WHY AM I SO DIFFER-ENT?
WHY ONLY ME?
DEAR GOD, WHY?
THIS CURSED COLOR...
I'LL NEVER BE ACCEPTED WITH IT.
BUT I'LL MAKE THEM RECOGNIZE ME...

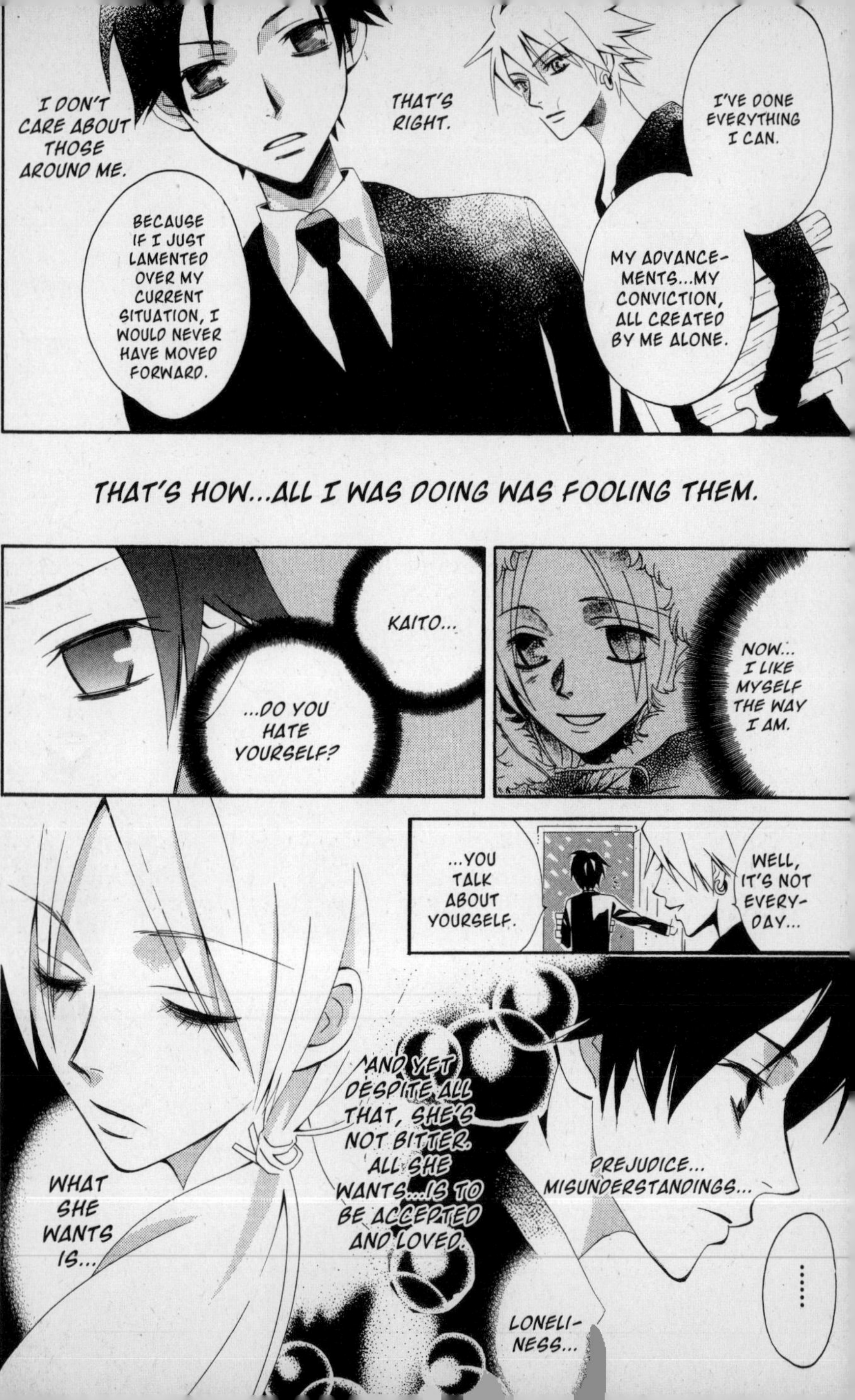
I'VE DONE EVERYTHING I CAN.
MY ADVANCEMENTS...MY CONVICTION, ALL CREATED BY ME ALONE.
THAT'S RIGHT.
I DON'T CARE ABOUT THOSE AROUND ME.
BECAUSE IF I JUST LAMENTED OVER MY CURRENT SITUATION, I WOULD NEVER HAVE MOVED FORWARD.
THAT'S HOW...ALL I WAS DOING WAS FOOLING THEM.
NOW... I LIKE MYSELF THE WAY I AM.
KAITO...
...DO YOU HATE YOURSELF?
WELL, IT'S NOT EVERY-DAY...
...YOU TALK ABOUT YOURSELF.
PREJUDICE... MISUNDERSTANDINGS...
LONELI-NESS...
......
AND YET DESPITE ALL THAT, SHE'S NOT BITTER. ALL SHE WANTS...IS TO BE ACCEPTED AND LOVED.
WHAT SHE WANTS IS...

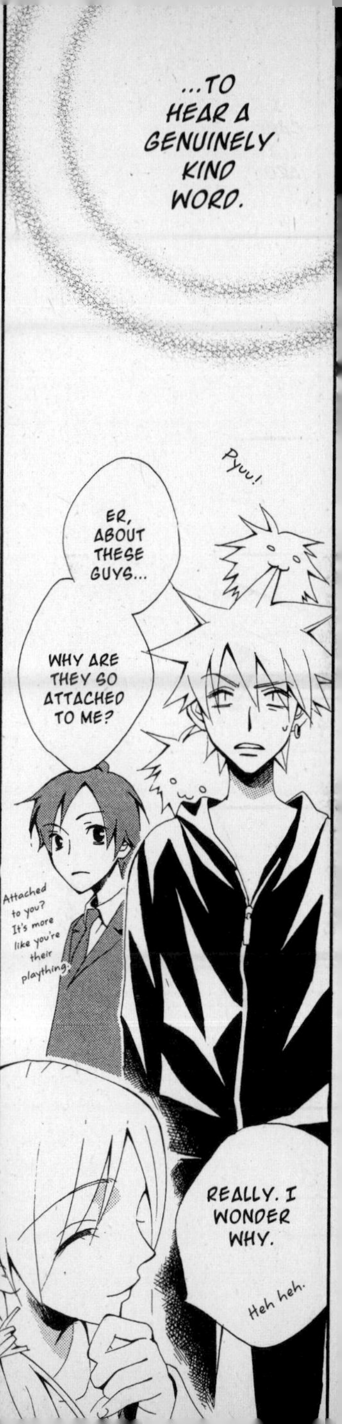
...TO HEAR A GENUINELY KIND WORD.
Pyuu!
ER, ABOUT THESE GUYS...
WHY ARE THEY SO ATTACHED TO ME?
Attached to you? It's more like you're their plaything.
REALLY. I WONDER WHY.
Heh heh.
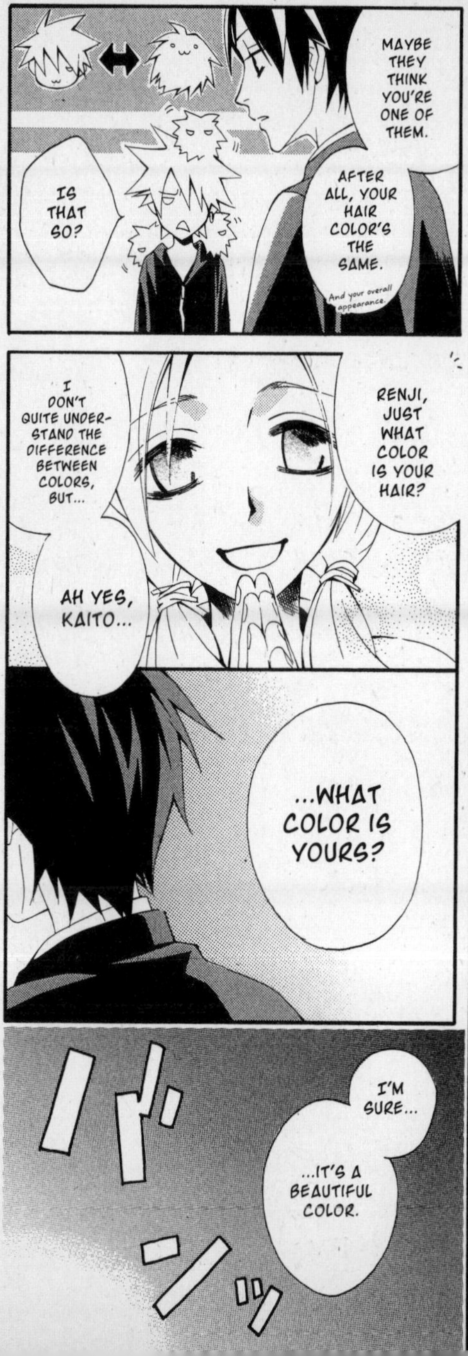
MAYBE THEY THINK YOU'RE ONE OF THEM.
AFTER ALL, YOUR HAIR COLOR'S THE SAME.
And your overall appearance.
IS THAT SO?
RENJI, JUST WHAT COLOR IS YOUR HAIR?
I DON'T QUITE UNDERSTAND THE DIFFERENCE BETWEEN COLORS, BUT...
AH YES, KAITO...
...WHAT COLOR IS YOURS?
I'M SURE...
...IT'S A BEAUTIFUL COLOR.

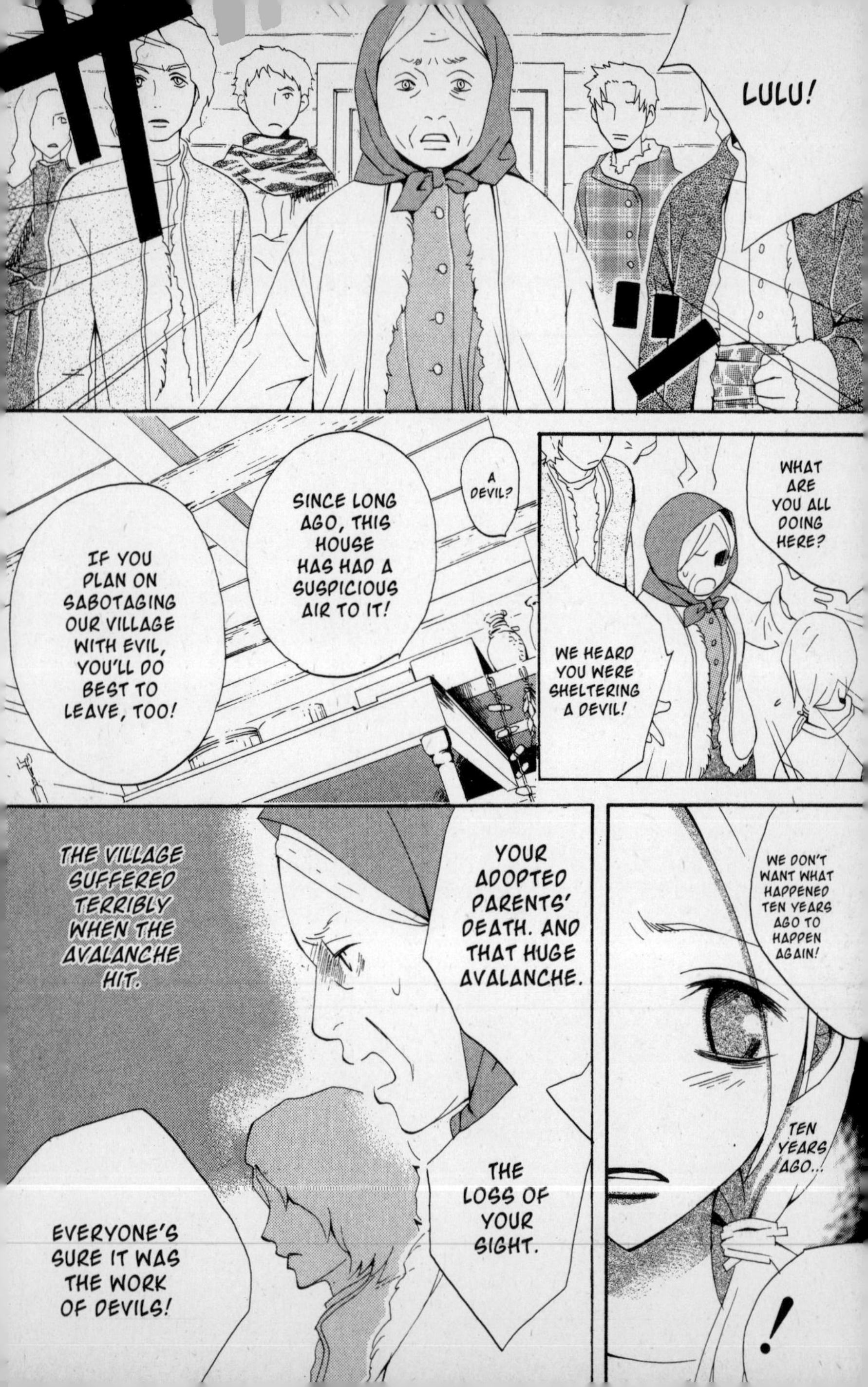
LULU!
WHAT ARE YOU ALL DOING HERE?
WE HEARD YOU WERE SHELTERING A DEVIL!
A DEVIL?
SINCE LONG AGO, THIS HOUSE HAS HAD A SUSPICIOUS AIR TO IT!
IF YOU PLAN ON SABOTAGING OUR VILLAGE WITH EVIL, YOU'LL DO BEST TO LEAVE, TOO!
WE DON'T WANT WHAT HAPPENED TEN YEARS AGO TO HAPPEN AGAIN!
TEN YEARS AGO...
!
YOUR ADOPTED PARENTS' DEATH. AND THAT HUGE AVALANCHE.
THE LOSS OF YOUR SIGHT.
THE VILLAGE SUFFERED TERRIBLY WHEN THE AVALANCHE HIT.
EVERYONE'S SURE IT WAS THE WORK OF DEVILS!

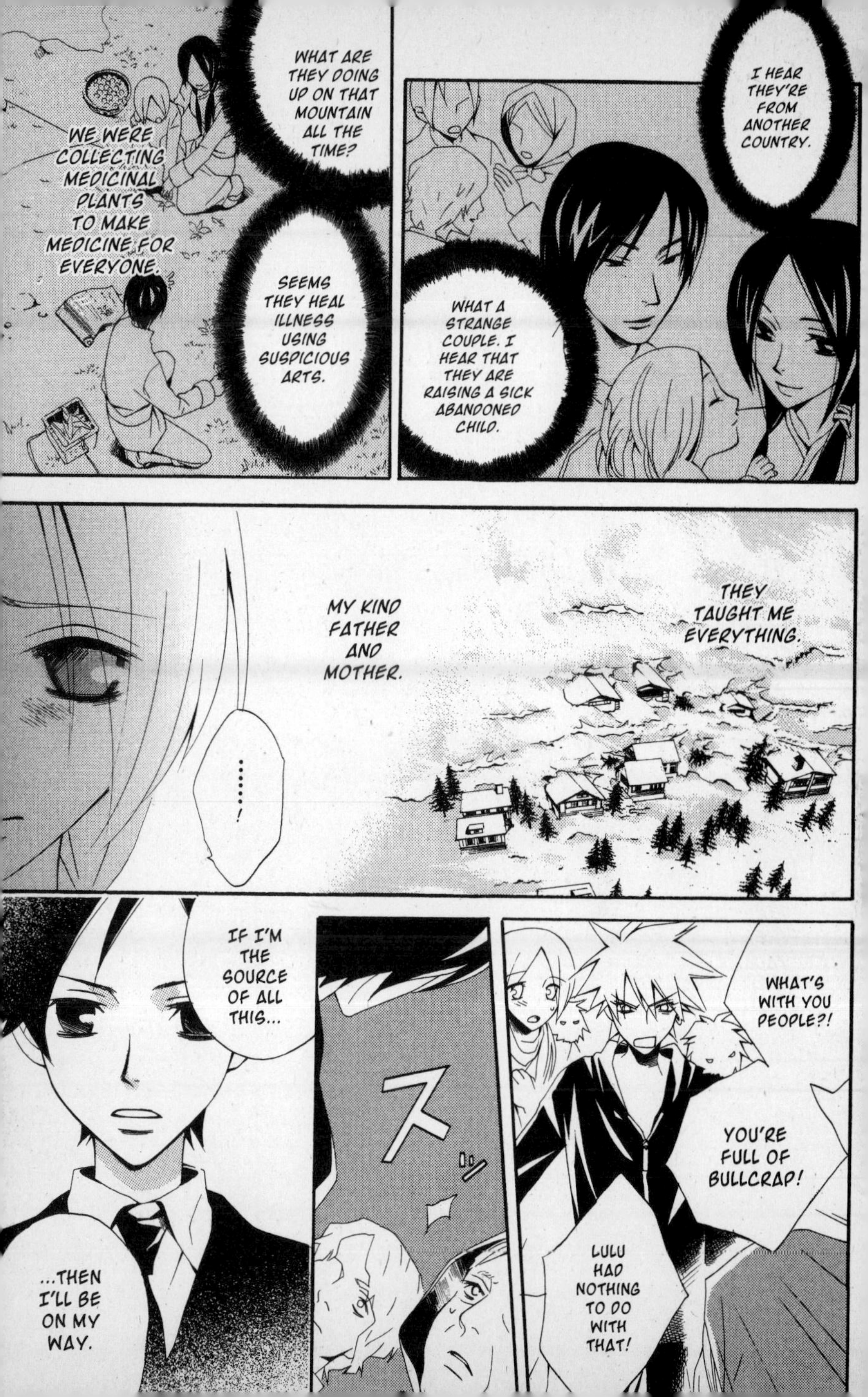
I HEAR THEY'RE FROM ANOTHER COUNTRY.
WHAT A STRANGE COUPLE. I HEAR THAT THEY ARE RAISING A SICK ABANDONED CHILD.
WHAT ARE THEY DOING UP ON THAT MOUNTAIN ALL THE TIME?
WE WERE COLLECTING MEDICINAL PLANTS TO MAKE MEDICINE FOR EVERYONE.
SEEMS THEY HEAL ILLNESS USING SUSPICIOUS ARTS.
THEY TAUGHT ME EVERYTHING.
MY KIND FATHER AND MOTHER.
......!
WHAT'S WITH YOU PEOPLE?!
YOU'RE FULL OF BULLCRAP!
LULU HAD NOTHING TO DO WITH THAT!
ス
IF I'M THE SOURCE OF ALL THIS...
...THEN I'LL BE ON MY WAY.

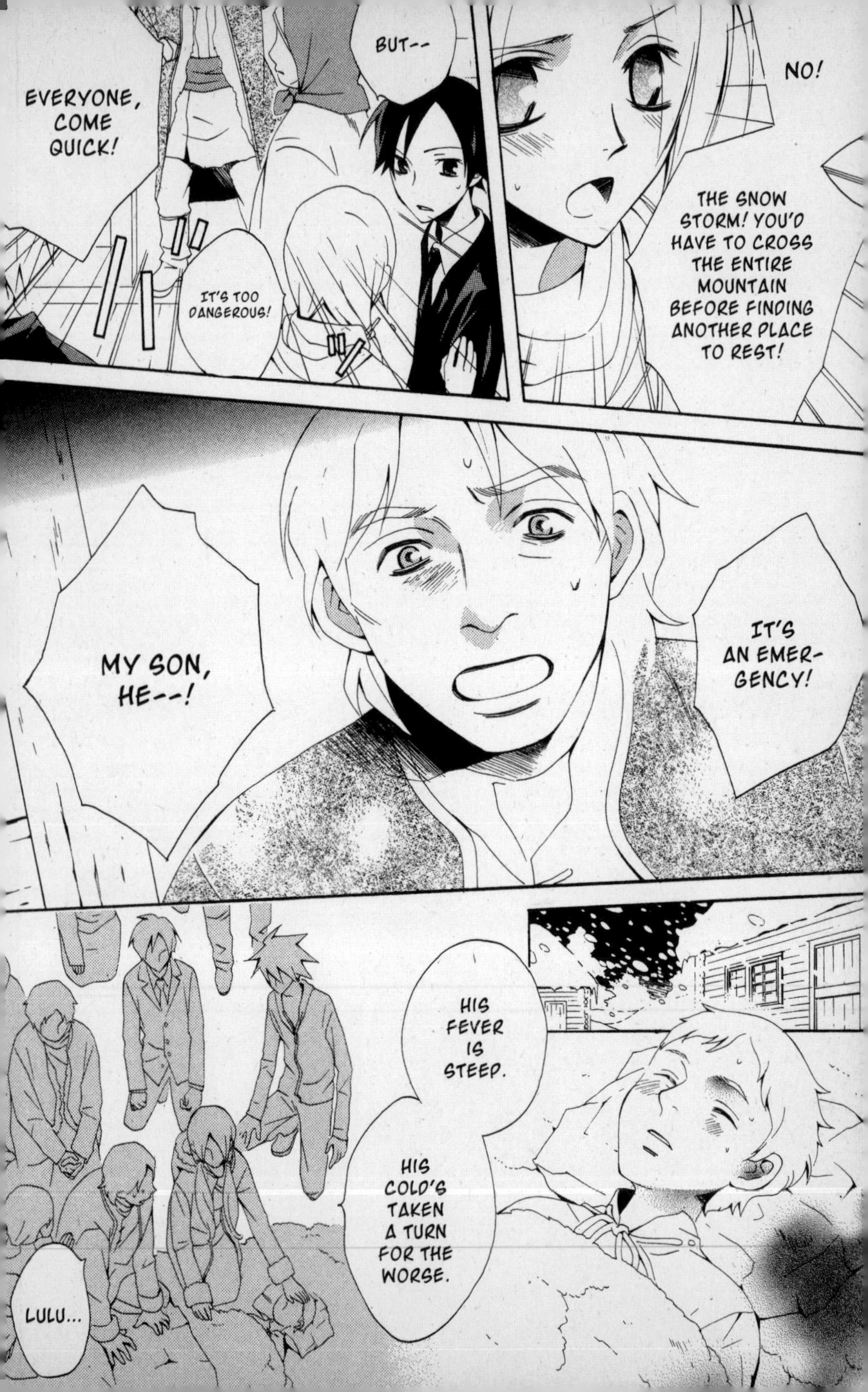
NO!
THE SNOW STORM! YOU'D HAVE TO CROSS THE ENTIRE MOUNTAIN BEFORE FINDING ANOTHER PLACE TO REST!
BUT--
EVERYONE, COME QUICK!
IT'S TOO DANGEROUS!
IT'S AN EMER-GENCY!
MY SON, HE--!
HIS FEVER IS STEEP.
HIS COLD'S TAKEN A TURN FOR THE WORSE.
LULU...

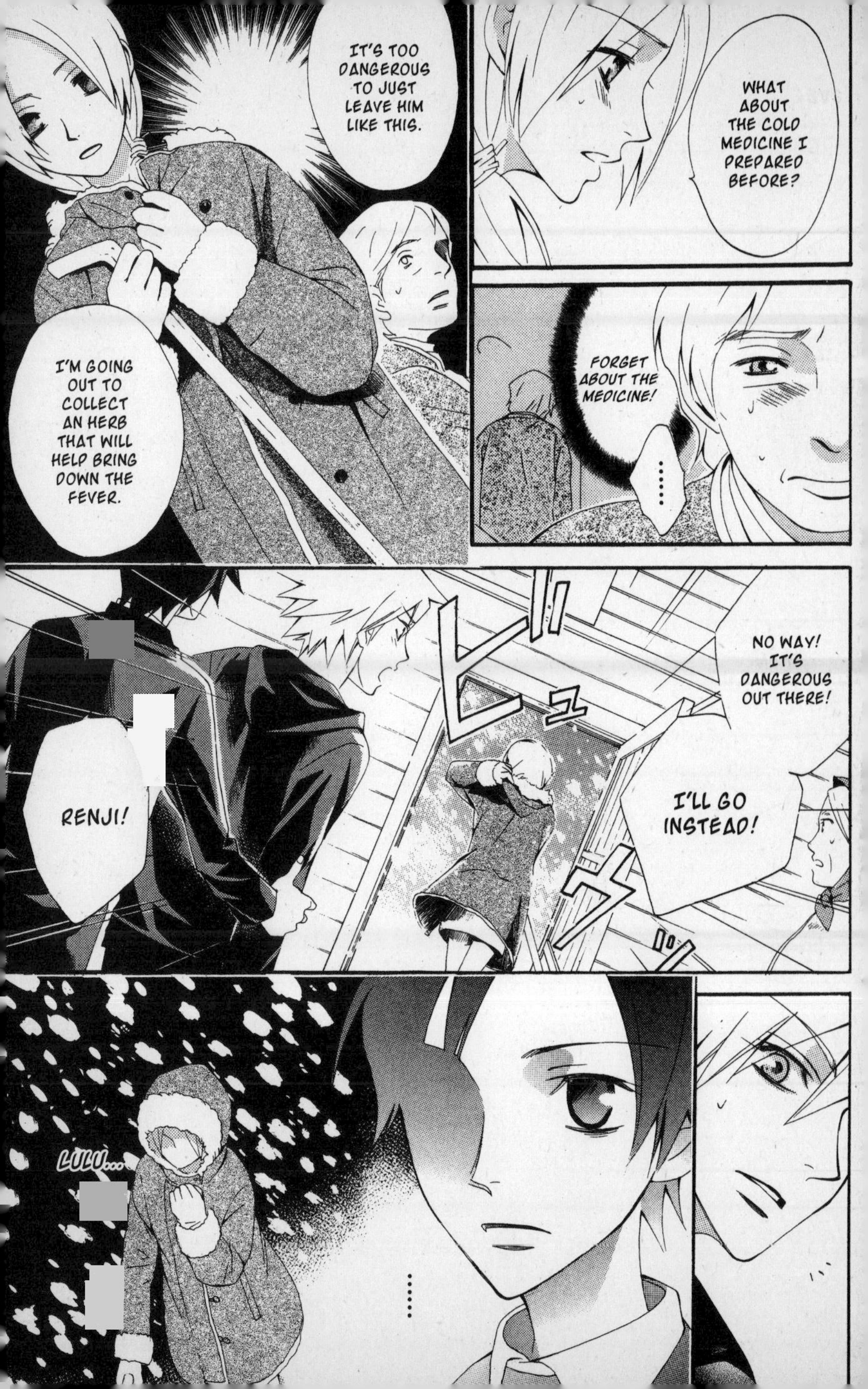
WHAT ABOUT THE COLD MEDICINE I PREPARED BEFORE?
FORGET ABOUT THE MEDICINE!
......
IT'S TOO DANGEROUS TO JUST LEAVE HIM LIKE THIS.
I'M GOING OUT TO COLLECT AN HERB THAT WILL HELP BRING DOWN THE FEVER.
NO WAY! IT'S DANGEROUS OUT THERE!
I'LL GO INSTEAD!
RENJI!
LULU...
......

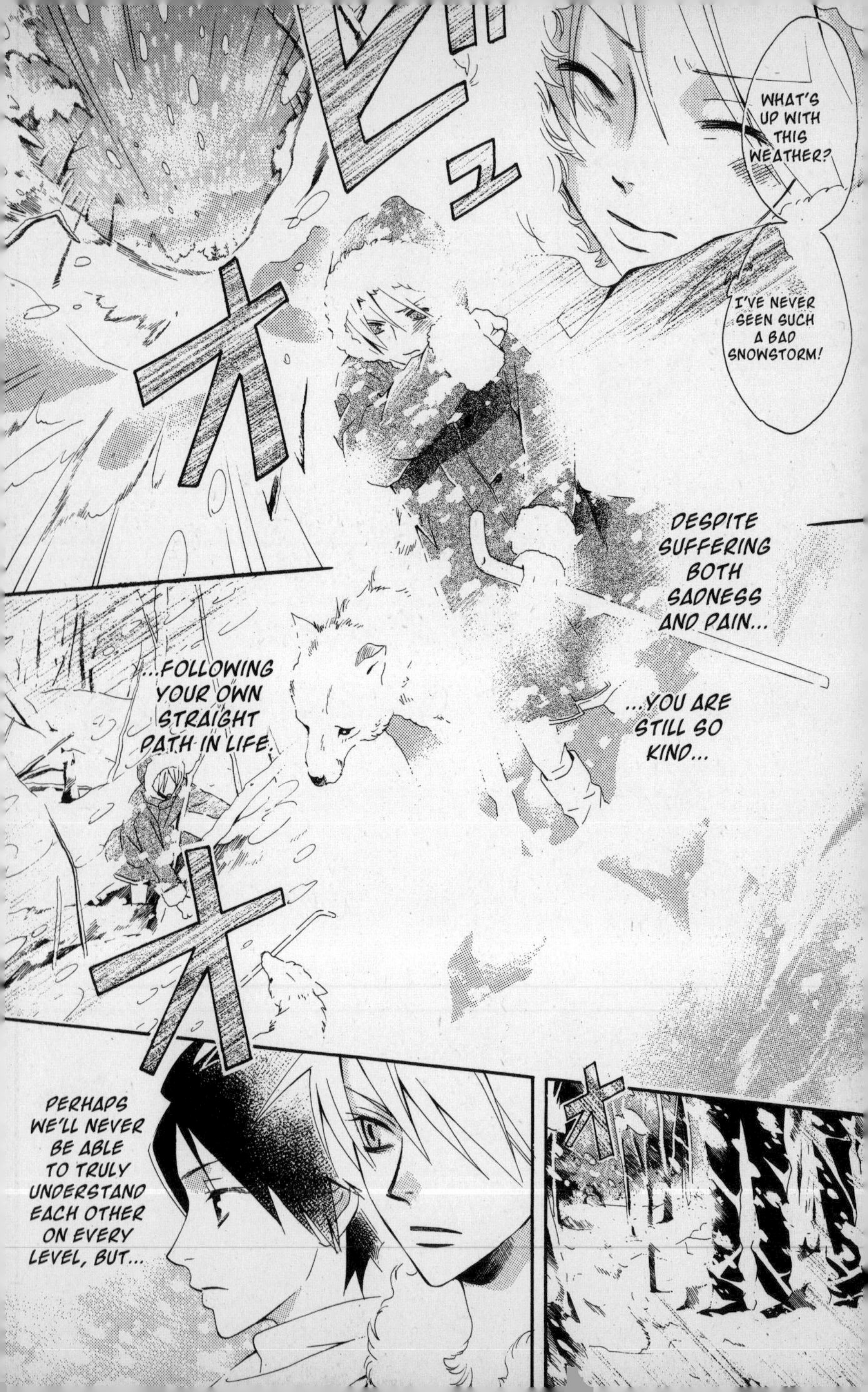
WHAT'S UP WITH THIS WEATHER?
I'VE NEVER SEEN SUCH A BAD SNOWSTORM!
DESPITE SUFFERING BOTH SADNESS AND PAIN...
...YOU ARE STILL SO KIND...
...FOLLOWING YOUR OWN STRAIGHT PATH IN LIFE.
PERHAPS WE'LL NEVER BE ABLE TO TRULY UNDERSTAND EACH OTHER ON EVERY LEVEL, BUT...

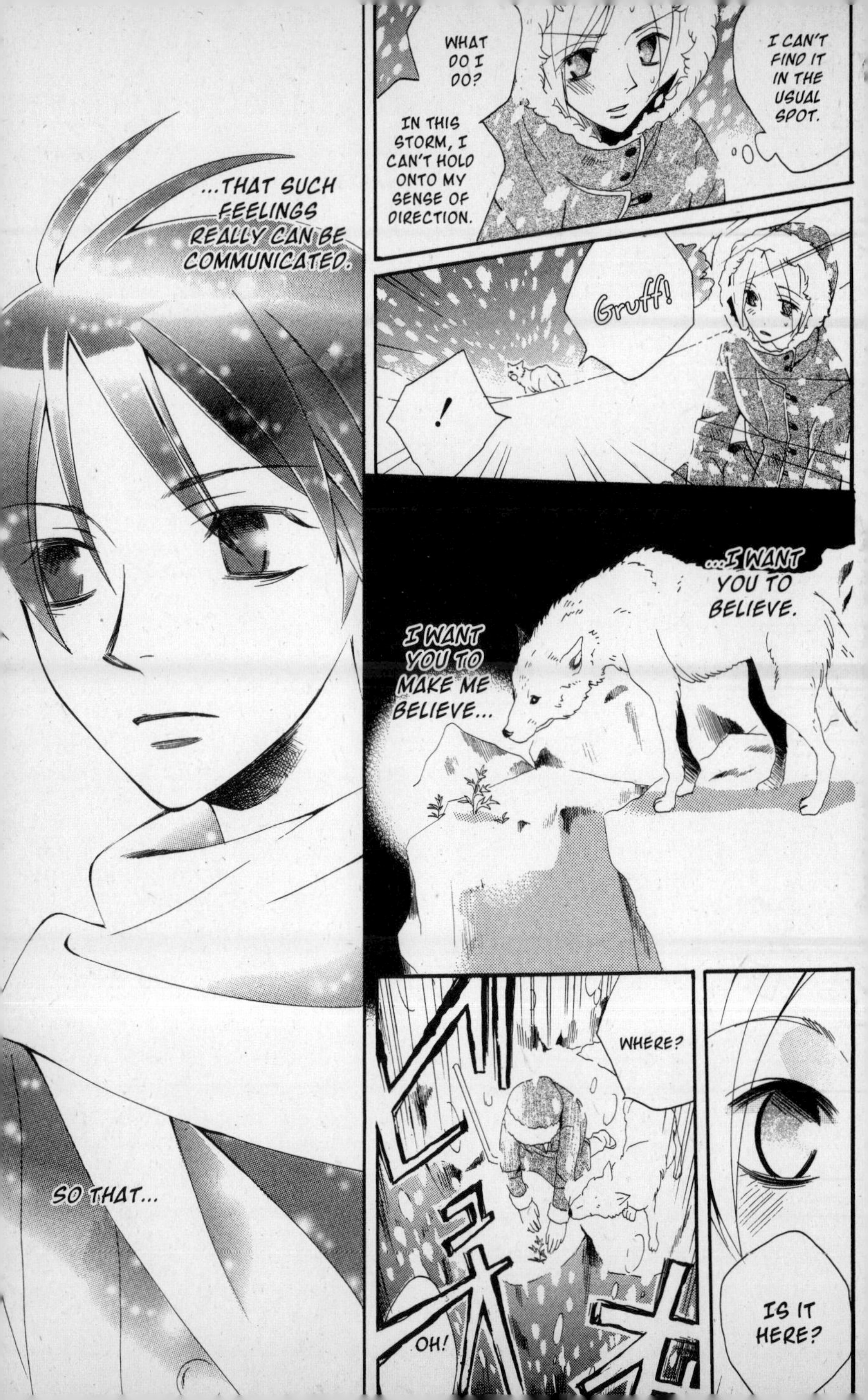
I CAN'T FIND IT IN THE USUAL SPOT.
WHAT DO I DO?
IN THIS STORM, I CAN'T HOLD ONTO MY SENSE OF DIRECTION.
Gruff!
!
...I WANT YOU TO BELIEVE.
I WANT YOU TO MAKE ME BELIEVE...
IS IT HERE?
WHERE?
OH!
...THAT SUCH FEELINGS REALLY CAN BE COMMUNICATED.
SO THAT...

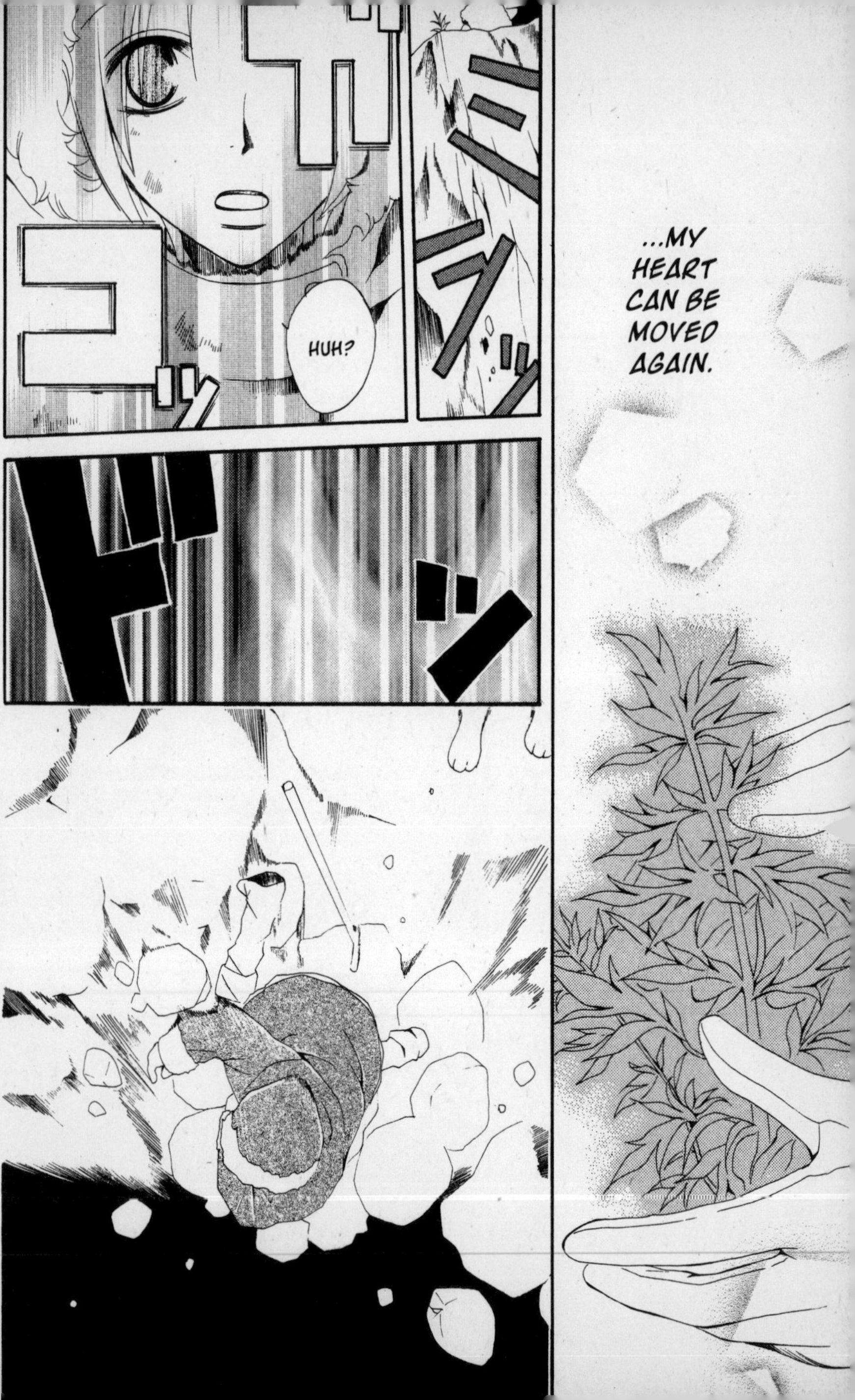
...MY HEART CAN BE MOVED AGAIN.
HUH?

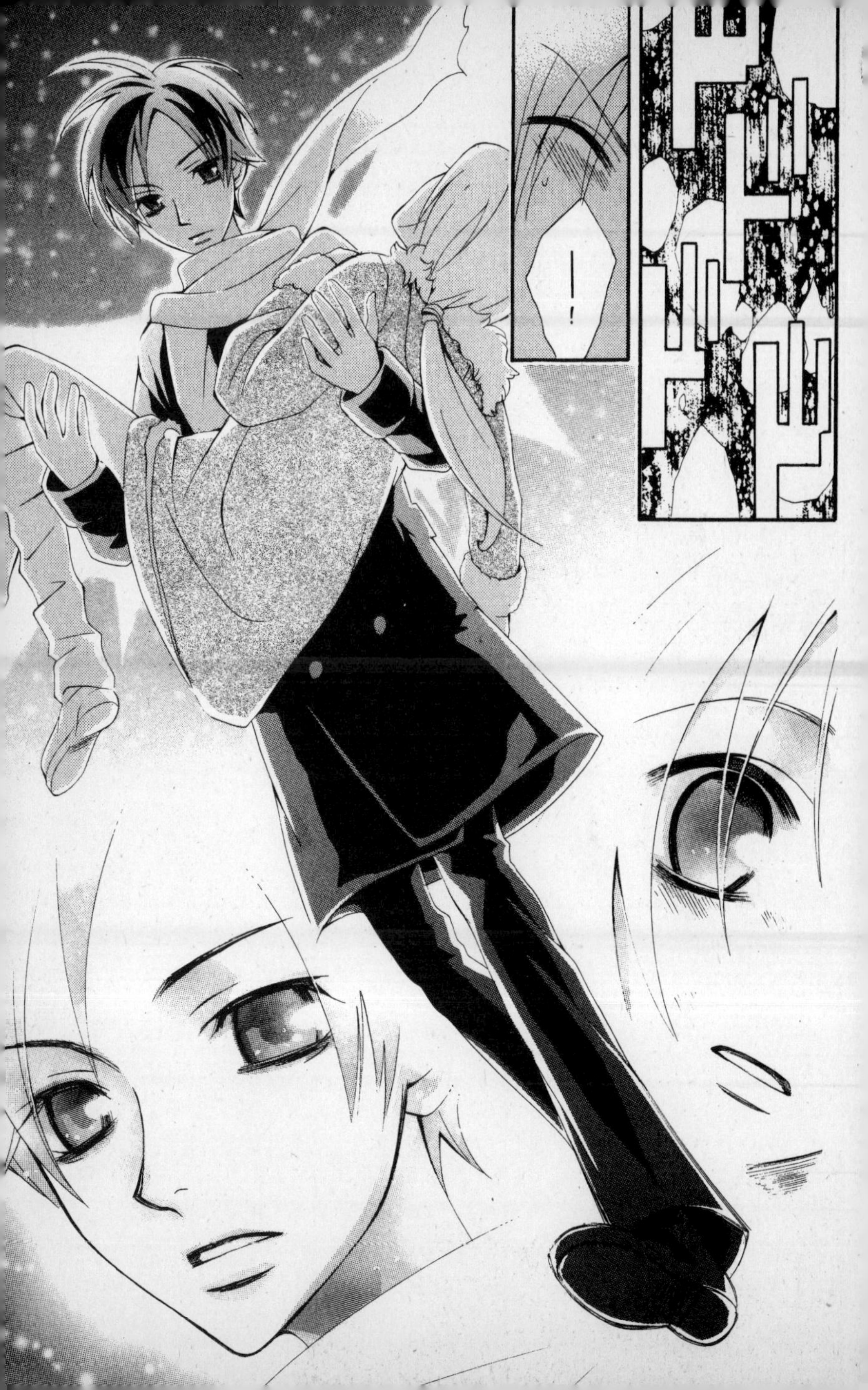
!

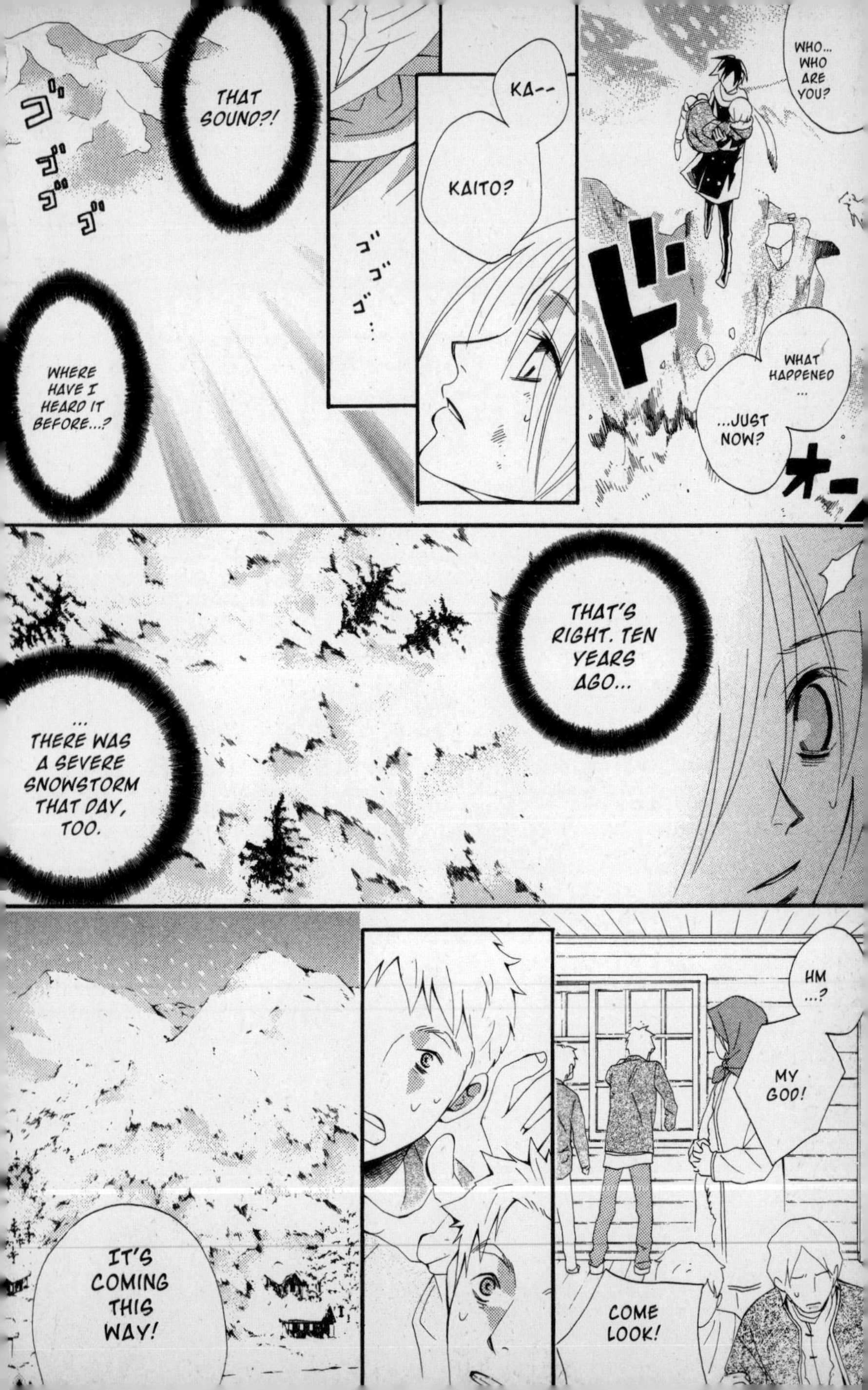
WHO... WHO ARE YOU?
ド
WHAT HAPPENED ... ...JUST NOW?
オー
KA--
KAITO?
ゴゴゴ...
THAT SOUND?!
ゴゴゴゴ
WHERE HAVE I HEARD IT BEFORE...?
THAT'S RIGHT. TEN YEARS AGO...
... THERE WAS A SEVERE SNOWSTORM THAT DAY, TOO.
HM ...?
MY GOD!
COME LOOK!
IT'S COMING THIS WAY!

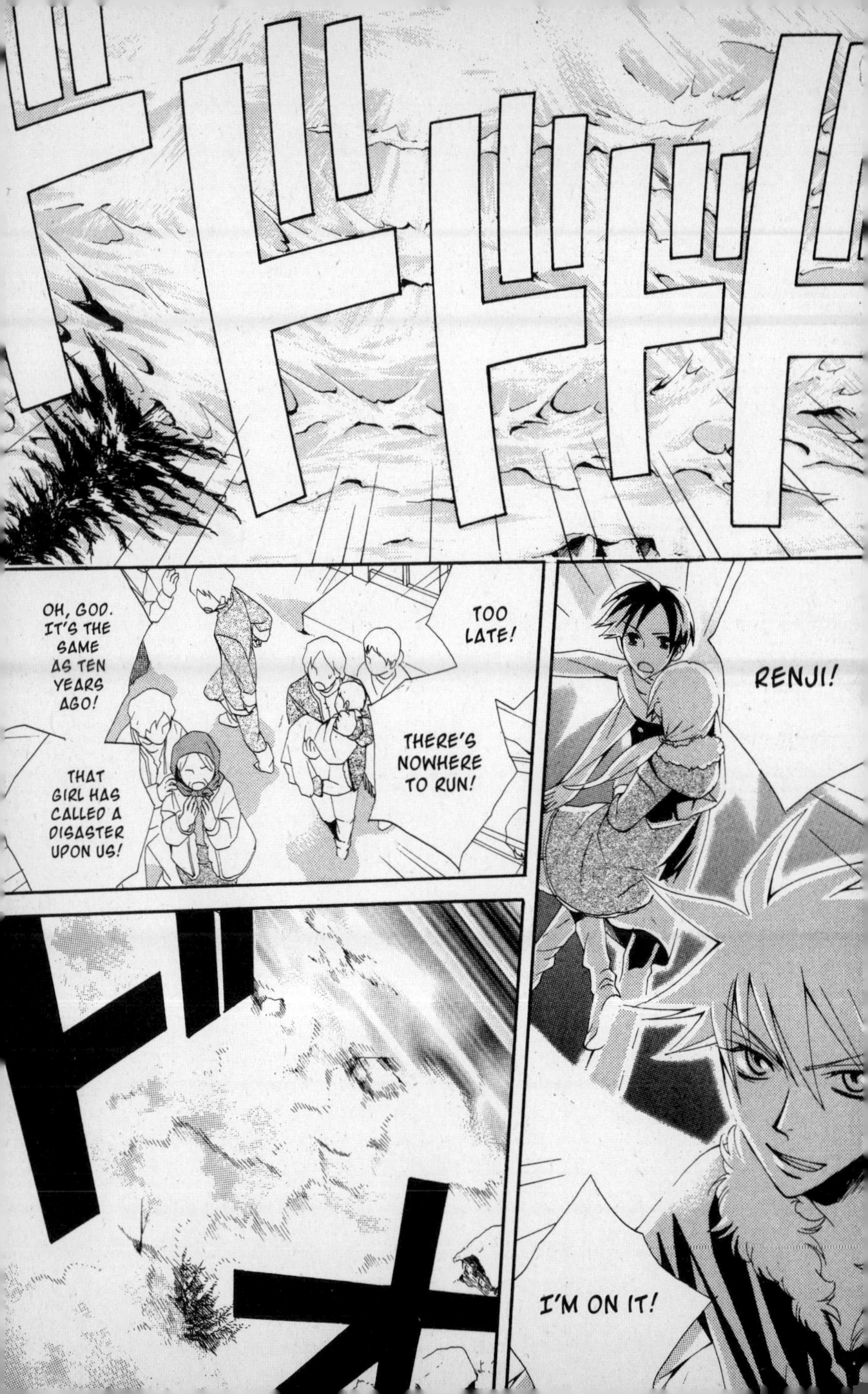
RENJI!
I'M ON IT!
TOO LATE!
THERE'S NOWHERE TO RUN!
OH, GOD. IT'S THE SAME AS TEN YEARS AGO!
THAT GIRL HAS CALLED A DISASTER UPON US!

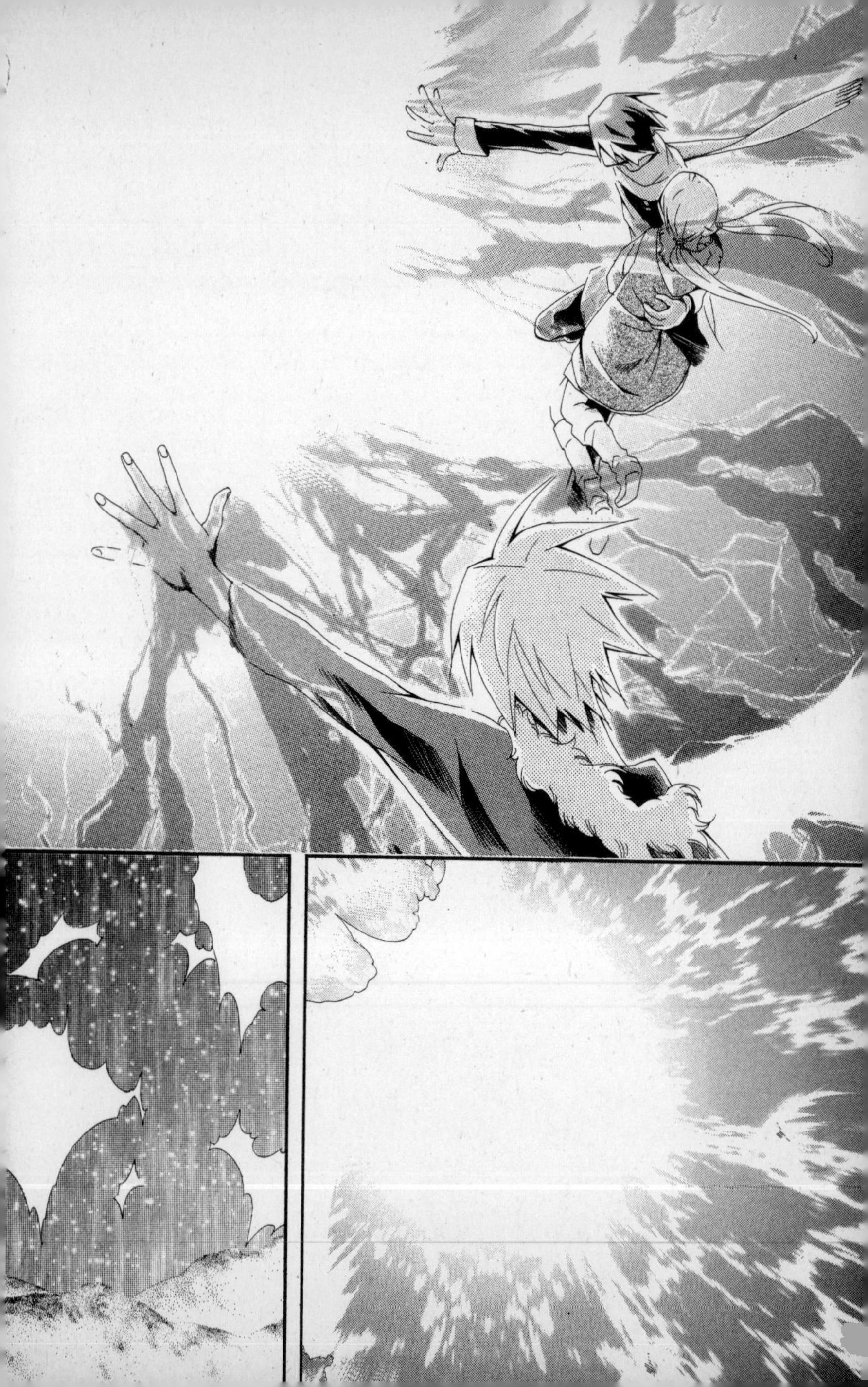

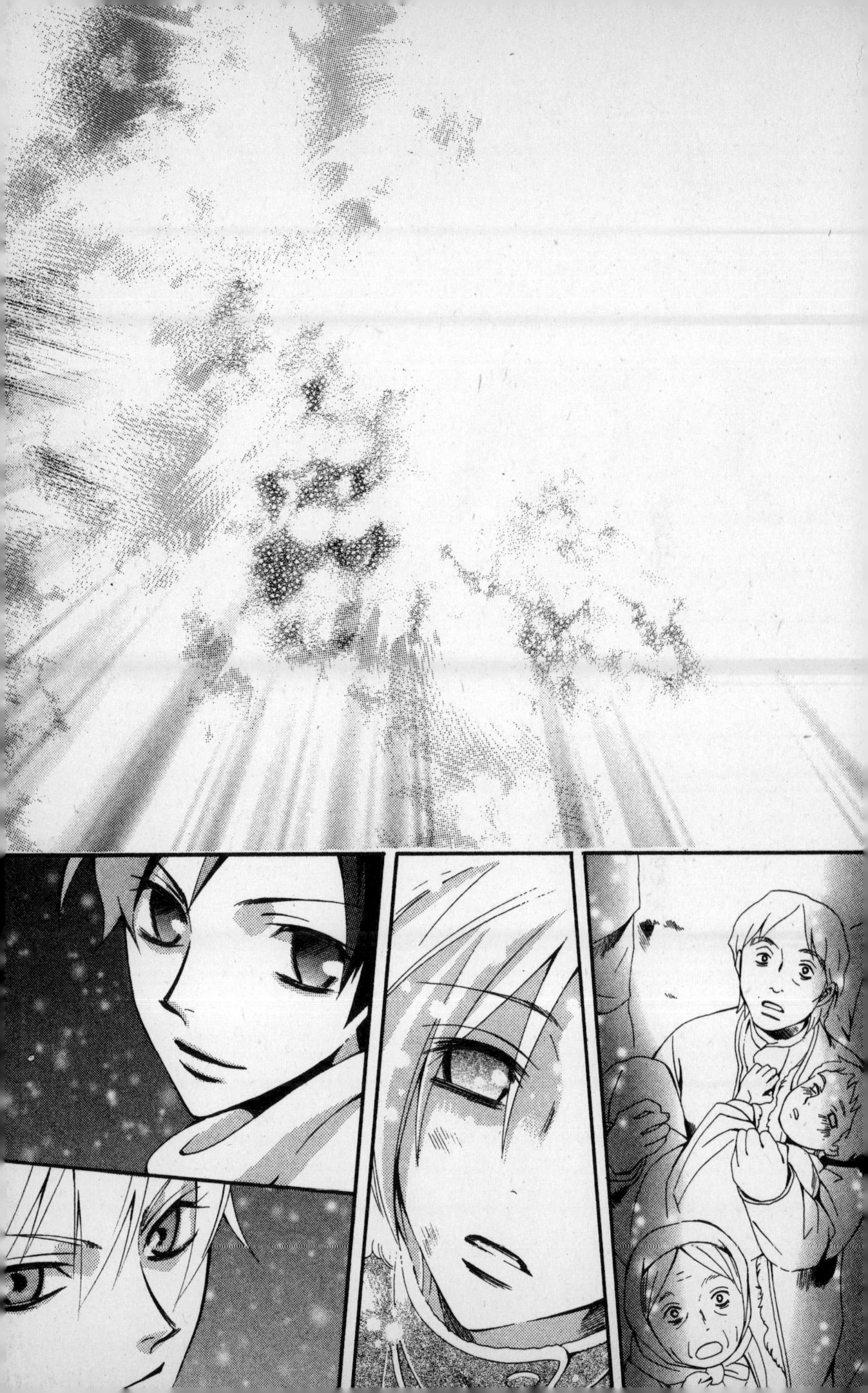

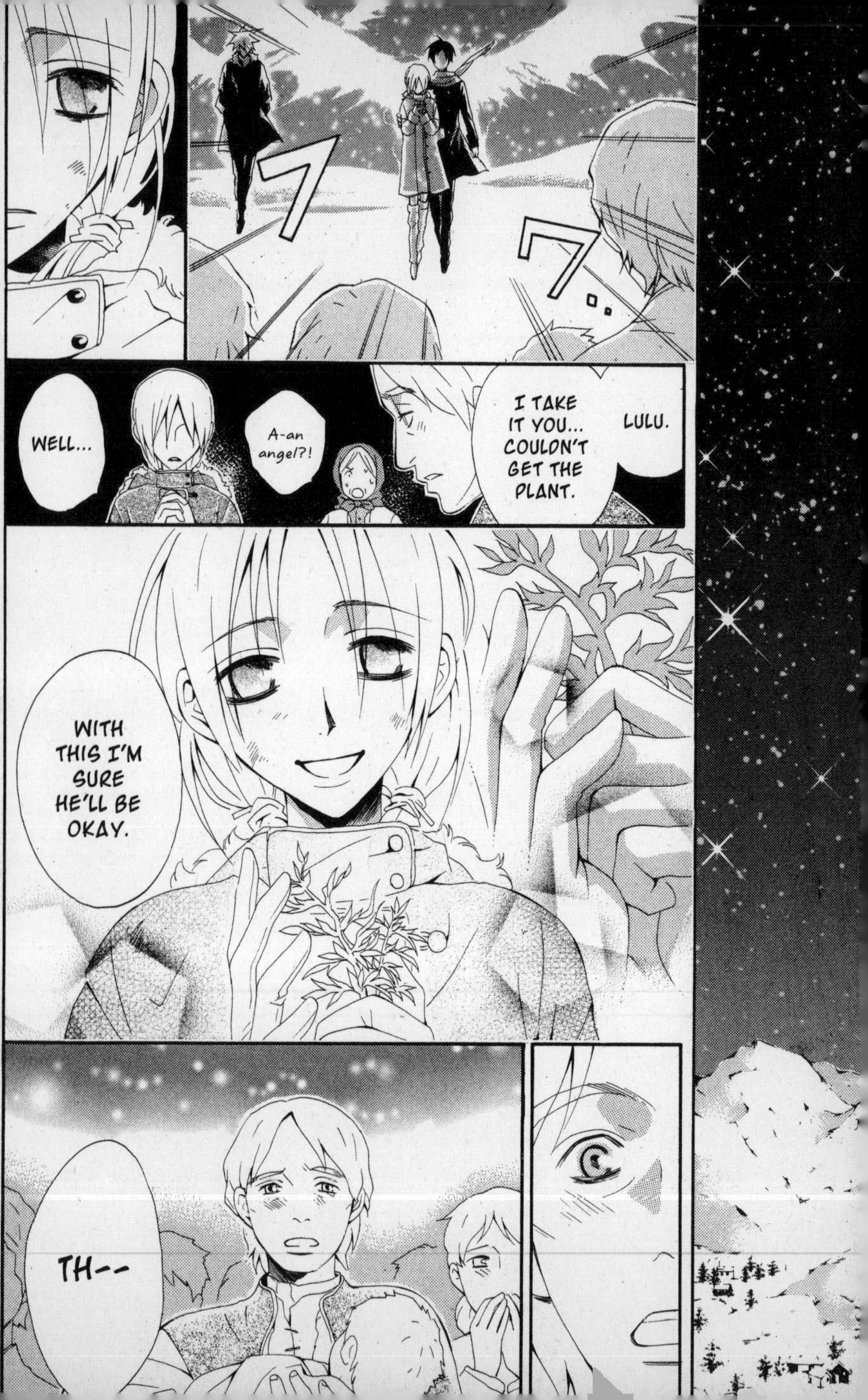
LULU.
I TAKE IT YOU... COULDN'T GET THE PLANT.
A-an angel?!
WELL...
WITH THIS I'M SURE HE'LL BE OKAY.
TH--

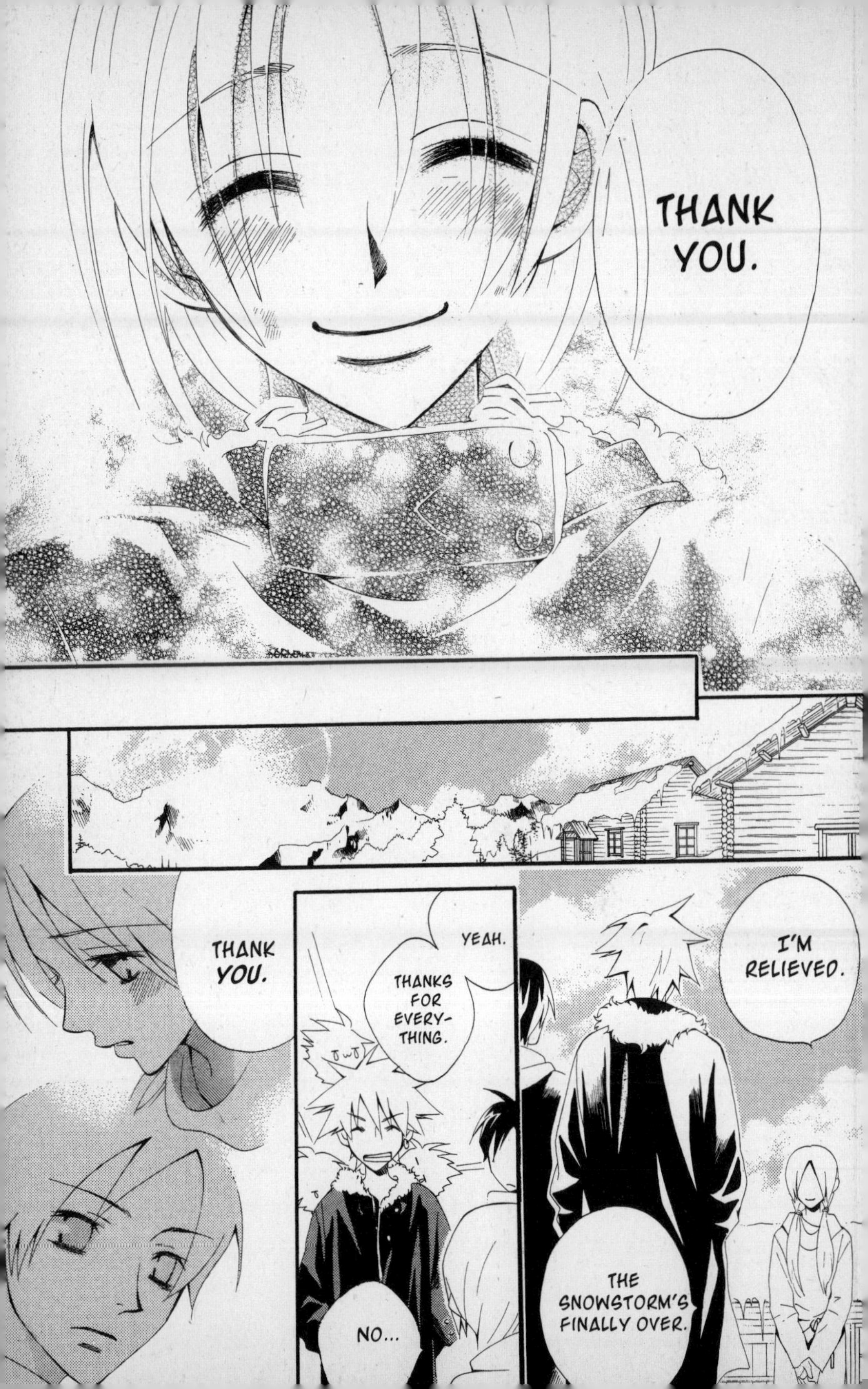
THANK YOU.
I'M RELIEVED.
THE SNOWSTORM'S FINALLY OVER.
YEAH.
THANKS FOR EVERYTHING.
NO...
THANK YOU.

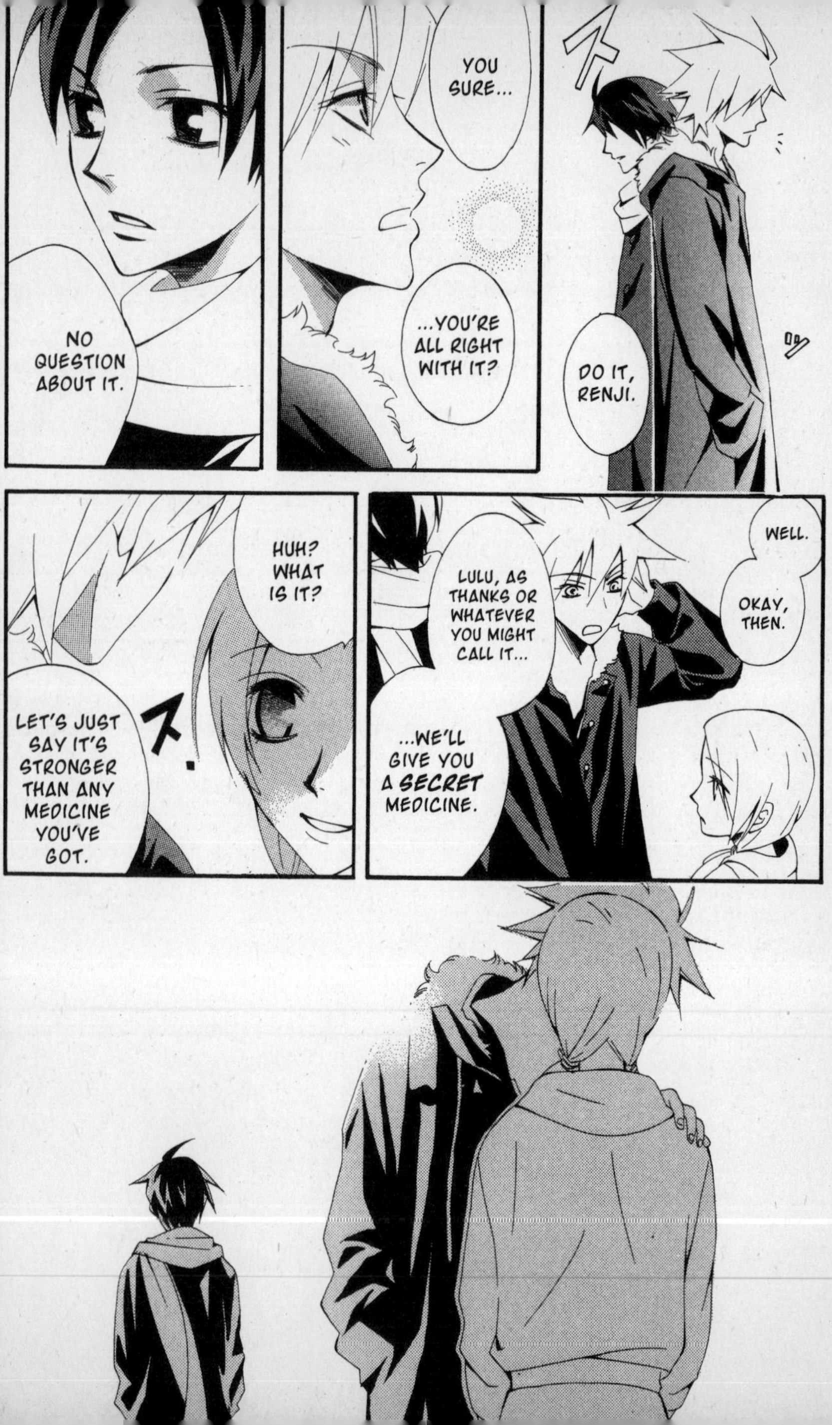
ス
ッ
DO IT, RENJI.
YOU SURE...
...YOU'RE ALL RIGHT WITH IT?
NO QUESTION ABOUT IT.
WELL.
OKAY, THEN.
LULU, AS THANKS OR WHATEVER YOU MIGHT CALL IT...
...WE'LL GIVE YOU A **SECRET** MEDICINE.
HUH? WHAT IS IT?
ス.
LET'S JUST SAY IT'S STRONGER THAN ANY MEDICINE YOU'VE GOT.

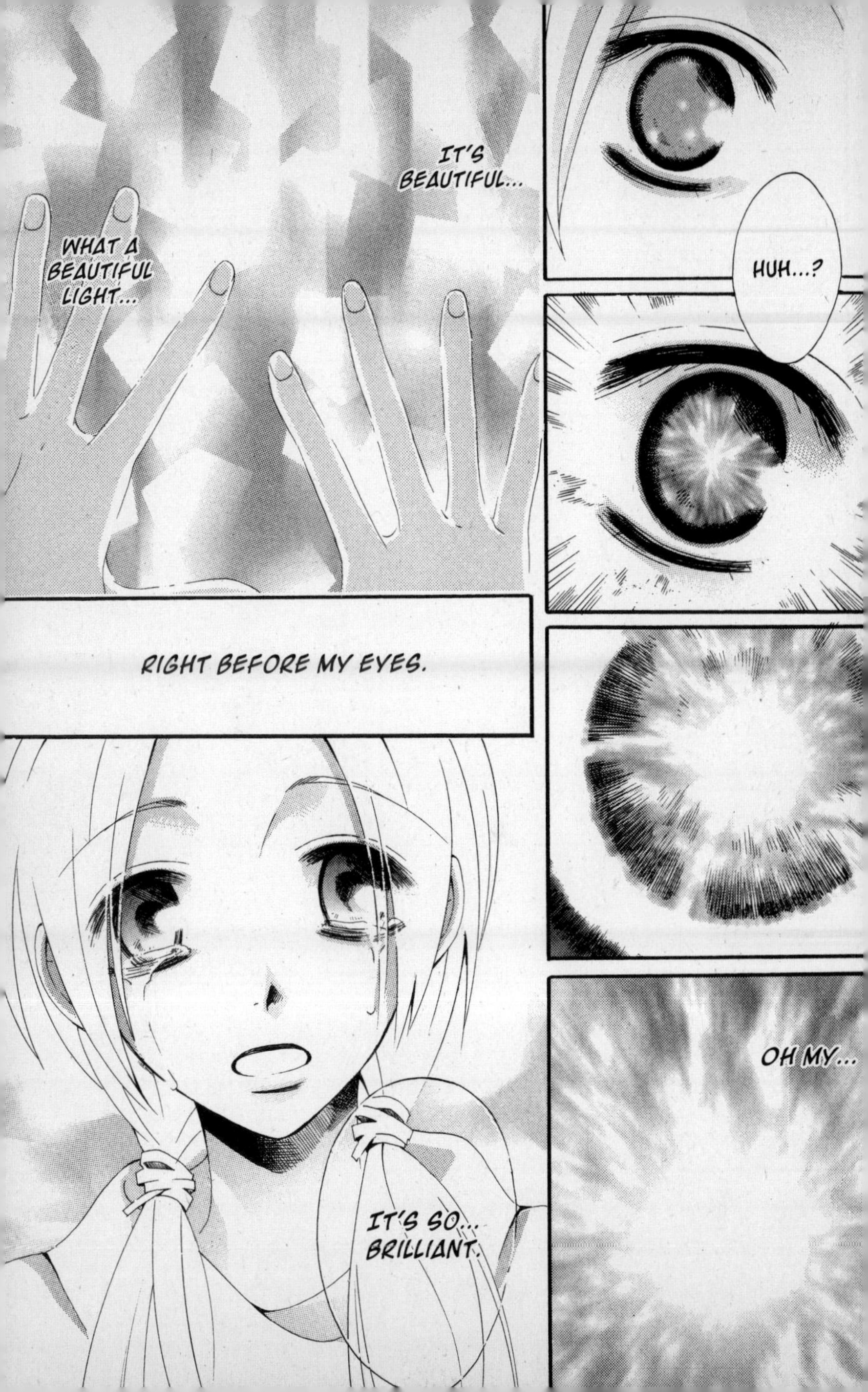
HUH...?
OH MY...
IT'S BEAUTIFUL...
WHAT A BEAUTIFUL LIGHT...
RIGHT BEFORE MY EYES.
IT'S SO... BRILLIANT.

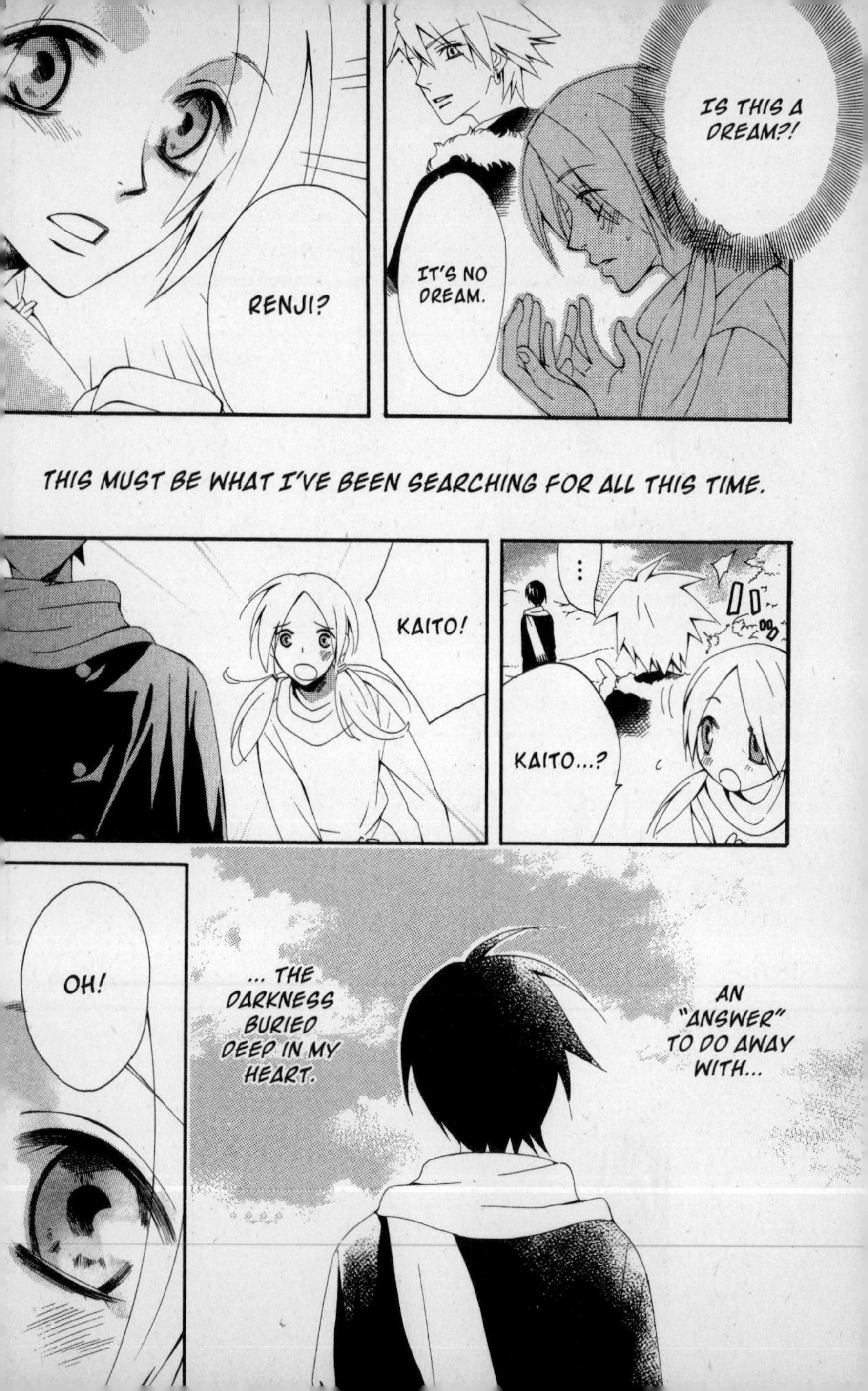
IS THIS A DREAM?!
IT'S NO DREAM.
RENJI?
THIS MUST BE WHAT I'VE BEEN SEARCHING FOR ALL THIS TIME.
...
KAITO...?
KAITO!
AN "ANSWER" TO DO AWAY WITH...
... THE DARKNESS BURIED DEEP IN MY HEART.
OH!

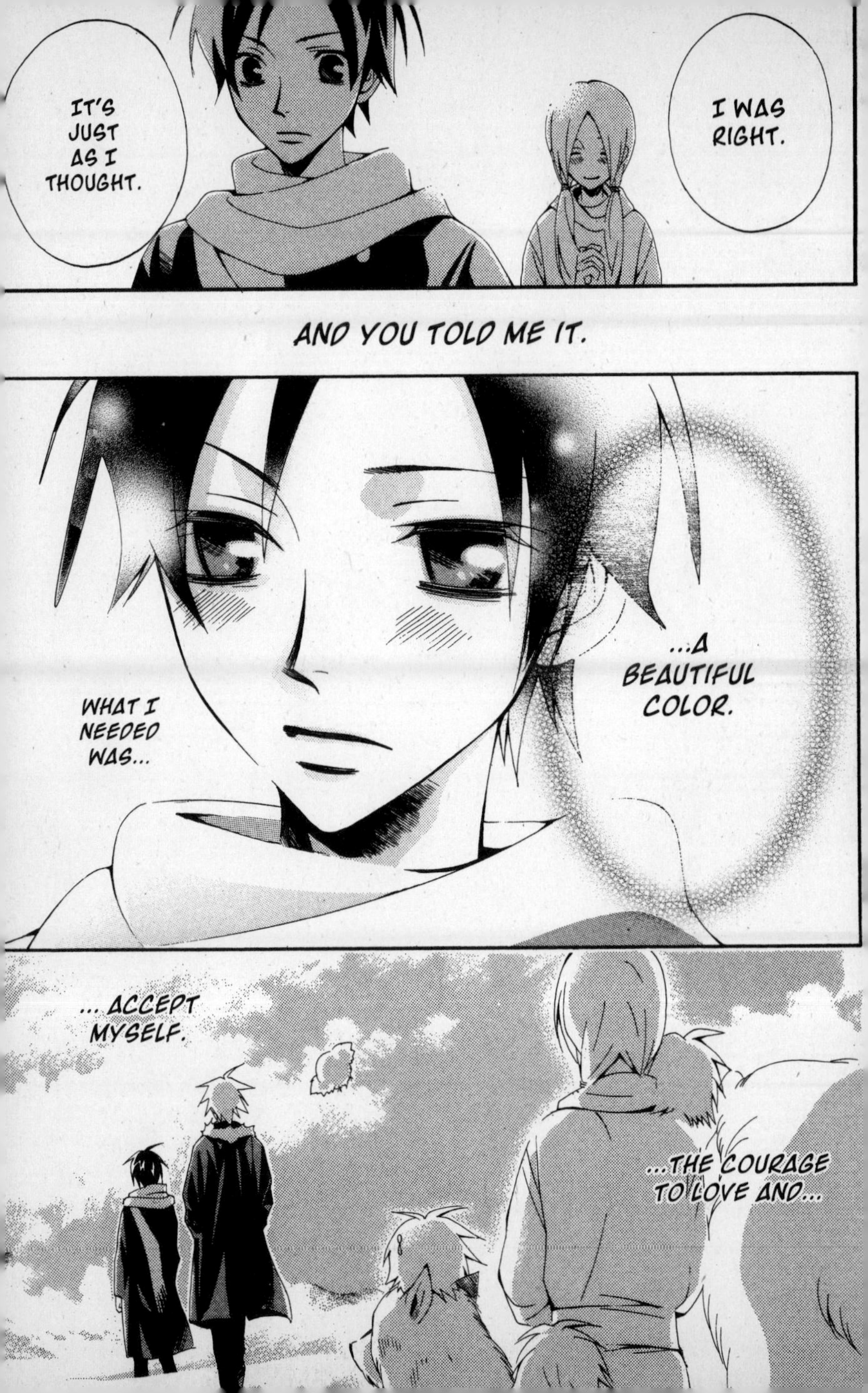
I WAS RIGHT.
IT'S JUST AS I THOUGHT.
AND YOU TOLD ME IT.
...A BEAUTIFUL COLOR.
WHAT I NEEDED WAS...
...THE COURAGE TO LOVE AND...
... ACCEPT MYSELF.

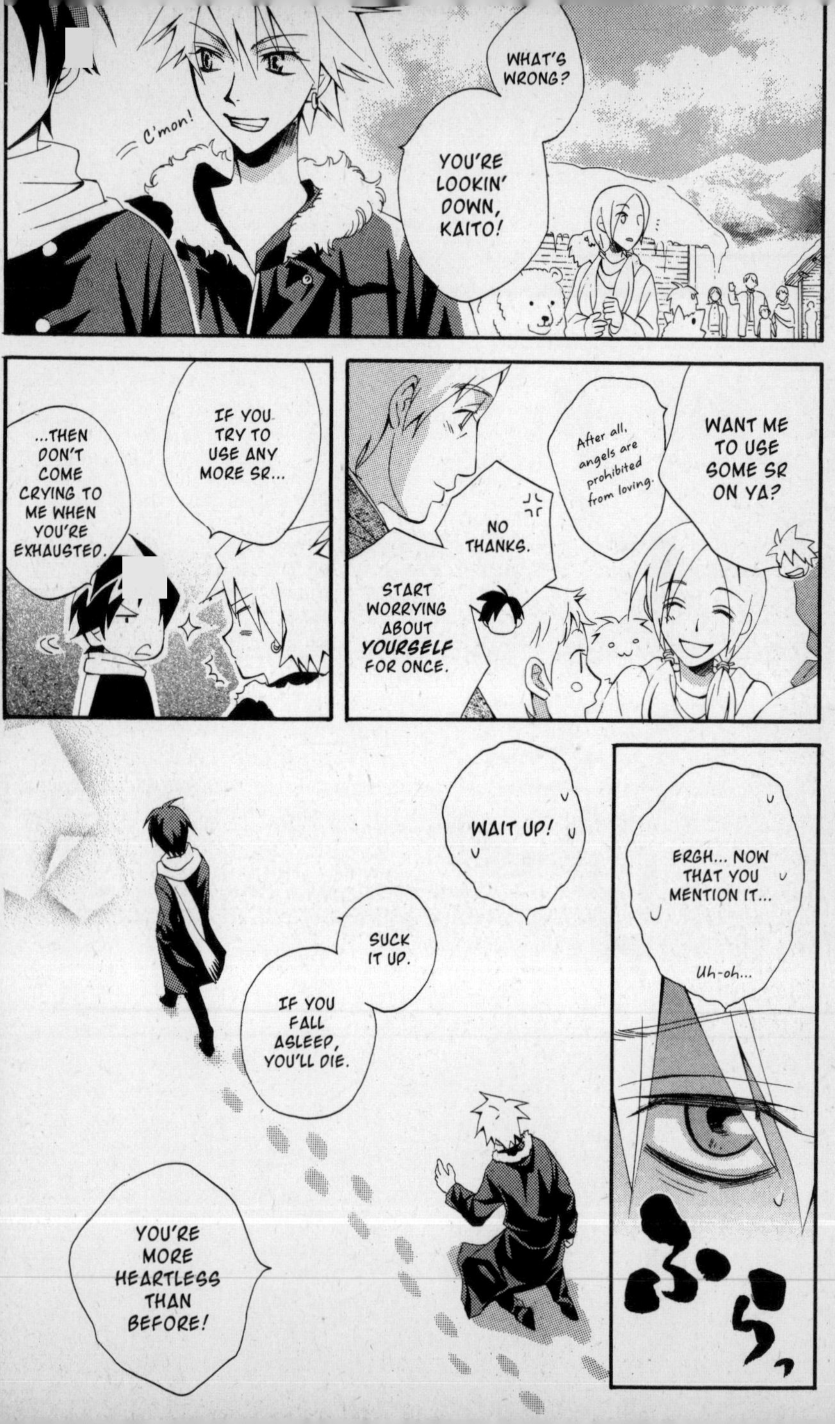
WHAT'S WRONG?
YOU'RE LOOKIN' DOWN, KAITO!
C'mon!
WANT ME TO USE SOME SR ON YA?
After all, angels are prohibited from loving.
NO THANKS.
START WORRYING ABOUT YOURSELF FOR ONCE.
IF YOU TRY TO USE ANY MORE SR...
...THEN DON'T COME CRYING TO ME WHEN YOU'RE EXHAUSTED.
ERGH... NOW THAT YOU MENTION IT...
Uh-oh...
ふらっ
WAIT UP!
SUCK IT UP.
IF YOU FALL ASLEEP, YOU'LL DIE.
YOU'RE MORE HEARTLESS THAN BEFORE!

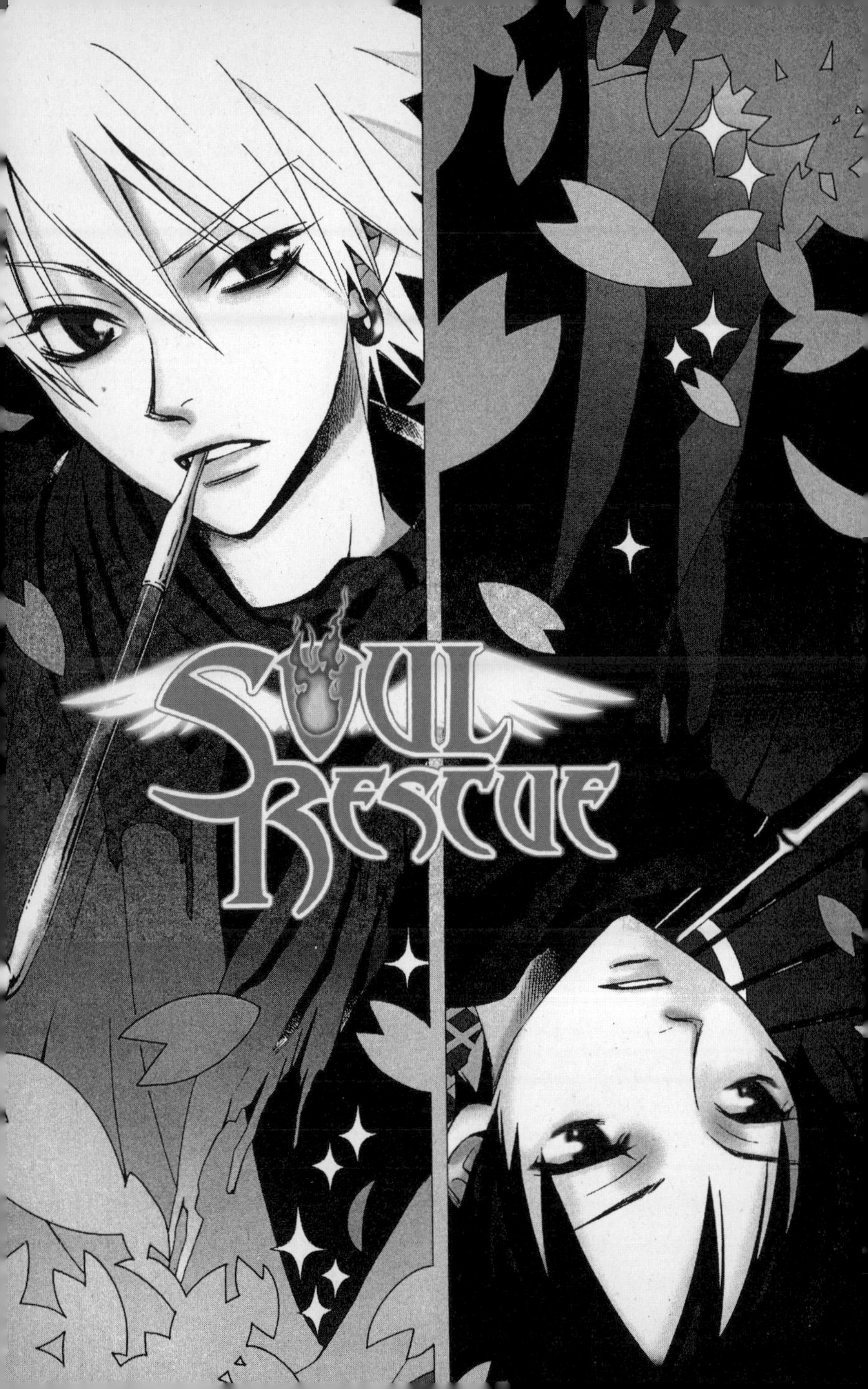
SOUL RESCUE

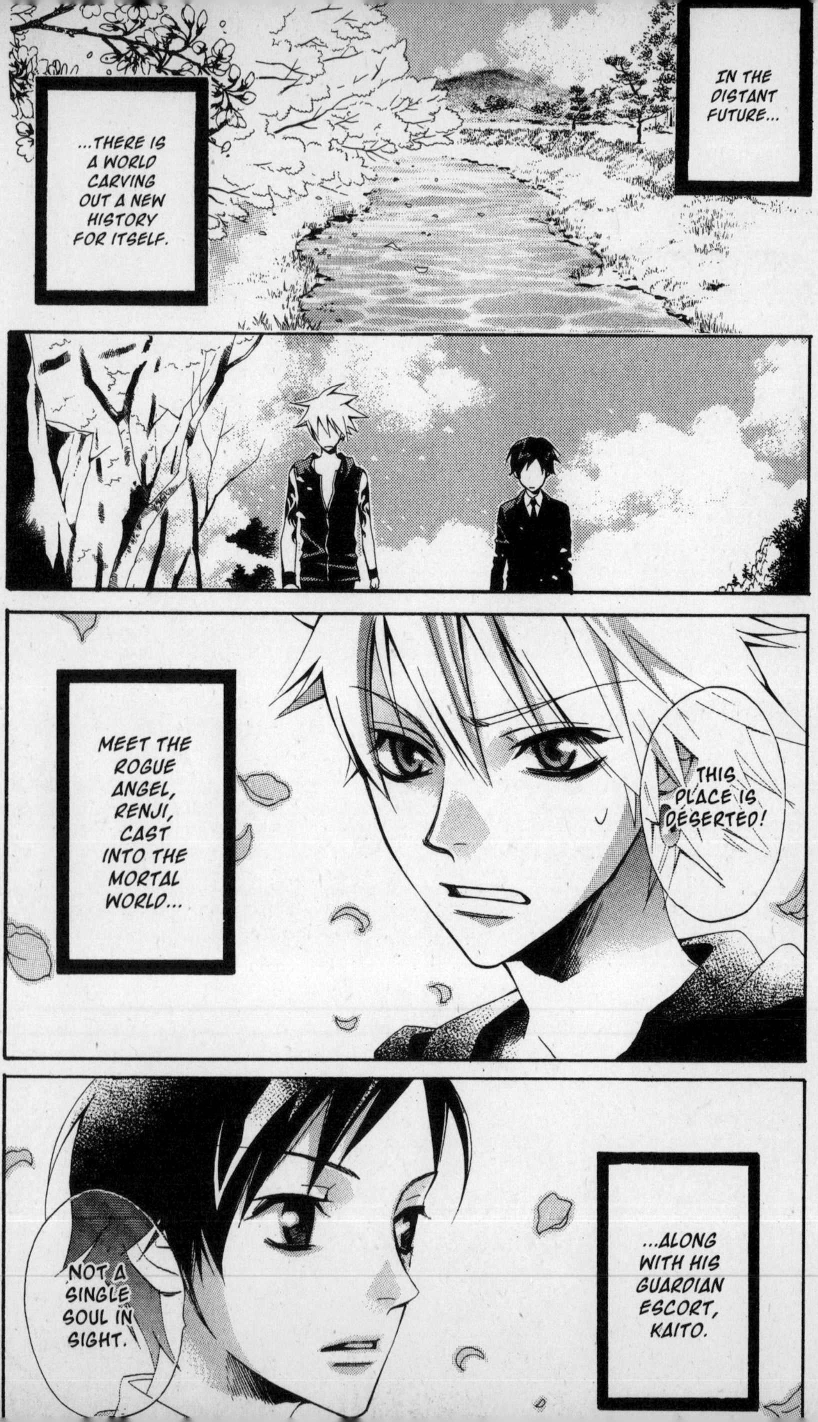
IN THE DISTANT FUTURE...
...THERE IS A WORLD CARVING OUT A NEW HISTORY FOR ITSELF.
THIS PLACE IS DESERTED!
MEET THE ROGUE ANGEL, RENJI, CAST INTO THE MORTAL WORLD...
...ALONG WITH HIS GUARDIAN ESCORT, KAITO.
NOT A SINGLE SOUL IN SIGHT.

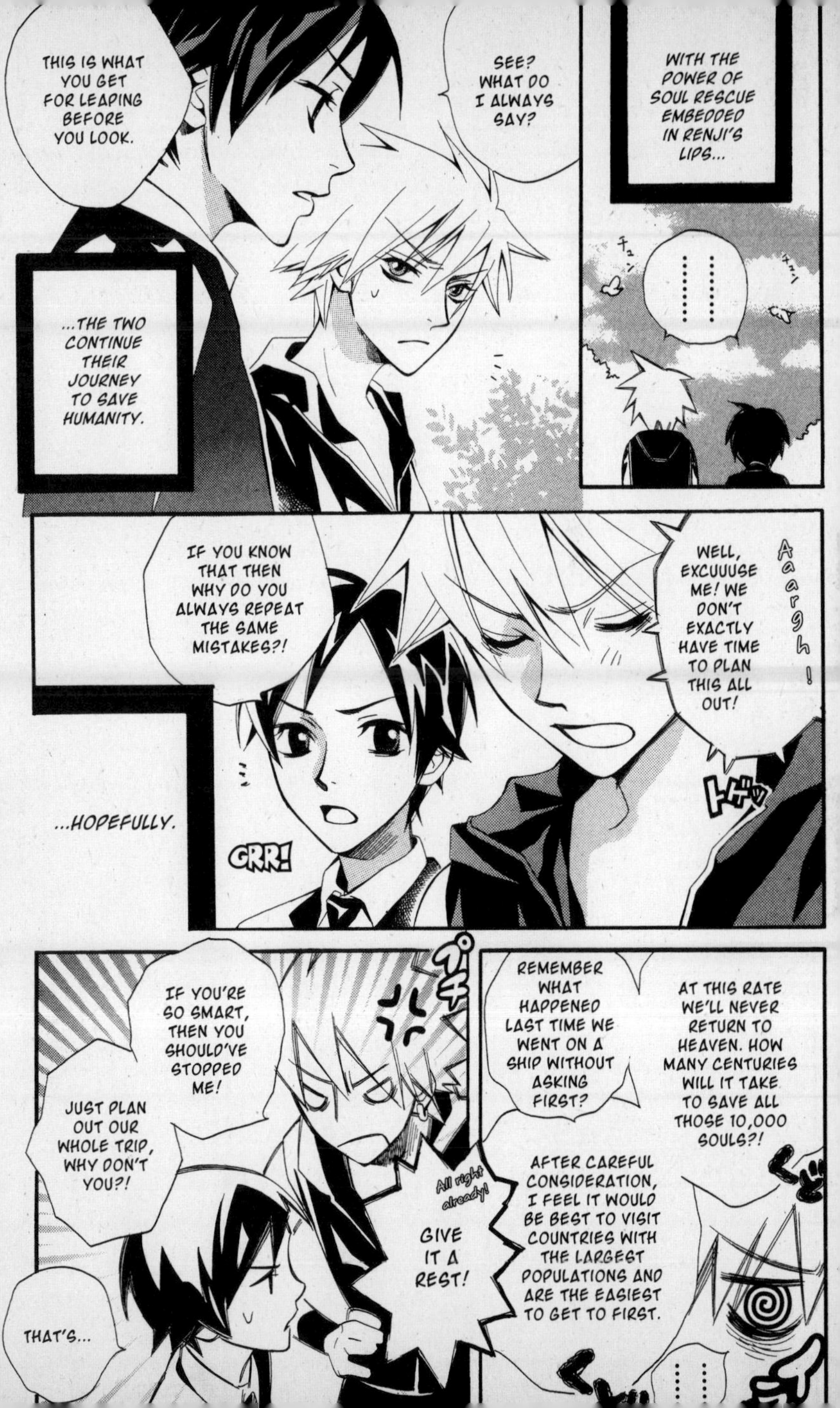
WITH THE POWER OF SOUL RESCUE EMBEDDED IN RENJI'S LIPS...
......
SEE? WHAT DO I ALWAYS SAY?
THIS IS WHAT YOU GET FOR LEAPING BEFORE YOU LOOK.
...THE TWO CONTINUE THEIR JOURNEY TO SAVE HUMANITY.
WELL, EXCUUUSE ME! WE DON'T EXACTLY HAVE TIME TO PLAN THIS ALL OUT!
Aaargh!
IF YOU KNOW THAT THEN WHY DO YOU ALWAYS REPEAT THE SAME MISTAKES?!
...HOPEFULLY.
GRR!
AT THIS RATE WE'LL NEVER RETURN TO HEAVEN. HOW MANY CENTURIES WILL IT TAKE TO SAVE ALL THOSE 10,000 SOULS?!
REMEMBER WHAT HAPPENED LAST TIME WE WENT ON A SHIP WITHOUT ASKING FIRST?
AFTER CAREFUL CONSIDERATION, I FEEL IT WOULD BE BEST TO VISIT COUNTRIES WITH THE LARGEST POPULATIONS AND ARE THE EASIEST TO GET TO FIRST.
......
IF YOU'RE SO SMART, THEN YOU SHOULD'VE STOPPED ME!
JUST PLAN OUT OUR WHOLE TRIP, WHY DON'T YOU?!
All right already!
GIVE IT A REST!
THAT'S...

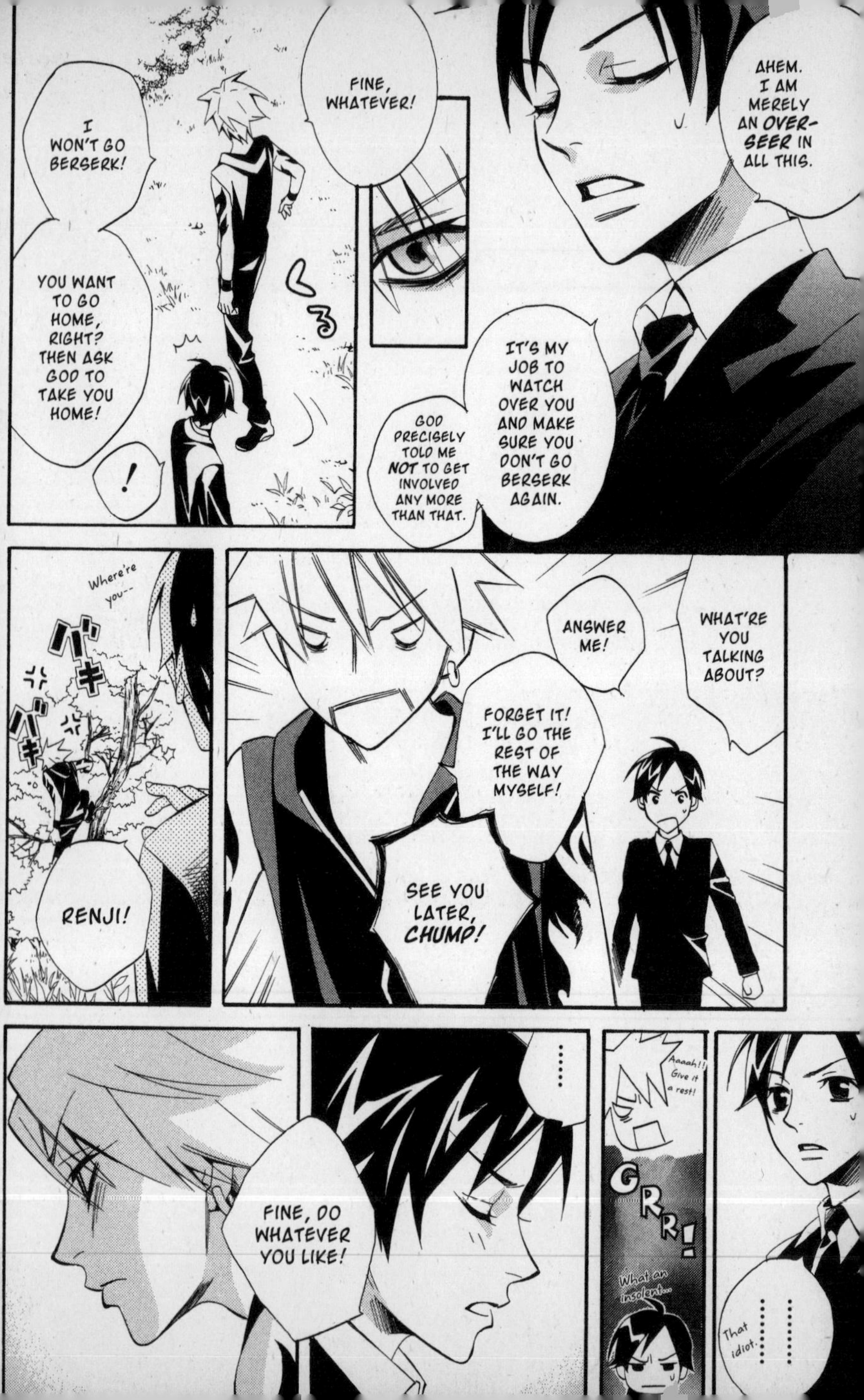
AHEM. I AM MERELY AN *OVERSEER* IN ALL THIS.
IT'S MY JOB TO WATCH OVER YOU AND MAKE SURE YOU DON'T GO BERSERK AGAIN.
GOD PRECISELY TOLD ME *NOT* TO GET INVOLVED ANY MORE THAN THAT.
FINE, WHATEVER!
I WON'T GO BERSERK!
YOU WANT TO GO HOME, RIGHT? THEN ASK GOD TO TAKE YOU HOME!
!
WHAT'RE YOU TALKING ABOUT?
ANSWER ME!
FORGET IT! I'LL GO THE REST OF THE WAY MYSELF!
SEE YOU LATER, *CHUMP*!
Where're you--
バキ
バキ
RENJI!
......
......
That idiot.
Aaaah!! Give it a rest!
GRR!
What an insolent...
......
FINE, DO WHATEVER YOU LIKE!

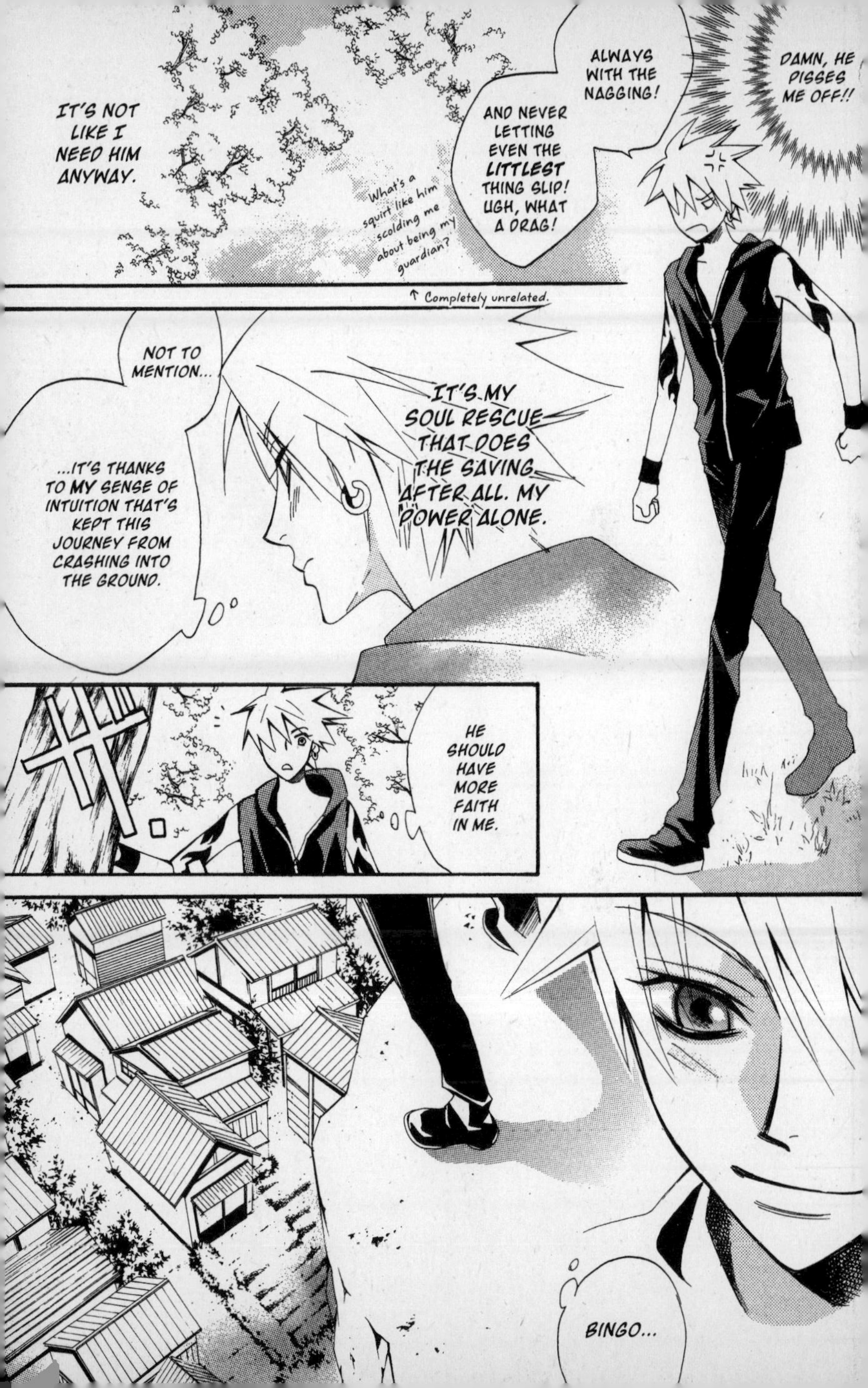
DAMN, HE PISSES ME OFF!!
ALWAYS WITH THE NAGGING!
AND NEVER LETTING EVEN THE LITTLEST THING SLIP! UGH, WHAT A DRAG!
What's a squirt like him scolding me about being my guardian?
IT'S NOT LIKE I NEED HIM ANYWAY.
↑ Completely unrelated.
IT'S MY SOUL RESCUE THAT DOES THE SAVING AFTER ALL. MY POWER ALONE.
NOT TO MENTION...
...IT'S THANKS TO MY SENSE OF INTUITION THAT'S KEPT THIS JOURNEY FROM CRASHING INTO THE GROUND.
HE SHOULD HAVE MORE FAITH IN ME.
BINGO...

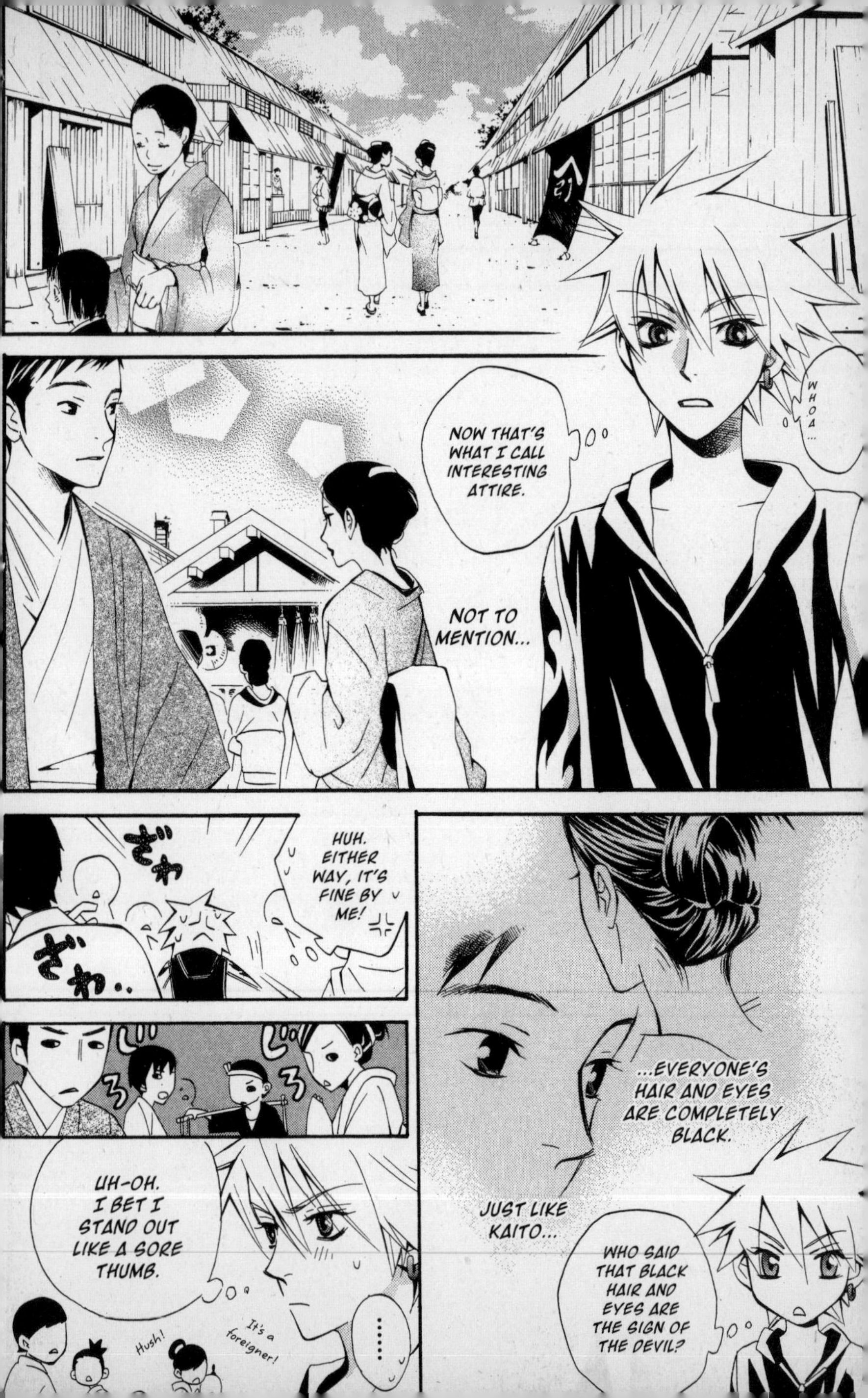
WHOA...
NOW THAT'S WHAT I CALL INTERESTING ATTIRE.
NOT TO MENTION...
...EVERYONE'S HAIR AND EYES ARE COMPLETELY BLACK.
JUST LIKE KAITO...
WHO SAID THAT BLACK HAIR AND EYES ARE THE SIGN OF THE DEVIL?
HUH. EITHER WAY, IT'S FINE BY ME!
ざわ
ざわ..
UH-OH. I BET I STAND OUT LIKE A SORE THUMB.
......
It's a foreigner!
Hush!

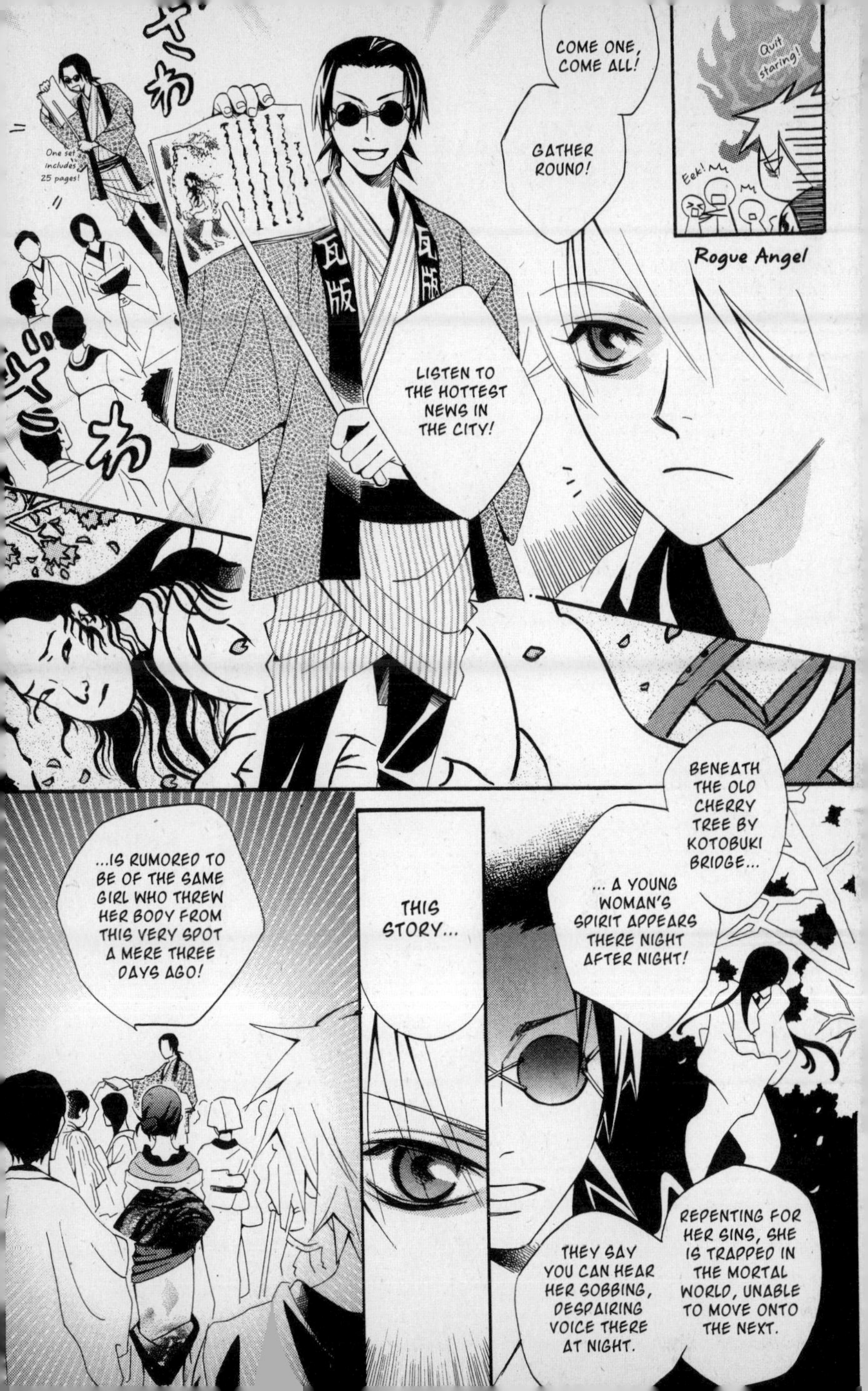
Quit staring!
Eek!
Rogue Angel
COME ONE, COME ALL!
GATHER ROUND!
LISTEN TO THE HOTTEST NEWS IN THE CITY!
ざわ
One set includes 25 pages!
ざわ
BENEATH THE OLD CHERRY TREE BY KOTOBUKI BRIDGE...
... A YOUNG WOMAN'S SPIRIT APPEARS THERE NIGHT AFTER NIGHT!
REPENTING FOR HER SINS, SHE IS TRAPPED IN THE MORTAL WORLD, UNABLE TO MOVE ONTO THE NEXT.
THEY SAY YOU CAN HEAR HER SOBBING, DESPAIRING VOICE THERE AT NIGHT.
THIS STORY...
...IS RUMORED TO BE OF THE SAME GIRL WHO THREW HER BODY FROM THIS VERY SPOT A MERE THREE DAYS AGO!

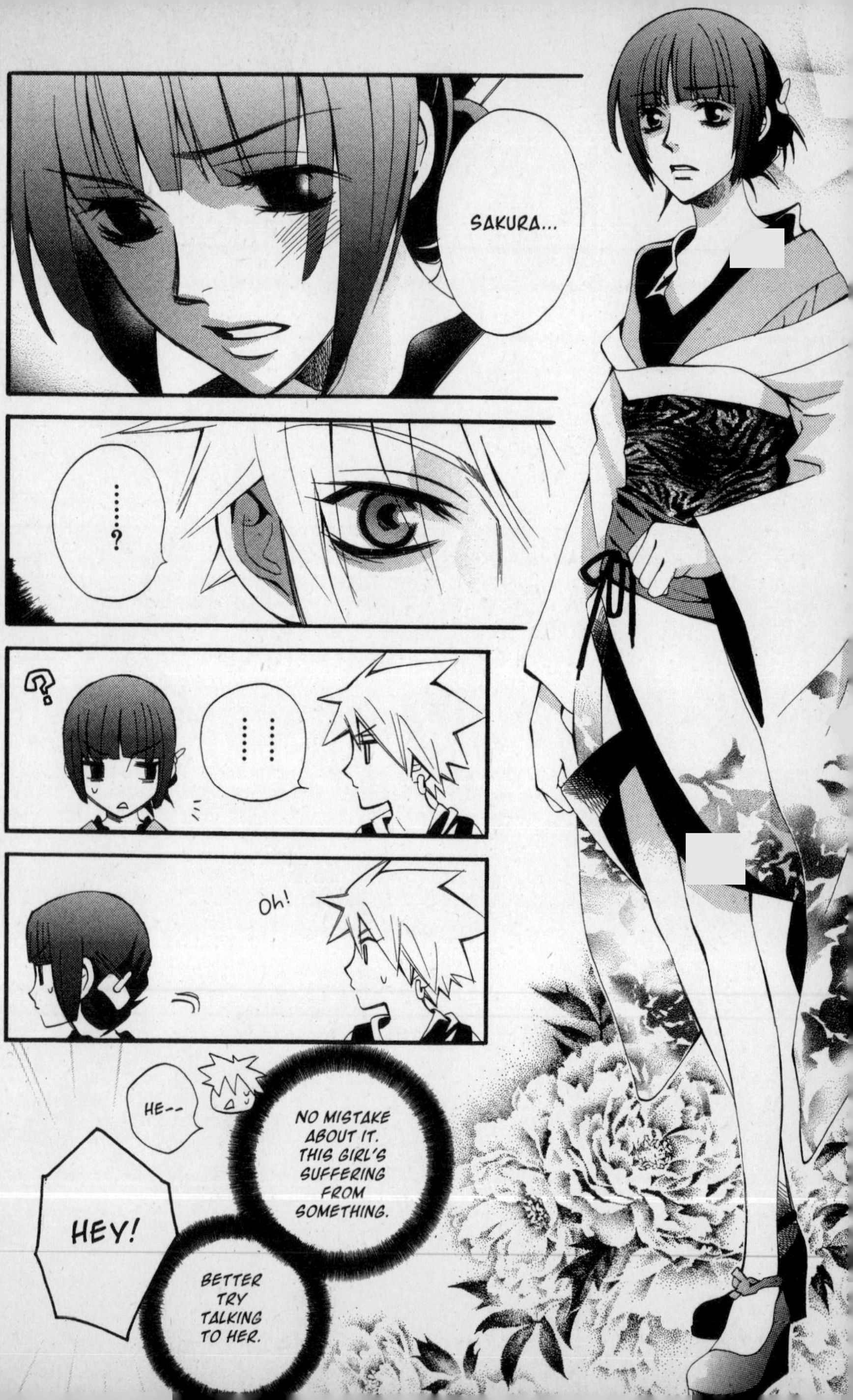
SAKURA...
......?
....
Oh!
NO MISTAKE ABOUT IT. THIS GIRL'S SUFFERING FROM SOMETHING.
BETTER TRY TALKING TO HER.
HE--
HEY!

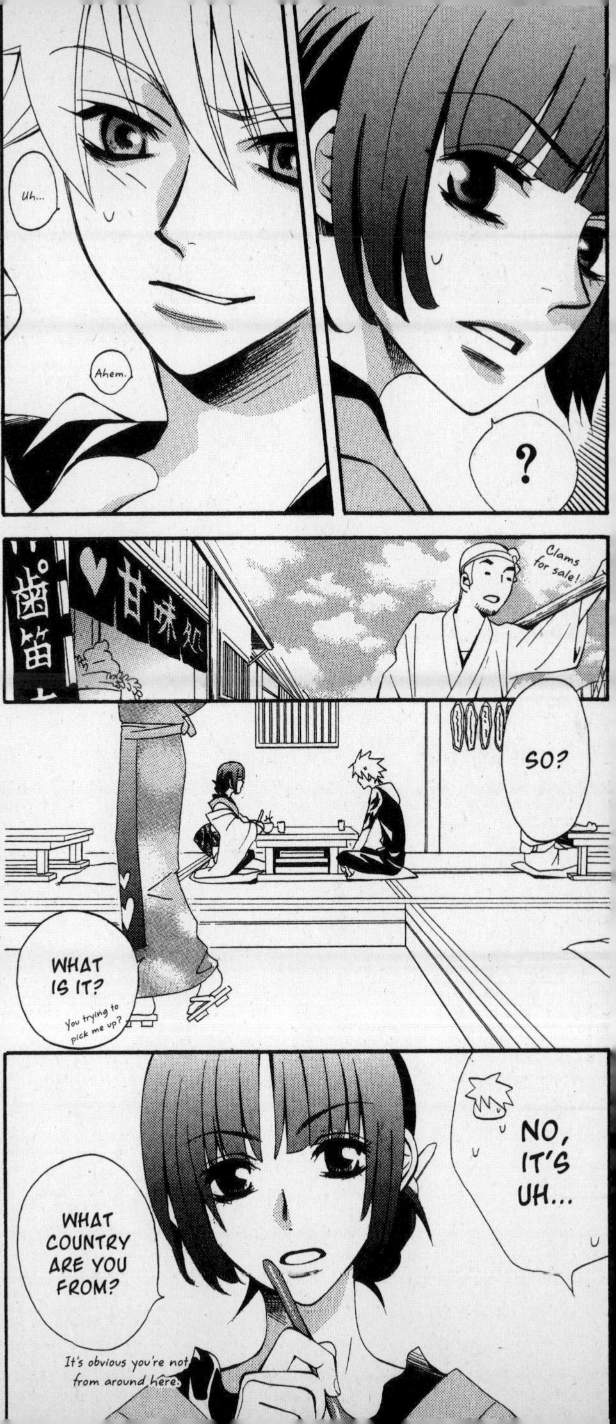
?
Uh...
Ahem.
甘味処
Clams for sale!
SO?
WHAT IS IT?
You trying to pick me up?
NO, IT'S UH...
WHAT COUNTRY ARE YOU FROM?
It's obvious you're not from around here.

SR

Japanese style!! You know I've been looking forward to doing it forever!

I enjoy period dramas like this. When I was in middle school, I'd watch historical plays and read historical novels almost everyday. So I was in heaven when my school trip took us to Kyoto... (← I was a Shinsengumi-maniac, you see.)

Since it seems the majority of my readers really enjoy kimonos, it's a good thing you're reading this chapter.

Though I often don't know what to think of it as a country, Japanese drawings and architecture and alphabets really are something beautiful, don't you think? I like that word "wa". 和's a great character. It not only means "Japan" but also "peace" and 'harmony."

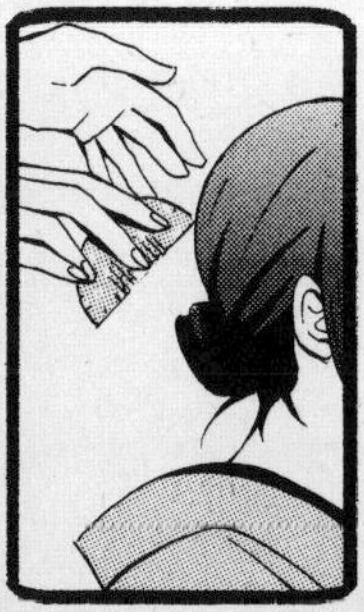

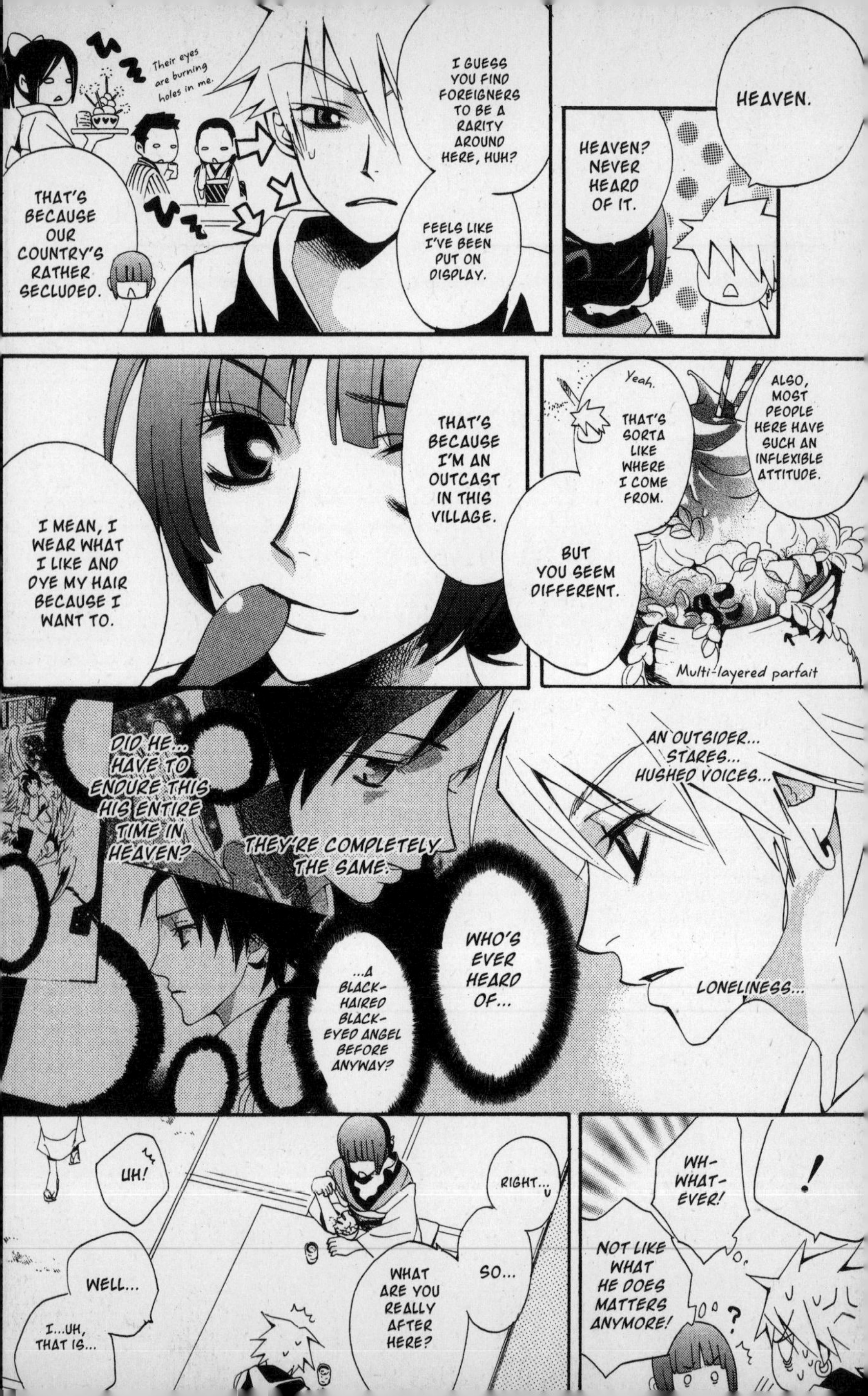
HEAVEN.
HEAVEN? NEVER HEARD OF IT.
I GUESS YOU FIND FOREIGNERS TO BE A RARITY AROUND HERE, HUH?
FEELS LIKE I'VE BEEN PUT ON DISPLAY.
Their eyes are burning holes in me.
THAT'S BECAUSE OUR COUNTRY'S RATHER SECLUDED.
ALSO, MOST PEOPLE HERE HAVE SUCH AN INFLEXIBLE ATTITUDE.
Yeah.
THAT'S SORTA LIKE WHERE I COME FROM.
BUT YOU SEEM DIFFERENT.
Multi-layered parfait
THAT'S BECAUSE I'M AN OUTCAST IN THIS VILLAGE.
I MEAN, I WEAR WHAT I LIKE AND DYE MY HAIR BECAUSE I WANT TO.
AN OUTSIDER... STARES... HUSHED VOICES...
LONELINESS...
WHO'S EVER HEARD OF...
...A BLACK-HAIRED BLACK-EYED ANGEL BEFORE ANYWAY?
THEY'RE COMPLETELY THE SAME.
DID HE... HAVE TO ENDURE THIS HIS ENTIRE TIME IN HEAVEN?
!
WH-WHAT-EVER!
NOT LIKE WHAT HE DOES MATTERS ANYMORE!
?
RIGHT...
SO...
WHAT ARE YOU REALLY AFTER HERE?
UH!
WELL...
I...UH, THAT IS...

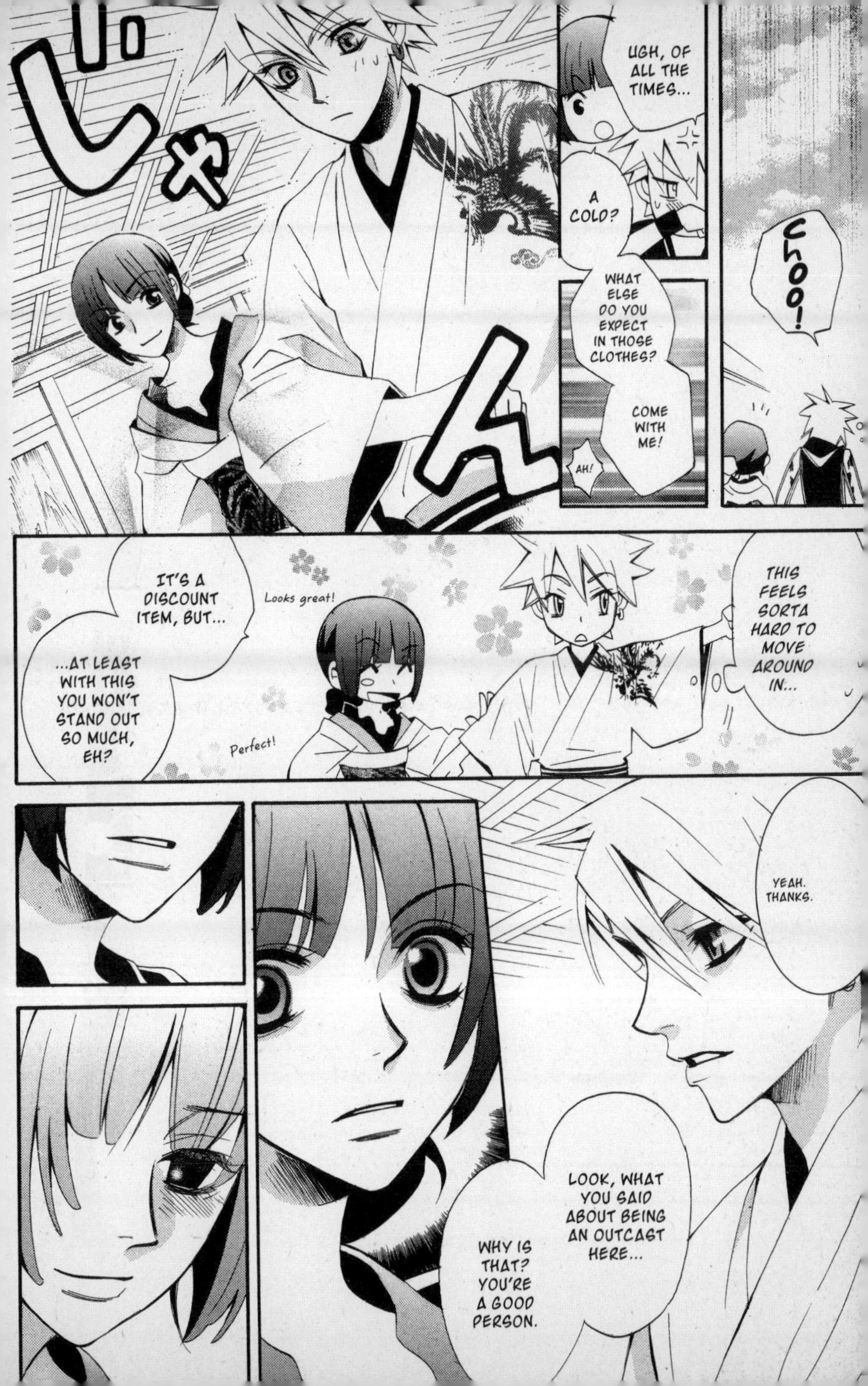
Choo!
UGH, OF ALL THE TIMES...
A COLD?
WHAT ELSE DO YOU EXPECT IN THOSE CLOTHES?
COME WITH ME!
AH!
しゃん
THIS FEELS SORTA HARD TO MOVE AROUND IN...
Looks great!
Perfect!
IT'S A DISCOUNT ITEM, BUT...
...AT LEAST WITH THIS YOU WON'T STAND OUT SO MUCH, EH?
YEAH. THANKS.
LOOK, WHAT YOU SAID ABOUT BEING AN OUTCAST HERE...
WHY IS THAT? YOU'RE A GOOD PERSON.

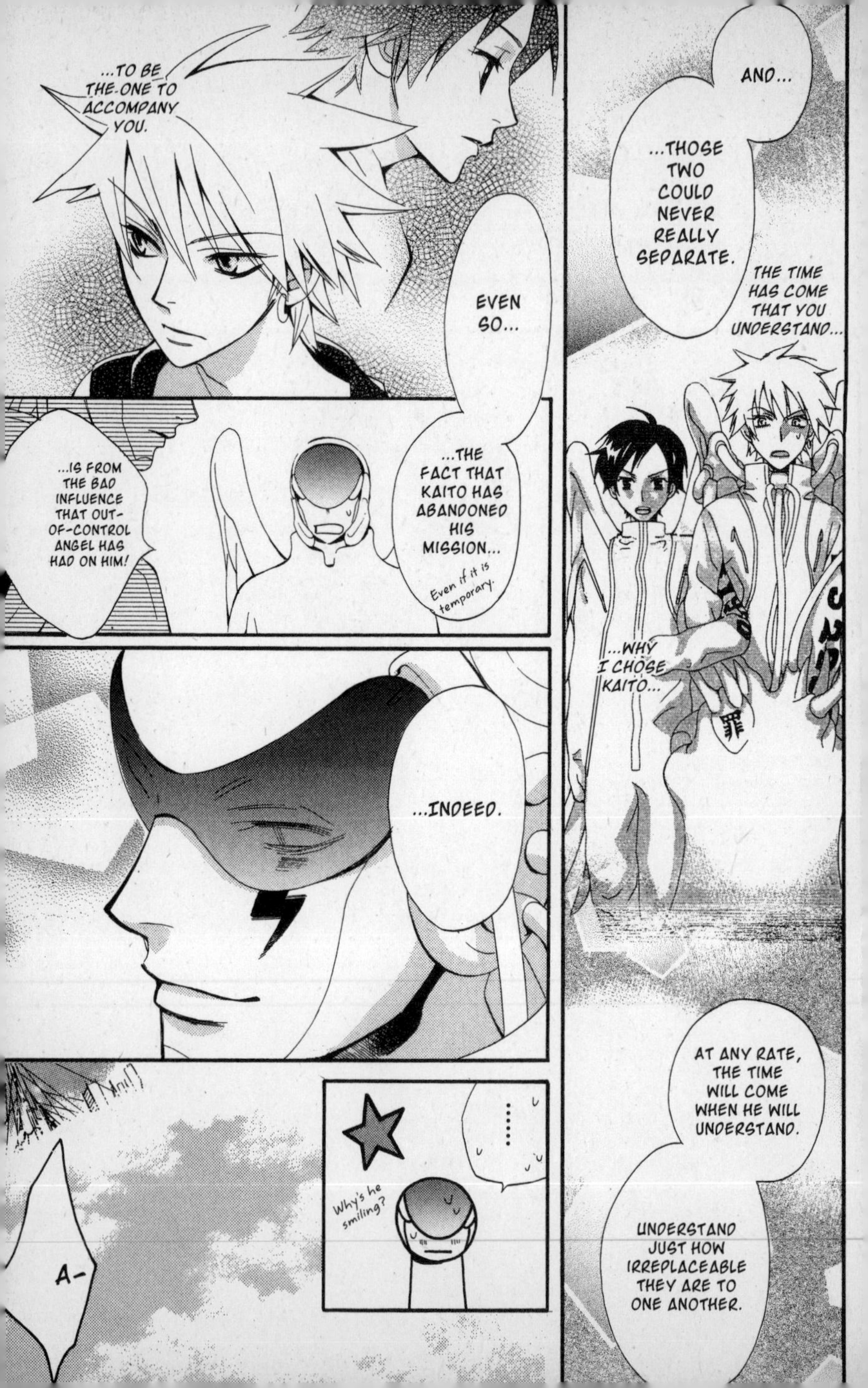
AND...
...THOSE TWO COULD NEVER REALLY SEPARATE.
THE TIME HAS COME THAT YOU UNDERSTAND...
...WHY I CHOSE KAITO...
AT ANY RATE, THE TIME WILL COME WHEN HE WILL UNDERSTAND.
UNDERSTAND JUST HOW IRREPLACEABLE THEY ARE TO ONE ANOTHER.
...TO BE THE-ONE TO ACCOMPANY YOU.
EVEN SO...
...THE FACT THAT KAITO HAS ABANDONED HIS MISSION...
Even if it is temporary.
...IS FROM THE BAD INFLUENCE THAT OUT-OF-CONTROL ANGEL HAS HAD ON HIM!
...INDEED.
......
Why's he smiling?
A-

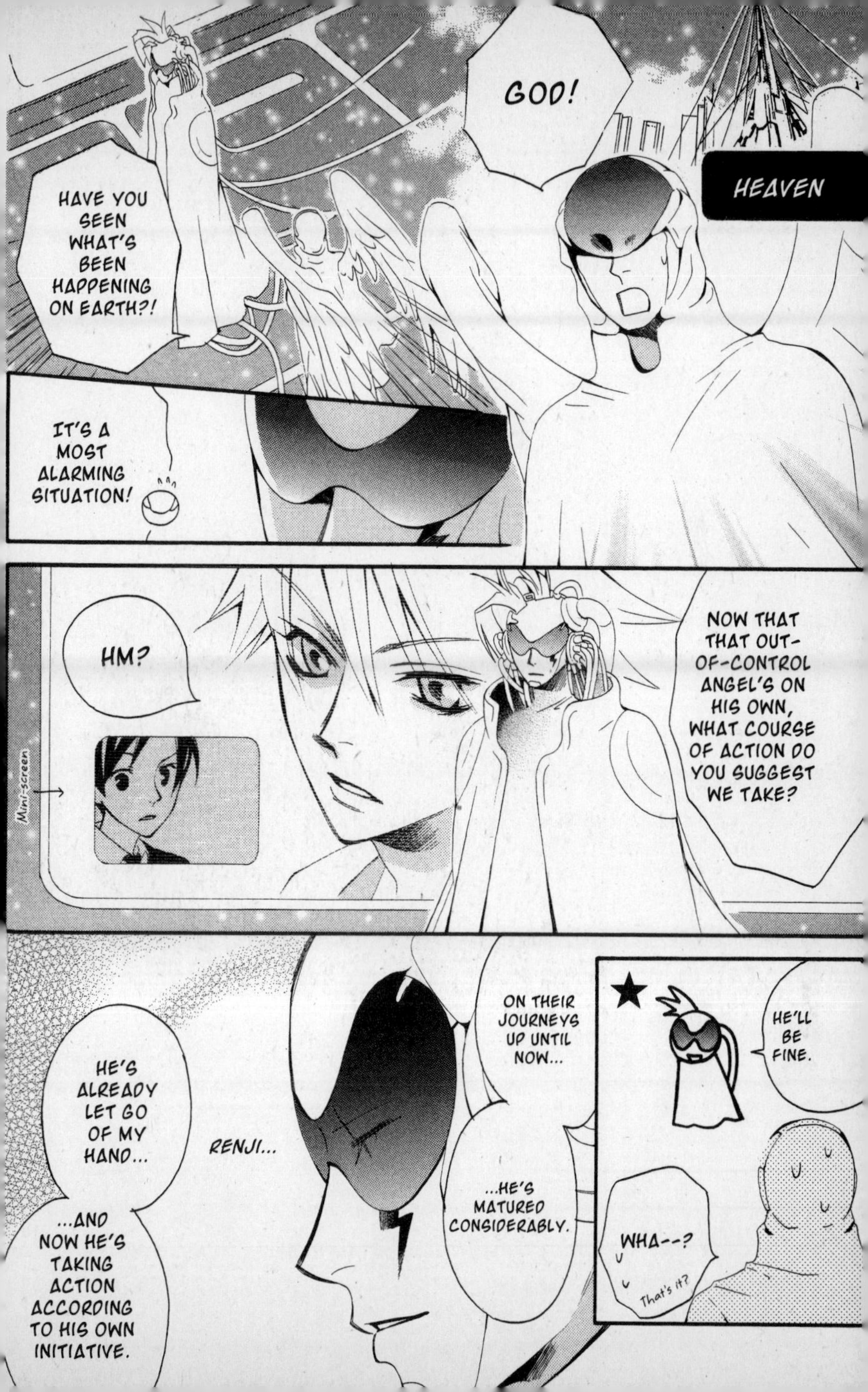
HEAVEN
GOD!
HAVE YOU SEEN WHAT'S BEEN HAPPENING ON EARTH?!
IT'S A MOST ALARMING SITUATION!
NOW THAT THAT OUT-OF-CONTROL ANGEL'S ON HIS OWN, WHAT COURSE OF ACTION DO YOU SUGGEST WE TAKE?
HM?
Mini-screen
HE'LL BE FINE.
WHA--?
That's it?
ON THEIR JOURNEYS UP UNTIL NOW...
...HE'S MATURED CONSIDERABLY.
RENJI...
HE'S ALREADY LET GO OF MY HAND...
...AND NOW HE'S TAKING ACTION ACCORDING TO HIS OWN INITIATIVE.

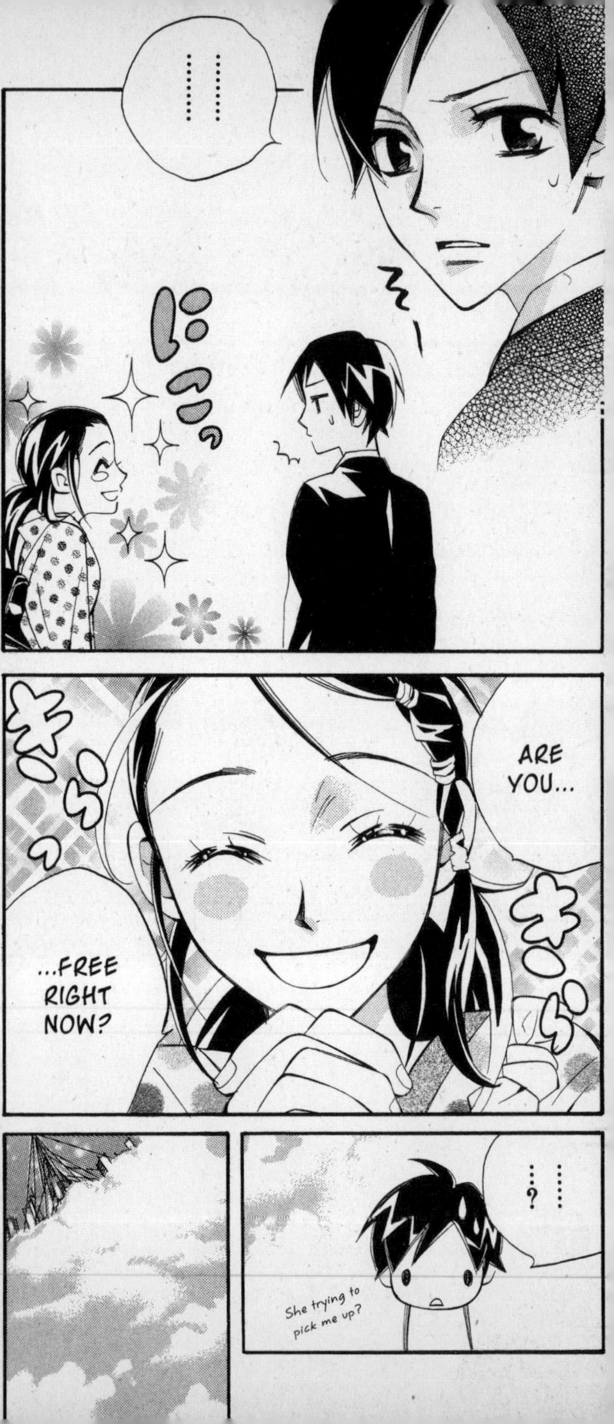
……
ARE YOU...
...FREE RIGHT NOW?
……?
She trying to pick me up?

SR

Uuuh...
Since I get quite a few letters from fans saying they want to know more about me, I'm going to tell you a little about myself now. A profile, you might call it. I'm sorry but anyone not interested can just skip over this part then. First off, my birthday is January 30th, and I was born in downtown Tokyo. I'm an Aquarius and my blood-type is AB. My hobbies include listening to music and going to live performances. How's that for the basic run-down? As for my personality, I've recently come to realize that I can be rather selfish. And then my little sister had to go and ask "You only realized **now?**" I need to grow up, and be more mature... even though it's next to impossible.

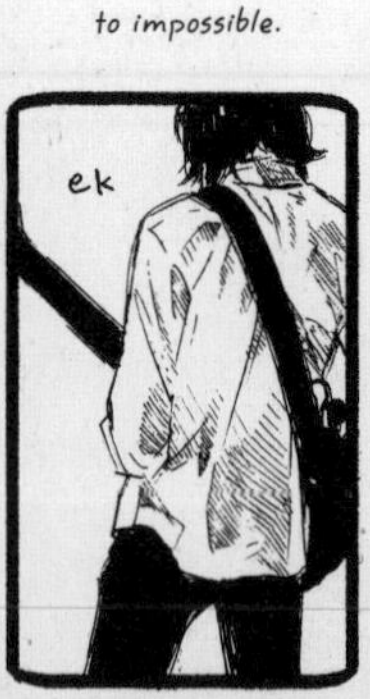
ek

I'm sorry it's not a manga drawing.

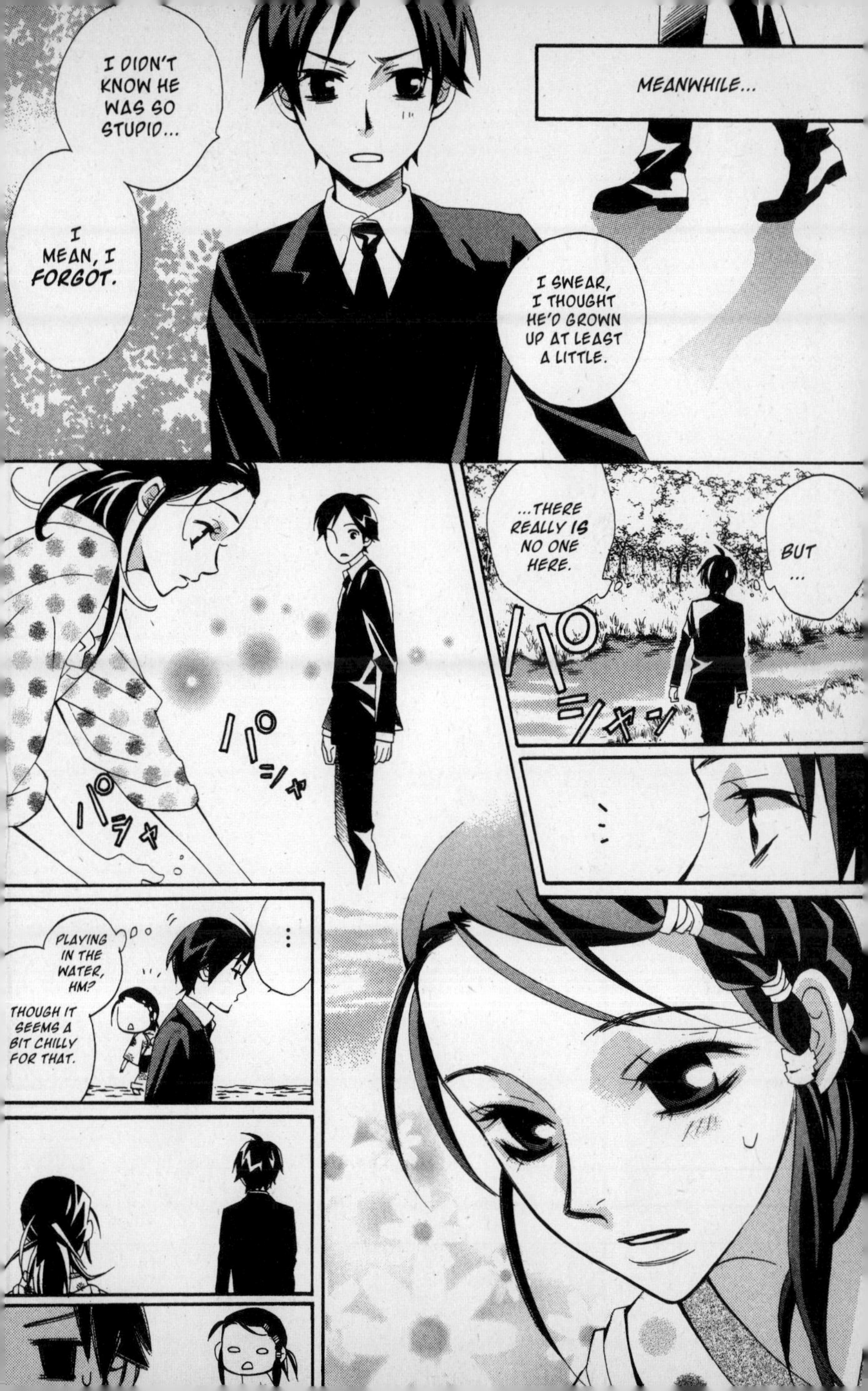
MEANWHILE...
I SWEAR, I THOUGHT HE'D GROWN UP AT LEAST A LITTLE.
I DIDN'T KNOW HE WAS SO STUPID...
I MEAN, I **FORGOT**.
BUT ...
...THERE REALLY **IS** NO ONE HERE.
パシャン
パシャ
パシャ
...
...
PLAYING IN THE WATER, HM?
THOUGH IT SEEMS A BIT CHILLY FOR THAT.

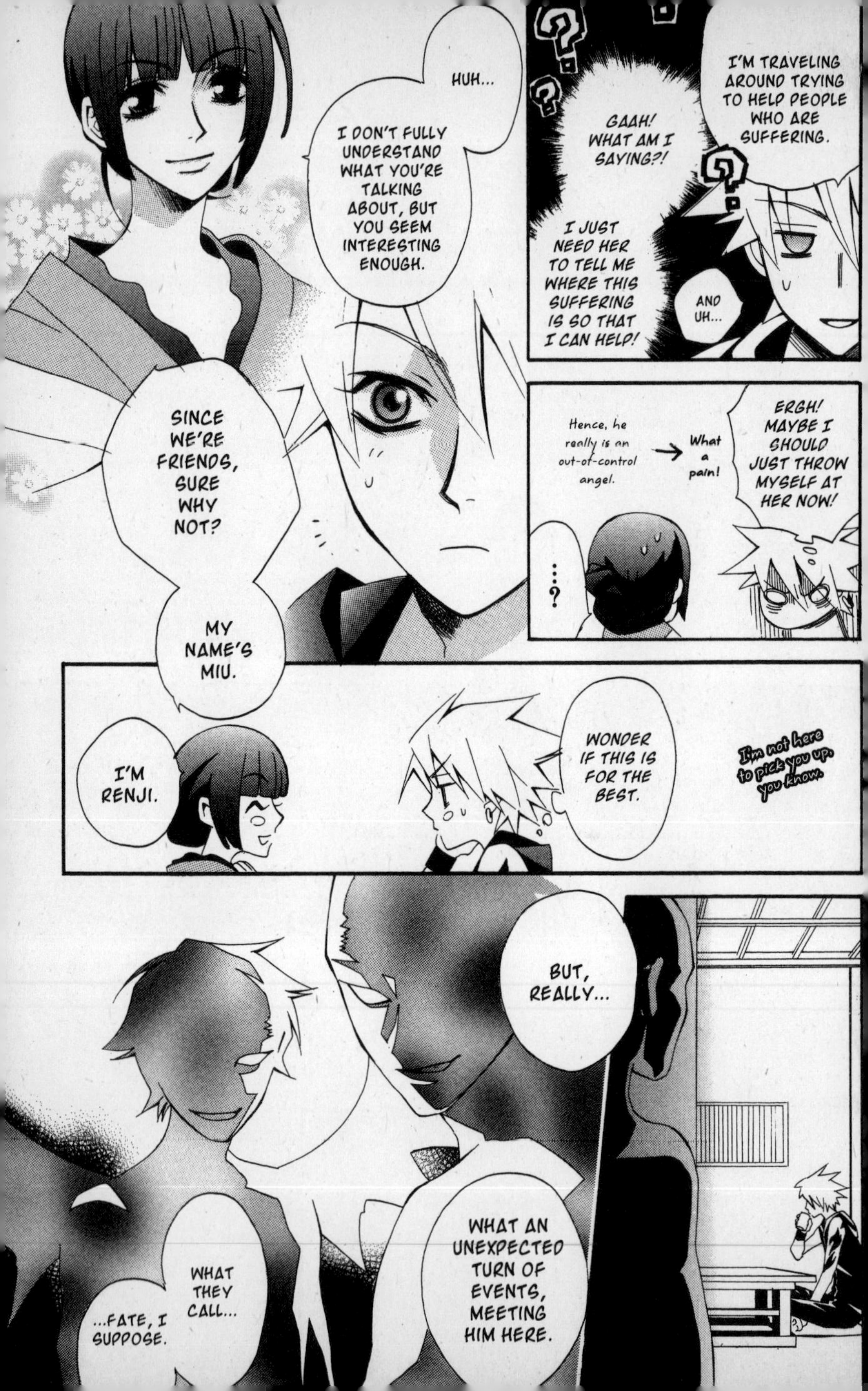
I'M TRAVELING AROUND TRYING TO HELP PEOPLE WHO ARE SUFFERING.
AND UH...
GAAH! WHAT AM I SAYING?!
I JUST NEED HER TO TELL ME WHERE THIS SUFFERING IS SO THAT I CAN HELP!
ERGH! MAYBE I SHOULD JUST THROW MYSELF AT HER NOW!
What a pain!
Hence, he really is an out-of-control angel.
...?
HUH...
I DON'T FULLY UNDERSTAND WHAT YOU'RE TALKING ABOUT, BUT YOU SEEM INTERESTING ENOUGH.
SINCE WE'RE FRIENDS, SURE WHY NOT?
MY NAME'S MIU.
I'm not here to pick you up, you know.
WONDER IF THIS IS FOR THE BEST.
I'M RENJI.
BUT, REALLY...
WHAT AN UNEXPECTED TURN OF EVENTS, MEETING HIM HERE.
WHAT THEY CALL...
...FATE, I SUPPOSE.

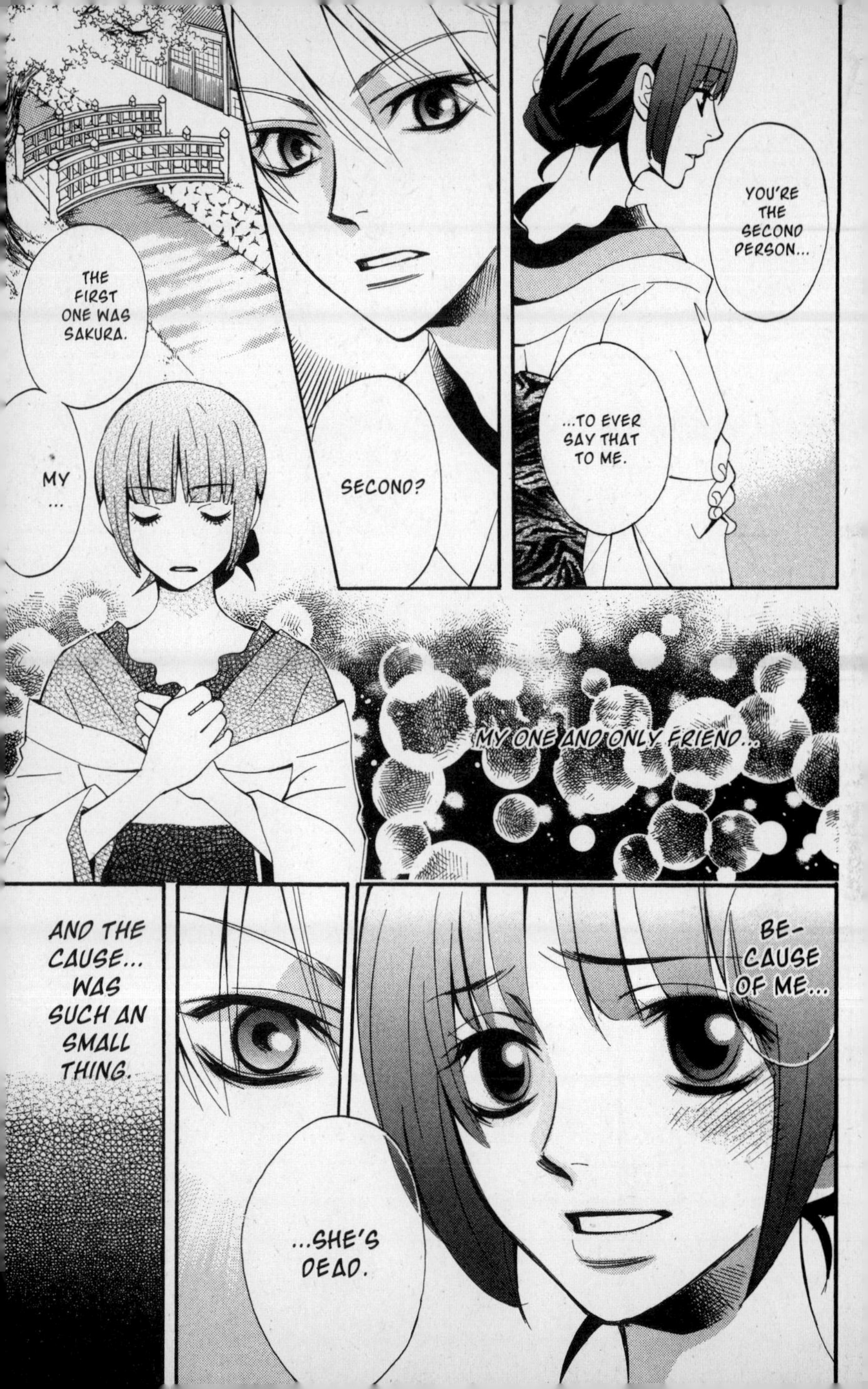
YOU'RE THE SECOND PERSON...
...TO EVER SAY THAT TO ME.
SECOND?
THE FIRST ONE WAS SAKURA.
MY ...
MY ONE AND ONLY FRIEND...
BE-CAUSE OF ME...
...SHE'S DEAD.
AND THE CAUSE... WAS SUCH AN SMALL THING.

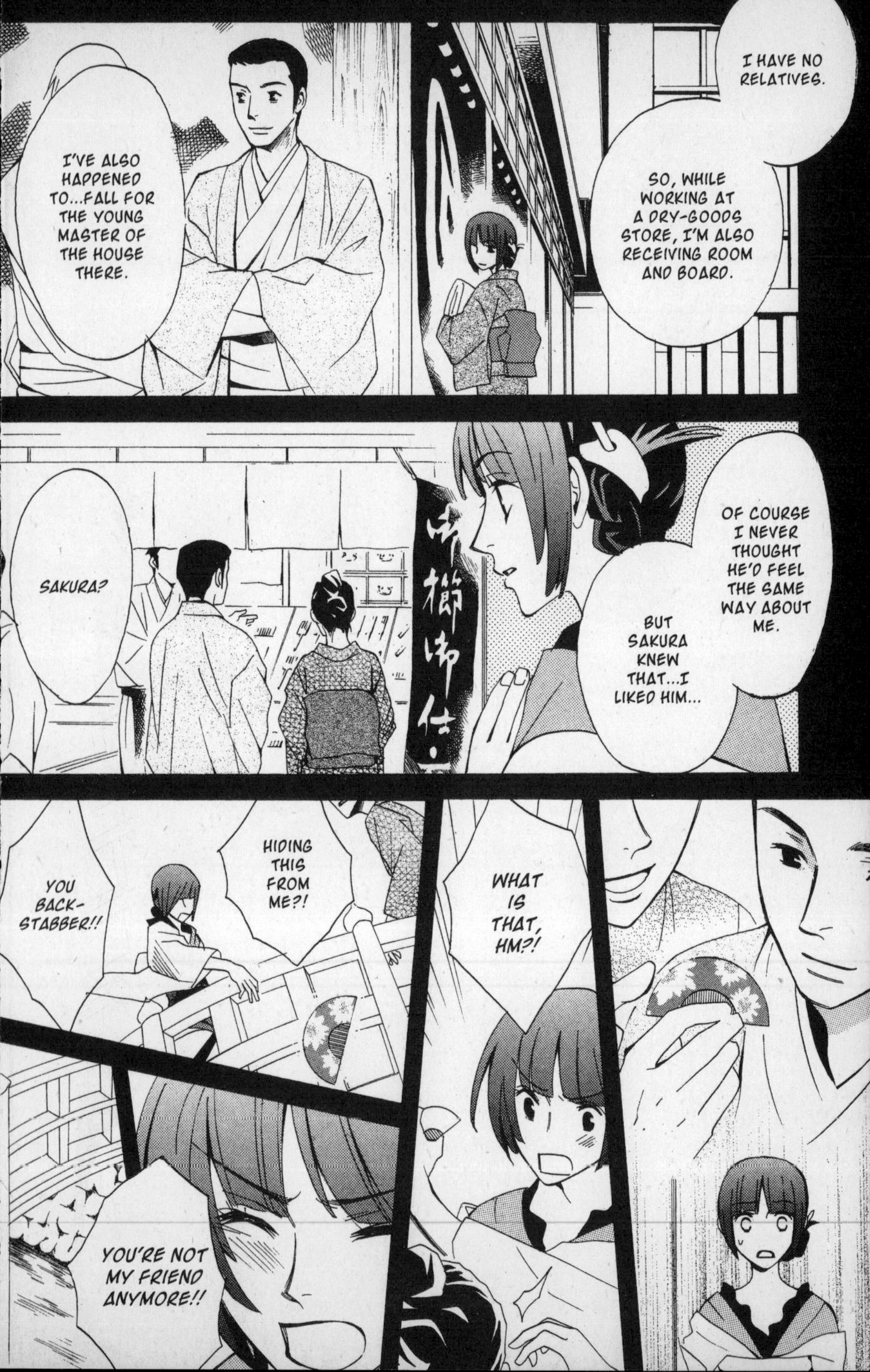
I HAVE NO RELATIVES.
SO, WHILE WORKING AT A DRY-GOODS STORE, I'M ALSO RECEIVING ROOM AND BOARD.
I'VE ALSO HAPPENED TO...FALL FOR THE YOUNG MASTER OF THE HOUSE THERE.
OF COURSE I NEVER THOUGHT HE'D FEEL THE SAME WAY ABOUT ME.
BUT SAKURA KNEW THAT...I LIKED HIM...
SAKURA?
WHAT IS THAT, HM?!
HIDING THIS FROM ME?!
YOU BACK-STABBER!!
YOU'RE NOT MY FRIEND ANYMORE!!

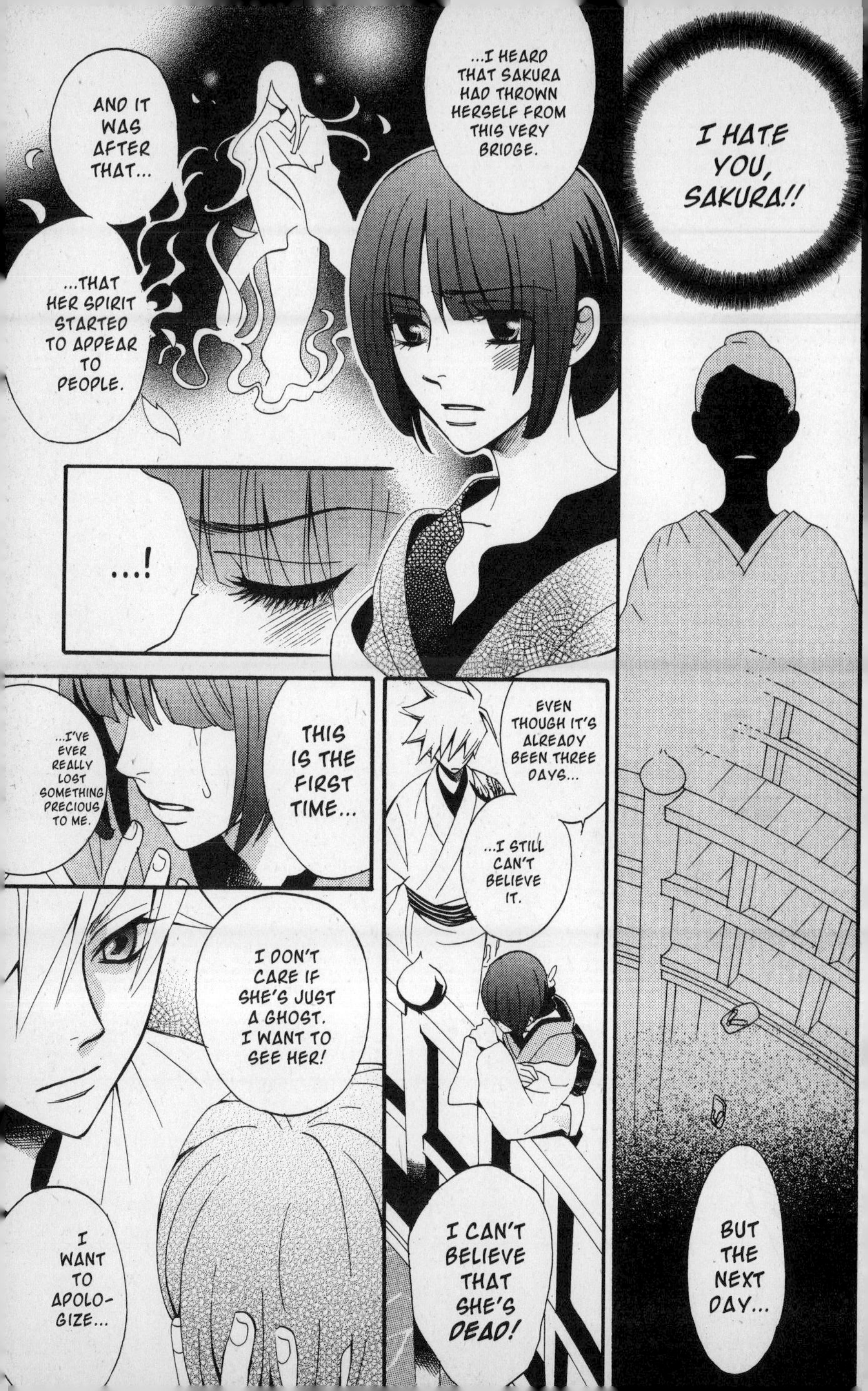
I HATE YOU, SAKURA!!
BUT THE NEXT DAY...
...I HEARD THAT SAKURA HAD THROWN HERSELF FROM THIS VERY BRIDGE.
AND IT WAS AFTER THAT...
...THAT HER SPIRIT STARTED TO APPEAR TO PEOPLE.
...!
EVEN THOUGH IT'S ALREADY BEEN THREE DAYS...
...I STILL CAN'T BELIEVE IT.
I CAN'T BELIEVE THAT SHE'S DEAD!
THIS IS THE FIRST TIME...
...I'VE EVER REALLY LOST SOMETHING PRECIOUS TO ME.
I DON'T CARE IF SHE'S JUST A GHOST. I WANT TO SEE HER!
I WANT TO APOLOGIZE...

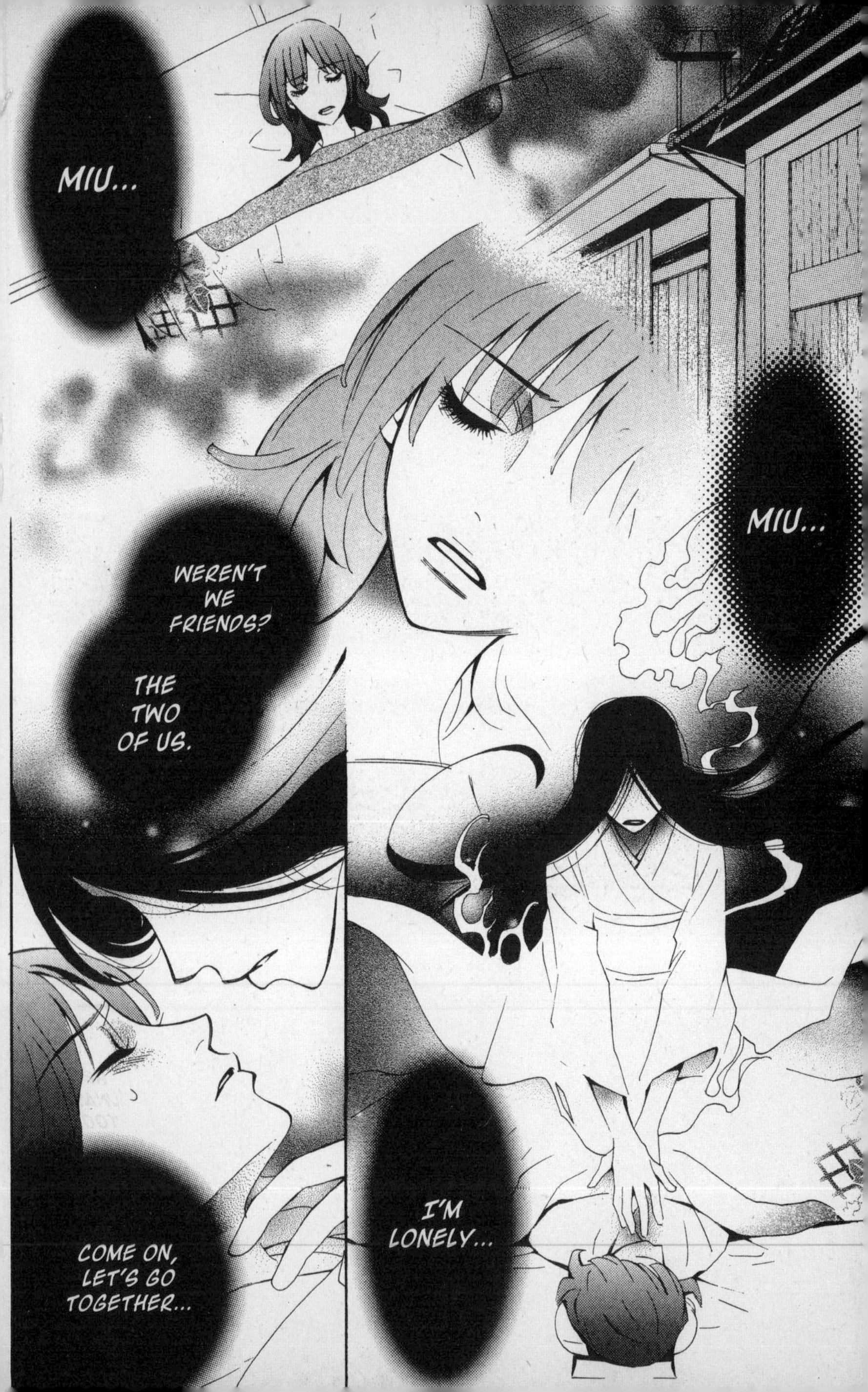
MIU...
MIU...
I'M LONELY...
WEREN'T WE FRIENDS?
THE TWO OF US.
COME ON, LET'S GO TOGETHER...

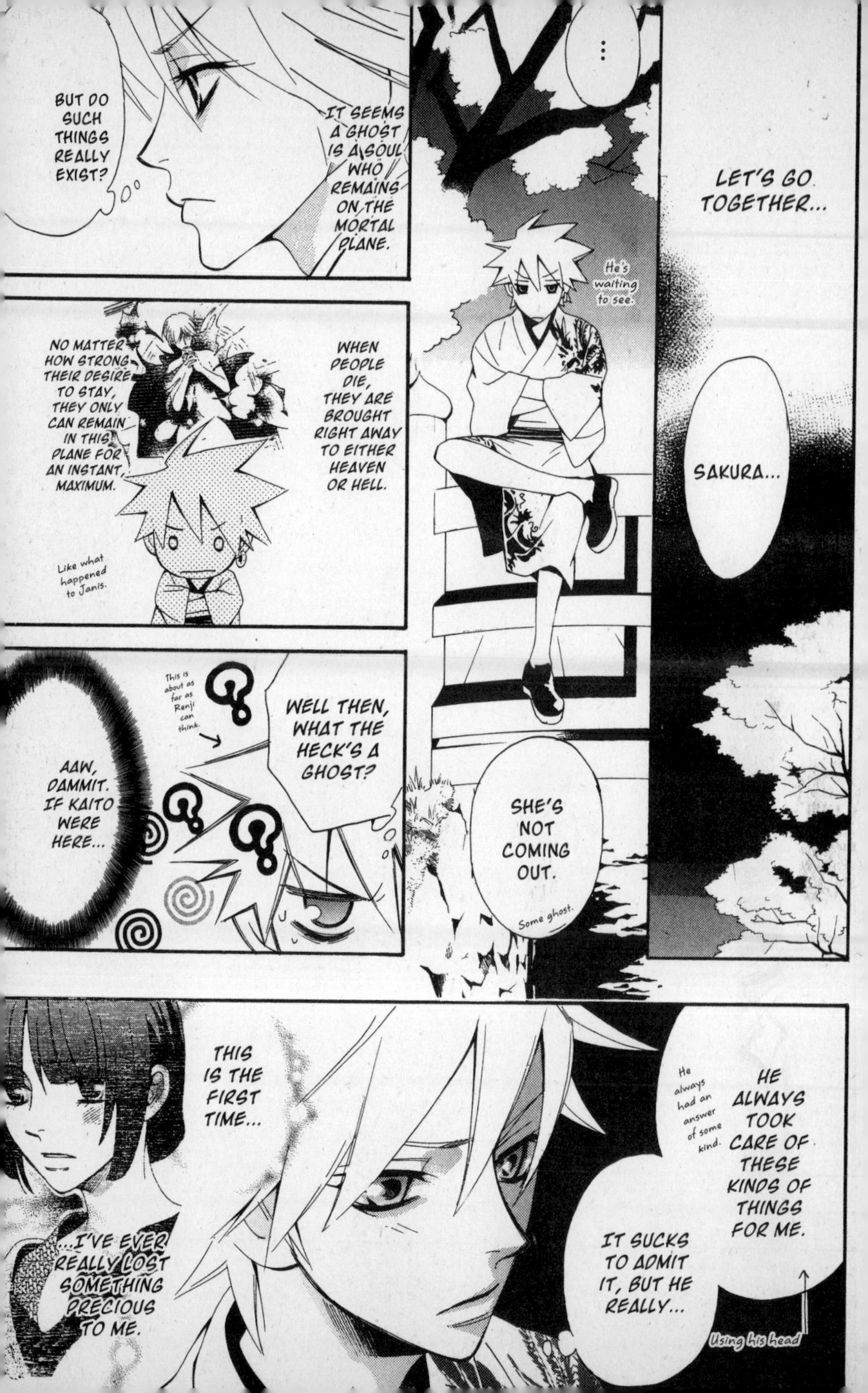
LET'S GO TOGETHER...
SAKURA...
...
He's waiting to see.
SHE'S NOT COMING OUT.
Some ghost.
IT SEEMS A GHOST IS A SOUL WHO REMAINS ON THE MORTAL PLANE.
BUT DO SUCH THINGS REALLY EXIST?
WHEN PEOPLE DIE, THEY ARE BROUGHT RIGHT AWAY TO EITHER HEAVEN OR HELL.
NO MATTER HOW STRONG THEIR DESIRE TO STAY, THEY ONLY CAN REMAIN IN THIS PLANE FOR AN INSTANT, MAXIMUM.
Like what happened to Janis.
WELL THEN, WHAT THE HECK'S A GHOST?
This is about as far as Renji can think.
AAW, DAMMIT. IF KAITO WERE HERE...
HE ALWAYS TOOK CARE OF THESE KINDS OF THINGS FOR ME.
He always had an answer of some kind.
IT SUCKS TO ADMIT IT, BUT HE REALLY...
Using his head
THIS IS THE FIRST TIME...
...I'VE EVER REALLY LOST SOMETHING PRECIOUS TO ME.

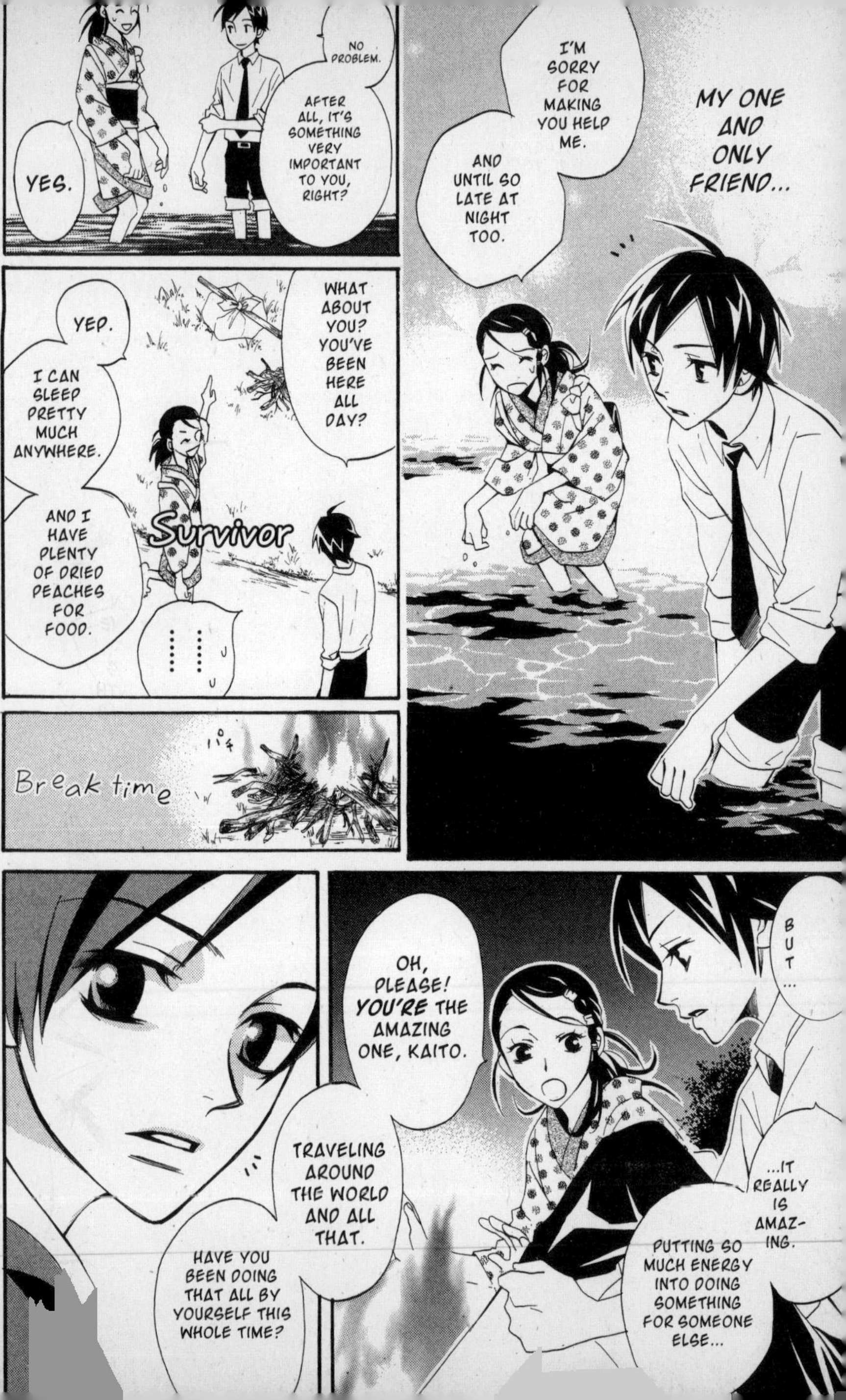

MY ONE AND ONLY FRIEND...
I'M SORRY FOR MAKING YOU HELP ME.
AND UNTIL SO LATE AT NIGHT TOO.
NO PROBLEM.
AFTER ALL, IT'S SOMETHING VERY IMPORTANT TO YOU, RIGHT?
YES.
WHAT ABOUT YOU? YOU'VE BEEN HERE ALL DAY?
YEP.
I CAN SLEEP PRETTY MUCH ANYWHERE.
AND I HAVE PLENTY OF DRIED PEACHES FOR FOOD.
Survivor
......
Break time
BUT...
OH, PLEASE! YOU'RE THE AMAZING ONE, KAITO.
TRAVELING AROUND THE WORLD AND ALL THAT.
...IT REALLY IS AMAZ-ING.
PUTTING SO MUCH ENERGY INTO DOING SOMETHING FOR SOMEONE ELSE...
HAVE YOU BEEN DOING THAT ALL BY YOURSELF THIS WHOLE TIME?

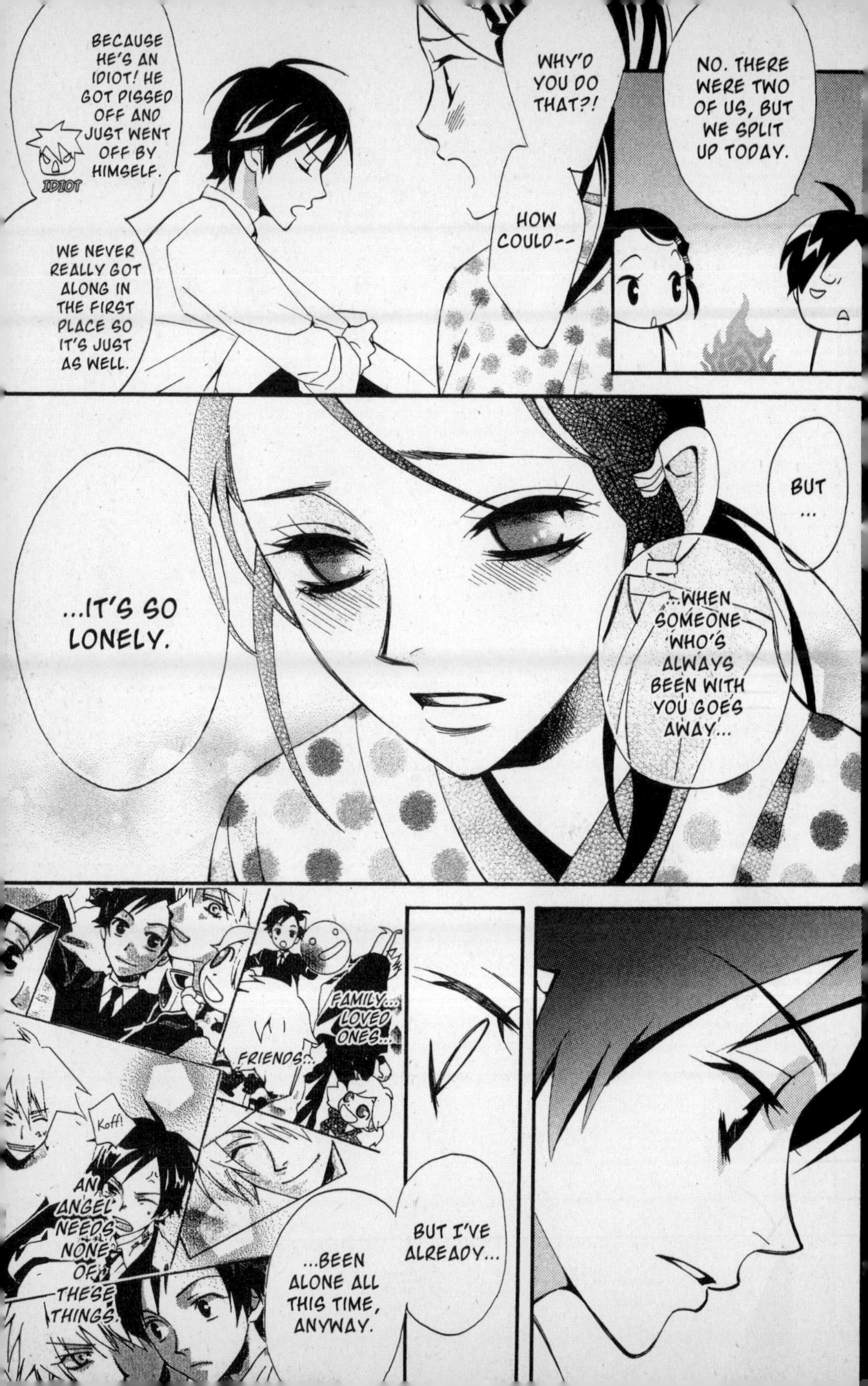
NO. THERE WERE TWO OF US, BUT WE SPLIT UP TODAY.
WHY'D YOU DO THAT?!
HOW COULD--
BECAUSE HE'S AN IDIOT! HE GOT PISSED OFF AND JUST WENT OFF BY HIMSELF.
IDIOT
WE NEVER REALLY GOT ALONG IN THE FIRST PLACE SO IT'S JUST AS WELL.
BUT ...
...WHEN SOMEONE WHO'S ALWAYS BEEN WITH YOU GOES AWAY...
...IT'S SO LONELY.
BUT I'VE ALREADY...
...BEEN ALONE ALL THIS TIME, ANYWAY.
FAMILY... LOVED ONES...
FRIENDS...
Koff!
AN ANGEL NEEDS NONE OF THESE THINGS.

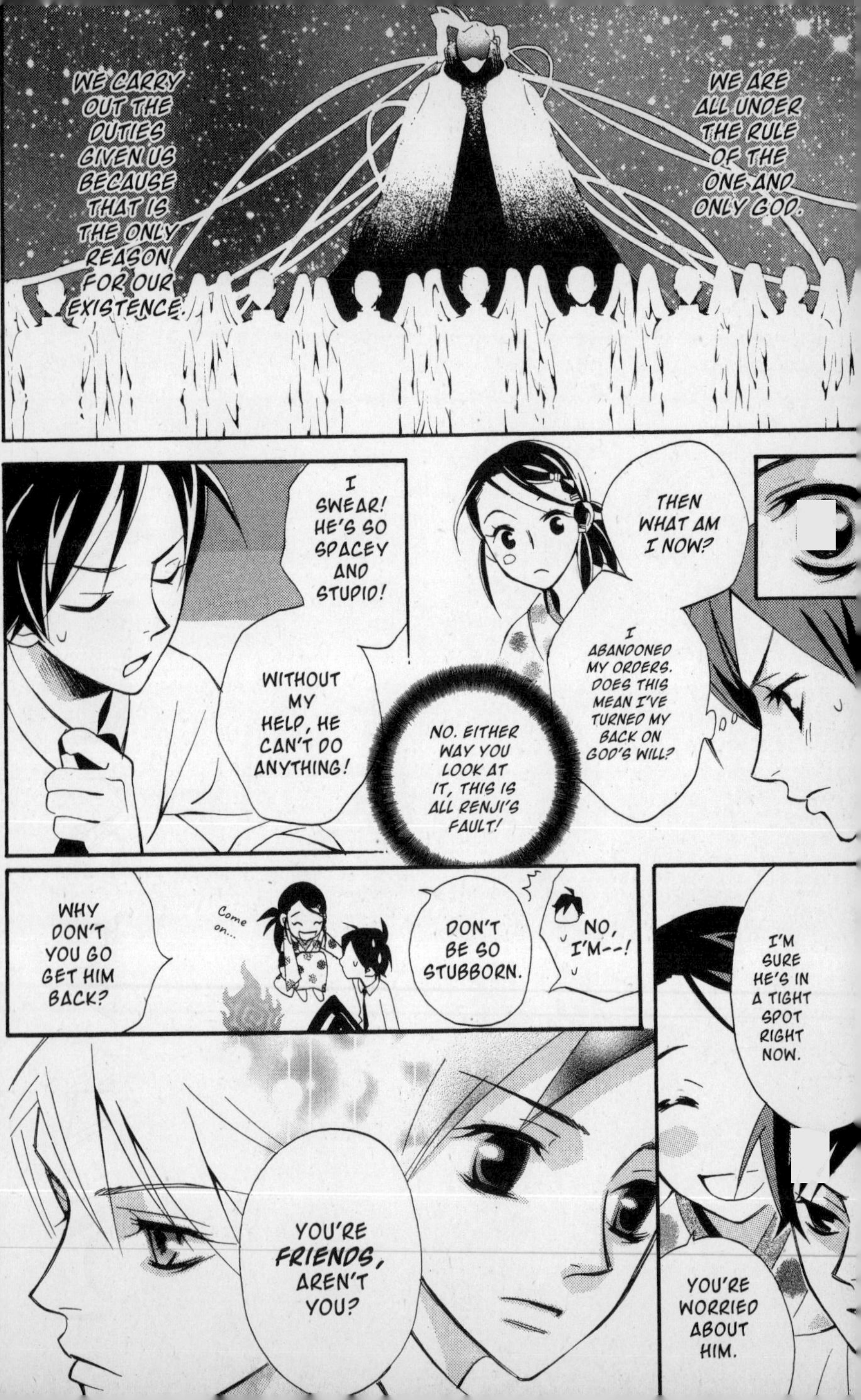
WE ARE ALL UNDER THE RULE OF THE ONE AND ONLY GOD.
WE CARRY OUT THE DUTIES GIVEN US BECAUSE THAT IS THE ONLY REASON FOR OUR EXISTENCE.
THEN WHAT AM I NOW?
I ABANDONED MY ORDERS. DOES THIS MEAN I'VE TURNED MY BACK ON GOD'S WILL?
NO. EITHER WAY YOU LOOK AT IT, THIS IS ALL RENJI'S FAULT!
I SWEAR! HE'S SO SPACEY AND STUPID!
WITHOUT MY HELP, HE CAN'T DO ANYTHING!
I'M SURE HE'S IN A TIGHT SPOT RIGHT NOW.
YOU'RE WORRIED ABOUT HIM.
NO, I'M--!
DON'T BE SO STUBBORN.
Come on...
WHY DON'T YOU GO GET HIM BACK?
YOU'RE FRIENDS, AREN'T YOU?

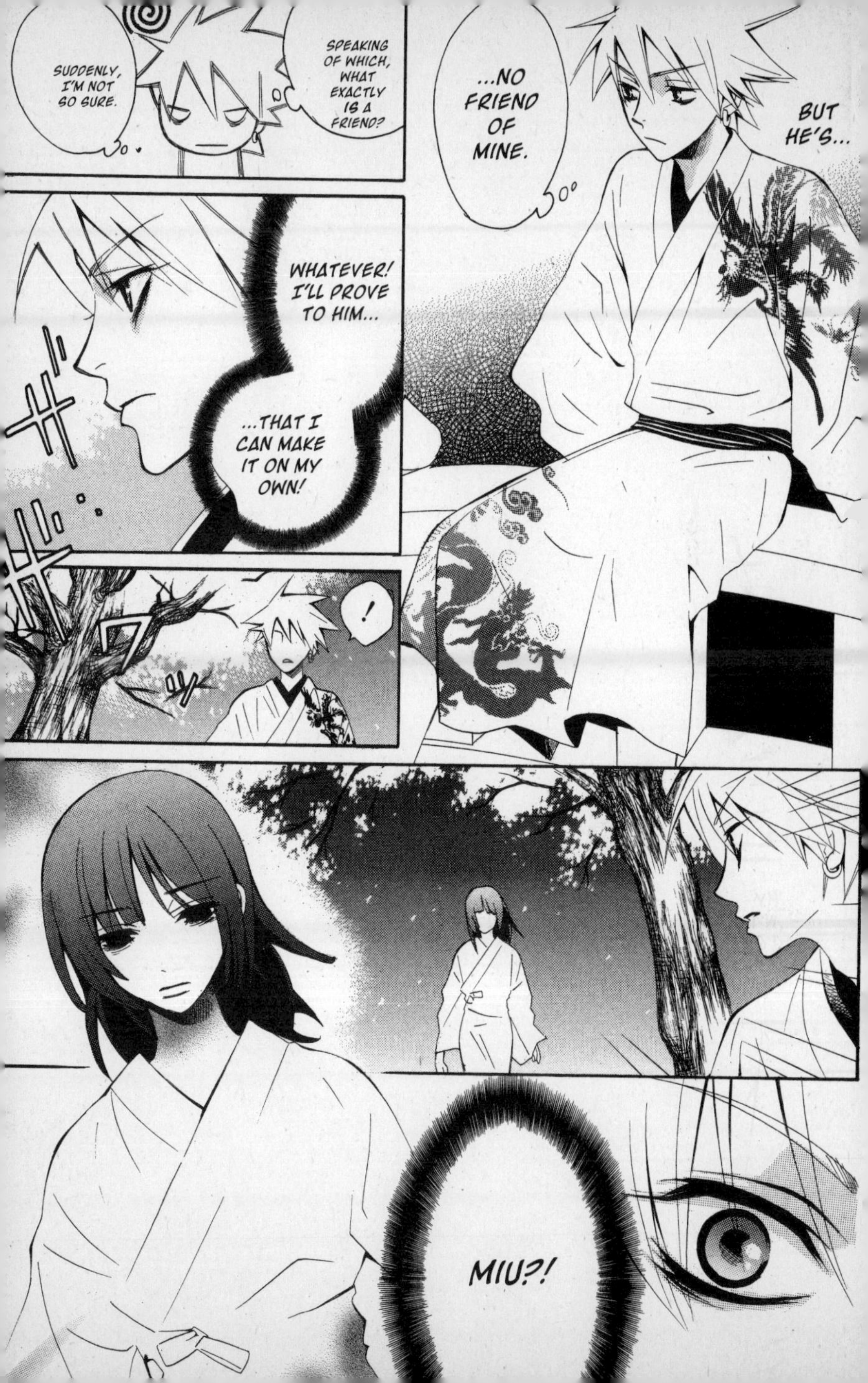
BUT HE'S...
...NO FRIEND OF MINE.
SPEAKING OF WHICH, WHAT EXACTLY IS A FRIEND?
SUDDENLY, I'M NOT SO SURE.
WHATEVER! I'LL PROVE TO HIM...
...THAT I CAN MAKE IT ON MY OWN!
!
MIU?!

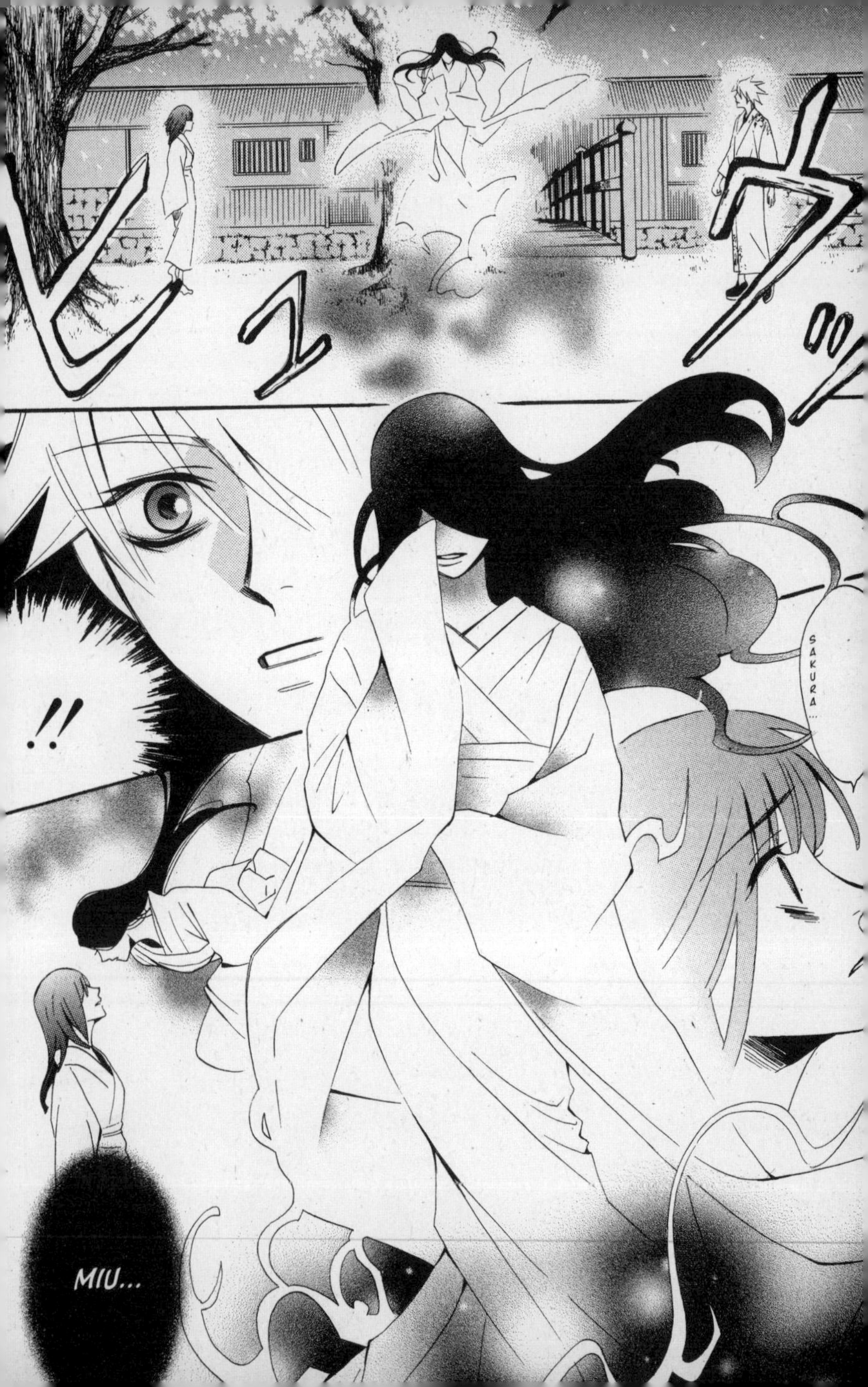
ビュゥ
SAKURA...
!!
MIU...

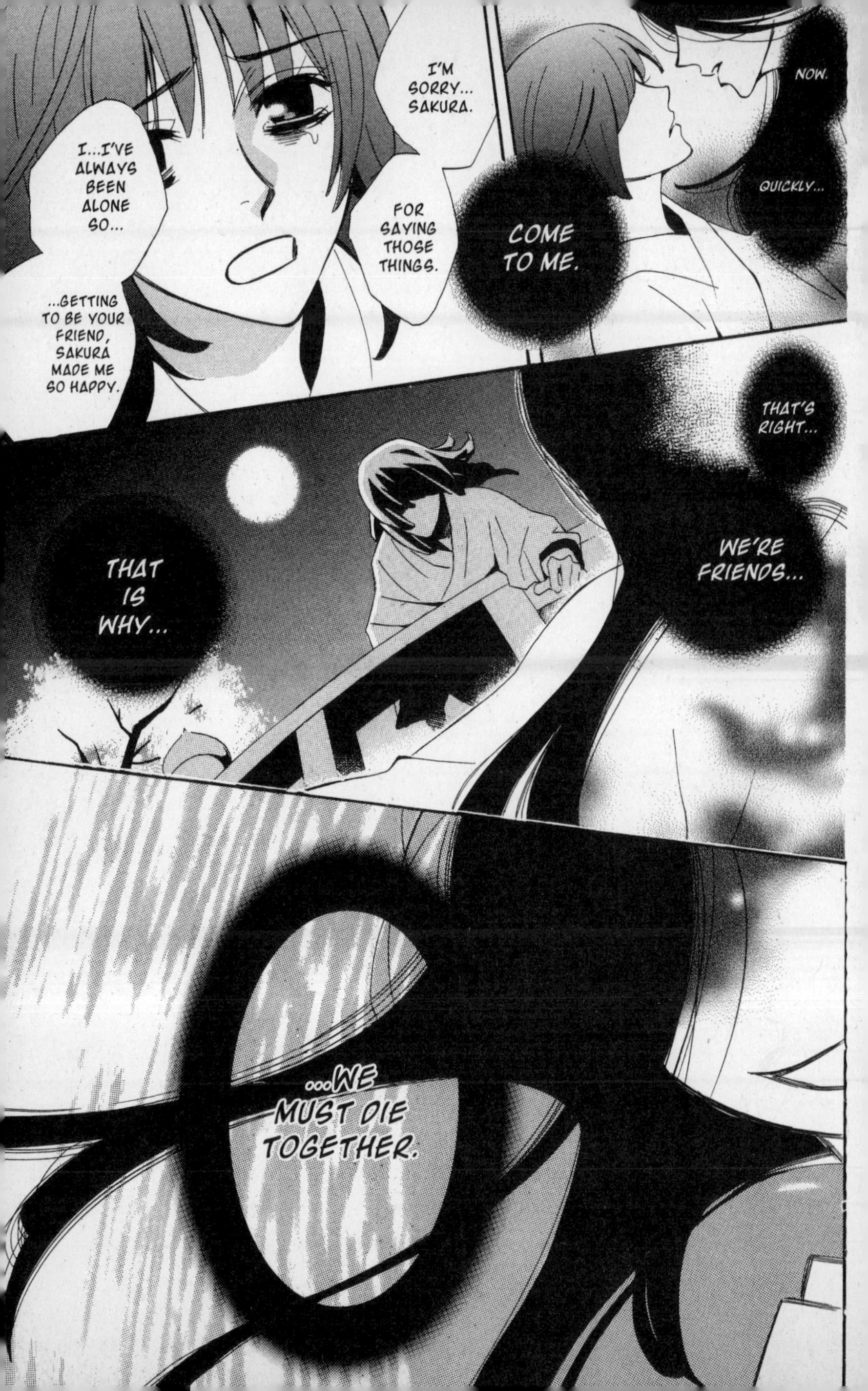
NOW.
QUICKLY...
COME TO ME.
I'M SORRY... SAKURA.
FOR SAYING THOSE THINGS.
I...I'VE ALWAYS BEEN ALONE SO...
...GETTING TO BE YOUR FRIEND, SAKURA MADE ME SO HAPPY.
THAT'S RIGHT...
WE'RE FRIENDS...
THAT IS WHY...
...WE MUST DIE TOGETHER.

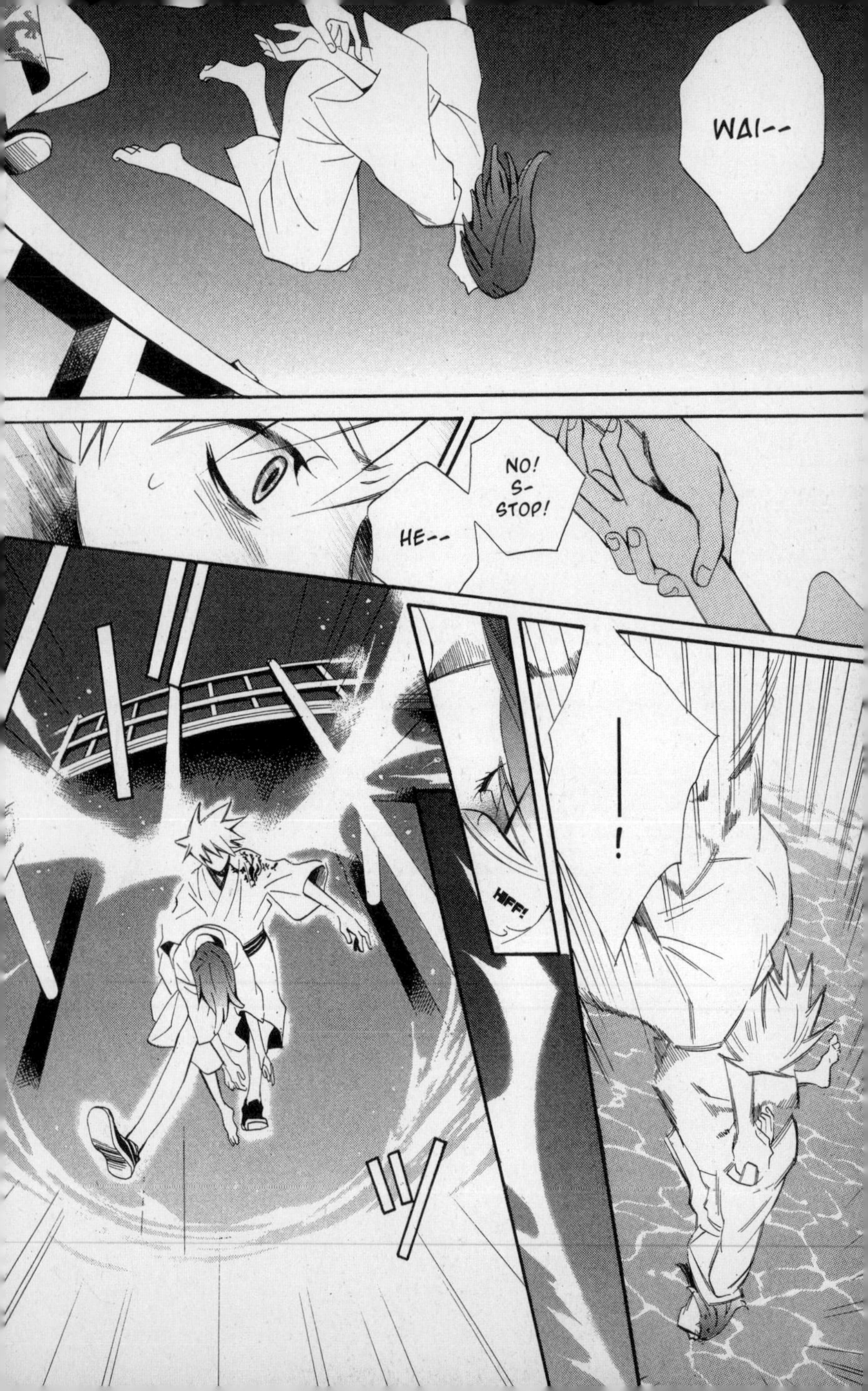
WAI--
NO! S- STOP!
HE--
!
HFF!

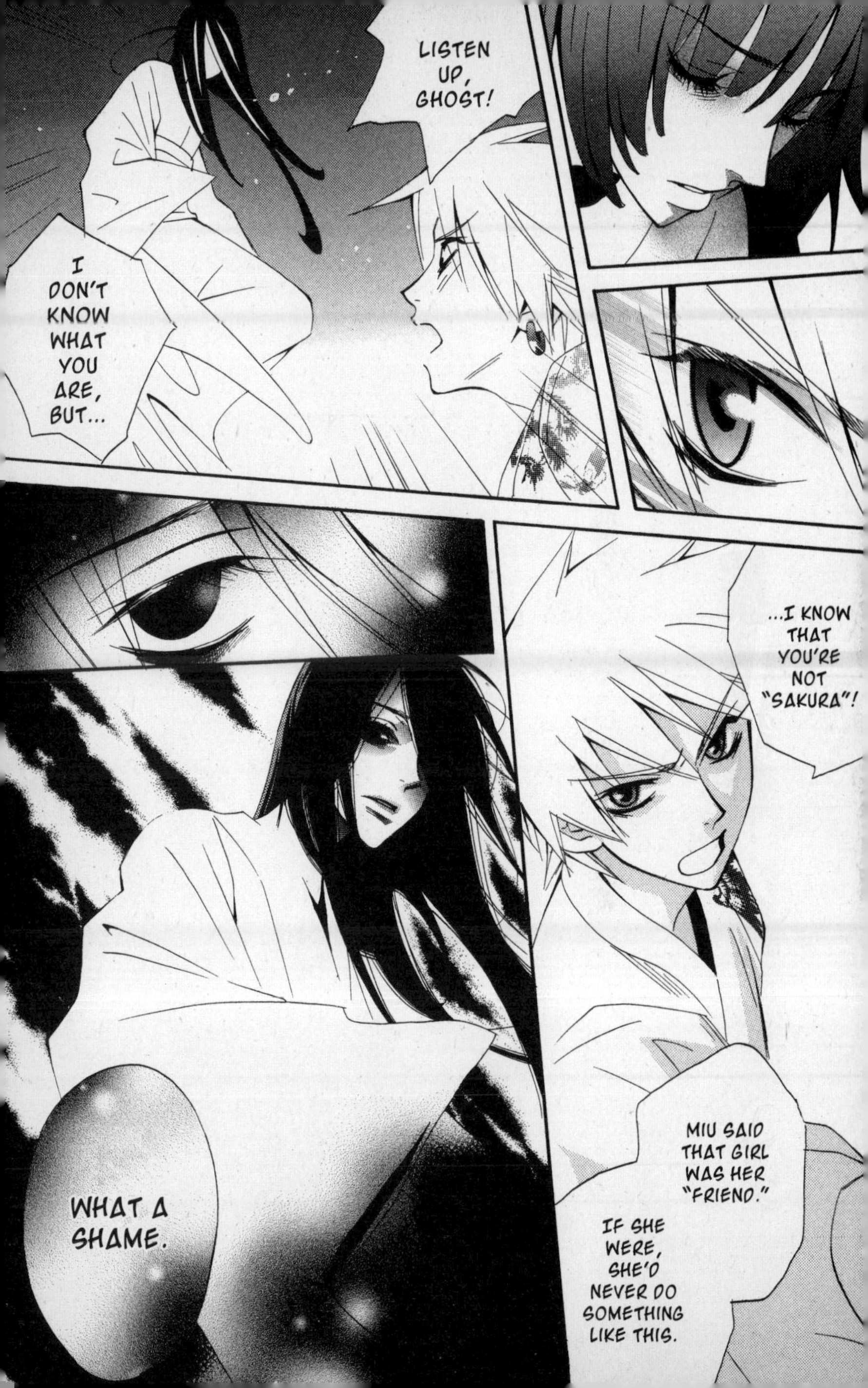
LISTEN UP, GHOST!
I DON'T KNOW WHAT YOU ARE, BUT...
...I KNOW THAT YOU'RE NOT "SAKURA"!
MIU SAID THAT GIRL WAS HER "FRIEND."
IF SHE WERE, SHE'D NEVER DO SOMETHING LIKE THIS.
WHAT A SHAME.

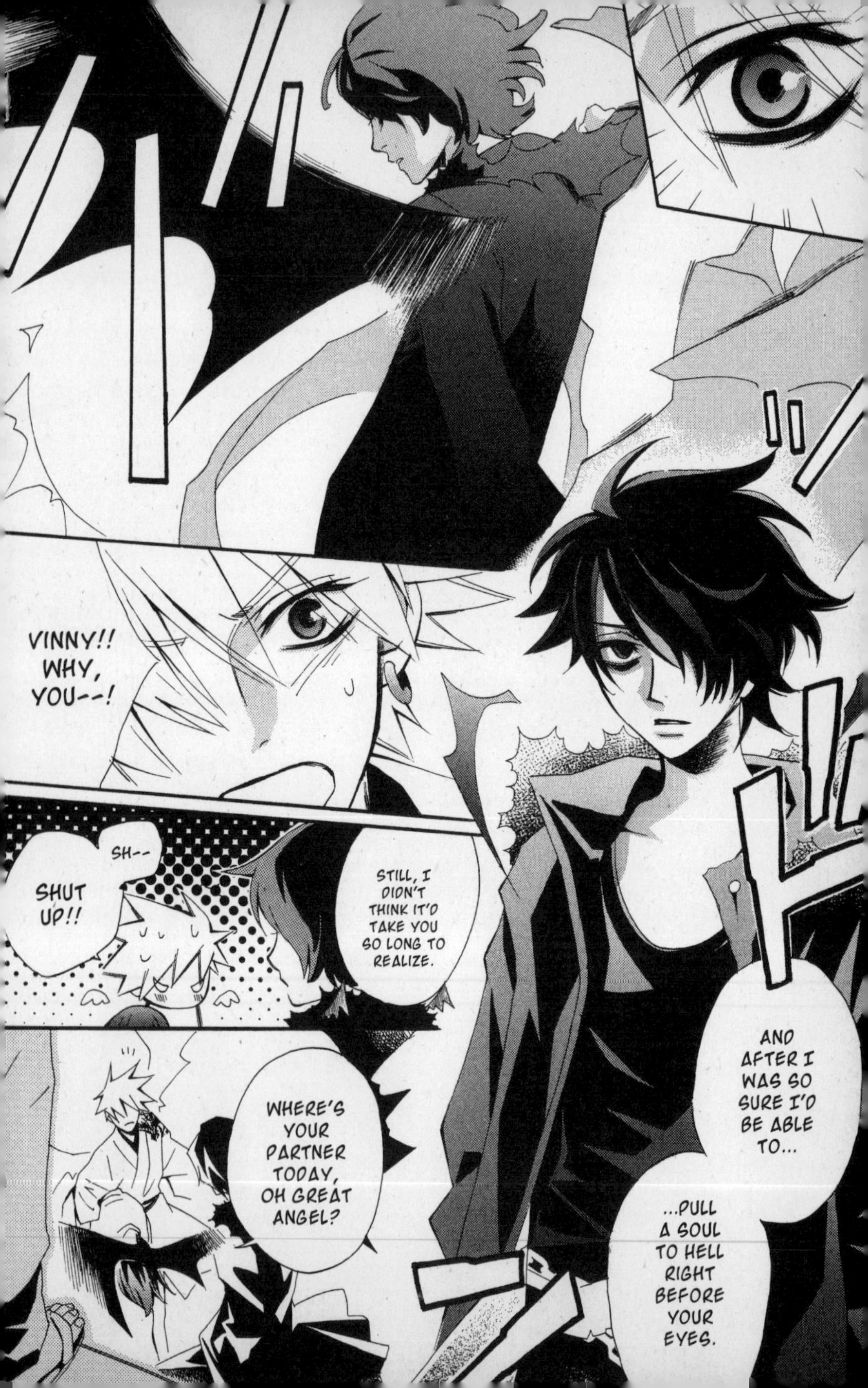
AND AFTER I WAS SO SURE I'D BE ABLE TO...
...PULL A SOUL TO HELL RIGHT BEFORE YOUR EYES.
VINNY!! WHY, YOU--!
STILL, I DIDN'T THINK IT'D TAKE YOU SO LONG TO REALIZE.
SH--
SHUT UP!!
WHERE'S YOUR PARTNER TODAY, OH GREAT ANGEL?

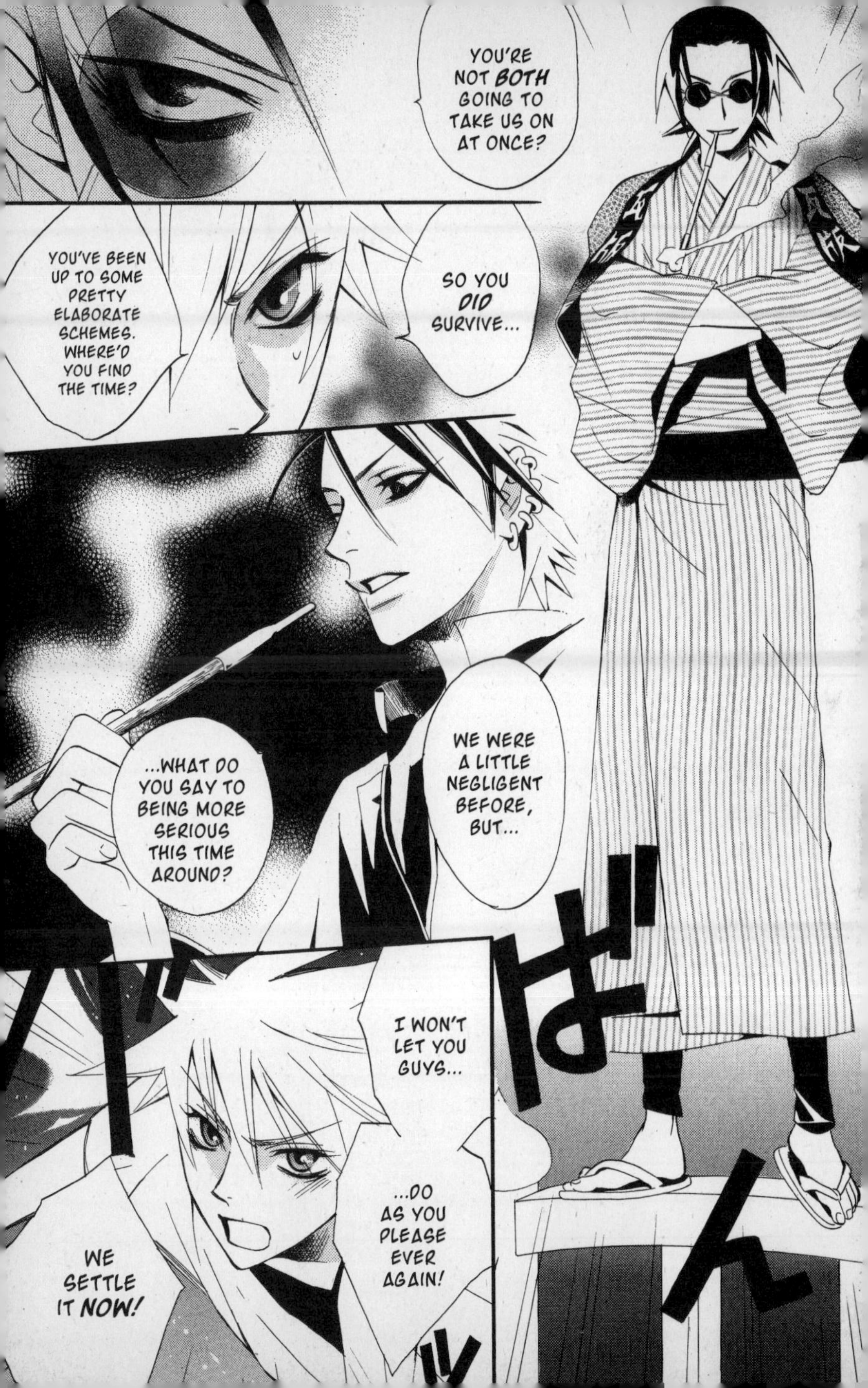

YOU'RE NOT BOTH GOING TO TAKE US ON AT ONCE?
SO YOU DID SURVIVE...
YOU'VE BEEN UP TO SOME PRETTY ELABORATE SCHEMES. WHERE'D YOU FIND THE TIME?
WE WERE A LITTLE NEGLIGENT BEFORE, BUT...
...WHAT DO YOU SAY TO BEING MORE SERIOUS THIS TIME AROUND?
I WON'T LET YOU GUYS...
...DO AS YOU PLEASE EVER AGAIN!
WE SETTLE IT NOW!

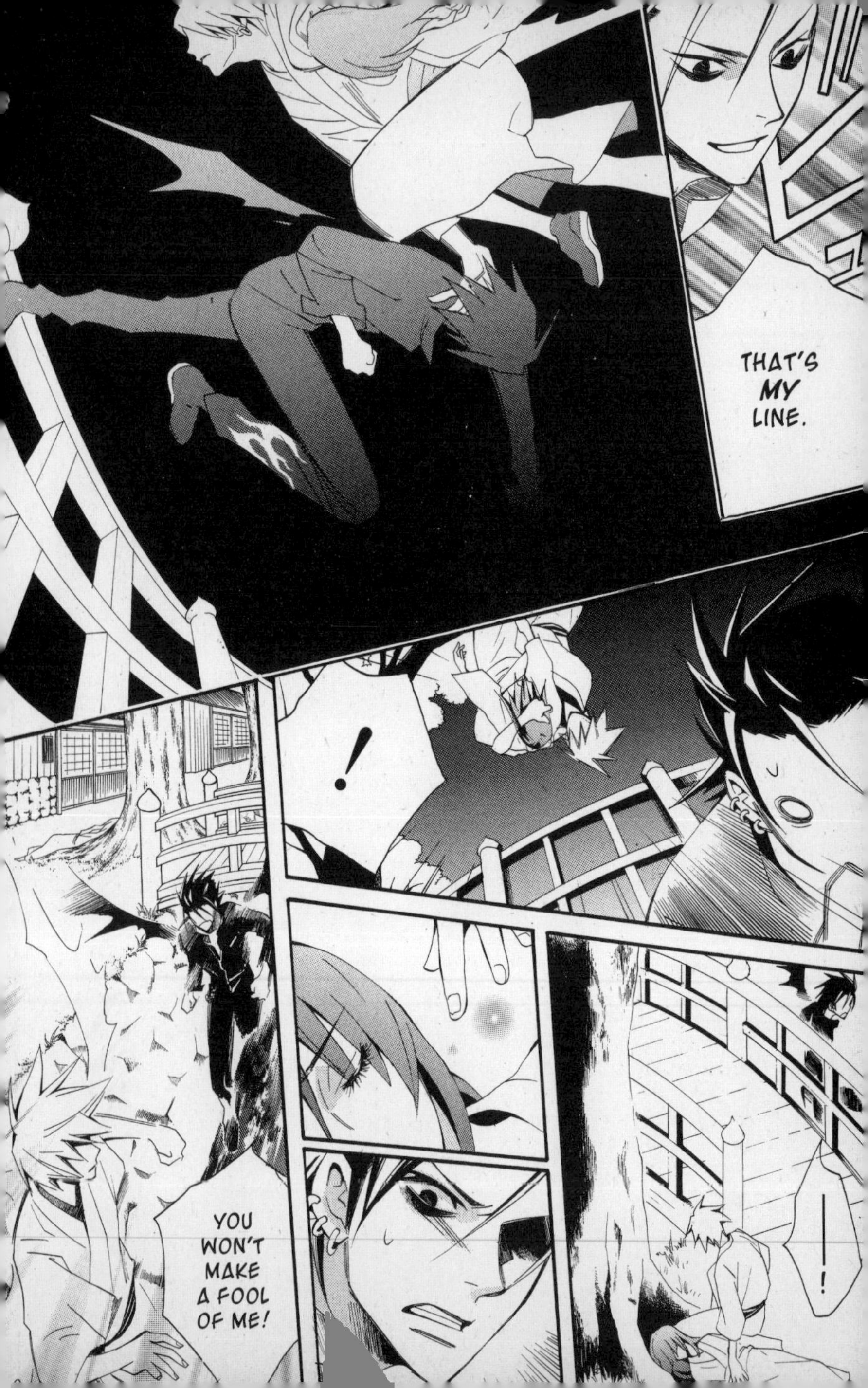
THAT'S MY LINE.
!
--!
YOU WON'T MAKE A FOOL OF ME!

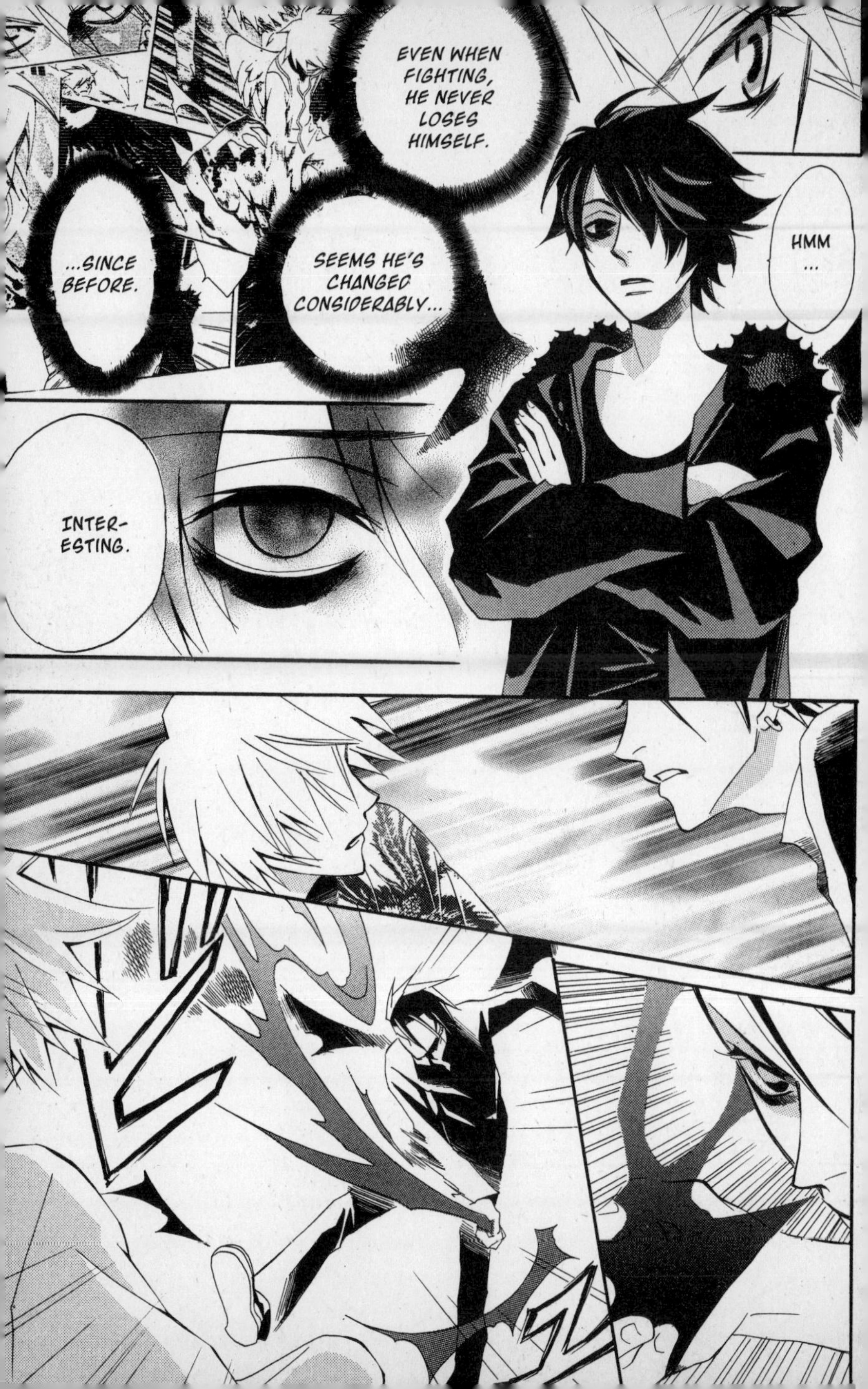
HMM ...
EVEN WHEN FIGHTING, HE NEVER LOSES HIMSELF.
SEEMS HE'S CHANGED CONSIDERABLY...
...SINCE BEFORE.
INTER-ESTING.

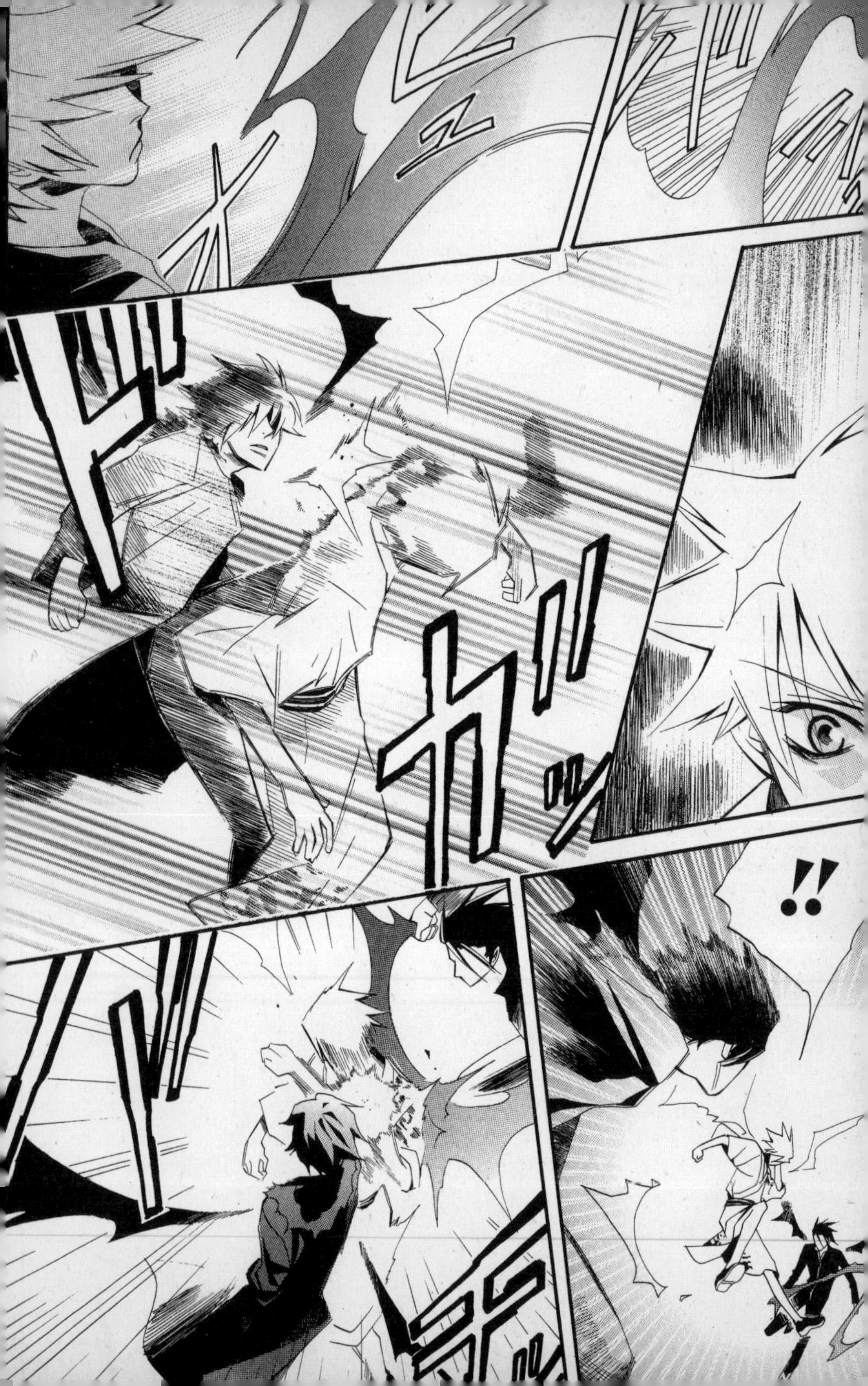
ビュオ
ドッ
ガッ
!!

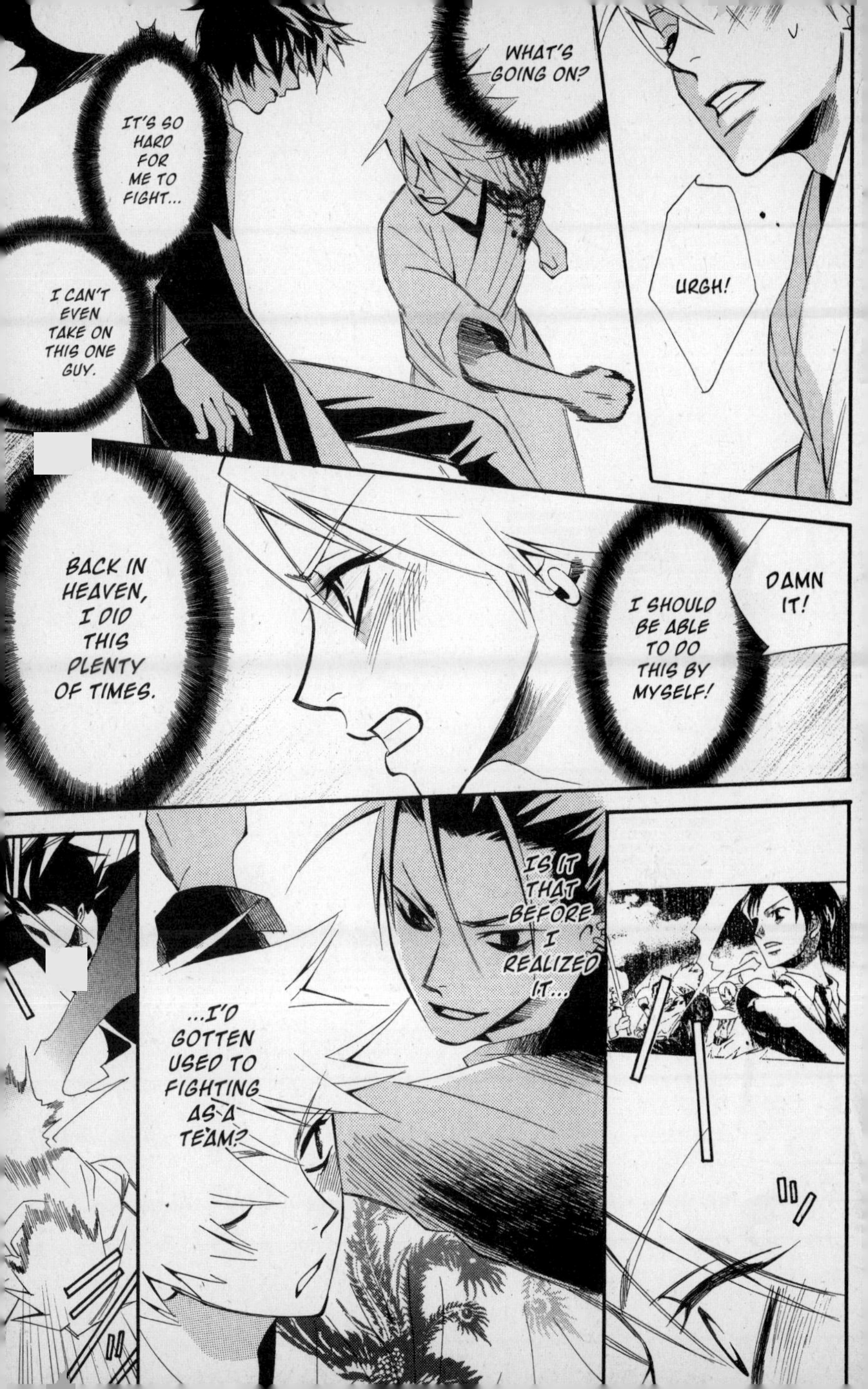
URGH!
WHAT'S GOING ON?
IT'S SO HARD FOR ME TO FIGHT...
I CAN'T EVEN TAKE ON THIS ONE GUY.
DAMN IT!
I SHOULD BE ABLE TO DO THIS BY MYSELF!
BACK IN HEAVEN, I DID THIS PLENTY OF TIMES.
IS IT THAT BEFORE I REALIZED IT...
...I'D GOTTEN USED TO FIGHTING AS A TEAM?

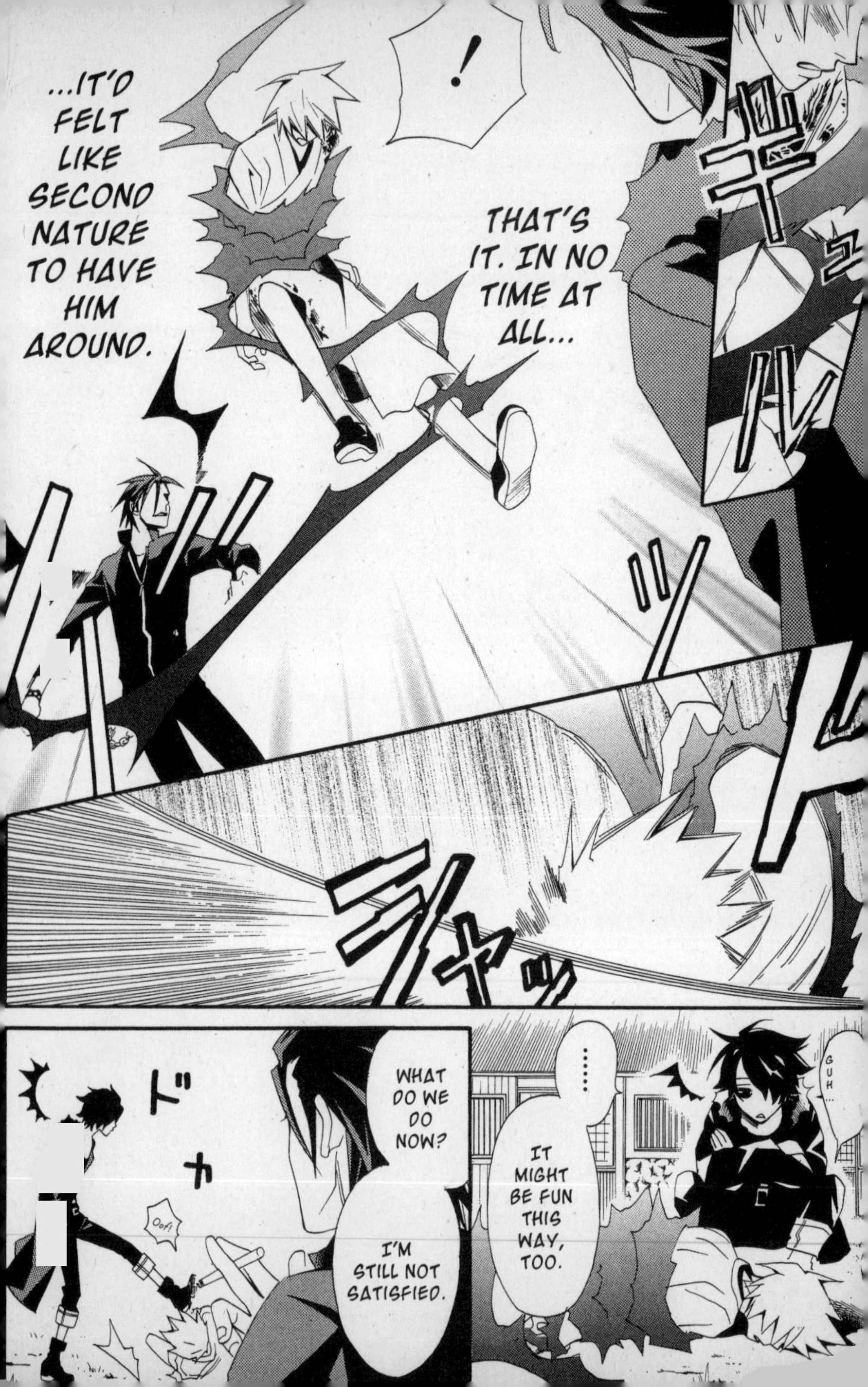
!
THAT'S IT. IN NO TIME AT ALL...
...IT'D FELT LIKE SECOND NATURE TO HAVE HIM AROUND.
GUH...
......
IT MIGHT BE FUN THIS WAY, TOO.
WHAT DO WE DO NOW?
I'M STILL NOT SATISFIED.
Oof!

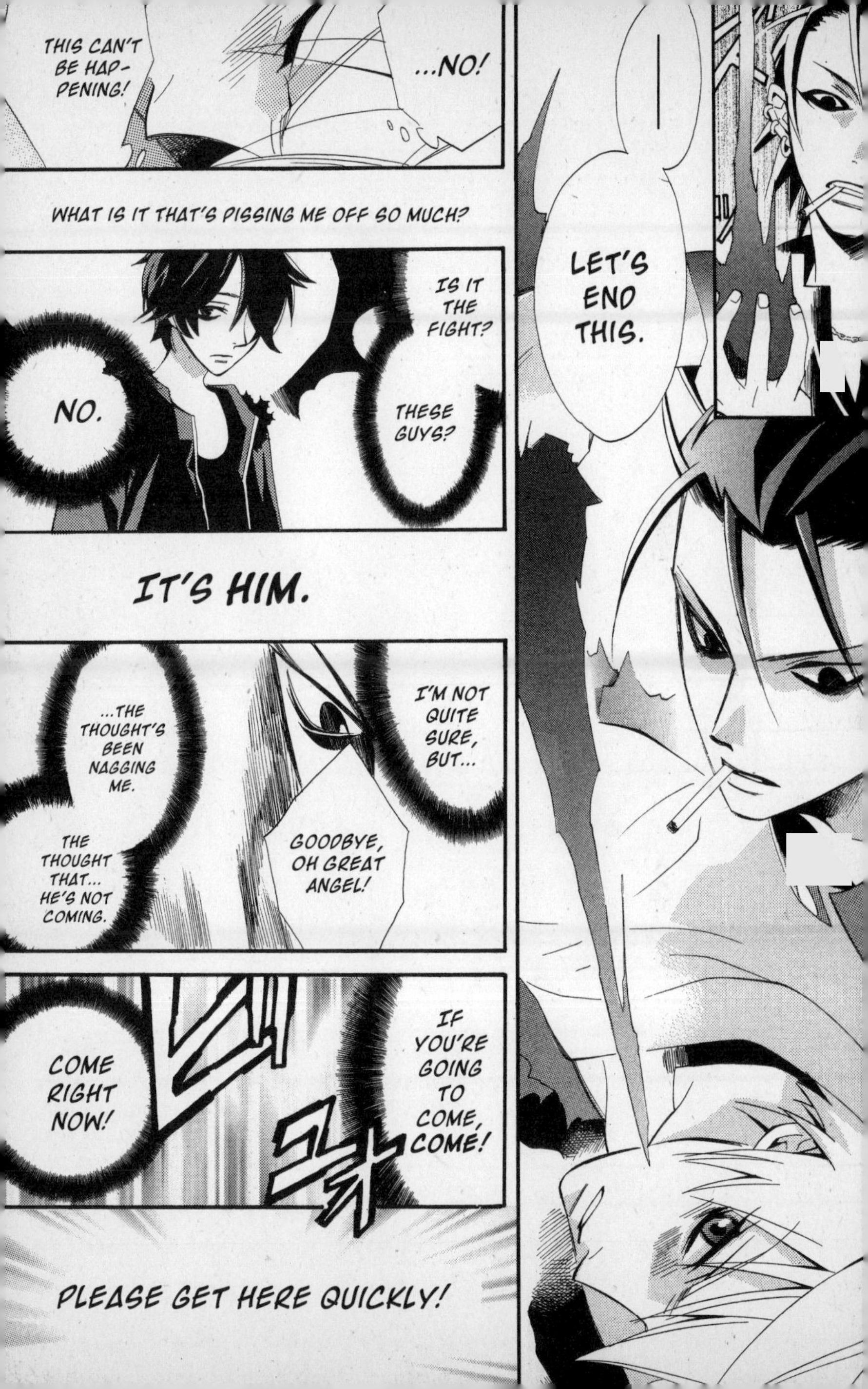
LET'S END THIS.
...NO!
THIS CAN'T BE HAP-PENING!
WHAT IS IT THAT'S PISSING ME OFF SO MUCH?
IS IT THE FIGHT?
THESE GUYS?
NO.
IT'S HIM.
I'M NOT QUITE SURE, BUT...
...THE THOUGHT'S BEEN NAGGING ME.
GOODBYE, OH GREAT ANGEL!
THE THOUGHT THAT... HE'S NOT COMING.
IF YOU'RE GOING TO COME, COME!
COME RIGHT NOW!
PLEASE GET HERE QUICKLY!

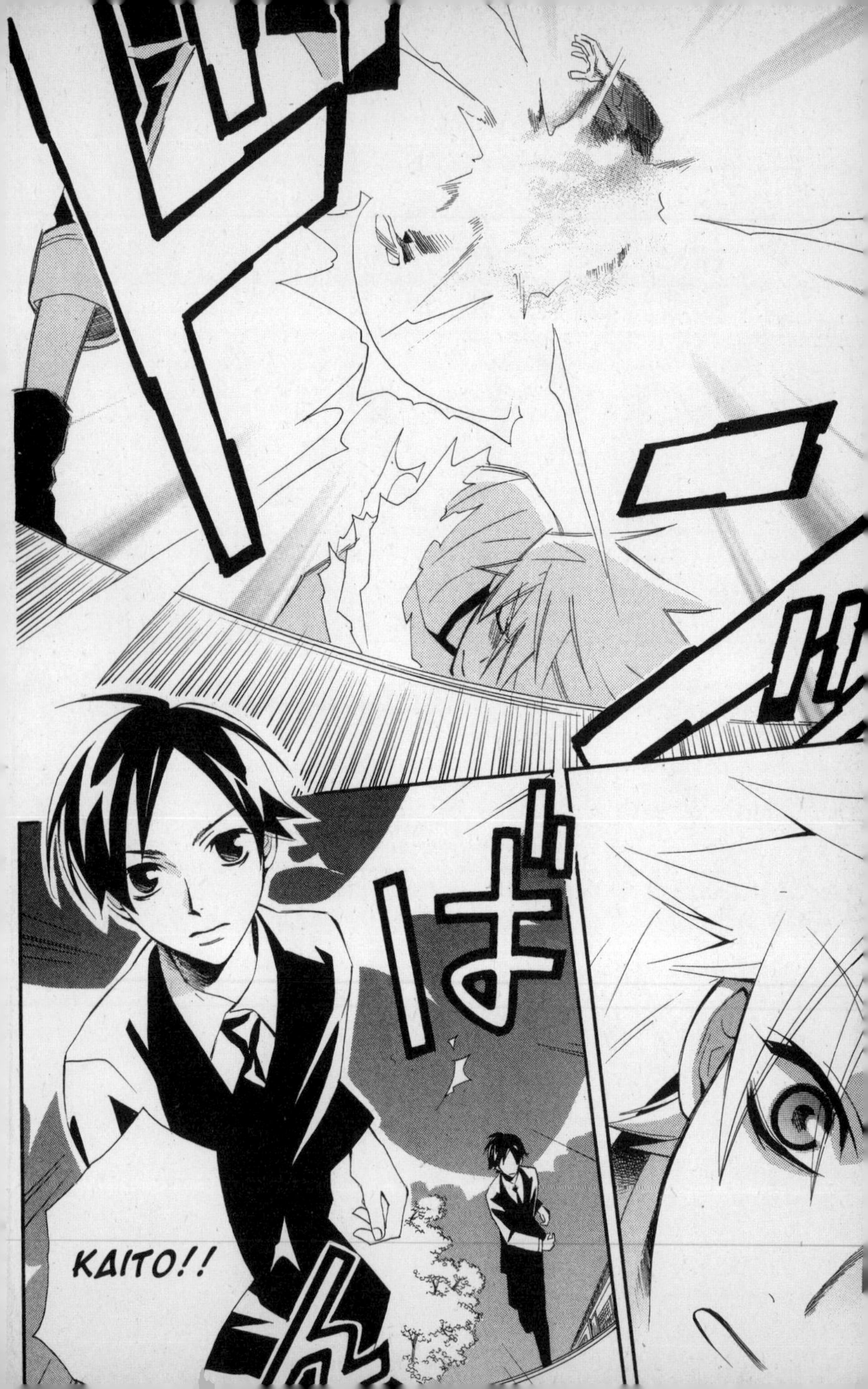
KAITO!!

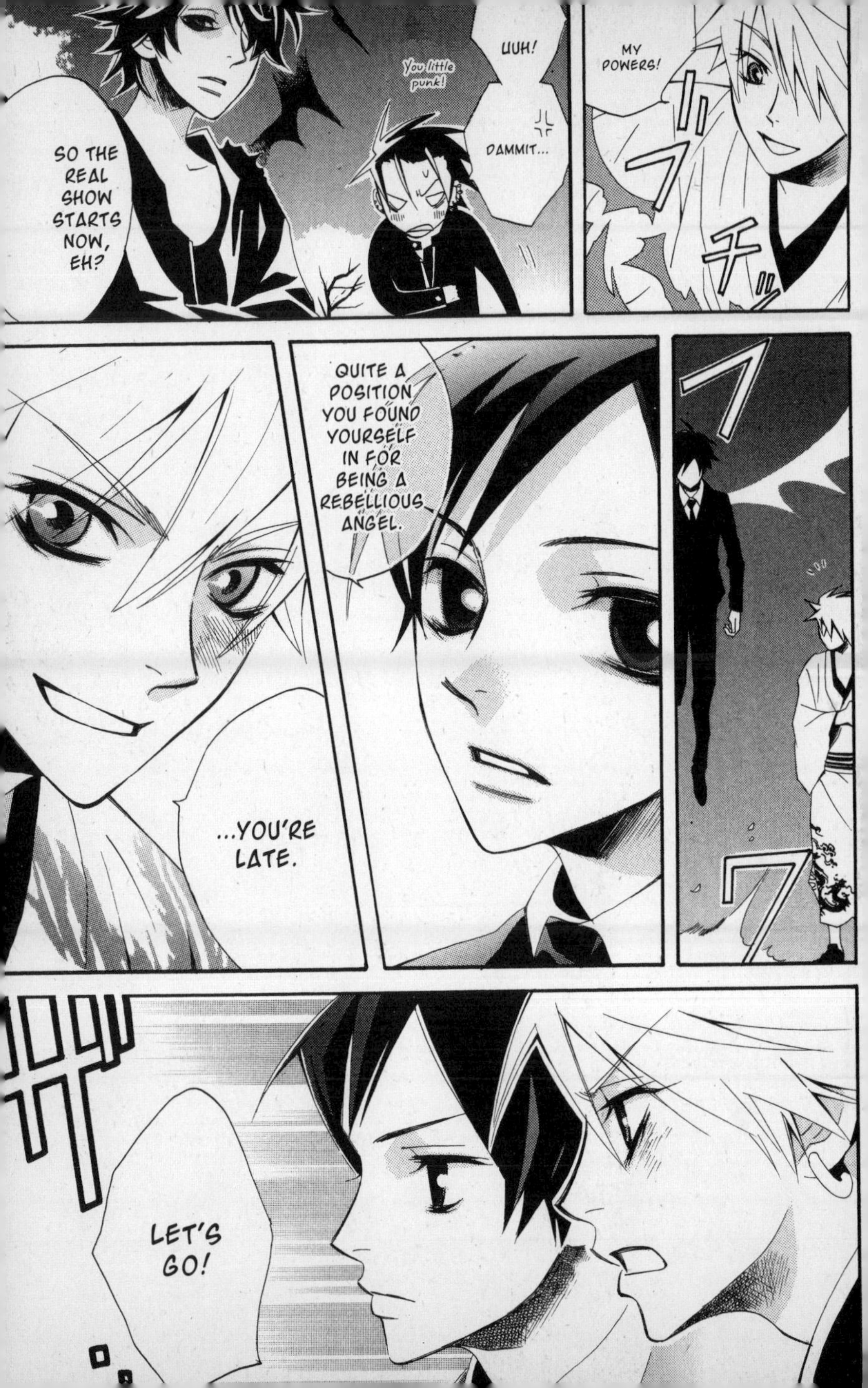
MY POWERS!
UUH!
You little punk!
DAMMIT...
SO THE REAL SHOW STARTS NOW, EH?
QUITE A POSITION YOU FOUND YOURSELF IN FOR BEING A REBELLIOUS ANGEL.
...YOU'RE LATE.
LET'S GO!

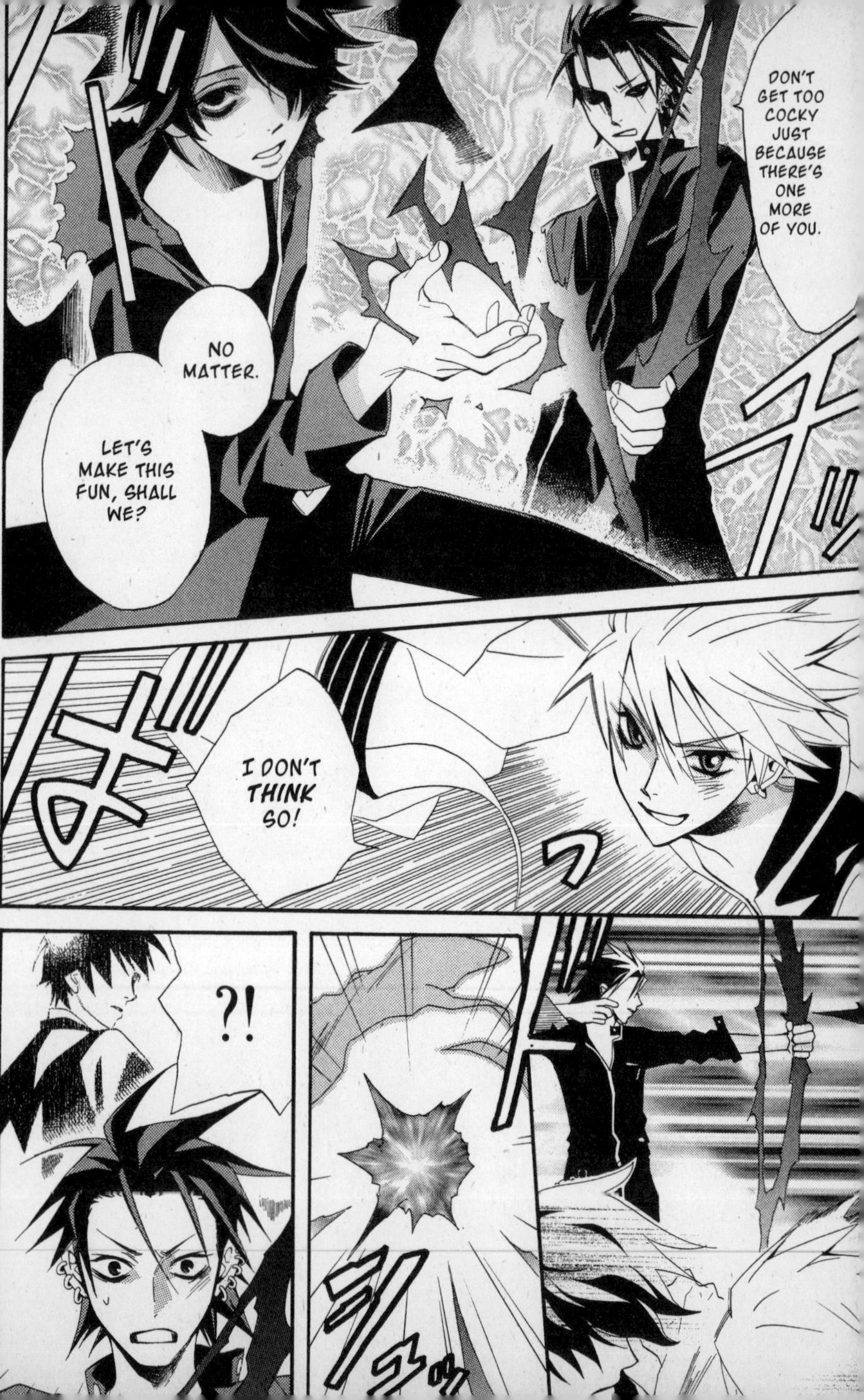
DON'T GET TOO COCKY JUST BECAUSE THERE'S ONE MORE OF YOU.
NO MATTER.
LET'S MAKE THIS FUN, SHALL WE?
I DON'T THINK SO!
?!

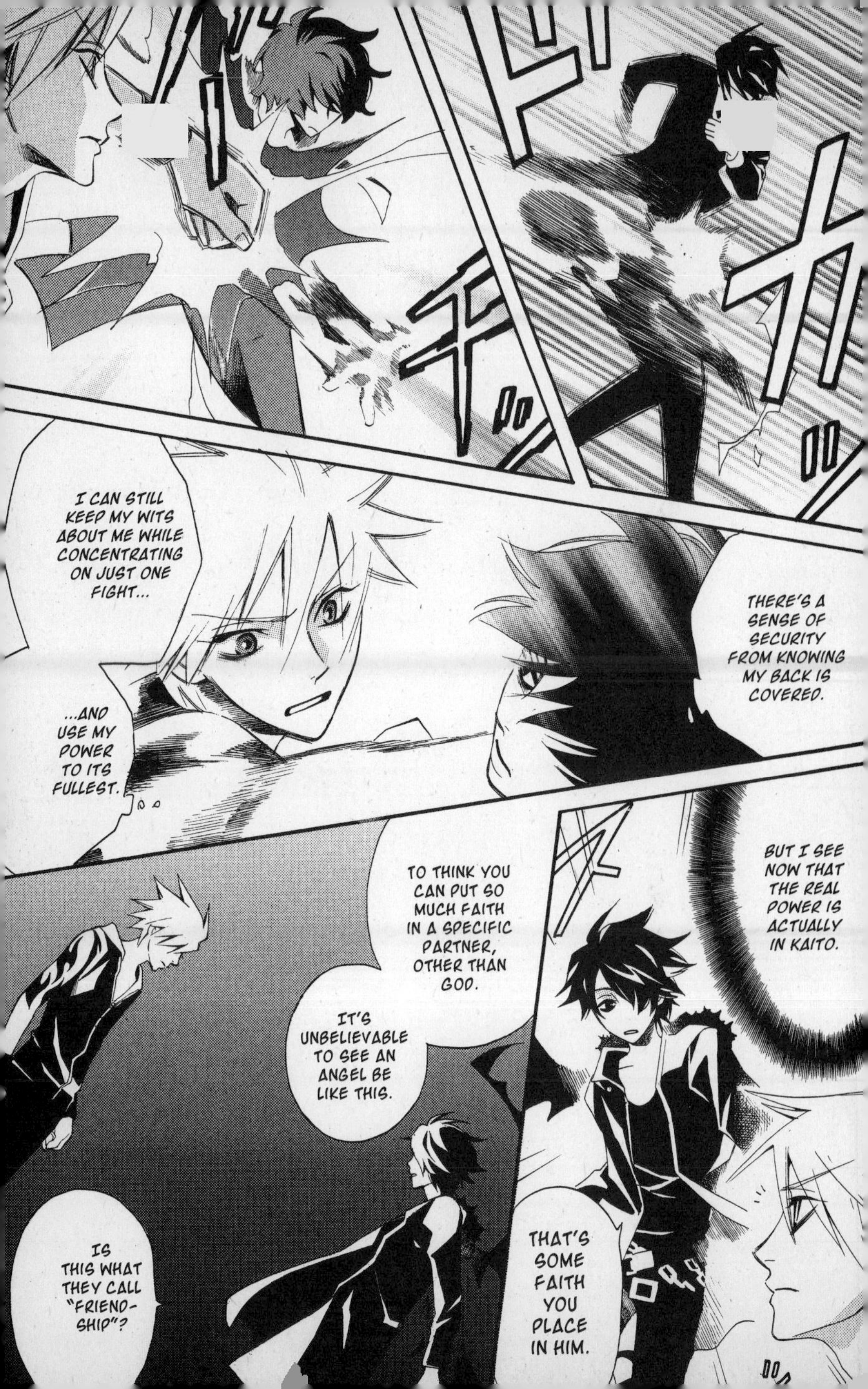
THERE'S A SENSE OF SECURITY FROM KNOWING MY BACK IS COVERED.
I CAN STILL KEEP MY WITS ABOUT ME WHILE CONCENTRATING ON JUST ONE FIGHT...
...AND USE MY POWER TO ITS FULLEST.
BUT I SEE NOW THAT THE REAL POWER IS ACTUALLY IN KAITO.
THAT'S SOME FAITH YOU PLACE IN HIM.
TO THINK YOU CAN PUT SO MUCH FAITH IN A SPECIFIC PARTNER, OTHER THAN GOD.
IT'S UNBELIEVABLE TO SEE AN ANGEL BE LIKE THIS.
IS THIS WHAT THEY CALL "FRIEND-SHIP"?

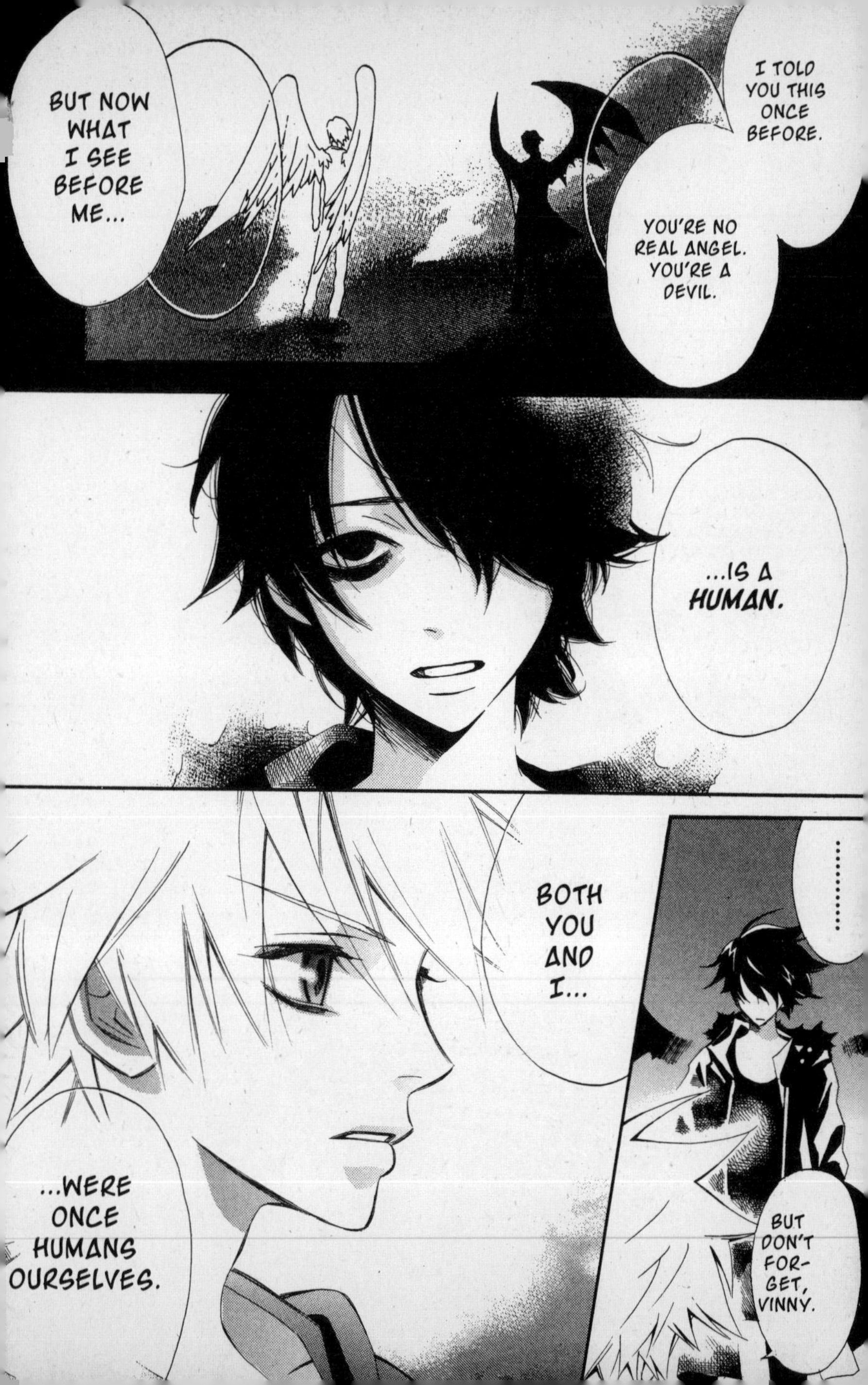
I TOLD YOU THIS ONCE BEFORE.
YOU'RE NO REAL ANGEL. YOU'RE A DEVIL.
BUT NOW WHAT I SEE BEFORE ME...
...IS A **HUMAN.**
....
BUT DON'T FOR-GET, VINNY.
BOTH YOU AND I...
...WERE ONCE HUMANS OURSELVES.

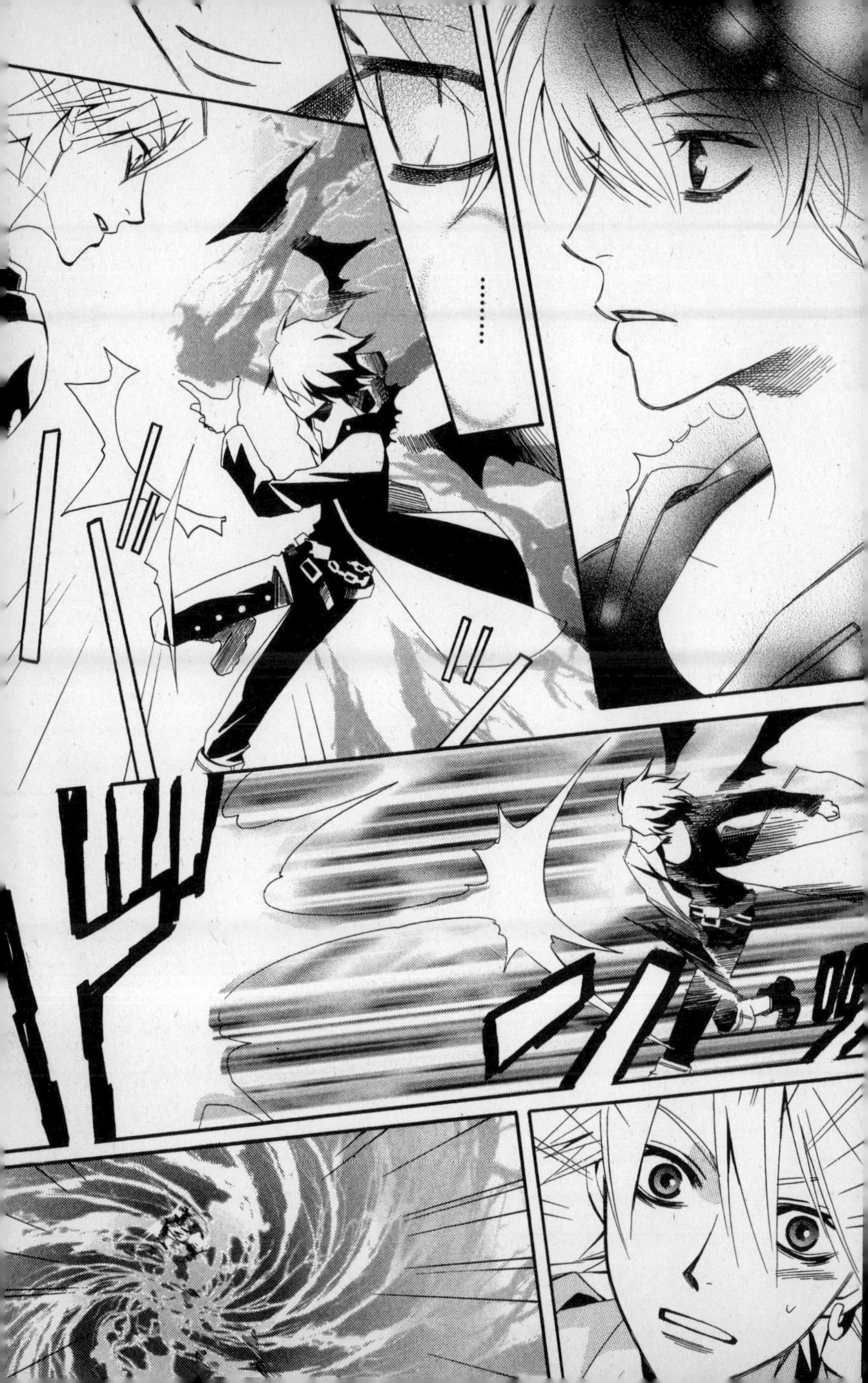
……

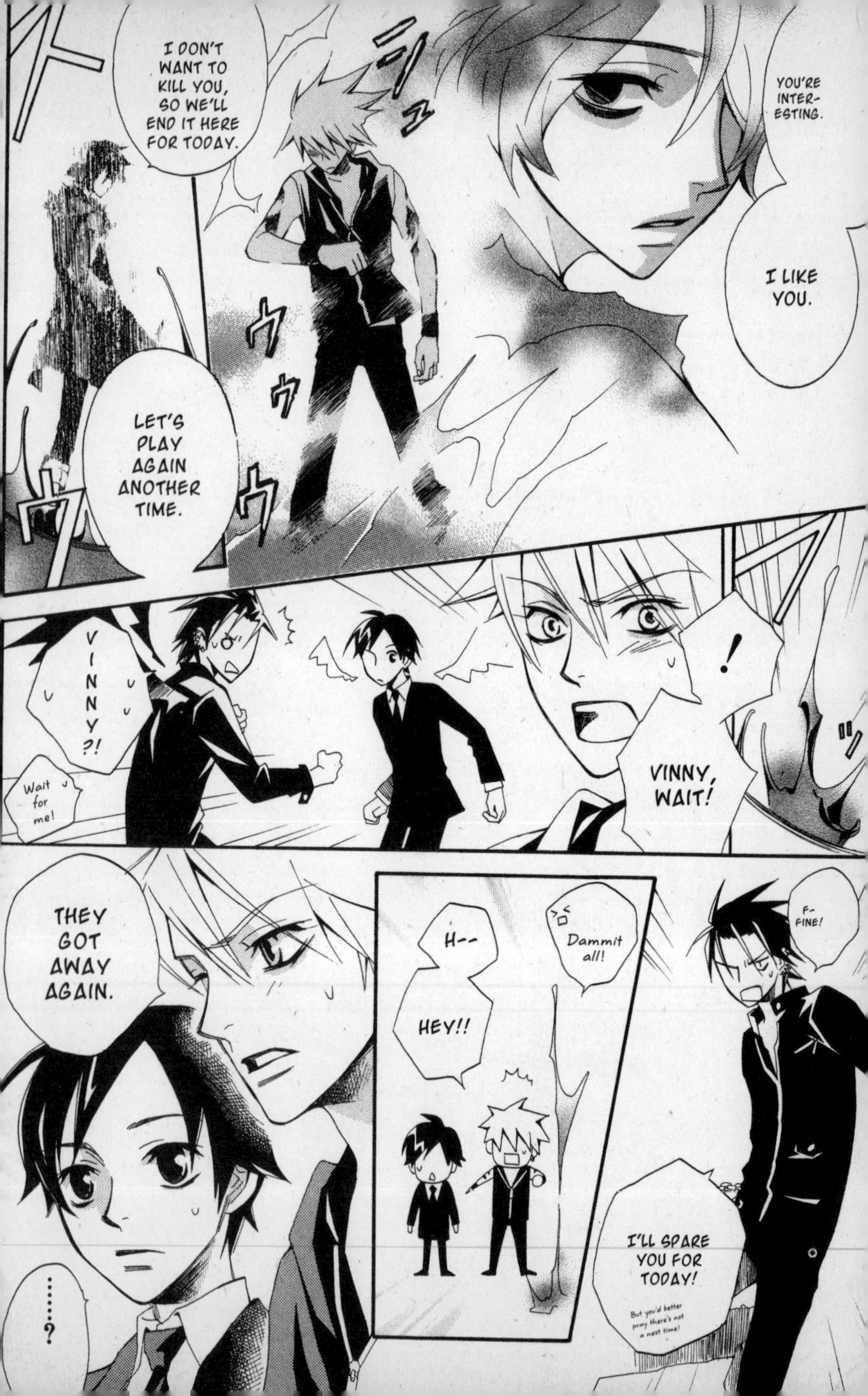
YOU'RE INTERESTING.
I LIKE YOU.
I DON'T WANT TO KILL YOU, SO WE'LL END IT HERE FOR TODAY.
LET'S PLAY AGAIN ANOTHER TIME.
!
VINNY, WAIT!
VINNY?!
Wait for me!
F-FINE!
I'LL SPARE YOU FOR TODAY!
But you'd better pray there's not a next time!
Dammit all!
H--
HEY!!
THEY GOT AWAY AGAIN.
......?

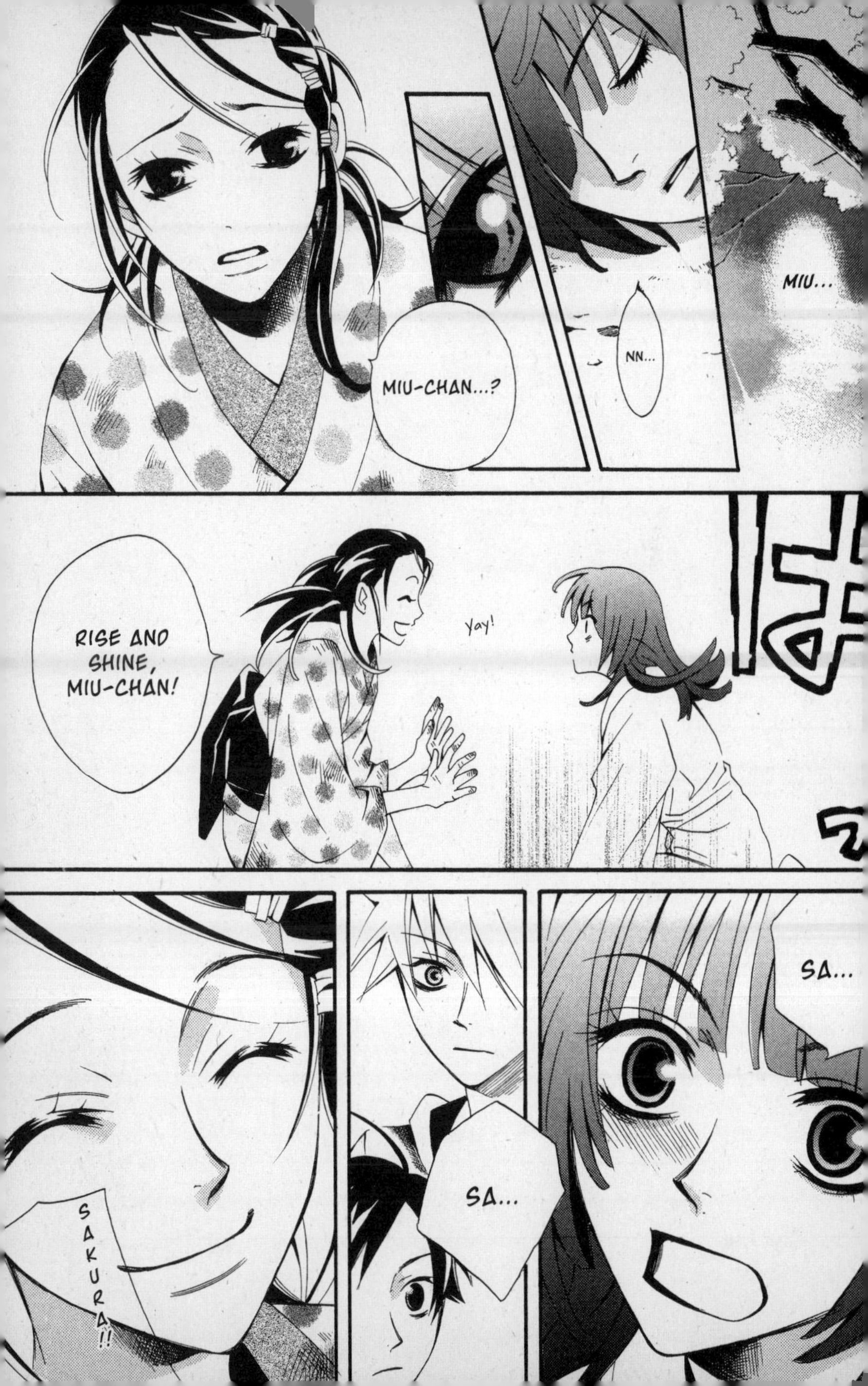
MIU...
NN...
MIU-CHAN...?
はっ
Yay!
RISE AND SHINE, MIU-CHAN!
SA...
SA...
SAKURA!!

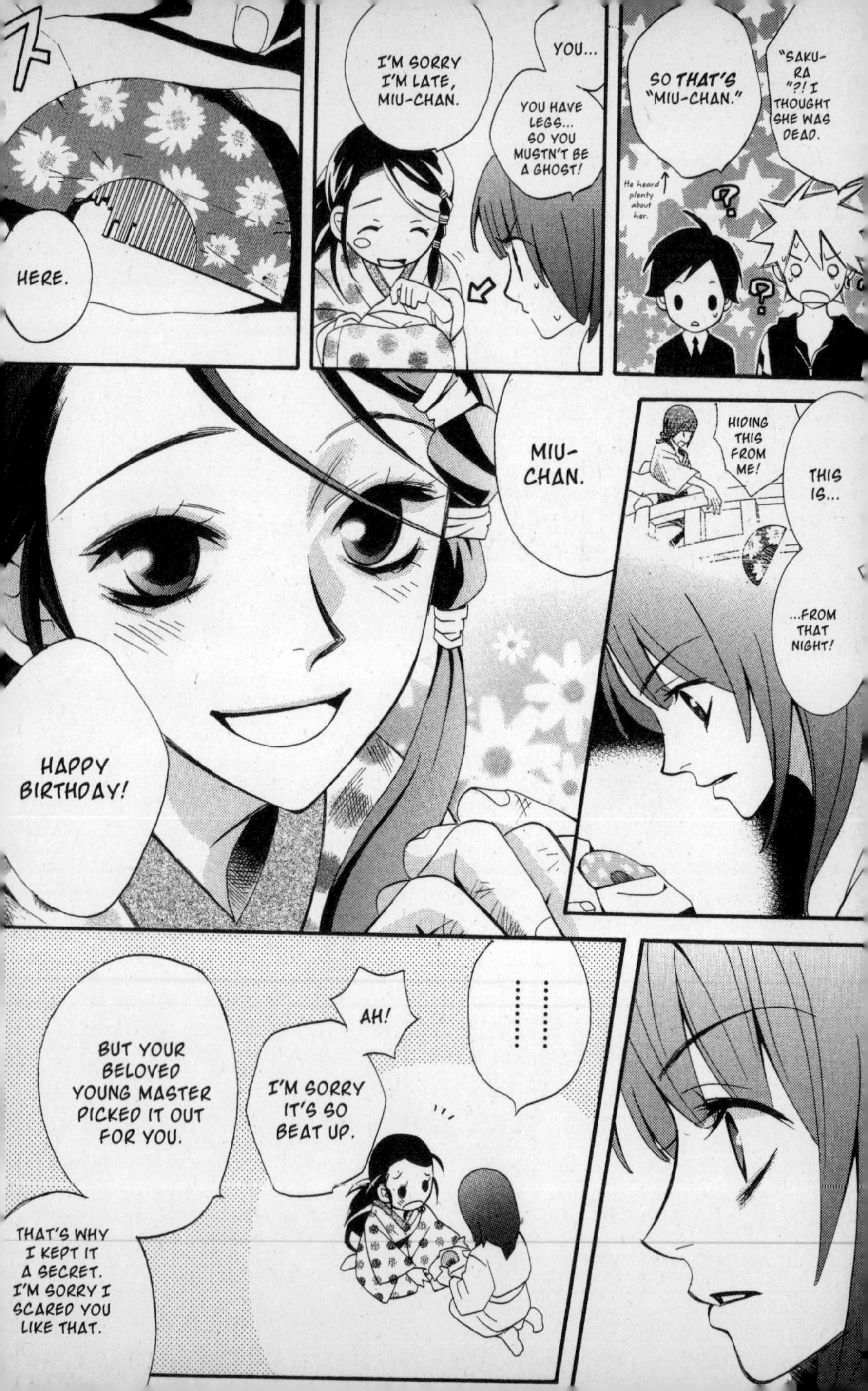

"SAKURA"?! I THOUGHT SHE WAS DEAD.
SO THAT'S "MIU-CHAN."
He heard plenty about her.
YOU...
YOU HAVE LEGS... SO YOU MUSTN'T BE A GHOST!
I'M SORRY I'M LATE, MIU-CHAN.
HERE.
THIS IS...
HIDING THIS FROM ME!
...FROM THAT NIGHT!
MIU-CHAN.
HAPPY BIRTHDAY!
......
AH!
I'M SORRY IT'S SO BEAT UP.
BUT YOUR BELOVED YOUNG MASTER PICKED IT OUT FOR YOU.
THAT'S WHY I KEPT IT A SECRET. I'M SORRY I SCARED YOU LIKE THAT.

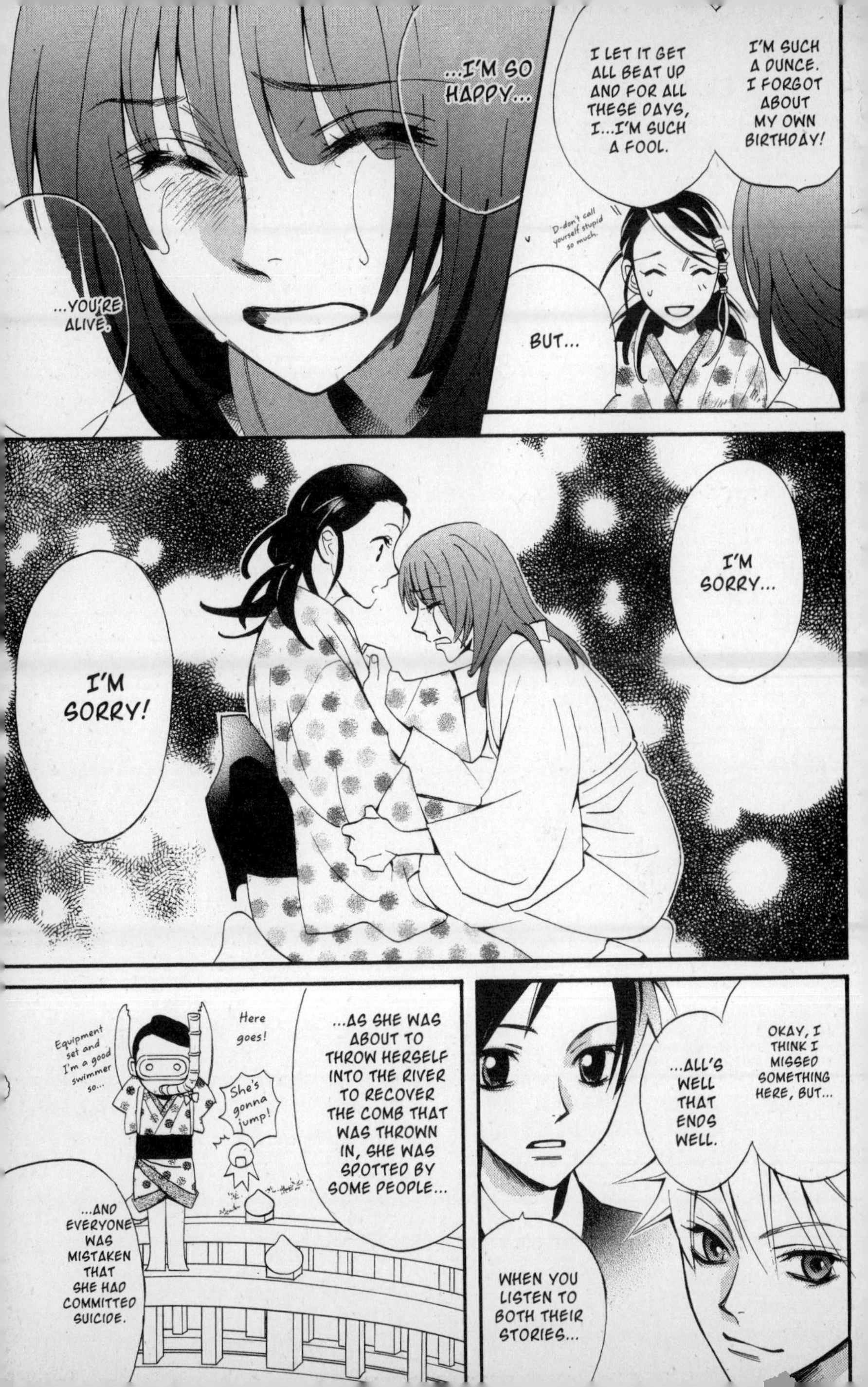
I'M SUCH A DUNCE. I FORGOT ABOUT MY OWN BIRTHDAY!
I LET IT GET ALL BEAT UP AND FOR ALL THESE DAYS, I...I'M SUCH A FOOL.
D-don't call yourself stupid so much.
BUT...
...I'M SO HAPPY...
...YOU'RE ALIVE.
I'M SORRY...
I'M SORRY!
OKAY, I THINK I MISSED SOMETHING HERE, BUT...
...ALL'S WELL THAT ENDS WELL.
WHEN YOU LISTEN TO BOTH THEIR STORIES...
...AS SHE WAS ABOUT TO THROW HERSELF INTO THE RIVER TO RECOVER THE COMB THAT WAS THROWN IN, SHE WAS SPOTTED BY SOME PEOPLE...
Here goes!
Equipment set and I'm a good swimmer so...
She's gonna jump!
...AND EVERYONE WAS MISTAKEN THAT SHE HAD COMMITTED SUICIDE.

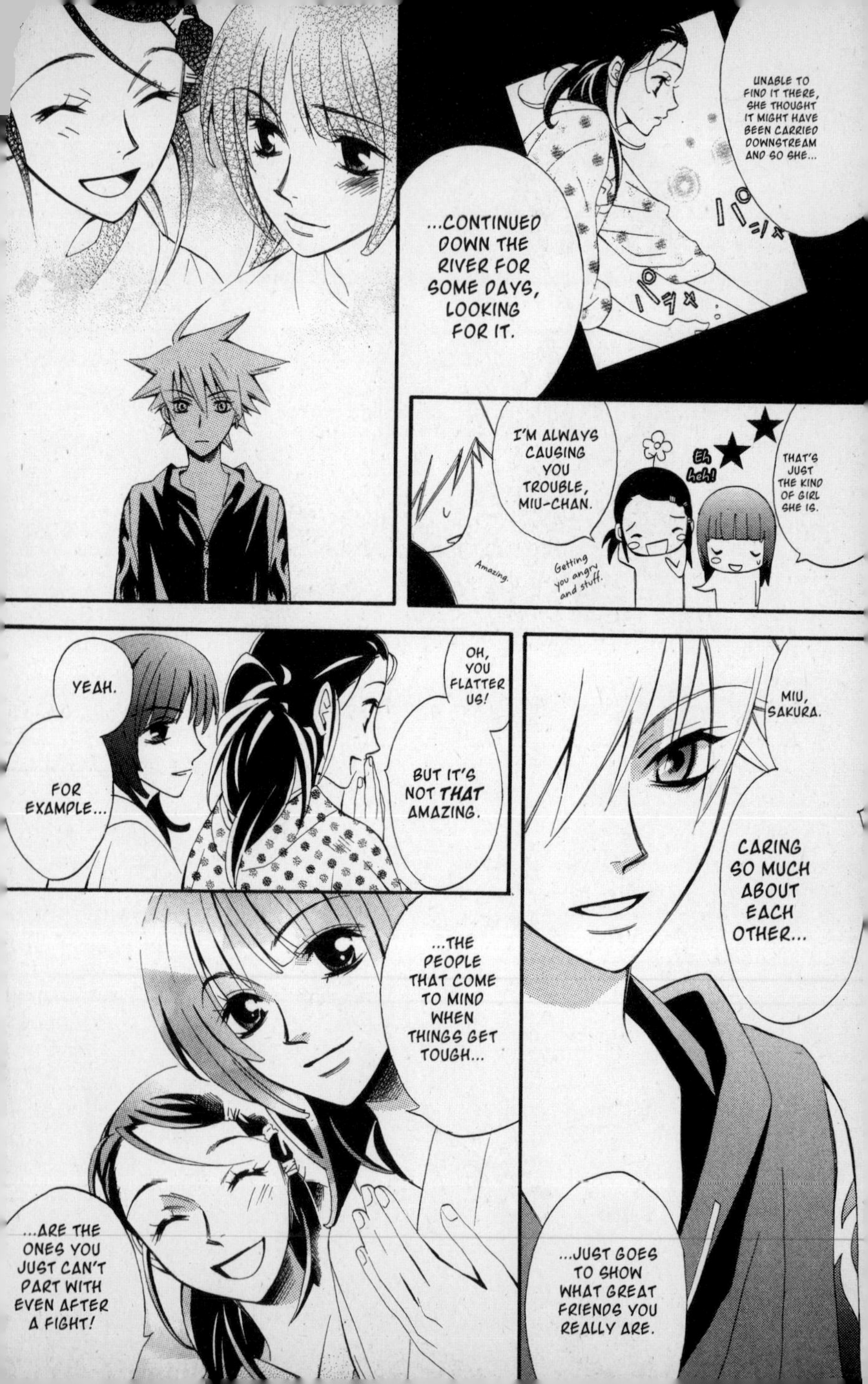

UNABLE TO FIND IT THERE, SHE THOUGHT IT MIGHT HAVE BEEN CARRIED DOWNSTREAM AND SO SHE...
...CONTINUED DOWN THE RIVER FOR SOME DAYS, LOOKING FOR IT.
THAT'S JUST THE KIND OF GIRL SHE IS.
Eh heh!
I'M ALWAYS CAUSING YOU TROUBLE, MIU-CHAN.
Getting you angry and stuff.
Amazing.
MIU, SAKURA.
CARING SO MUCH ABOUT EACH OTHER...
...JUST GOES TO SHOW WHAT GREAT FRIENDS YOU REALLY ARE.
OH, YOU FLATTER US!
BUT IT'S NOT *THAT* AMAZING.
YEAH.
FOR EXAMPLE...
...THE PEOPLE THAT COME TO MIND WHEN THINGS GET TOUGH...
...ARE THE ONES YOU JUST CAN'T PART WITH EVEN AFTER A FIGHT!

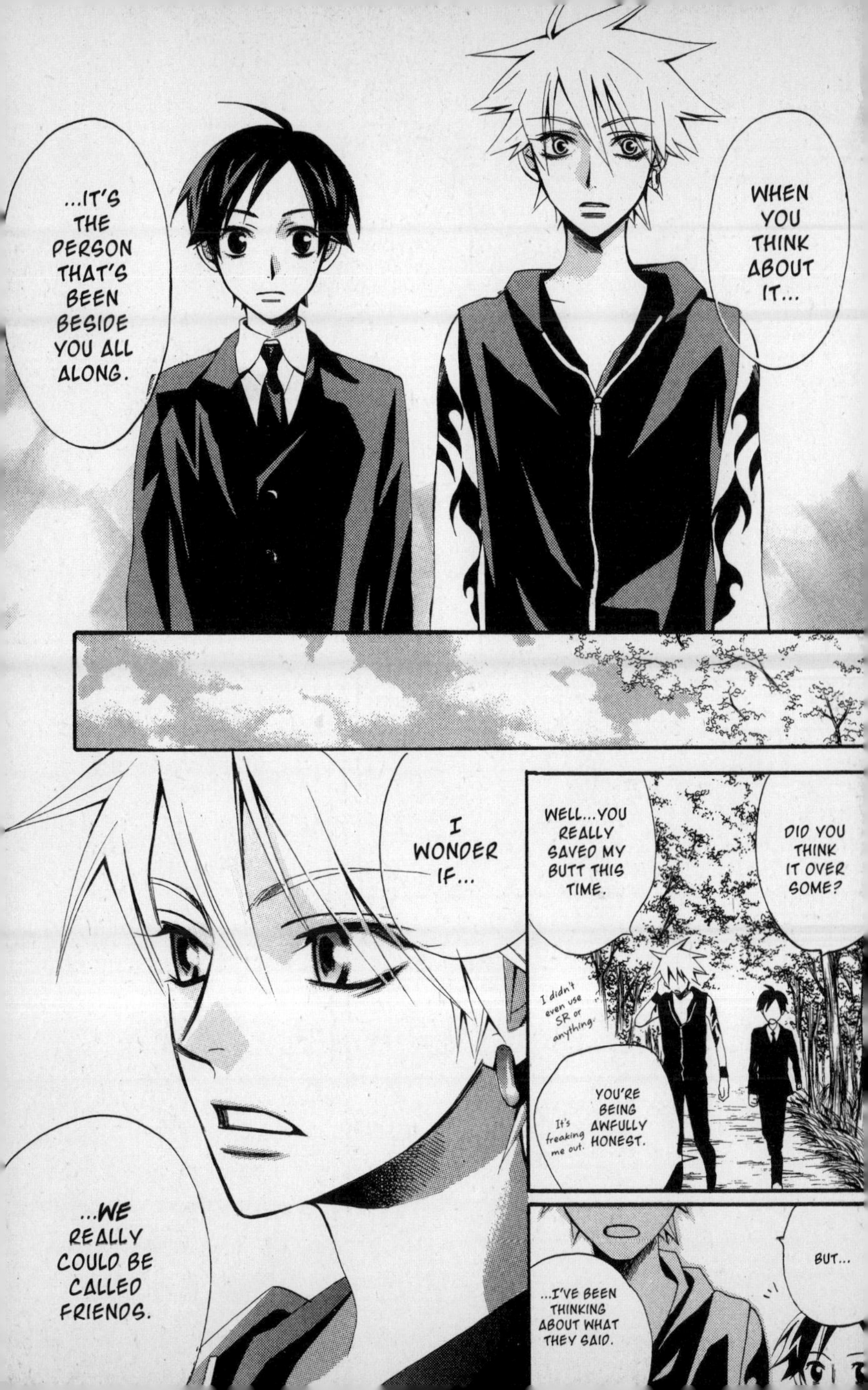
WHEN YOU THINK ABOUT IT...
...IT'S THE PERSON THAT'S BEEN BESIDE YOU ALL ALONG.
DID YOU THINK IT OVER SOME?
WELL...YOU REALLY SAVED MY BUTT THIS TIME.
I didn't even use SR or anything.
YOU'RE BEING AWFULLY HONEST.
It's freaking me out.
BUT...
...I'VE BEEN THINKING ABOUT WHAT THEY SAID.
I WONDER IF...
...WE REALLY COULD BE CALLED FRIENDS.

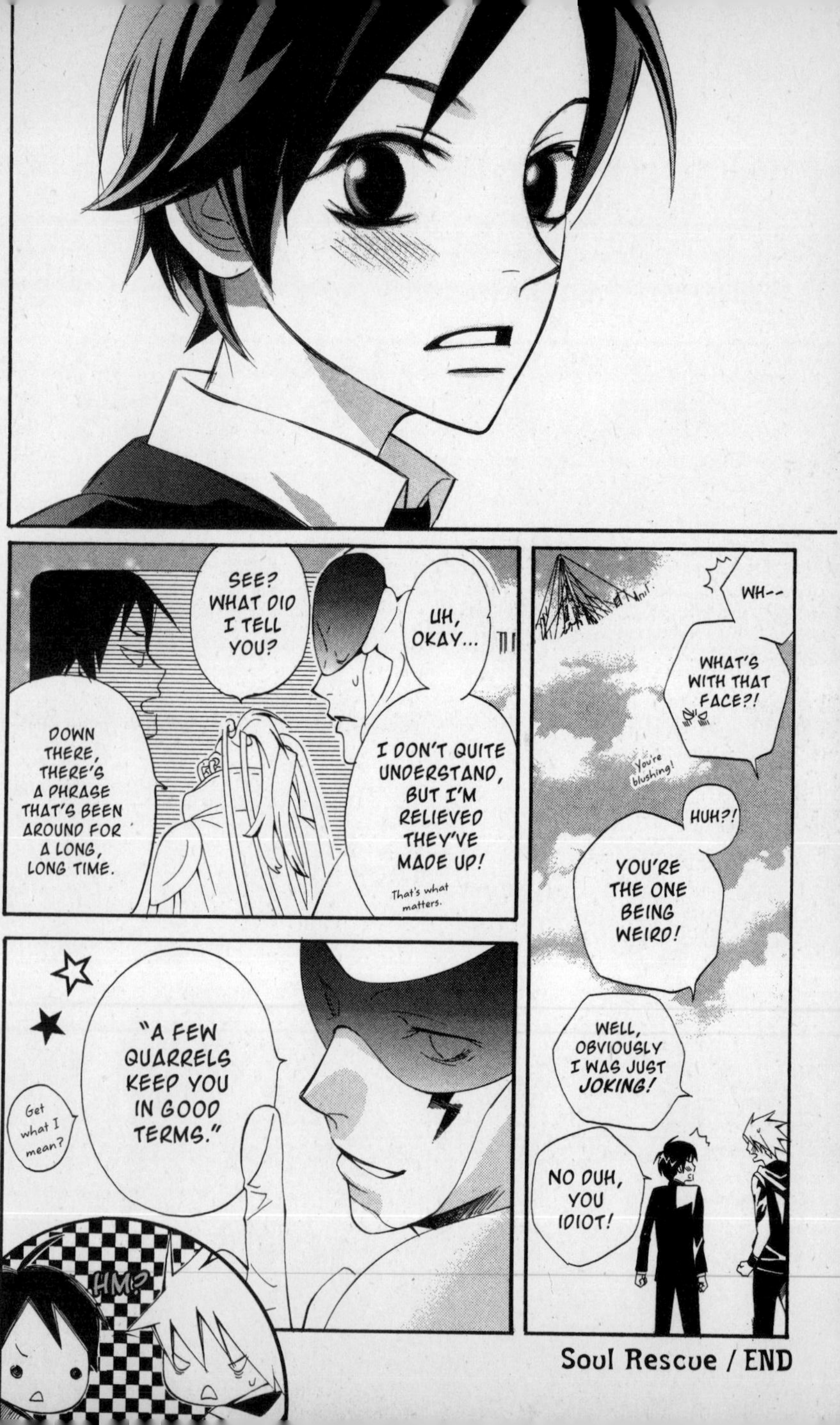
WH--
WHAT'S WITH THAT FACE?!
You're blushing!
HUH?!
YOU'RE THE ONE BEING WEIRD!
WELL, OBVIOUSLY I WAS JUST JOKING!
NO DUH, YOU IDIOT!
SEE? WHAT DID I TELL YOU?
UH, OKAY...
I DON'T QUITE UNDERSTAND, BUT I'M RELIEVED THEY'VE MADE UP!
That's what matters.
DOWN THERE, THERE'S A PHRASE THAT'S BEEN AROUND FOR A LONG, LONG TIME.
"A FEW QUARRELS KEEP YOU IN GOOD TERMS."
Get what I mean?
HM?

Soul Rescue / END

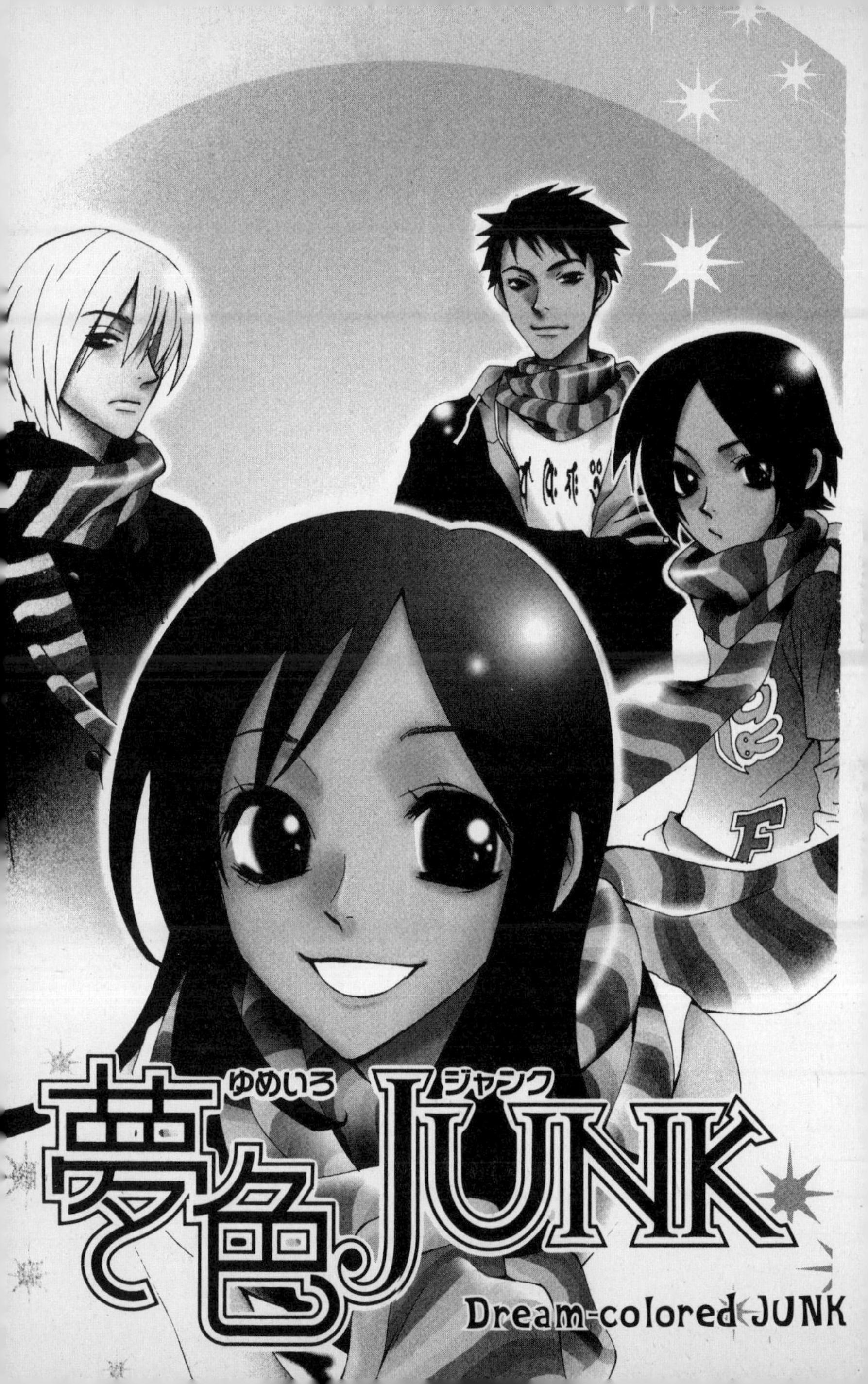
ゆめいろ
夢色
ジャンク
JUNK
Dream-colored JUNK

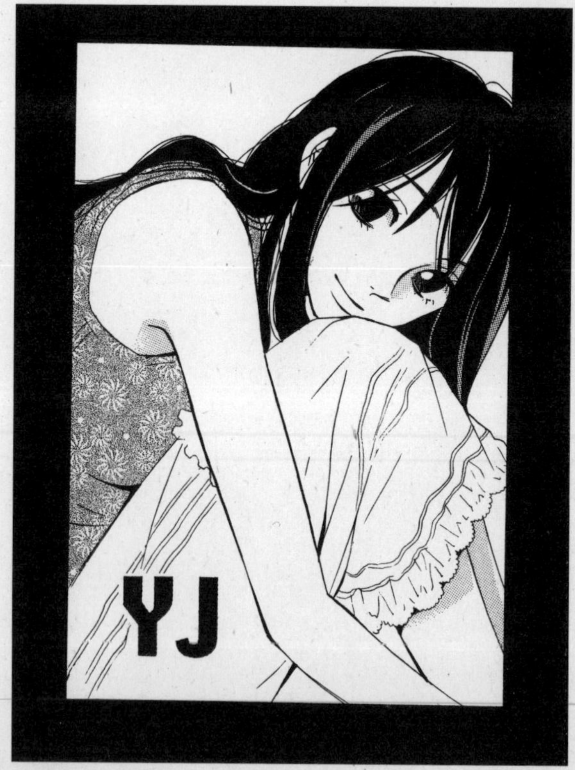
YJ

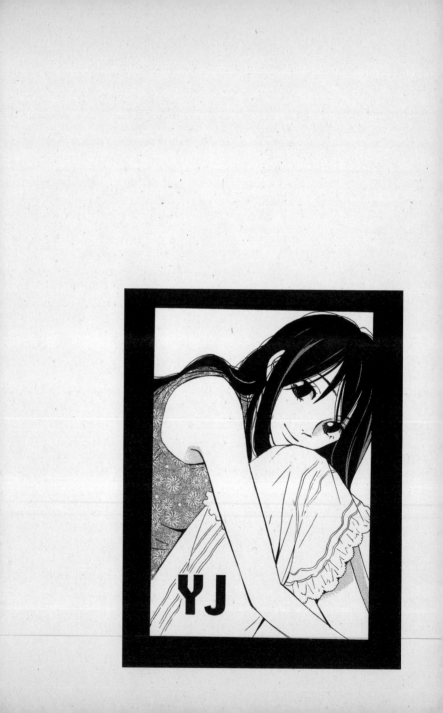

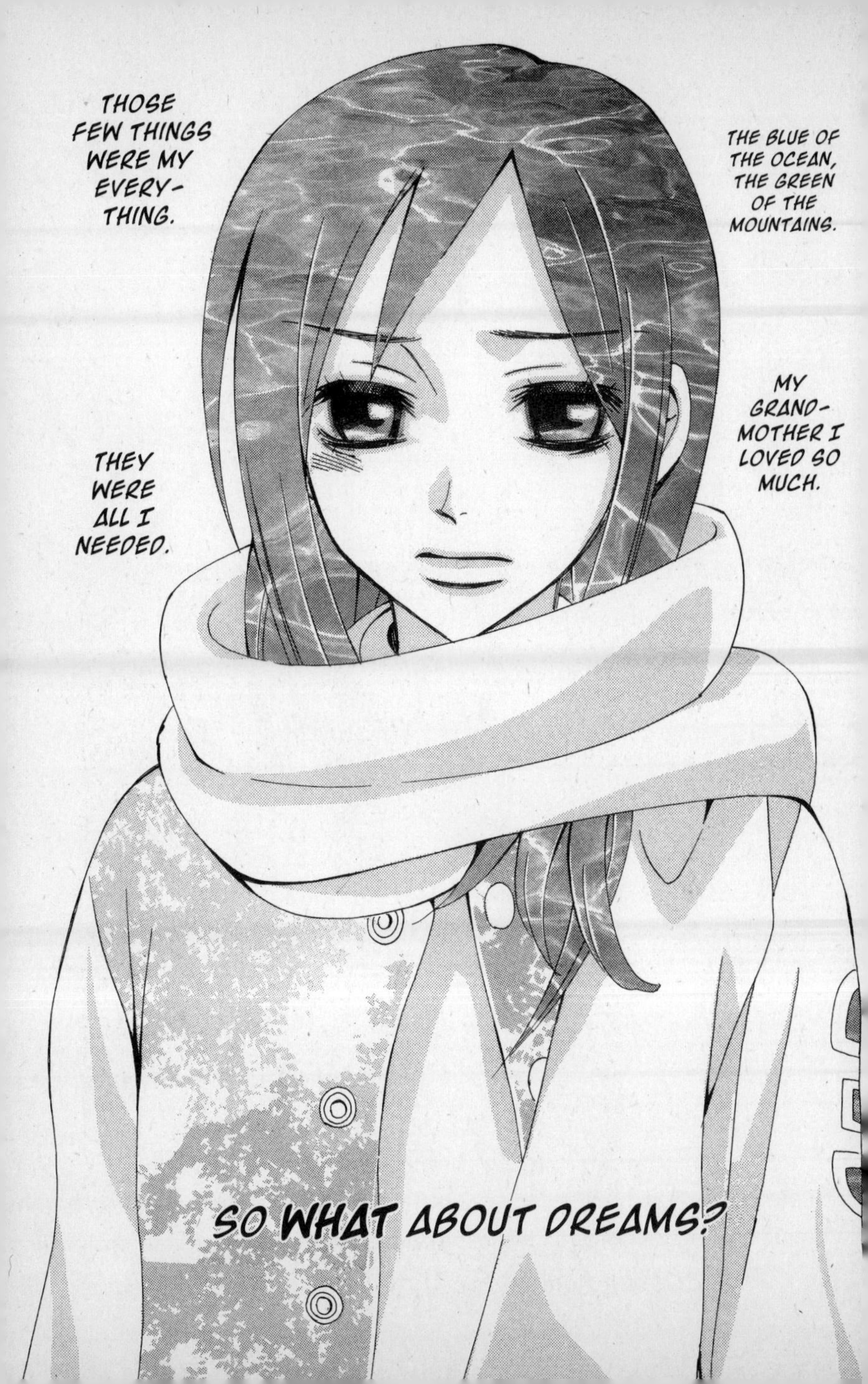
THE BLUE OF THE OCEAN, THE GREEN OF THE MOUNTAINS.
THOSE FEW THINGS WERE MY EVERYTHING.
MY GRANDMOTHER I LOVED SO MUCH.
THEY WERE ALL I NEEDED.
SO WHAT ABOUT DREAMS?

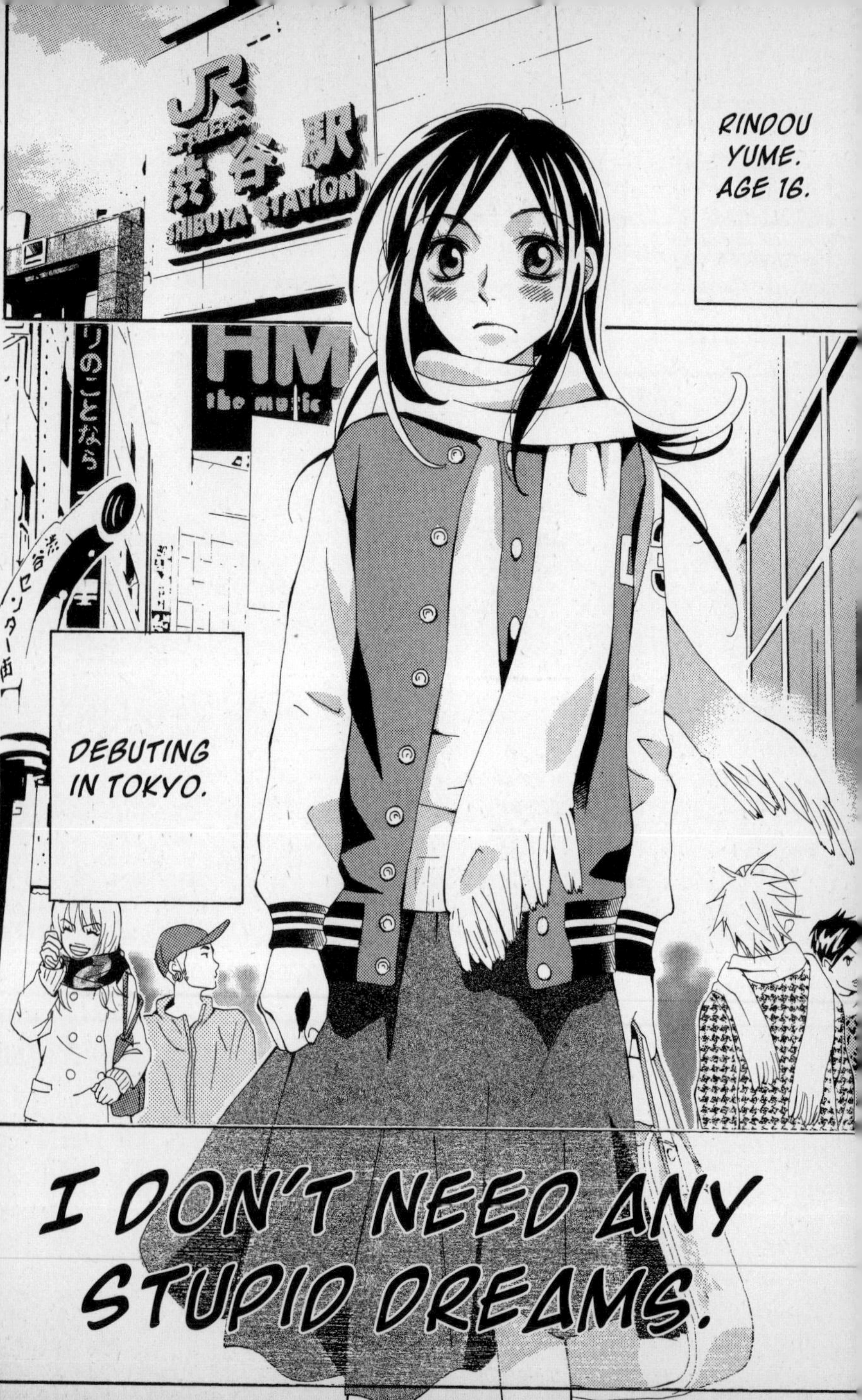
渋谷駅
SHIBUYA STATION
RINDOU YUME. AGE 16.
DEBUTING IN TOKYO.
I DON'T NEED ANY STUPID DREAMS.

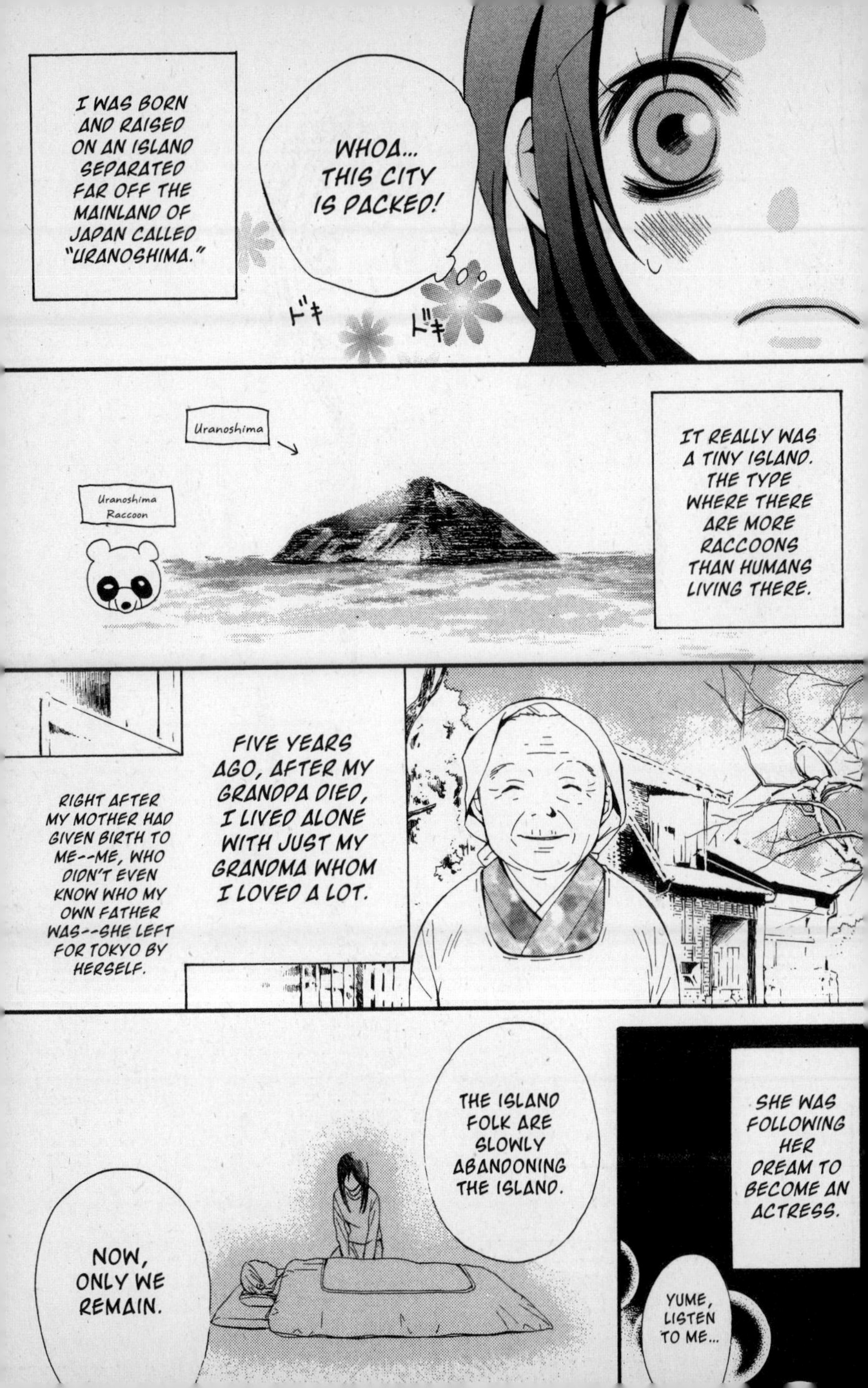
WHOA... THIS CITY IS PACKED!
I WAS BORN AND RAISED ON AN ISLAND SEPARATED FAR OFF THE MAINLAND OF JAPAN CALLED "URANOSHIMA."
ドキ
ドキ
IT REALLY WAS A TINY ISLAND. THE TYPE WHERE THERE ARE MORE RACCOONS THAN HUMANS LIVING THERE.
Uranoshima
Uranoshima Raccoon
FIVE YEARS AGO, AFTER MY GRANDPA DIED, I LIVED ALONE WITH JUST MY GRANDMA WHOM I LOVED A LOT.
RIGHT AFTER MY MOTHER HAD GIVEN BIRTH TO ME--ME, WHO DIDN'T EVEN KNOW WHO MY OWN FATHER WAS--SHE LEFT FOR TOKYO BY HERSELF.
SHE WAS FOLLOWING HER DREAM TO BECOME AN ACTRESS.
YUME, LISTEN TO ME...
THE ISLAND FOLK ARE SLOWLY ABANDONING THE ISLAND.
NOW, ONLY WE REMAIN.

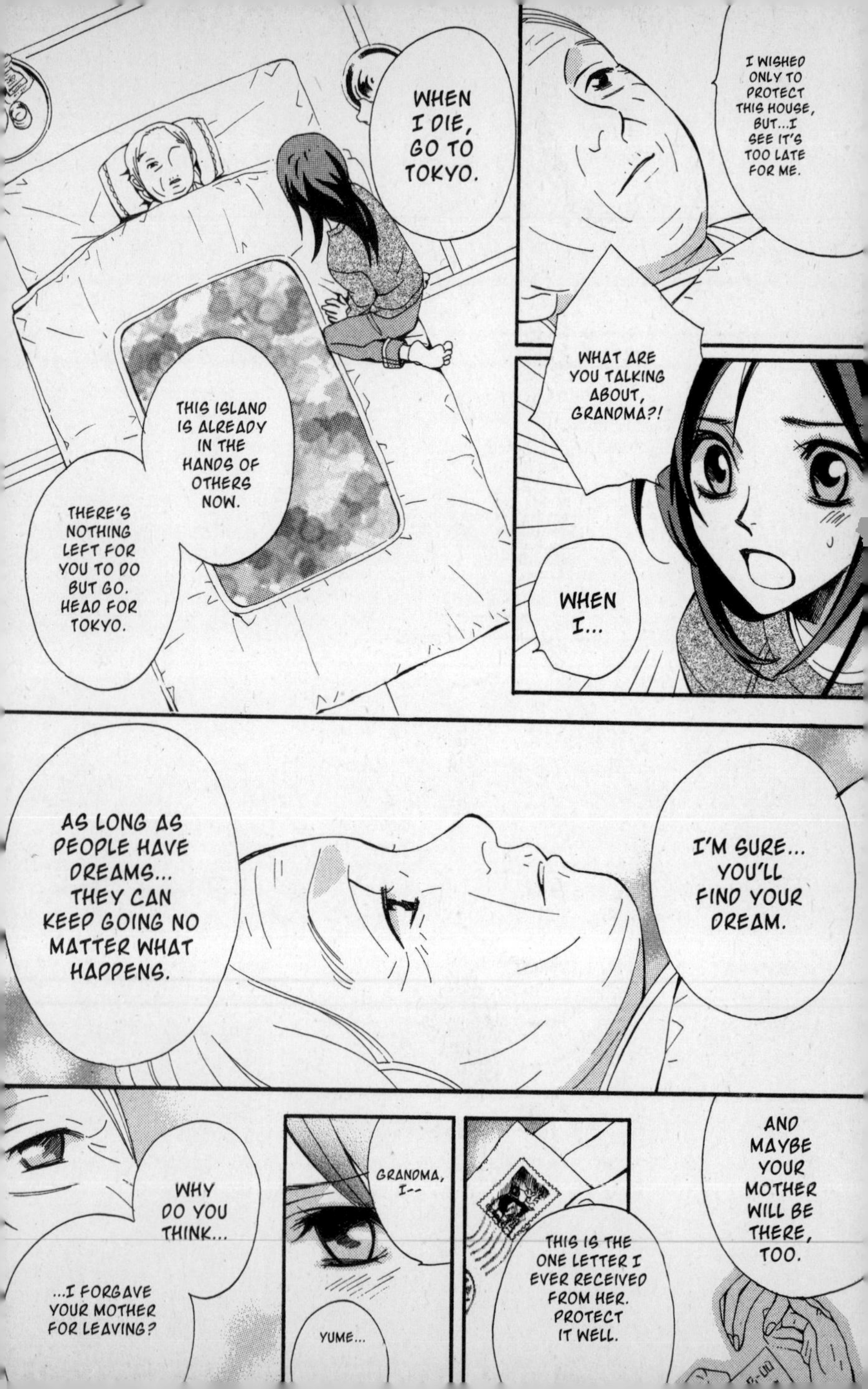
I WISHED ONLY TO PROTECT THIS HOUSE, BUT...I SEE IT'S TOO LATE FOR ME.
WHAT ARE YOU TALKING ABOUT, GRANDMA?!
WHEN I...
WHEN I DIE, GO TO TOKYO.
THIS ISLAND IS ALREADY IN THE HANDS OF OTHERS NOW.
THERE'S NOTHING LEFT FOR YOU TO DO BUT GO. HEAD FOR TOKYO.
I'M SURE... YOU'LL FIND YOUR DREAM.
AS LONG AS PEOPLE HAVE DREAMS... THEY CAN KEEP GOING NO MATTER WHAT HAPPENS.
AND MAYBE YOUR MOTHER WILL BE THERE, TOO.
THIS IS THE ONE LETTER I EVER RECEIVED FROM HER. PROTECT IT WELL.
GRANDMA, I--
YUME...
WHY DO YOU THINK...
...I FORGAVE YOUR MOTHER FOR LEAVING?

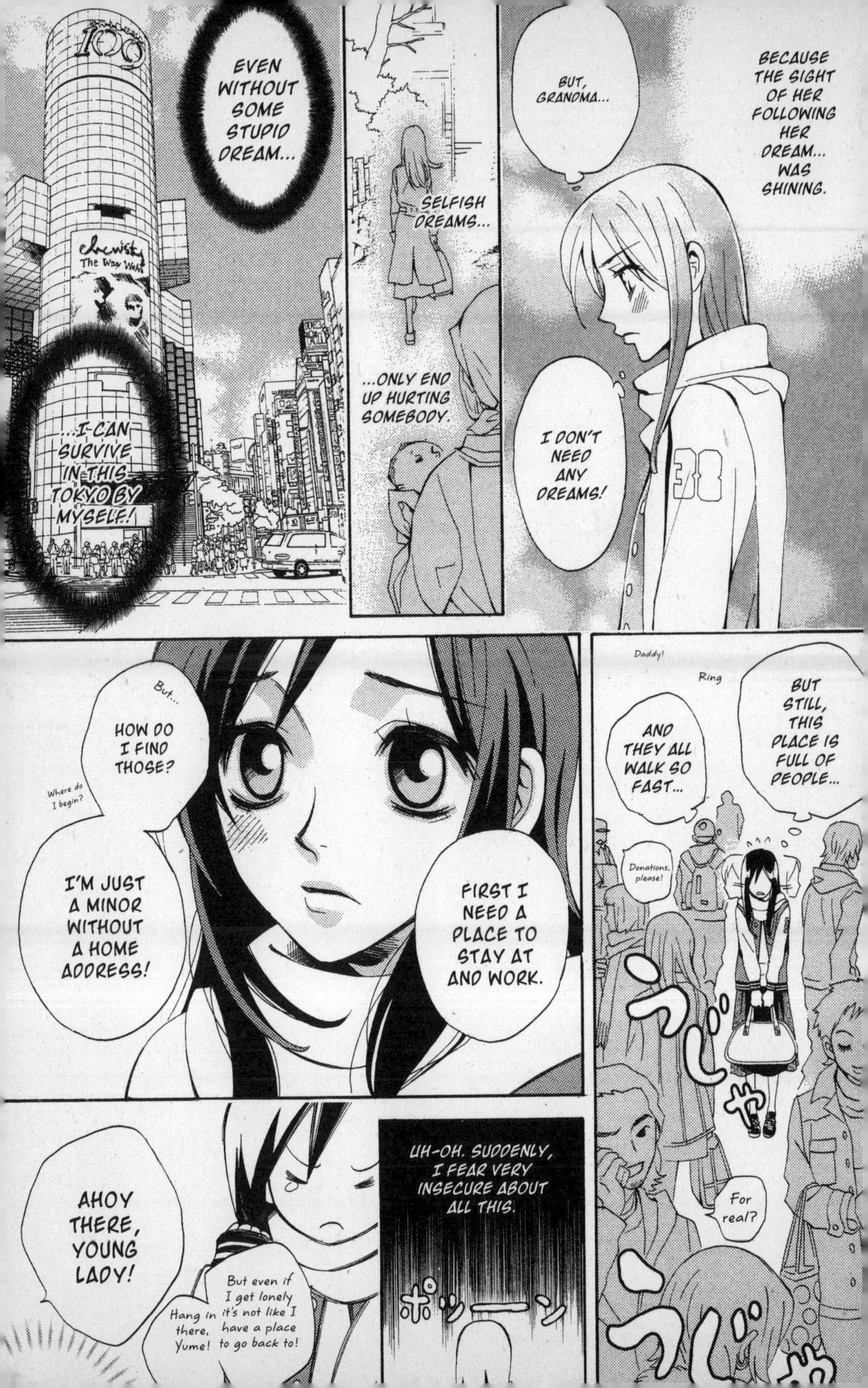
BECAUSE THE SIGHT OF HER FOLLOWING HER DREAM... WAS SHINING.
BUT, GRANDMA...
I DON'T NEED ANY DREAMS!
SELFISH DREAMS...
...ONLY END UP HURTING SOMEBODY.
EVEN WITHOUT SOME STUPID DREAM...
...I CAN SURVIVE IN THIS TOKYO BY MYSELF!
Daddy!
Ring
BUT STILL, THIS PLACE IS FULL OF PEOPLE...
AND THEY ALL WALK SO FAST...
Donations, please!
For real?
But...
HOW DO I FIND THOSE?
Where do I begin?
FIRST I NEED A PLACE TO STAY AT AND WORK.
I'M JUST A MINOR WITHOUT A HOME ADDRESS!
UH-OH. SUDDENLY, I FEAR VERY INSECURE ABOUT ALL THIS.
AHOY THERE, YOUNG LADY!
But even if I get lonely it's not like I have a place to go back to!
Hang in there, Yume!

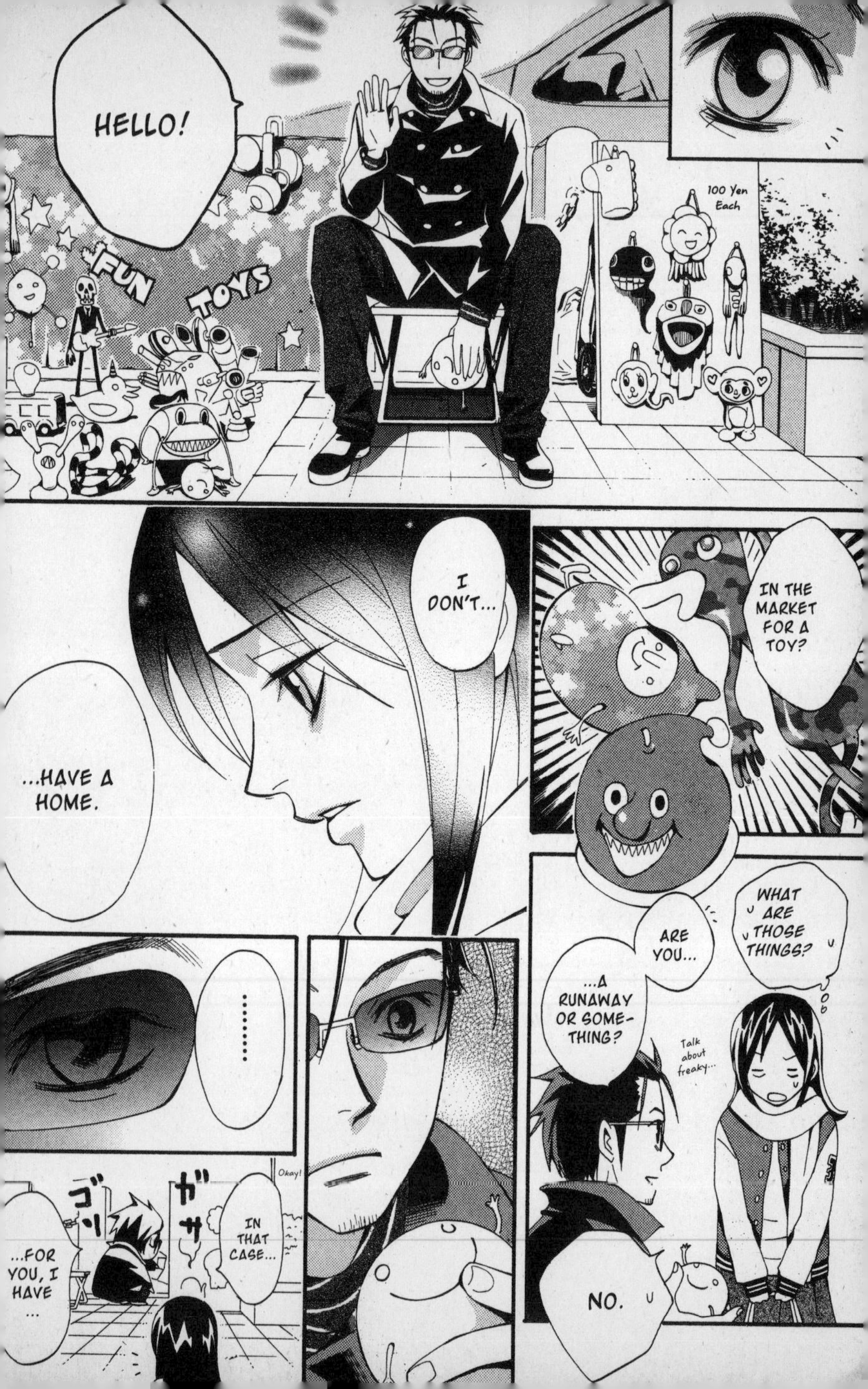
HELLO!
100 Yen Each
FUN TOYS
IN THE MARKET FOR A TOY?
I DON'T...
...HAVE A HOME.
WHAT ARE THOSE THINGS?
ARE YOU...
...A RUNAWAY OR SOME-THING?
Talk about freaky...
NO.
......
Okay!
IN THAT CASE...
ガサ
ゴソ
...FOR YOU, I HAVE ...

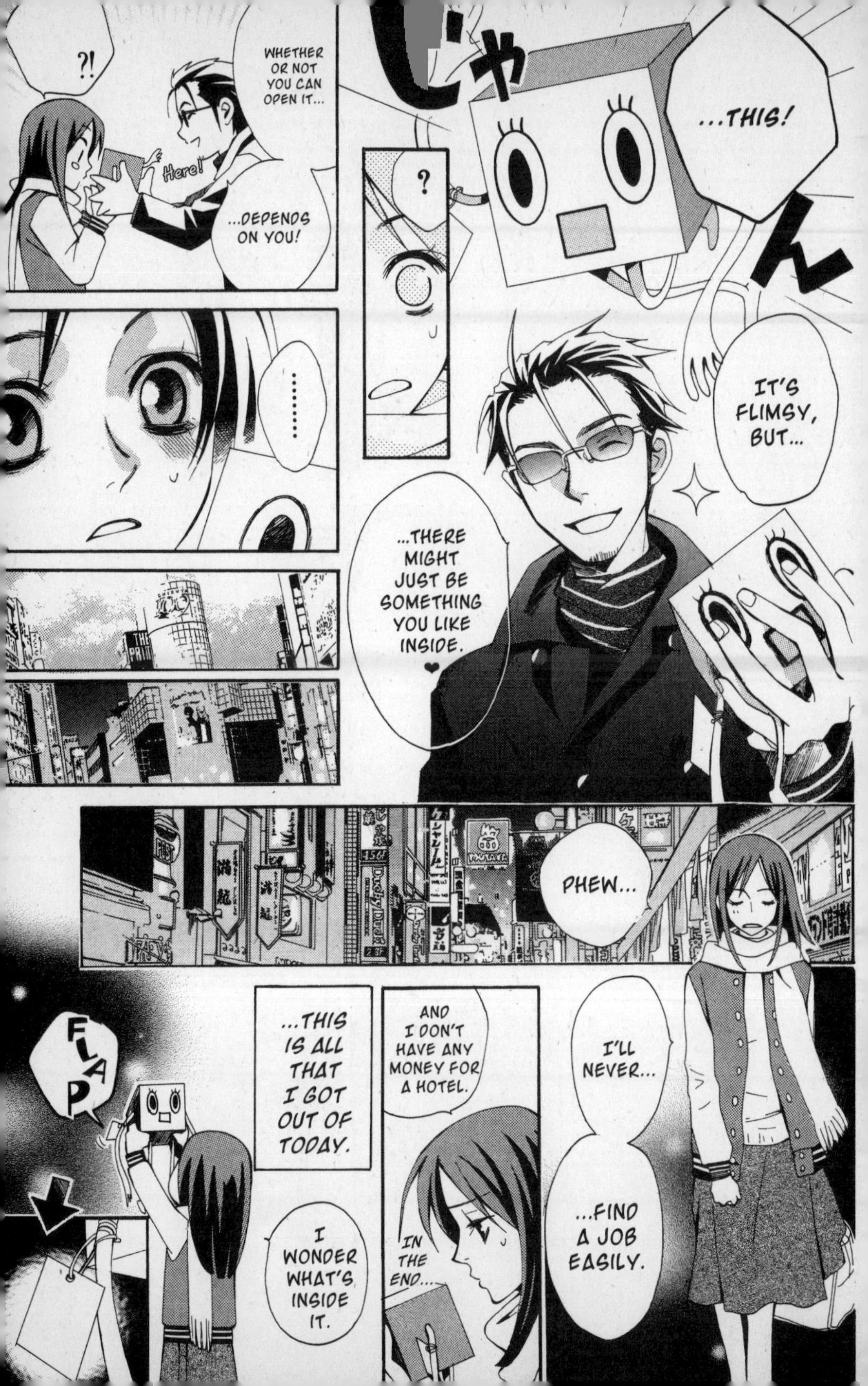

じゃん
...THIS!
?
WHETHER OR NOT YOU CAN OPEN IT...
...DEPENDS ON YOU!
Here!
?!
IT'S FLIMSY, BUT...
...THERE MIGHT JUST BE SOMETHING YOU LIKE INSIDE.
......
PHEW...
I'LL NEVER...
...FIND A JOB EASILY.
AND I DON'T HAVE ANY MONEY FOR A HOTEL.
IN THE END...
...THIS IS ALL THAT I GOT OUT OF TODAY.
FLAP
I WONDER WHAT'S INSIDE IT.

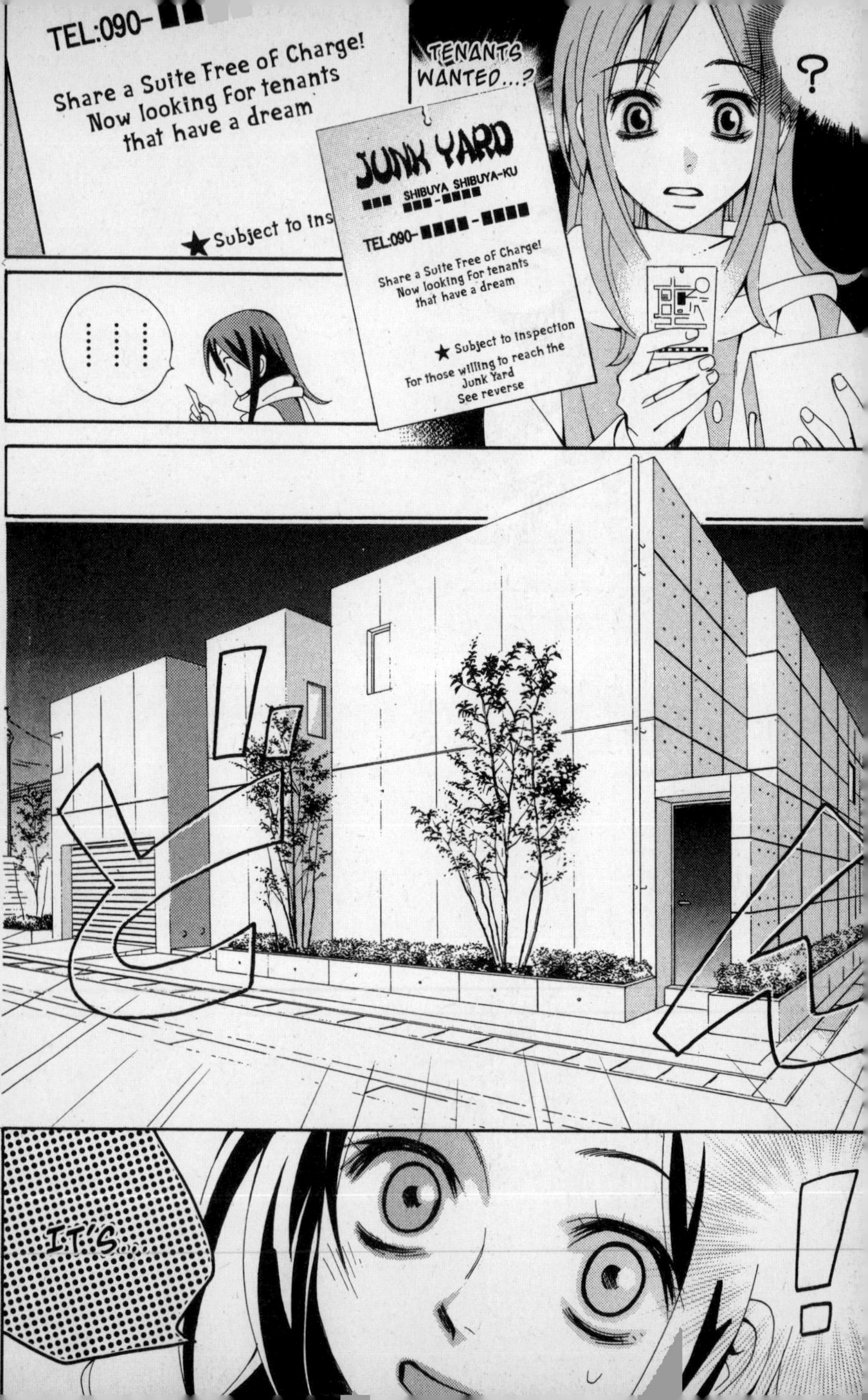
TENANTS WANTED...?
?
JUNK YARD
[redacted] SHIBUYA SHIBUYA-KU [redacted]
TEL:090-[redacted]
Share a Suite Free of Charge! Now looking for tenants that have a dream
★ Subject to inspection
For those willing to reach the Junk Yard See reverse
TEL:090-[redacted]
Share a Suite Free of Charge! Now looking for tenants that have a dream
★ Subject to ins
......
IT'S...
!

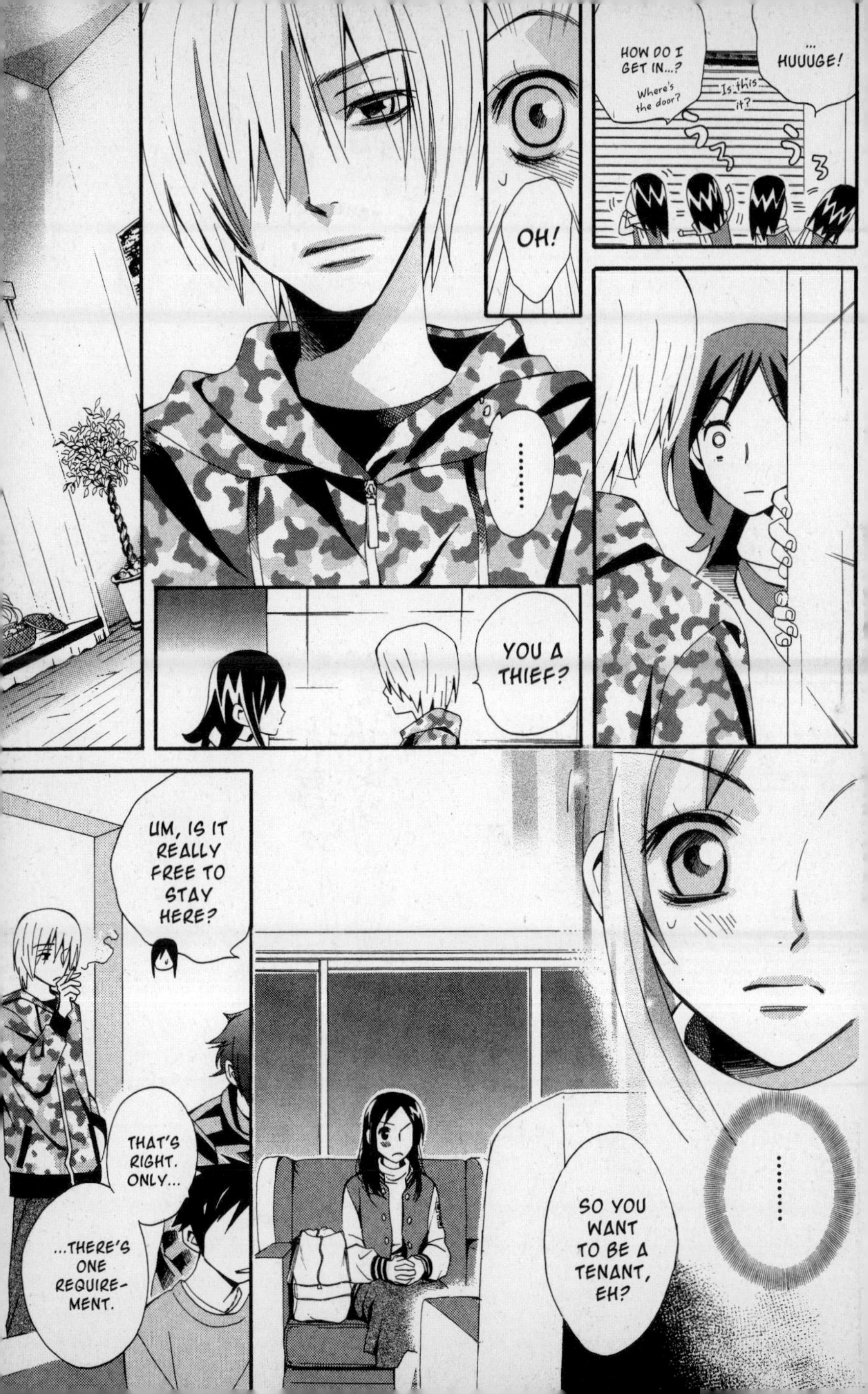
... HUUUGE!
HOW DO I GET IN...?
Where's the door?
Is this it?
OH!
......
YOU A THIEF?
......
SO YOU WANT TO BE A TENANT, EH?
UM, IS IT REALLY FREE TO STAY HERE?
THAT'S RIGHT. ONLY...
...THERE'S ONE REQUIREMENT.

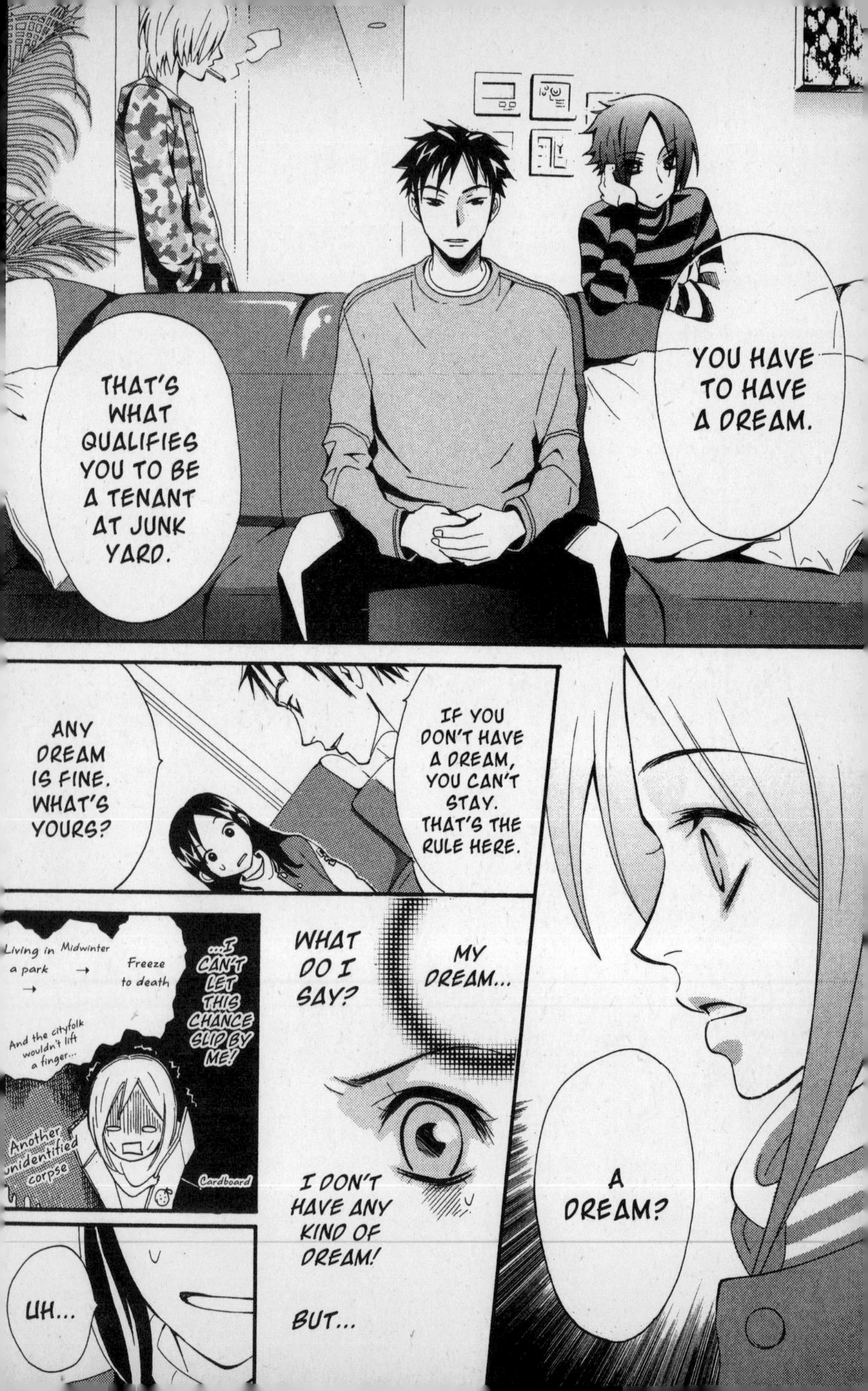
YOU HAVE TO HAVE A DREAM.
THAT'S WHAT QUALIFIES YOU TO BE A TENANT AT JUNK YARD.
A DREAM?
IF YOU DON'T HAVE A DREAM, YOU CAN'T STAY. THAT'S THE RULE HERE.
ANY DREAM IS FINE. WHAT'S YOURS?
MY DREAM...
WHAT DO I SAY?
I DON'T HAVE ANY KIND OF DREAM!
BUT...
...I CAN'T LET THIS CHANCE SLIP BY ME!
Living in a park → Midwinter → Freeze to death
And the cityfolk wouldn't lift a finger...
Another unidentified corpse
Cardboard
UH...

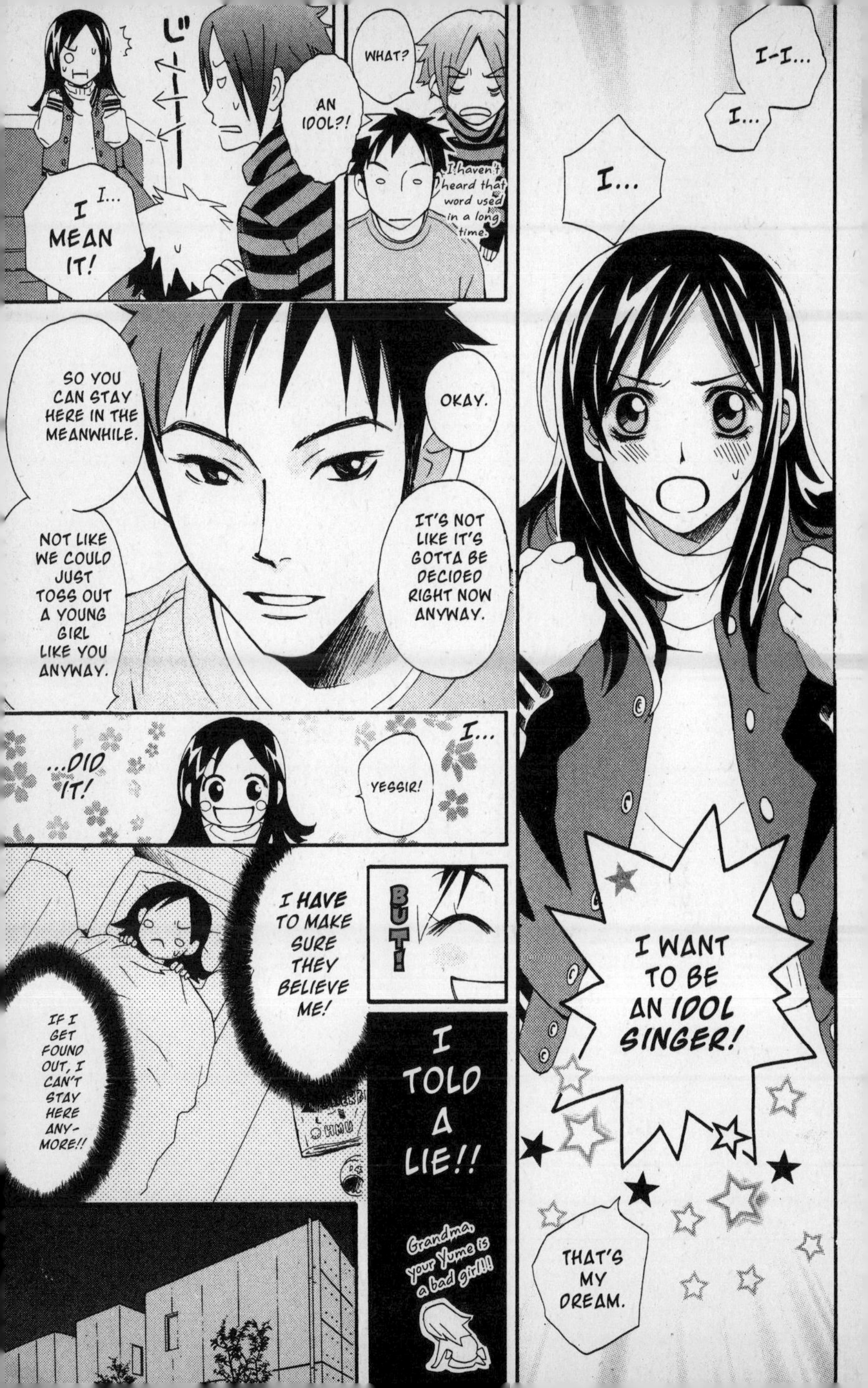
I-I...
I...
I...
I WANT TO BE AN IDOL SINGER!
THAT'S MY DREAM.
WHAT?
AN IDOL?!
I haven't heard that word used in a long time.
ジーー
I... I MEAN IT!
OKAY.
IT'S NOT LIKE IT'S GOTTA BE DECIDED RIGHT NOW ANYWAY.
SO YOU CAN STAY HERE IN THE MEANWHILE.
NOT LIKE WE COULD JUST TOSS OUT A YOUNG GIRL LIKE YOU ANYWAY.
I...
YESSIR!
...DID IT!
BUT!
I TOLD A LIE!!
Grandma, your Yume is a bad girl!!
I HAVE TO MAKE SURE THEY BELIEVE ME!
IF I GET FOUND OUT, I CAN'T STAY HERE ANYMORE!!

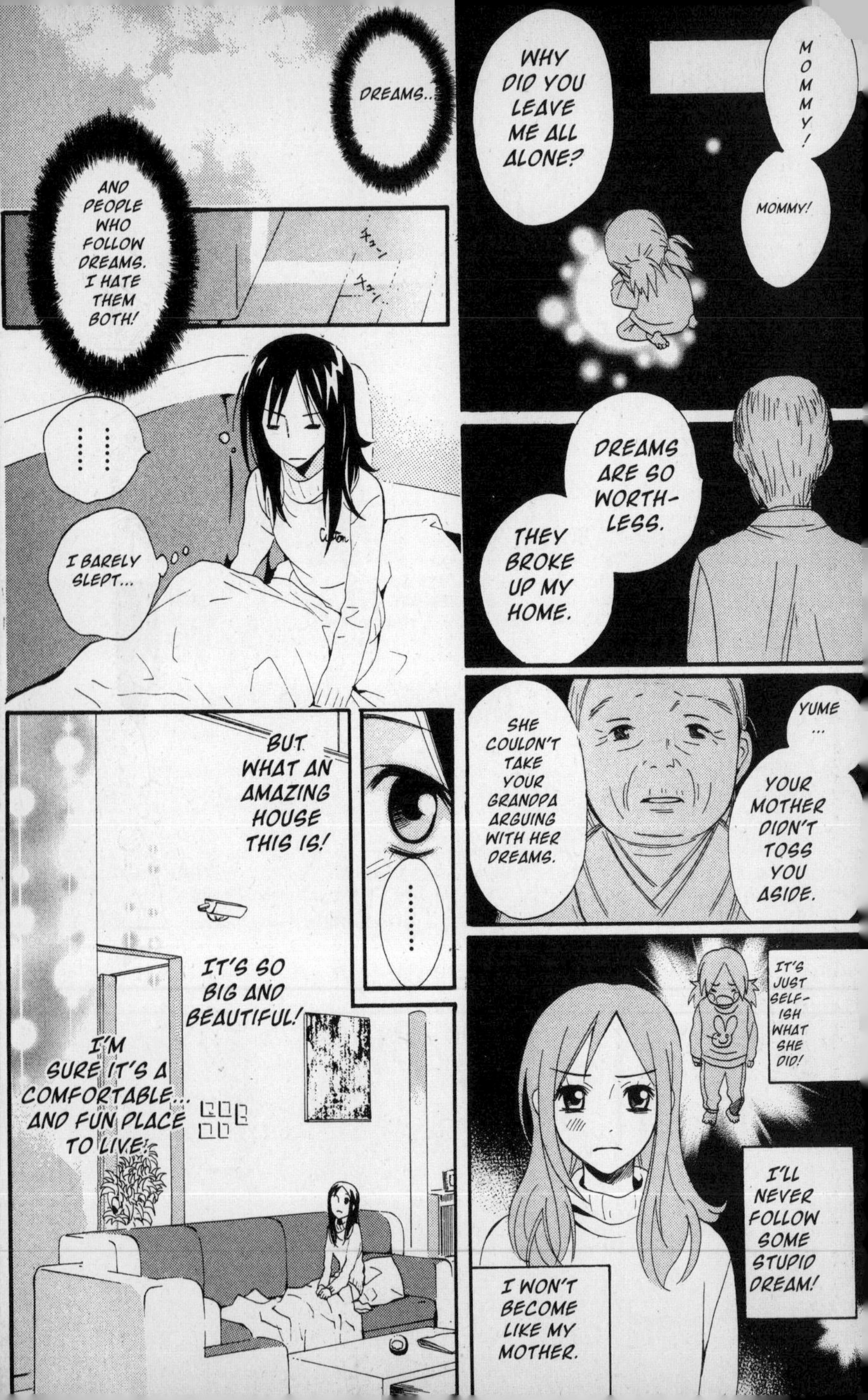
MOMMY!
MOMMY!
WHY DID YOU LEAVE ME ALL ALONE?
DREAMS ARE SO WORTHLESS.
THEY BROKE UP MY HOME.
YUME...
YOUR MOTHER DIDN'T TOSS YOU ASIDE.
SHE COULDN'T TAKE YOUR GRANDPA ARGUING WITH HER DREAMS.
IT'S JUST SELFISH WHAT SHE DID!
I'LL NEVER FOLLOW SOME STUPID DREAM!
I WON'T BECOME LIKE MY MOTHER.
DREAMS...
AND PEOPLE WHO FOLLOW DREAMS. I HATE THEM BOTH!
......
I BARELY SLEPT...
BUT WHAT AN AMAZING HOUSE THIS IS!
......
IT'S SO BIG AND BEAUTIFUL!
I'M SURE IT'S A COMFORTABLE... AND FUN PLACE TO LIVE!

SR

Dream-colored Junk!!

It's a standalone story, and it's the first time I have a girl as a protagonist. It was a lot of fun, but a lot of trouble at the same time. I based the island's dialect off my father's hometown. Dialects are always so much fun! I just can't get enough of them! In this story, aside from Yume, I thought up a **ton** of plot for all the other characters, so now it feels like sort of a waste not to write it. Speaking of which, this guy's (look down) beard is totally not popular with people, but I still like it... Beards are what make the ideal man! Most of my characters have a model they're based off of, but Chika-chan was pretty much...me. (And I don't mean looks.) I guess that's why she was so easy to draw. So, what did you think of the story?

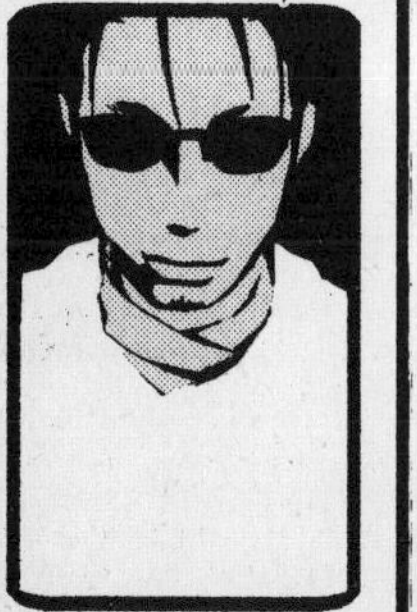

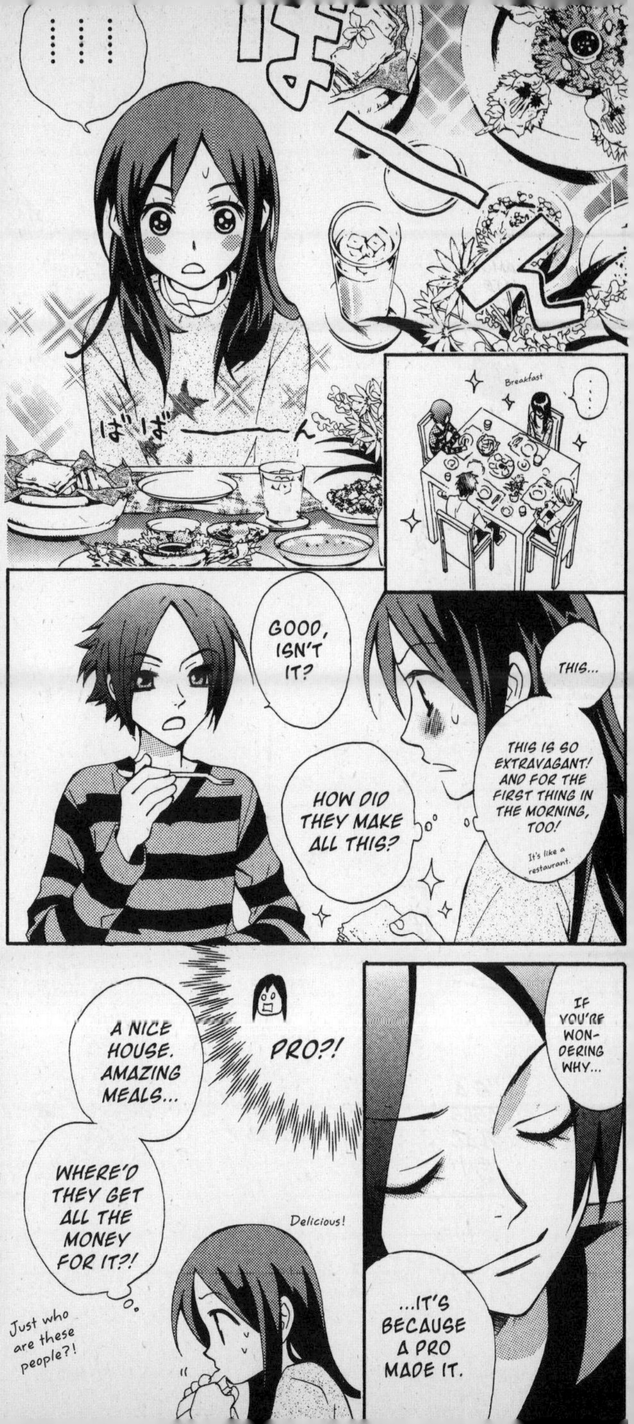

......
ぽーん
ばばーーーん
Breakfast
......
THIS...
THIS IS SO EXTRAVAGANT! AND FOR THE FIRST THING IN THE MORNING, TOO!
It's like a restaurant.
HOW DID THEY MAKE ALL THIS?
GOOD, ISN'T IT?
IF YOU'RE WON-DERING WHY...
...IT'S BECAUSE A PRO MADE IT.
PRO?!
A NICE HOUSE. AMAZING MEALS...
WHERE'D THEY GET ALL THE MONEY FOR IT?!
Delicious!
Just who are these people?!

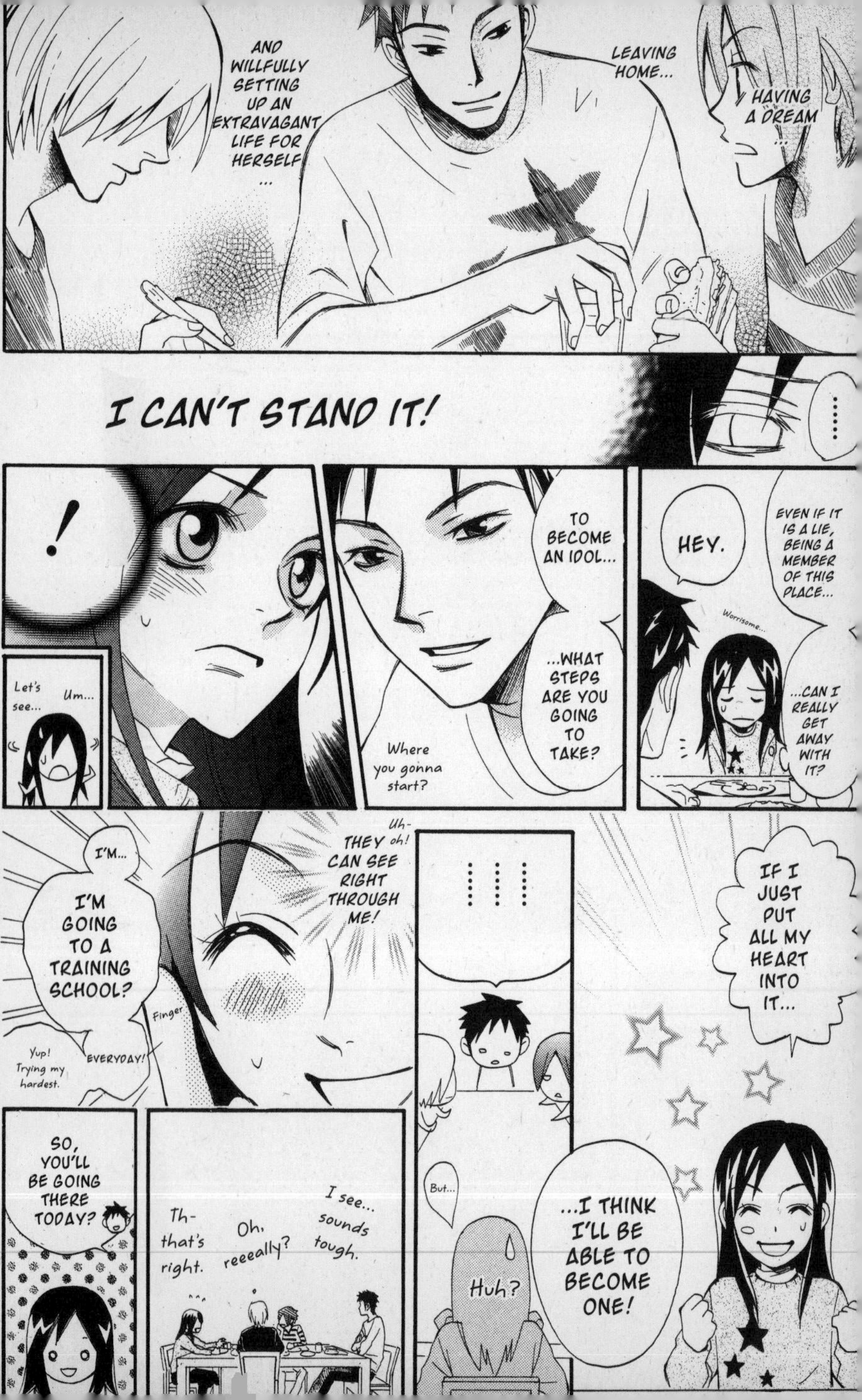
LEAVING HOME...
HAVING A DREAM...
AND WILLFULLY SETTING UP AN EXTRAVAGANT LIFE FOR HERSELF...
......
I CAN'T STAND IT!
EVEN IF IT IS A LIE, BEING A MEMBER OF THIS PLACE...
HEY.
Worrisome...
...CAN I REALLY GET AWAY WITH IT?
TO BECOME AN IDOL...
...WHAT STEPS ARE YOU GOING TO TAKE?
Where you gonna start?
!
Um...
Let's see...
IF I JUST PUT ALL MY HEART INTO IT...
...I THINK I'LL BE ABLE TO BECOME ONE!
...!!!
But...
Huh?
Uh-oh!
THEY CAN SEE RIGHT THROUGH ME!
I'M...
I'M GOING TO A TRAINING SCHOOL?
Finger
EVERYDAY!
Yup! Trying my hardest.
I see... sounds tough.
Oh, reeeally?
Th- that's right.
SO, YOU'LL BE GOING THERE TODAY?

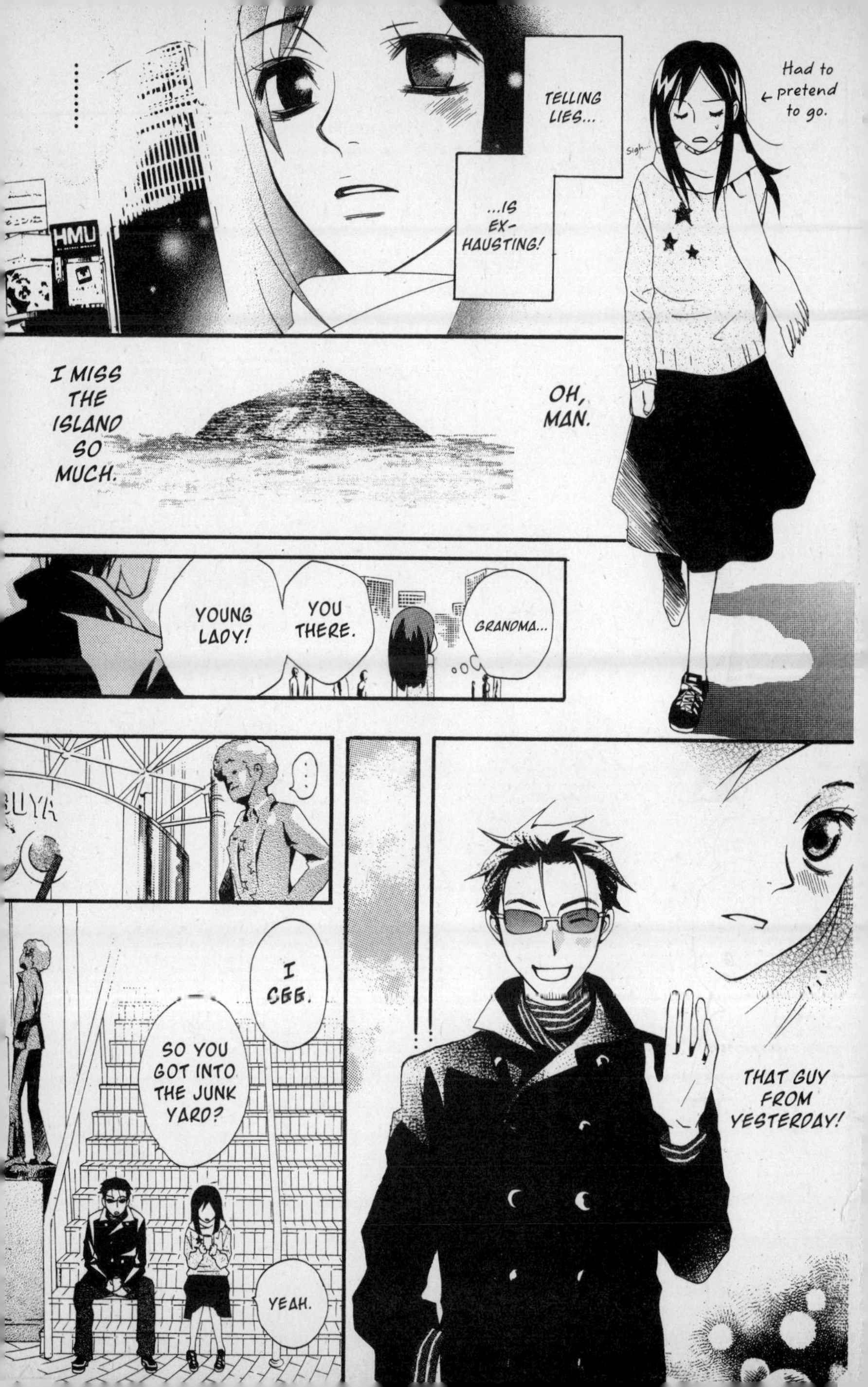

Had to pretend to go.
Sigh...
TELLING LIES...
...IS EX-HAUSTING!
OH, MAN.
I MISS THE ISLAND SO MUCH.
GRANDMA...
YOU THERE.
YOUNG LADY!
THAT GUY FROM YESTERDAY!
!!
...
I SEE.
SO YOU GOT INTO THE JUNK YARD?
YEAH.

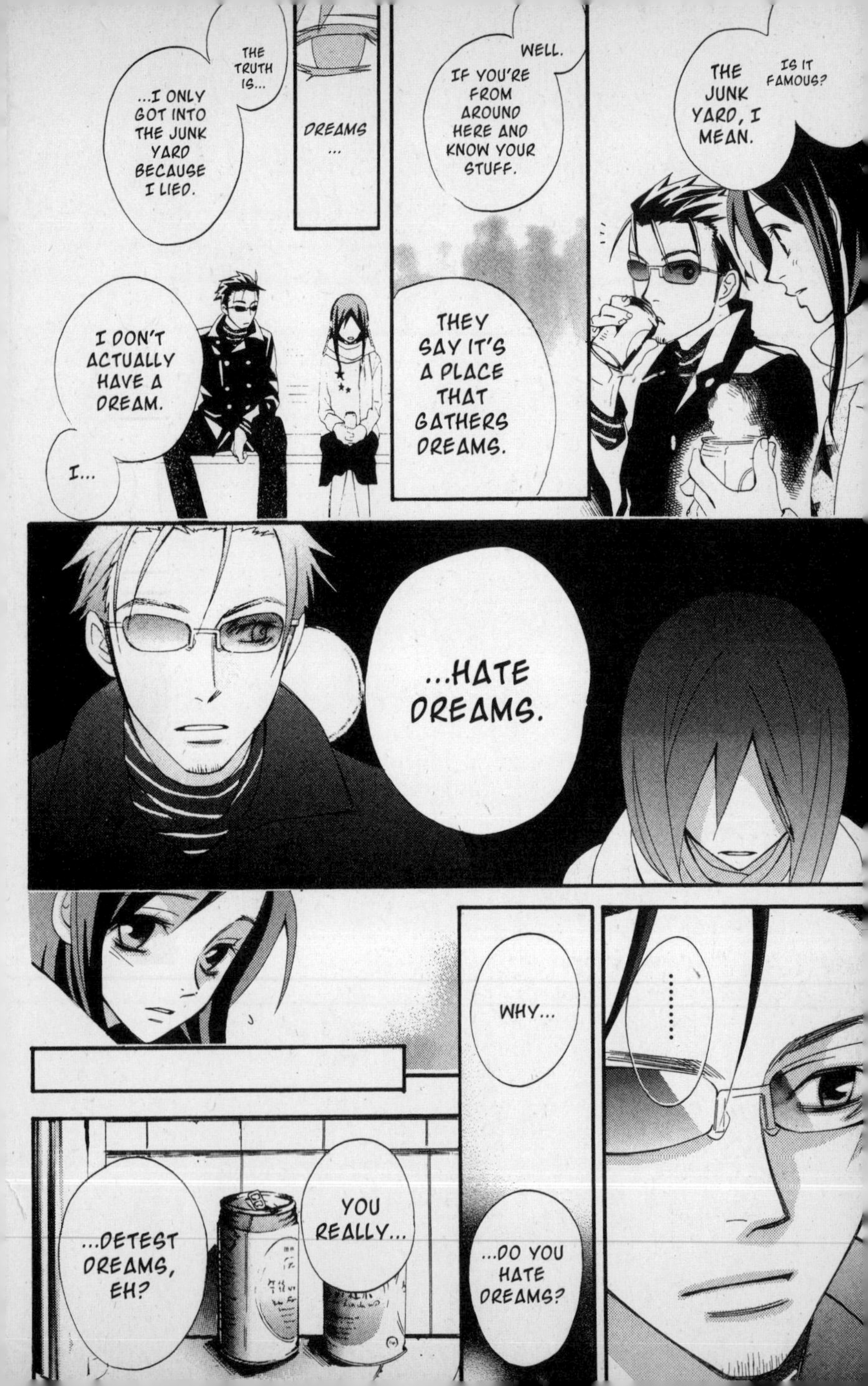
IS IT FAMOUS?
THE JUNK YARD, I MEAN.
WELL.
IF YOU'RE FROM AROUND HERE AND KNOW YOUR STUFF.
THEY SAY IT'S A PLACE THAT GATHERS DREAMS.
DREAMS...
THE TRUTH IS...
...I ONLY GOT INTO THE JUNK YARD BECAUSE I LIED.
I DON'T ACTUALLY HAVE A DREAM.
I...
...HATE DREAMS.
......
WHY...
...DO YOU HATE DREAMS?
YOU REALLY...
...DETEST DREAMS, EH?

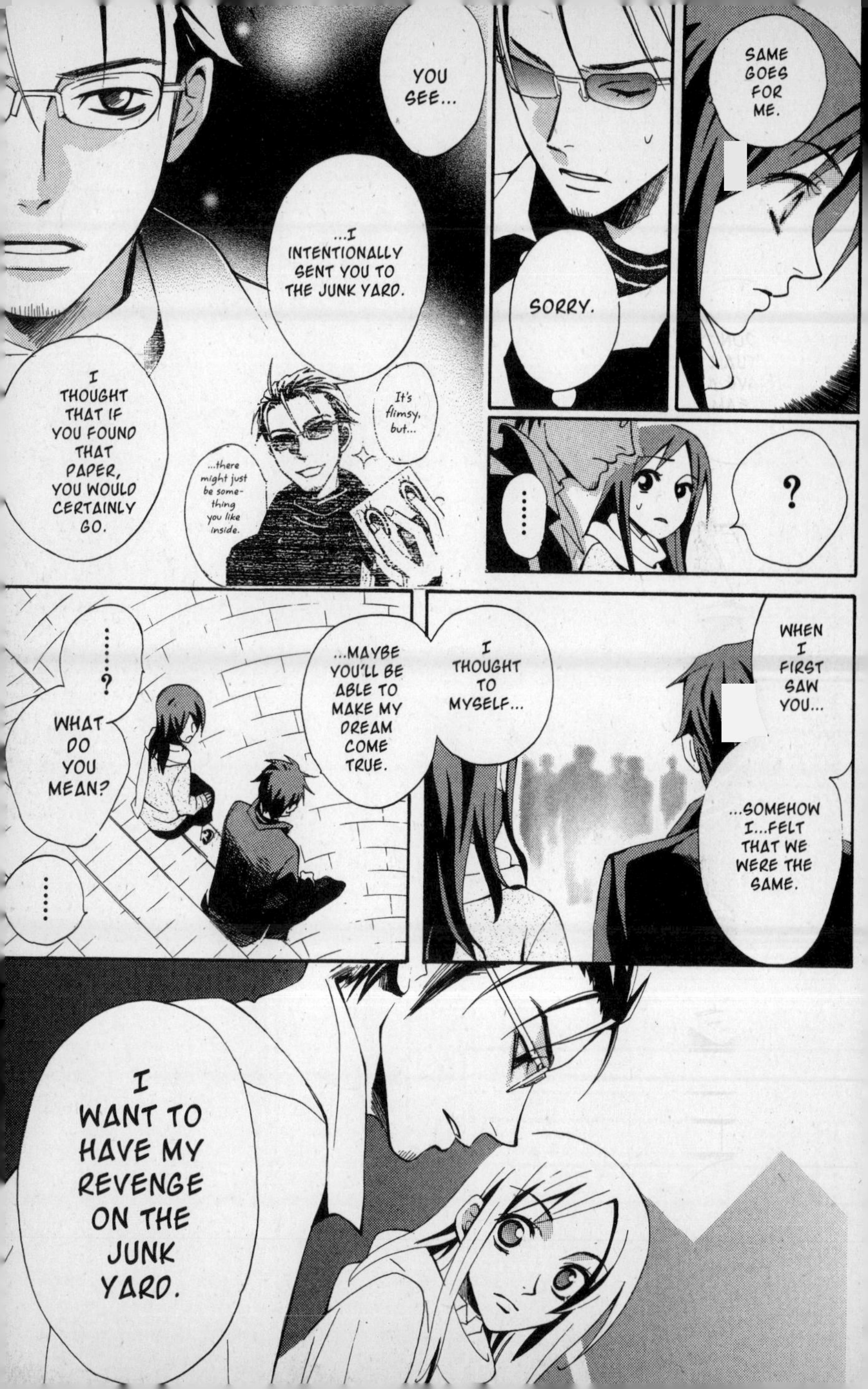
SAME GOES FOR ME.
SORRY.
?
......
YOU SEE...
...I INTENTIONALLY SENT YOU TO THE JUNK YARD.
I THOUGHT THAT IF YOU FOUND THAT PAPER, YOU WOULD CERTAINLY GO.
It's flimsy, but...
...there might just be something you like inside.
WHEN I FIRST SAW YOU...
...SOMEHOW I...FELT THAT WE WERE THE SAME.
I THOUGHT TO MYSELF...
...MAYBE YOU'LL BE ABLE TO MAKE MY DREAM COME TRUE.
......?
WHAT DO YOU MEAN?
......
I WANT TO HAVE MY REVENGE ON THE JUNK YARD.

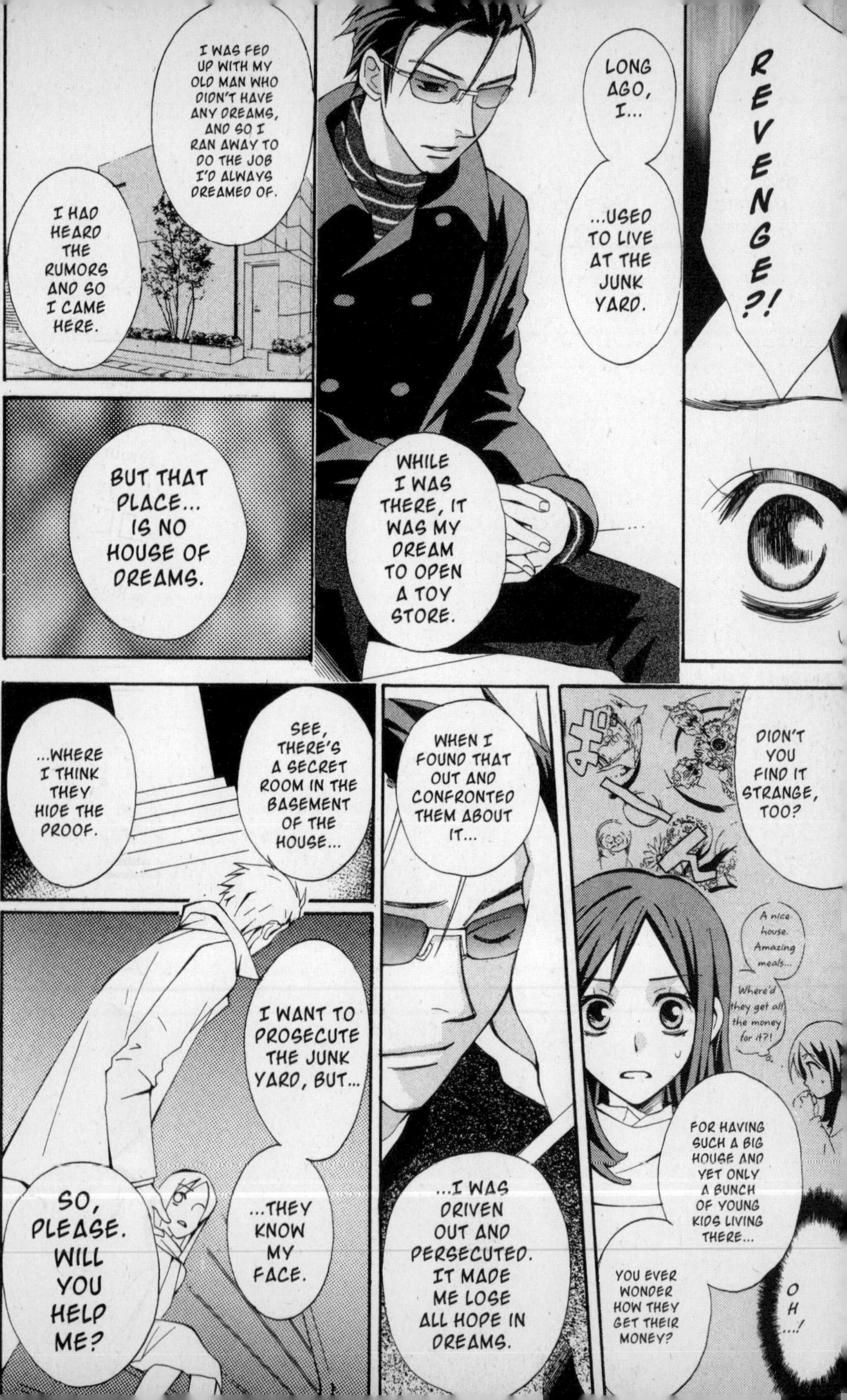

REVENGE?!
LONG AGO, I...
...USED TO LIVE AT THE JUNK YARD.
I WAS FED UP WITH MY OLD MAN WHO DIDN'T HAVE ANY DREAMS, AND SO I RAN AWAY TO DO THE JOB I'D ALWAYS DREAMED OF.
I HAD HEARD THE RUMORS AND SO I CAME HERE.
WHILE I WAS THERE, IT WAS MY DREAM TO OPEN A TOY STORE.
BUT THAT PLACE... IS NO HOUSE OF DREAMS.
DIDN'T YOU FIND IT STRANGE, TOO?
A nice house. Amazing meals...
Where'd they get all the money for it?!
FOR HAVING SUCH A BIG HOUSE AND YET ONLY A BUNCH OF YOUNG KIDS LIVING THERE...
YOU EVER WONDER HOW THEY GET THEIR MONEY?
OH...!
WHEN I FOUND THAT OUT AND CONFRONTED THEM ABOUT IT...
...I WAS DRIVEN OUT AND PERSECUTED. IT MADE ME LOSE ALL HOPE IN DREAMS.
SEE, THERE'S A SECRET ROOM IN THE BASEMENT OF THE HOUSE...
...WHERE I THINK THEY HIDE THE PROOF.
I WANT TO PROSECUTE THE JUNK YARD, BUT...
...THEY KNOW MY FACE.
SO, PLEASE. WILL YOU HELP ME?

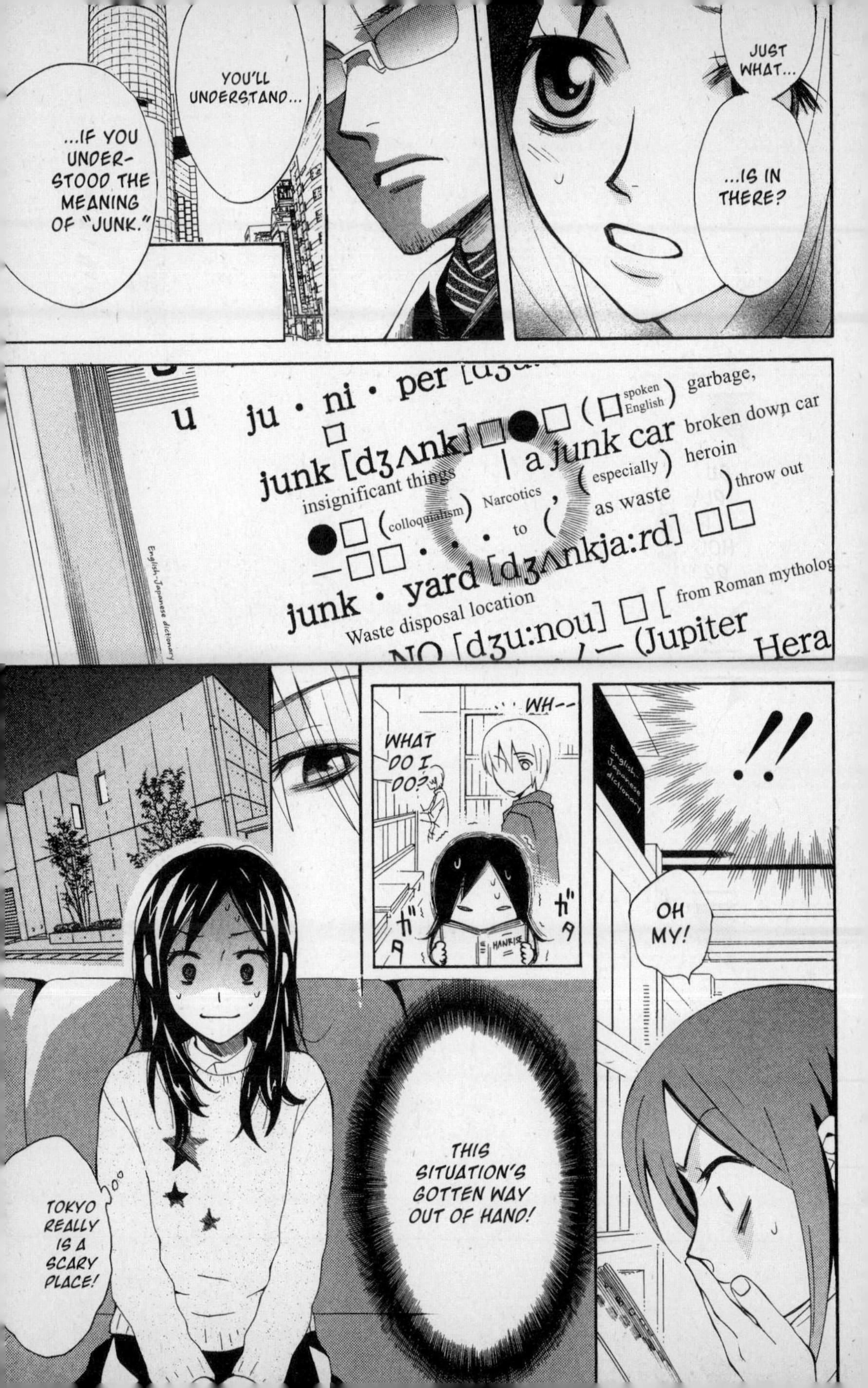
JUST WHAT...
...IS IN THERE?
YOU'LL UNDERSTAND...
...IF YOU UNDER-STOOD THE MEANING OF "JUNK."
ju · ni · per
spoken English
garbage,
junk [dʒʌnk]
a junk car
broken down car
insignificant things
especially
heroin
colloquialism
Narcotics
to
as waste
throw out
junk · yard [dʒʌnkja:rd]
Waste disposal location
from Roman mytholog
NO [dʒu:nou]
(Jupiter
Hera
English-Japanese dictionary
!!
English-Japanese dictionary
OH MY!
...WH--
WHAT DO I DO?
ガタ
ガタ
HANRISE
THIS SITUATION'S GOTTEN WAY OUT OF HAND!
TOKYO REALLY IS A SCARY PLACE!

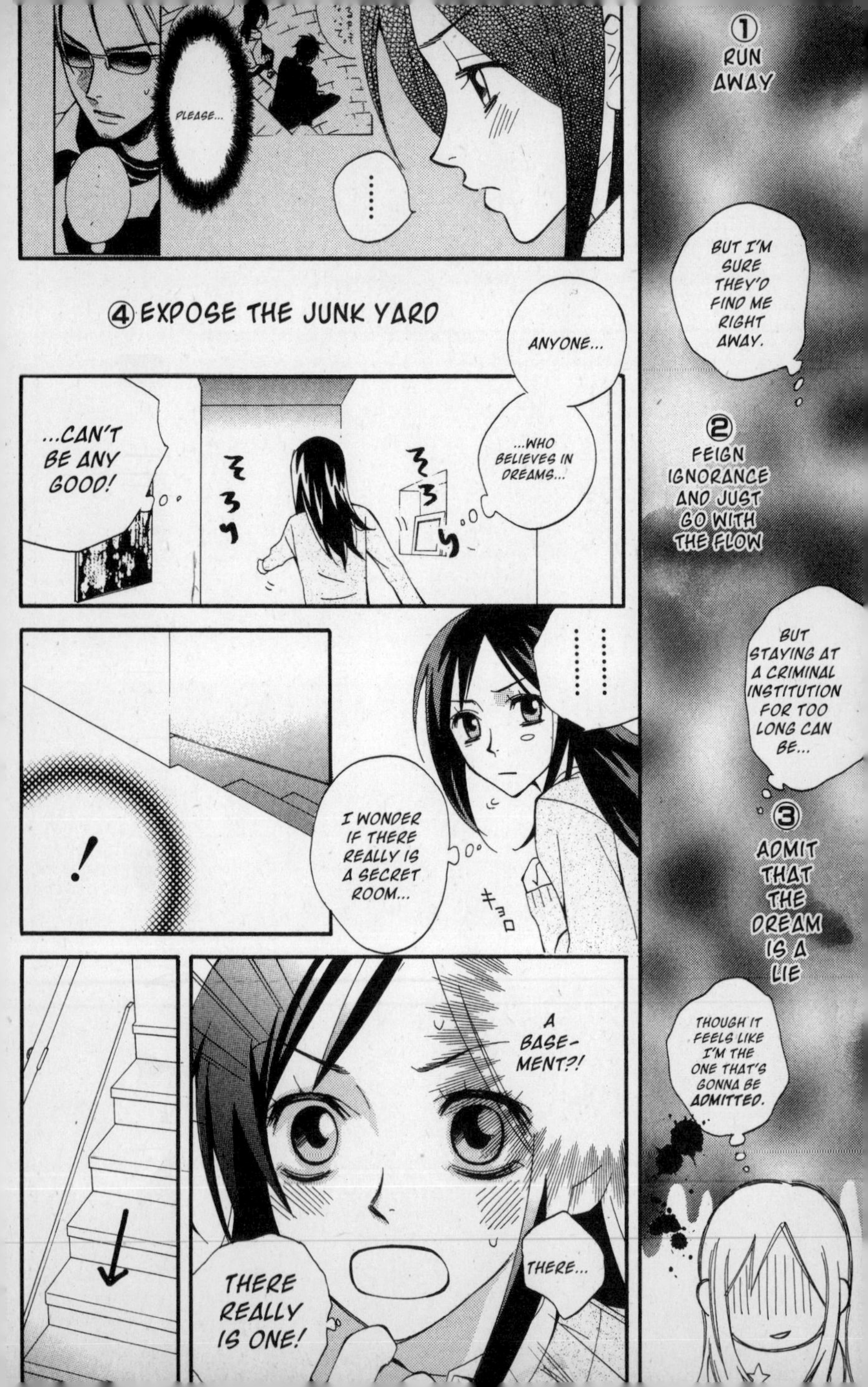
① RUN AWAY
BUT I'M SURE THEY'D FIND ME RIGHT AWAY.
② FEIGN IGNORANCE AND JUST GO WITH THE FLOW
BUT STAYING AT A CRIMINAL INSTITUTION FOR TOO LONG CAN BE...
③ ADMIT THAT THE DREAM IS A LIE
THOUGH IT FEELS LIKE I'M THE ONE THAT'S GONNA BE ADMITTED.
......
PLEASE...
④ EXPOSE THE JUNK YARD
ANYONE...
...WHO BELIEVES IN DREAMS...
...CAN'T BE ANY GOOD!
......
I WONDER IF THERE REALLY IS A SECRET ROOM...
!
A BASEMENT?!
THERE...
THERE REALLY IS ONE!

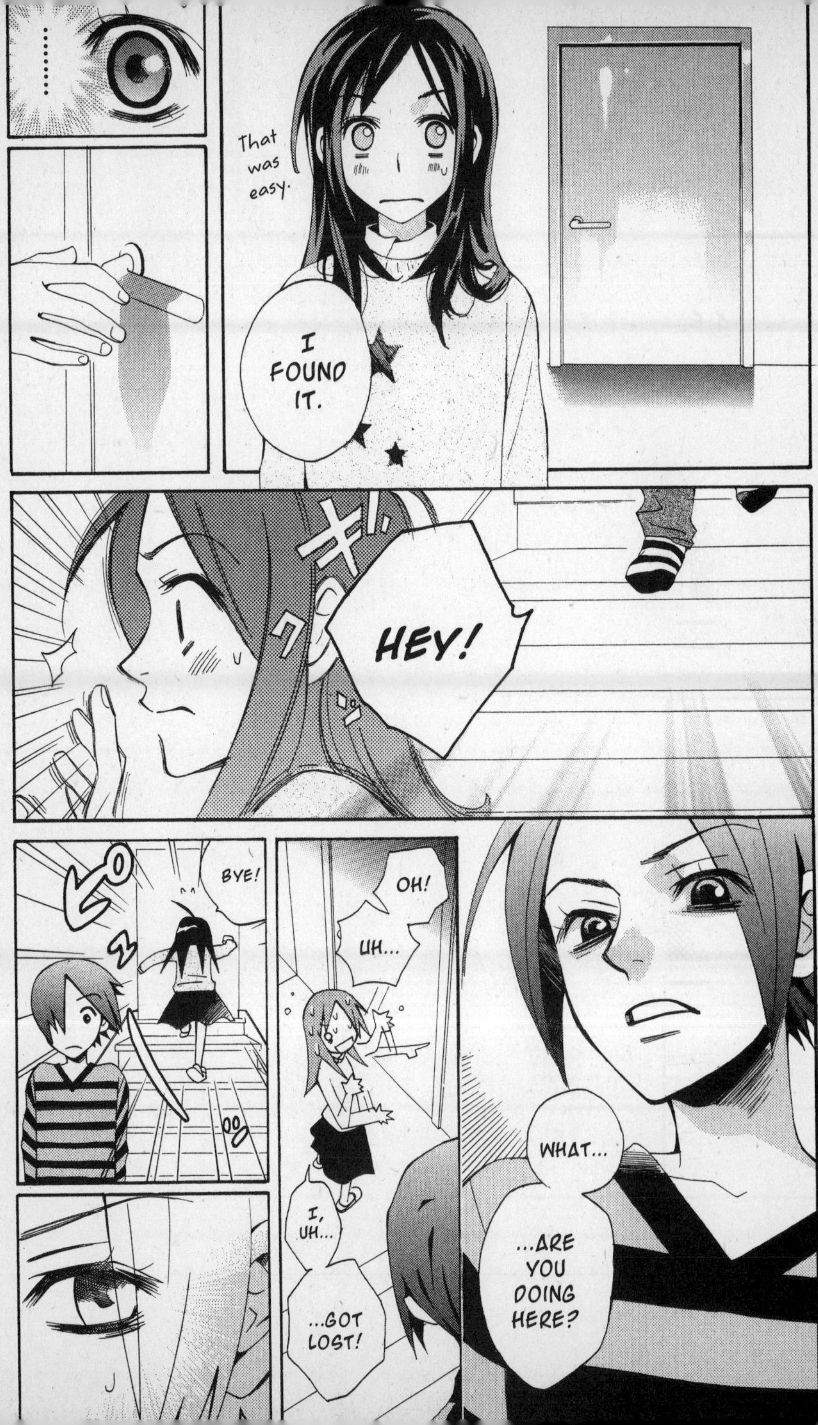
That was easy.
I FOUND IT.
HEY!
WHAT...
...ARE YOU DOING HERE?
OH!
UH...
I, UH...
...GOT LOST!
BYE!

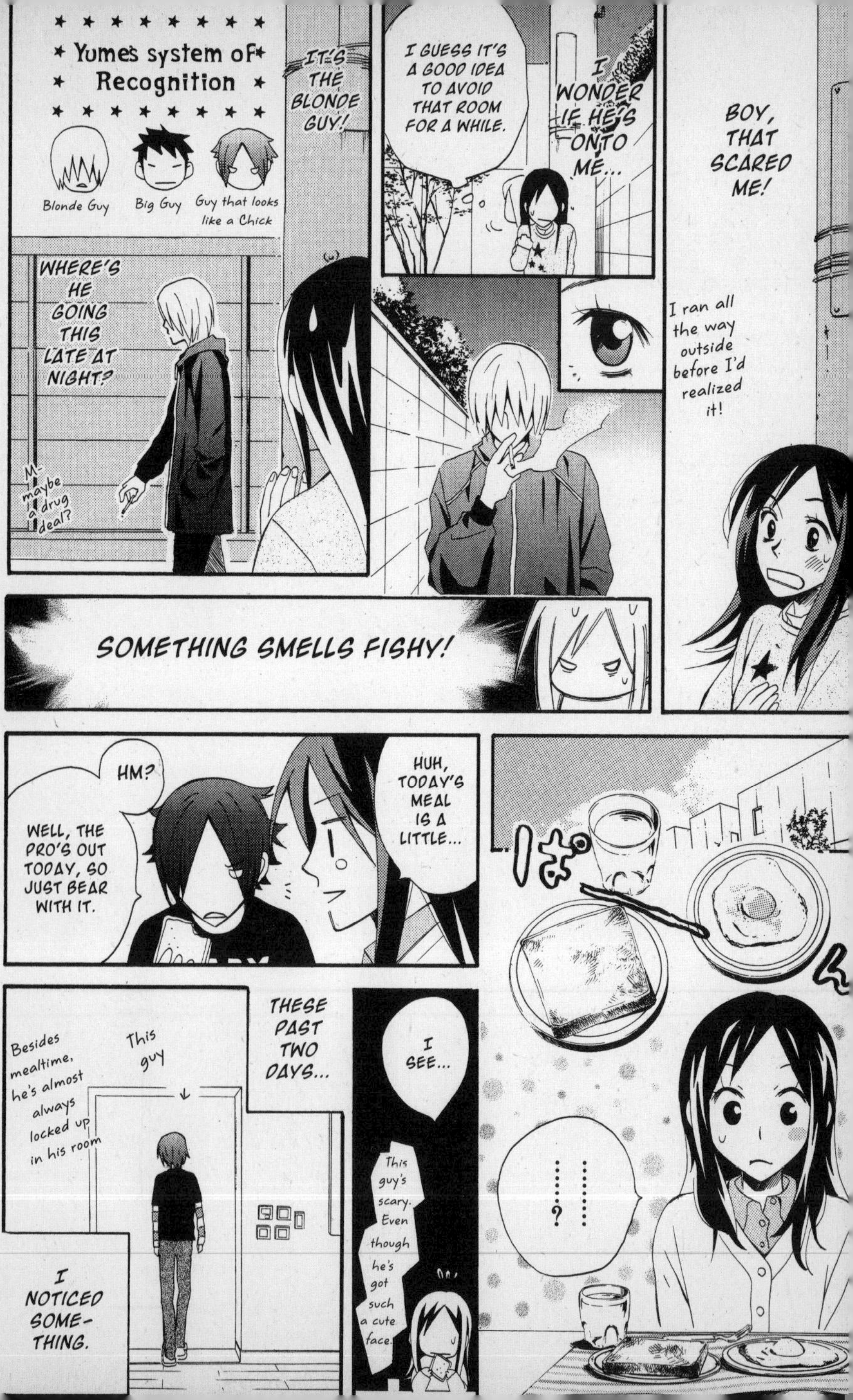
BOY, THAT SCARED ME!
I ran all the way outside before I'd realized it!
I GUESS IT'S A GOOD IDEA TO AVOID THAT ROOM FOR A WHILE.
I WONDER IF HE'S ONTO ME...
IT'S THE BLONDE GUY!
★ Yume's system of Recognition ★
Blonde Guy
Big Guy
Guy that looks like a Chick
WHERE'S HE GOING THIS LATE AT NIGHT?
M-maybe a drug deal?
SOMETHING SMELLS FISHY!
HUH, TODAY'S MEAL IS A LITTLE...
HM?
WELL, THE PRO'S OUT TODAY, SO JUST BEAR WITH IT.
......?
I SEE...
This guy's scary. Even though he's got such a cute face.
THESE PAST TWO DAYS...
This guy
Besides mealtime, he's almost always locked up in his room
I NOTICED SOME-THING.

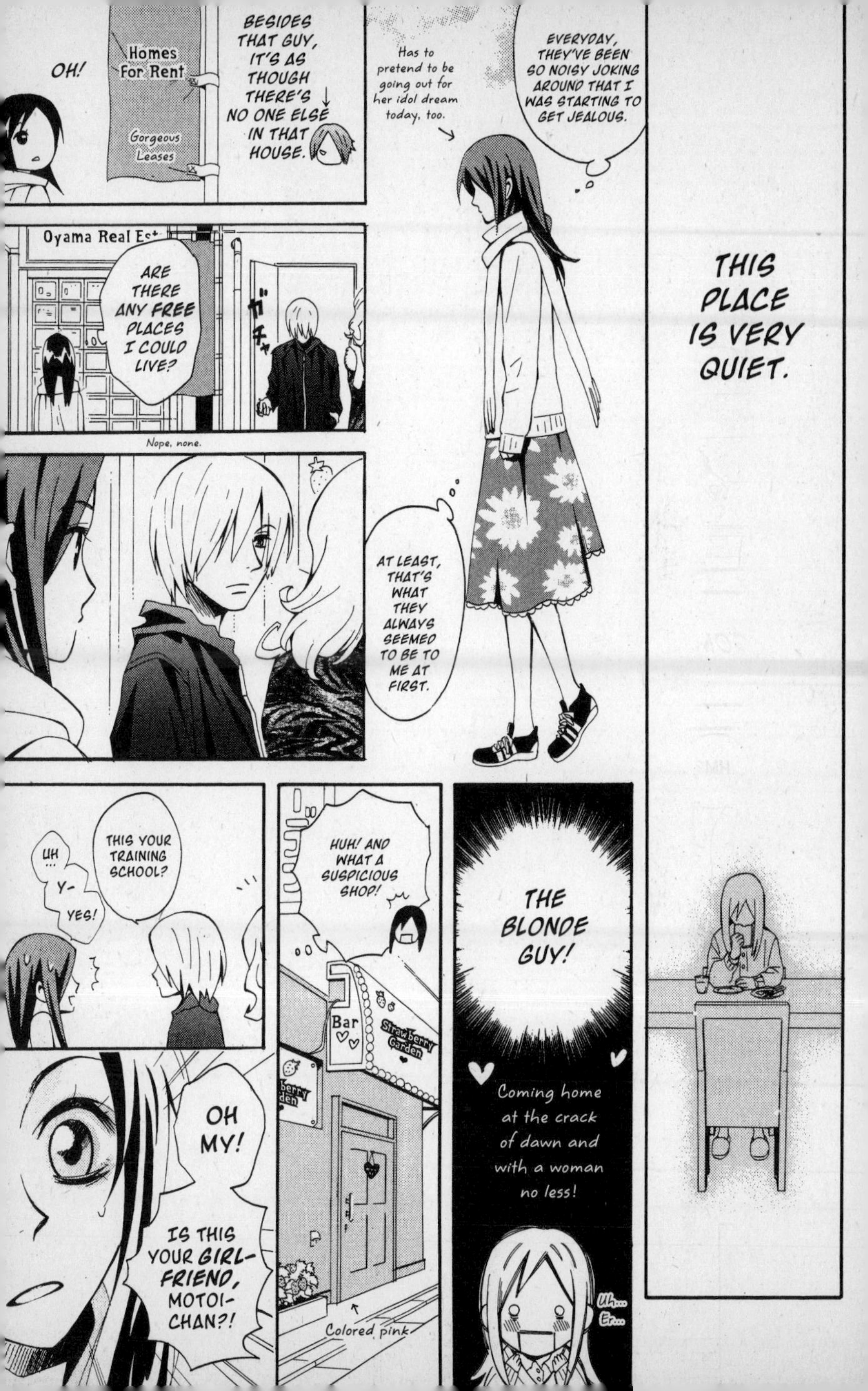
THIS PLACE IS VERY QUIET.
EVERYDAY, THEY'VE BEEN SO NOISY JOKING AROUND THAT I WAS STARTING TO GET JEALOUS.
Has to pretend to be going out for her idol dream today, too.
AT LEAST, THAT'S WHAT THEY ALWAYS SEEMED TO BE TO ME AT FIRST.
BESIDES THAT GUY, IT'S AS THOUGH THERE'S NO ONE ELSE IN THAT HOUSE.
Homes For Rent
Gorgeous Leases
OH!
ガチャ
ARE THERE ANY FREE PLACES I COULD LIVE?
Oyama Real Est
Nope, none.
THE BLONDE GUY!
Coming home at the crack of dawn and with a woman no less!
Uh... Er...
HUH! AND WHAT A SUSPICIOUS SHOP!
Bar
Strawberry Garden
Colored pink
THIS YOUR TRAINING SCHOOL?
UH ...
Y- YES!
OH MY!
IS THIS YOUR GIRL-FRIEND, MOTOI-CHAN?!

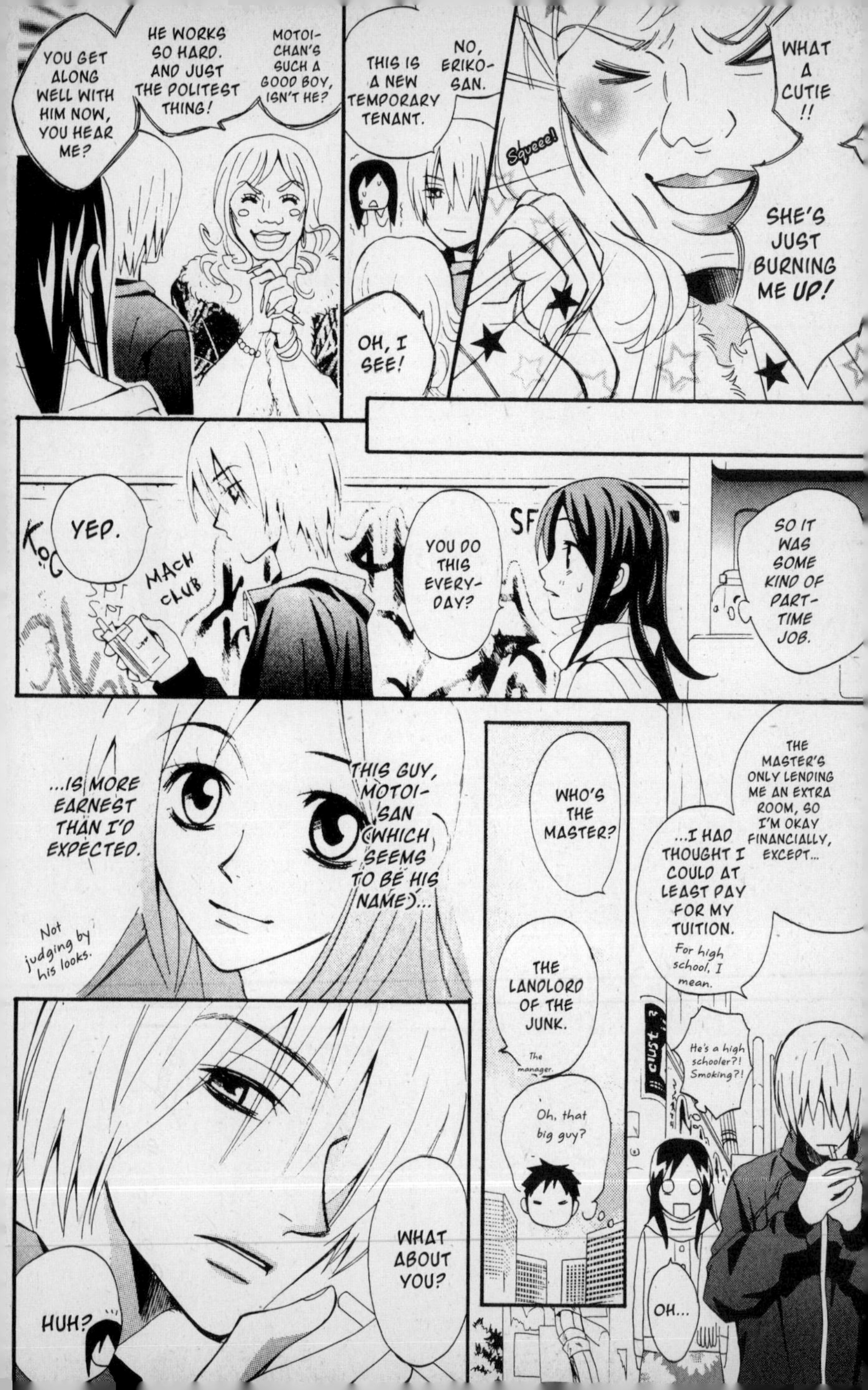
WHAT A CUTIE!!
Squeee!
SHE'S JUST BURNING ME UP!
NO, ERIKO-SAN.
THIS IS A NEW TEMPORARY TENANT.
OH, I SEE!
MOTOI-CHAN'S SUCH A GOOD BOY, ISN'T HE?
HE WORKS SO HARD. AND JUST THE POLITEST THING!
YOU GET ALONG WELL WITH HIM NOW, YOU HEAR ME?
SO IT WAS SOME KIND OF PART-TIME JOB.
SF
YOU DO THIS EVERY-DAY?
MACH CLUB
YEP.
SPT SPT
THE MASTER'S ONLY LENDING ME AN EXTRA ROOM, SO I'M OKAY FINANCIALLY, EXCEPT...
...I HAD THOUGHT I COULD AT LEAST PAY FOR MY TUITION.
For high school, I mean.
He's a high schooler?! Smoking?!
OH...
WHO'S THE MASTER?
THE LANDLORD OF THE JUNK.
The manager.
Oh, that big guy?
THIS GUY, MOTOI-SAN (WHICH SEEMS TO BE HIS NAME)...
...IS MORE EARNEST THAN I'D EXPECTED.
Not judging by his looks.
WHAT ABOUT YOU?
HUH?

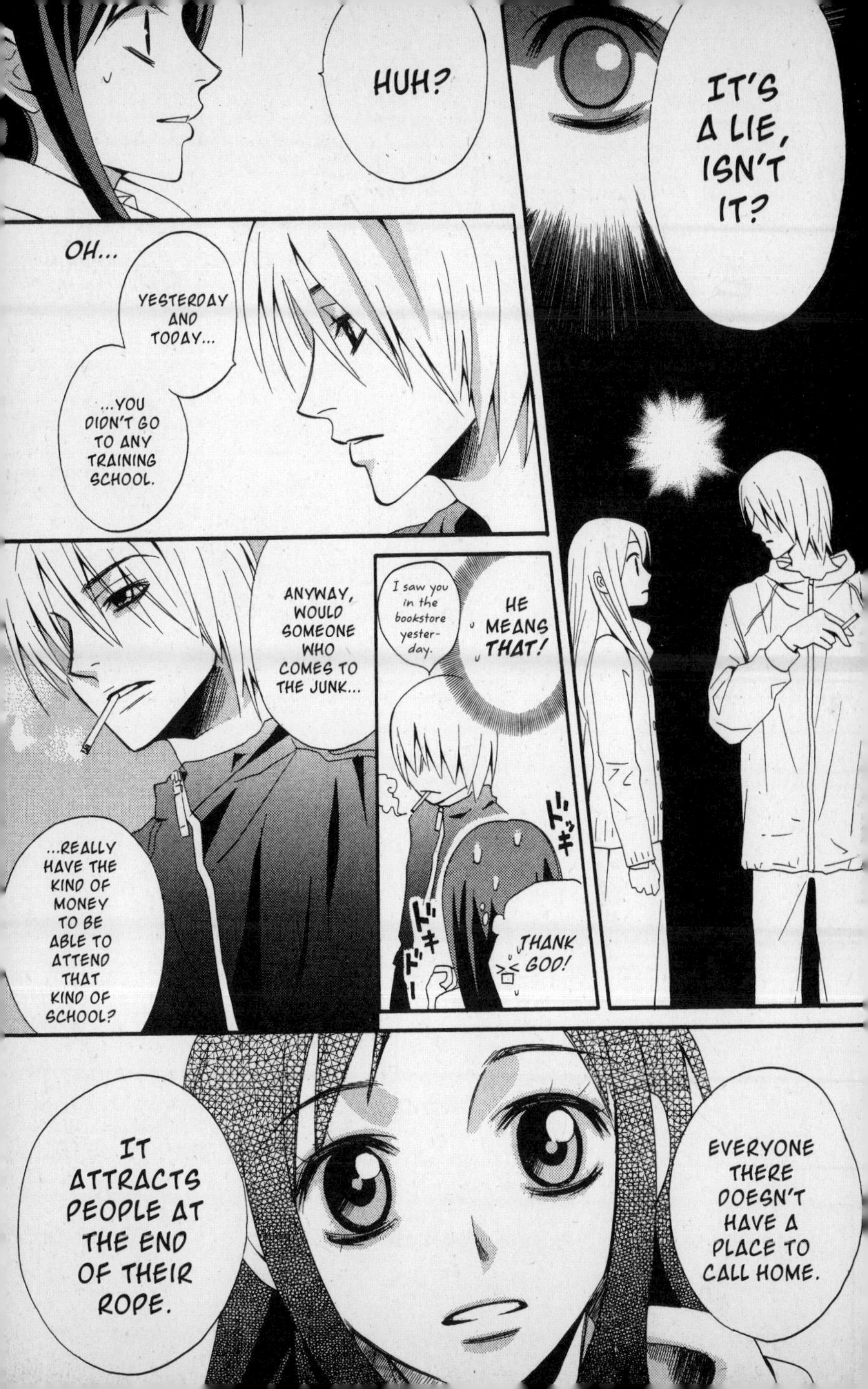
IT'S A LIE, ISN'T IT?
HUH?
OH...
YESTERDAY AND TODAY...
...YOU DIDN'T GO TO ANY TRAINING SCHOOL.
I saw you in the bookstore yester-day.
HE MEANS THAT!
ドキッ
THANK GOD!
ANYWAY, WOULD SOMEONE WHO COMES TO THE JUNK...
...REALLY HAVE THE KIND OF MONEY TO BE ABLE TO ATTEND THAT KIND OF SCHOOL?
EVERYONE THERE DOESN'T HAVE A PLACE TO CALL HOME.
IT ATTRACTS PEOPLE AT THE END OF THEIR ROPE.

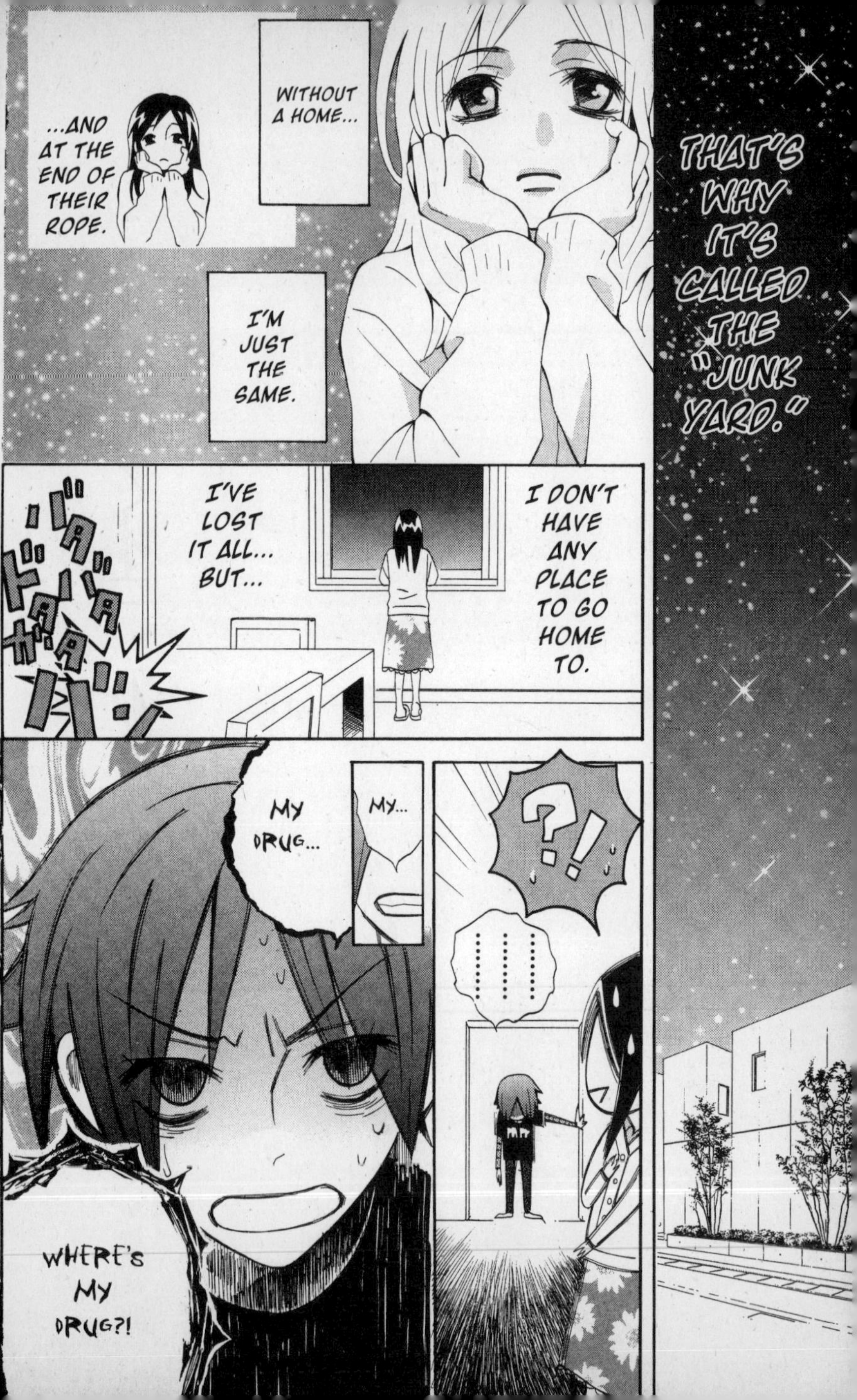
THAT'S WHY IT'S CALLED THE "JUNK YARD."
WITHOUT A HOME...
...AND AT THE END OF THEIR ROPE.
I'M JUST THE SAME.
I DON'T HAVE ANY PLACE TO GO HOME TO.
I'VE LOST IT ALL... BUT...
?!
......
MY...
MY DRUG...
WHERE'S MY DRUG?!

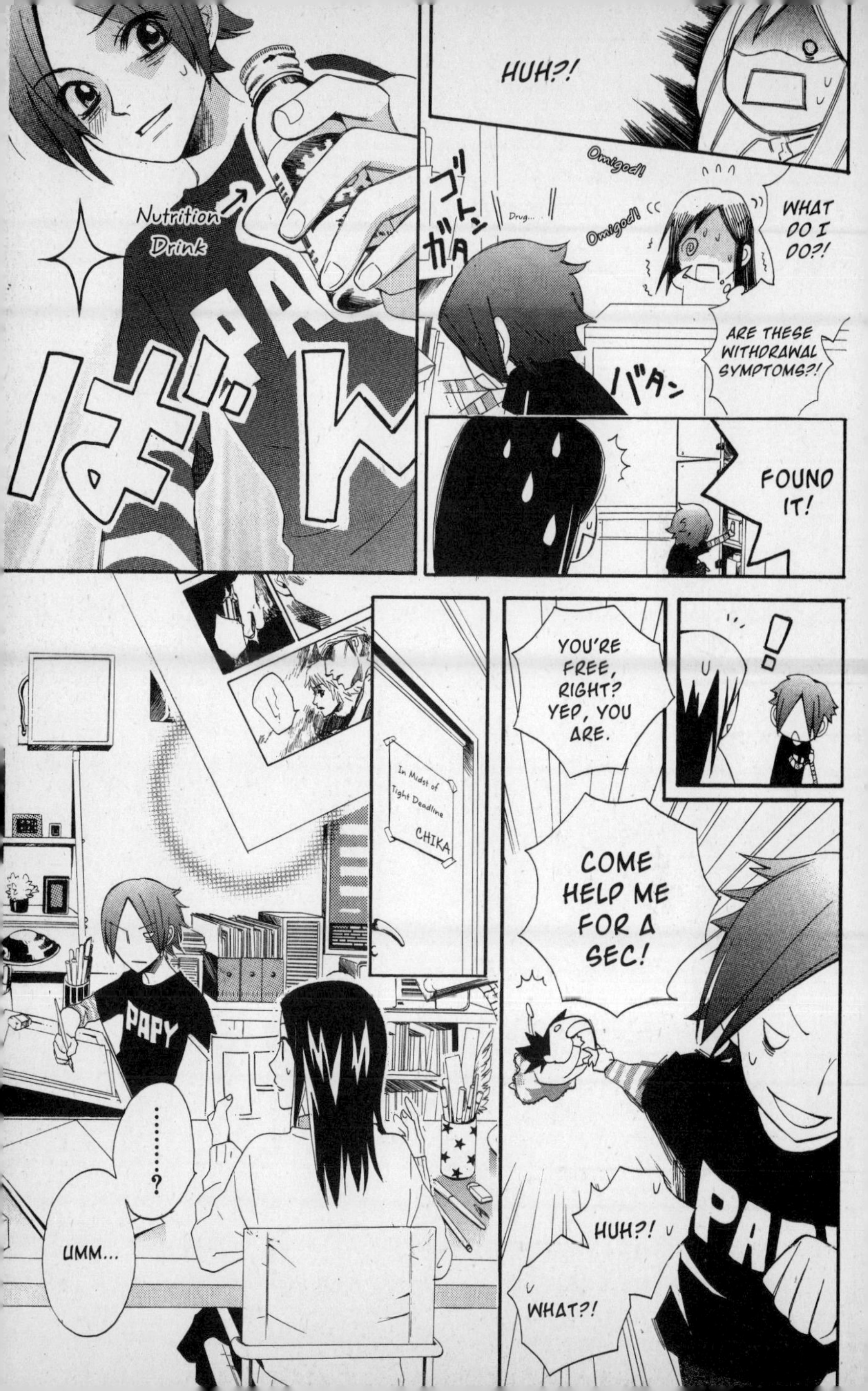
HUH?!
Omigod!
Omigod!
Drug...
ゴトン
ガタ
WHAT DO I DO?!
ARE THESE WITHDRAWAL SYMPTOMS?!
バタン
FOUND IT!
Nutrition Drink
!
YOU'RE FREE, RIGHT? YEP, YOU ARE.
COME HELP ME FOR A SEC!
HUH?!
WHAT?!
In Midst of Tight Deadline CHIKA
PAPY
......?
UMM...

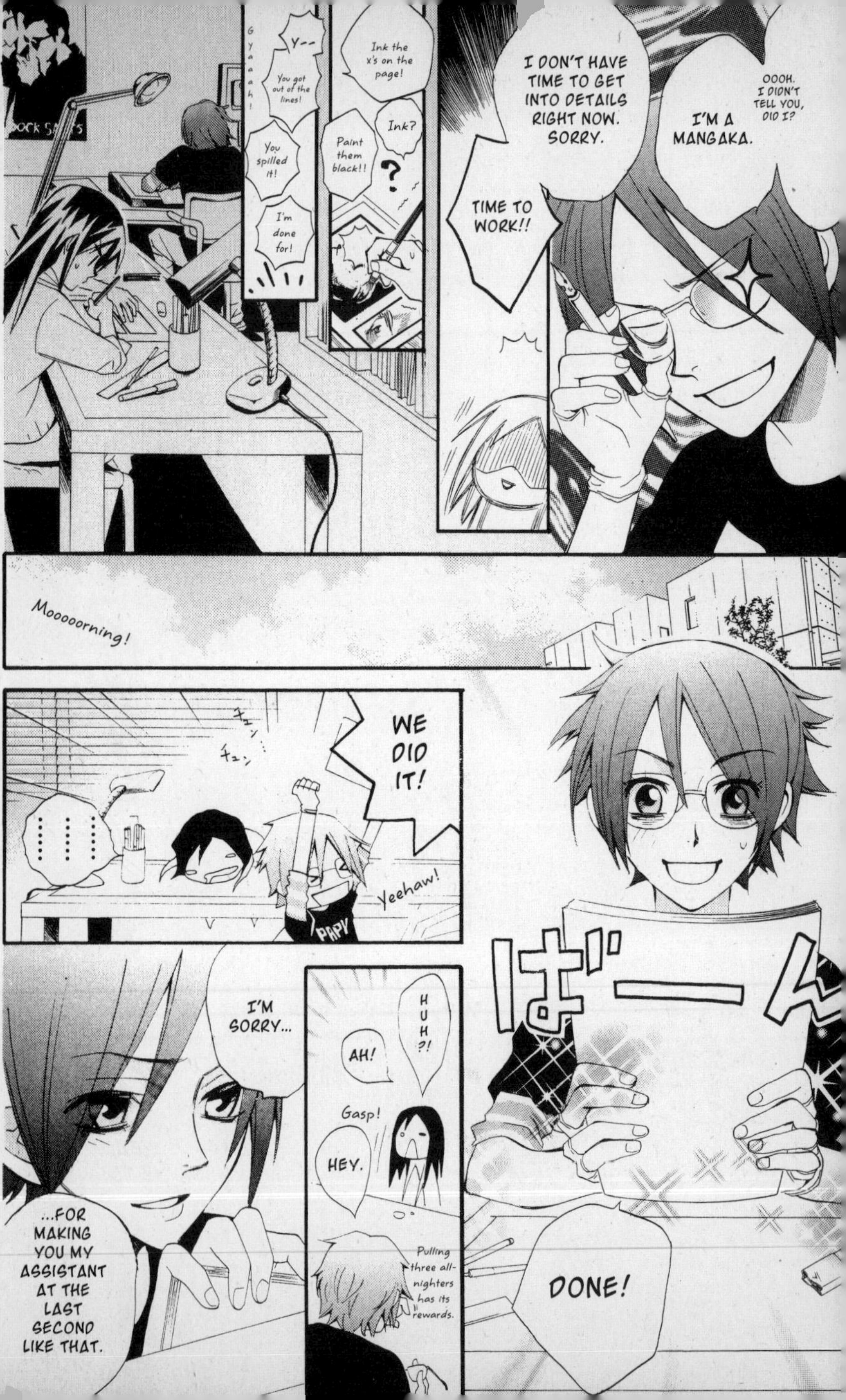

OOOH. I DIDN'T TELL YOU, DID I?
I'M A MANGAKA.
I DON'T HAVE TIME TO GET INTO DETAILS RIGHT NOW. SORRY.
TIME TO WORK!!
Ink the x's on the page!
Ink?
Paint them black!!
?
Y--
Gyaaah!
You got out of the lines!
You spilled it!
I'm done for!
Moooorning!
ばーん
DONE!
WE DID IT!
チュン… チュン
......
Yeehaw!
PAPY
HUH?!
AH!
Gasp!
HEY.
Pulling three all-nighters has its rewards.
I'M SORRY...
...FOR MAKING YOU MY ASSISTANT AT THE LAST SECOND LIKE THAT.

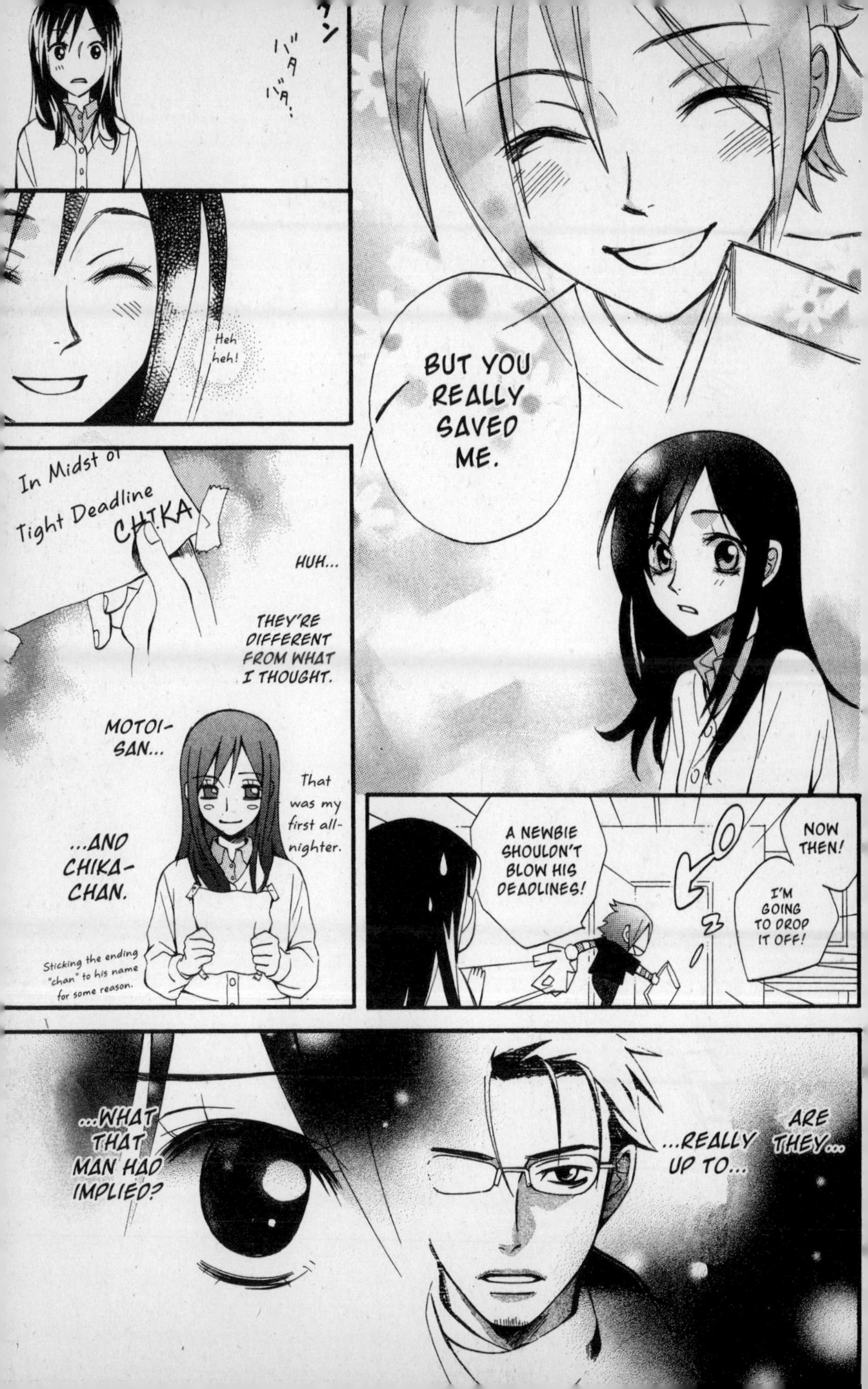
BUT YOU REALLY SAVED ME.
NOW THEN!
I'M GOING TO DROP IT OFF!
A NEWBIE SHOULDN'T BLOW HIS DEADLINES!
バタバタ
Heh heh!
In Midst of Tight Deadline
CHIKA
HUH...
THEY'RE DIFFERENT FROM WHAT I THOUGHT.
MOTOI-SAN...
...AND CHIKA-CHAN.
That was my first all-nighter.
Sticking the ending "chan" to his name for some reason.
ARE THEY...
...REALLY UP TO...
...WHAT THAT MAN HAD IMPLIED?

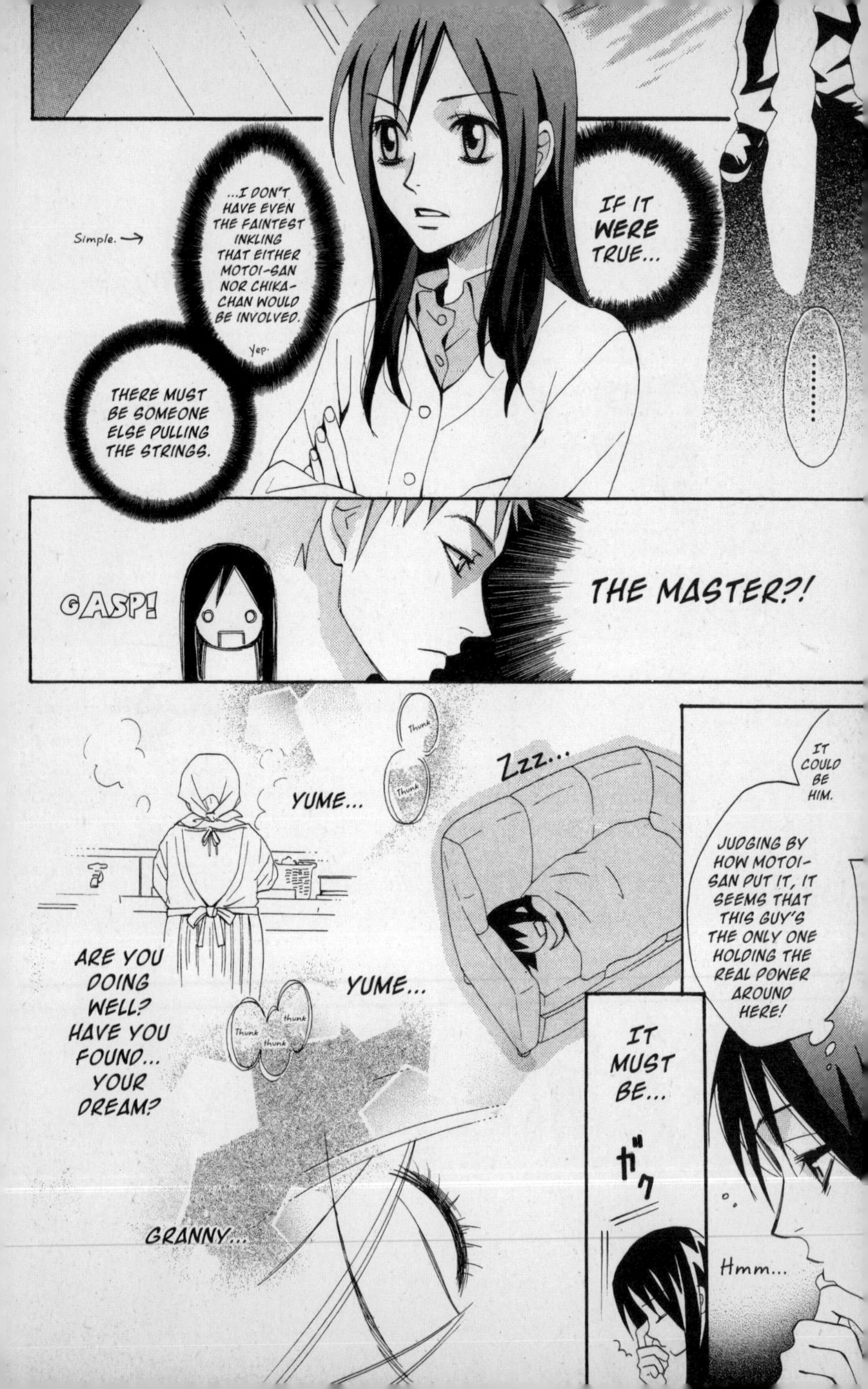
......
IF IT WERE TRUE...
...I DON'T HAVE EVEN THE FAINTEST INKLING THAT EITHER MOTOI-SAN NOR CHIKA-CHAN WOULD BE INVOLVED.
Simple. →
Yep.
THERE MUST BE SOMEONE ELSE PULLING THE STRINGS.
THE MASTER?!
GASP!
IT COULD BE HIM.
JUDGING BY HOW MOTOI-SAN PUT IT, IT SEEMS THAT THIS GUY'S THE ONLY ONE HOLDING THE REAL POWER AROUND HERE!
IT MUST BE...
ガク
Hmm...
Zzz...
Thunk
Thunk
YUME...
ARE YOU DOING WELL? HAVE YOU FOUND... YOUR DREAM?
YUME...
Thunk
thunk
thunk
GRANNY...

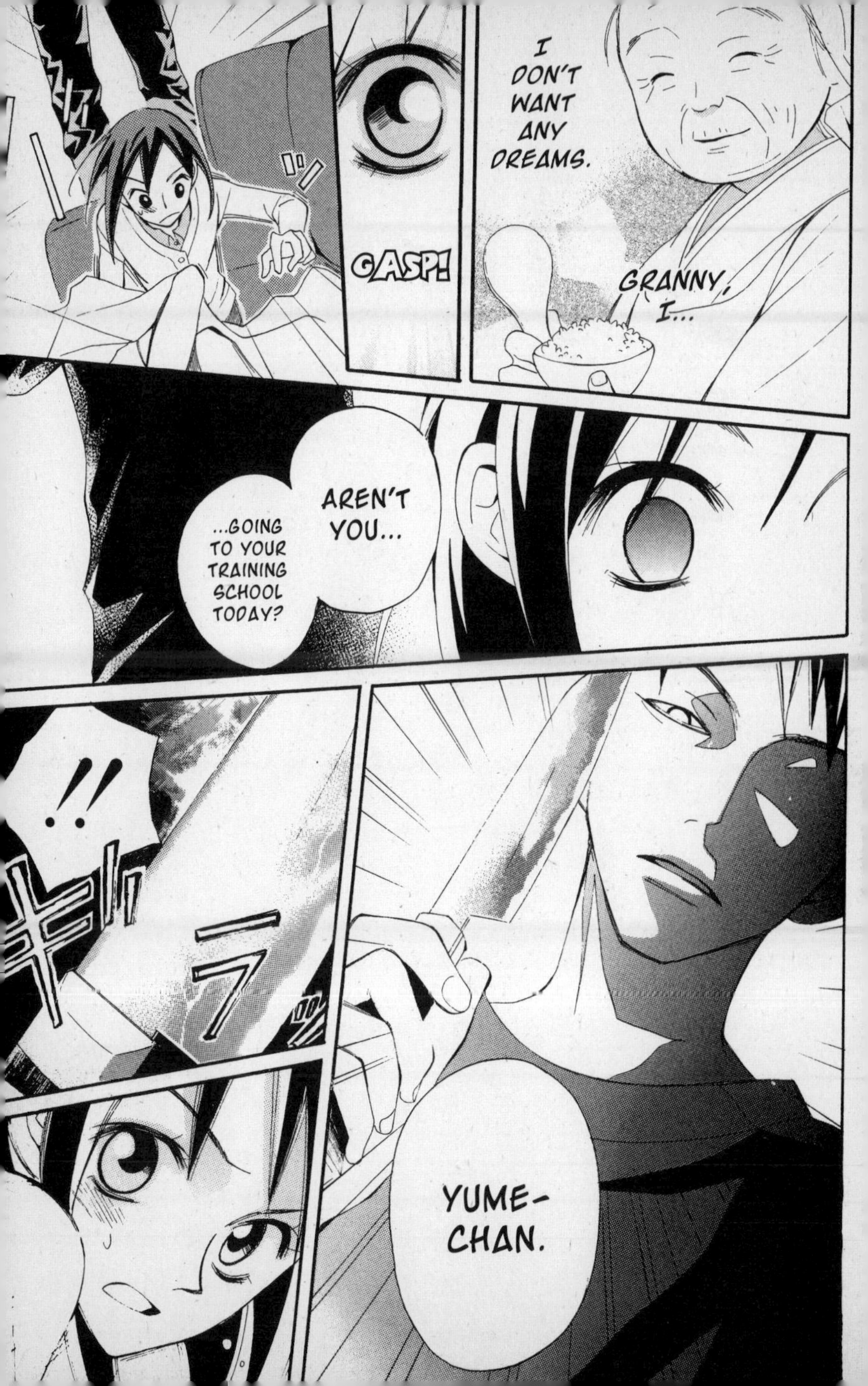
I DON'T WANT ANY DREAMS.
GRANNY, I...
GASP!
ARE N'T YOU...
...GOING TO YOUR TRAINING SCHOOL TODAY?
YUME-CHAN.
!!

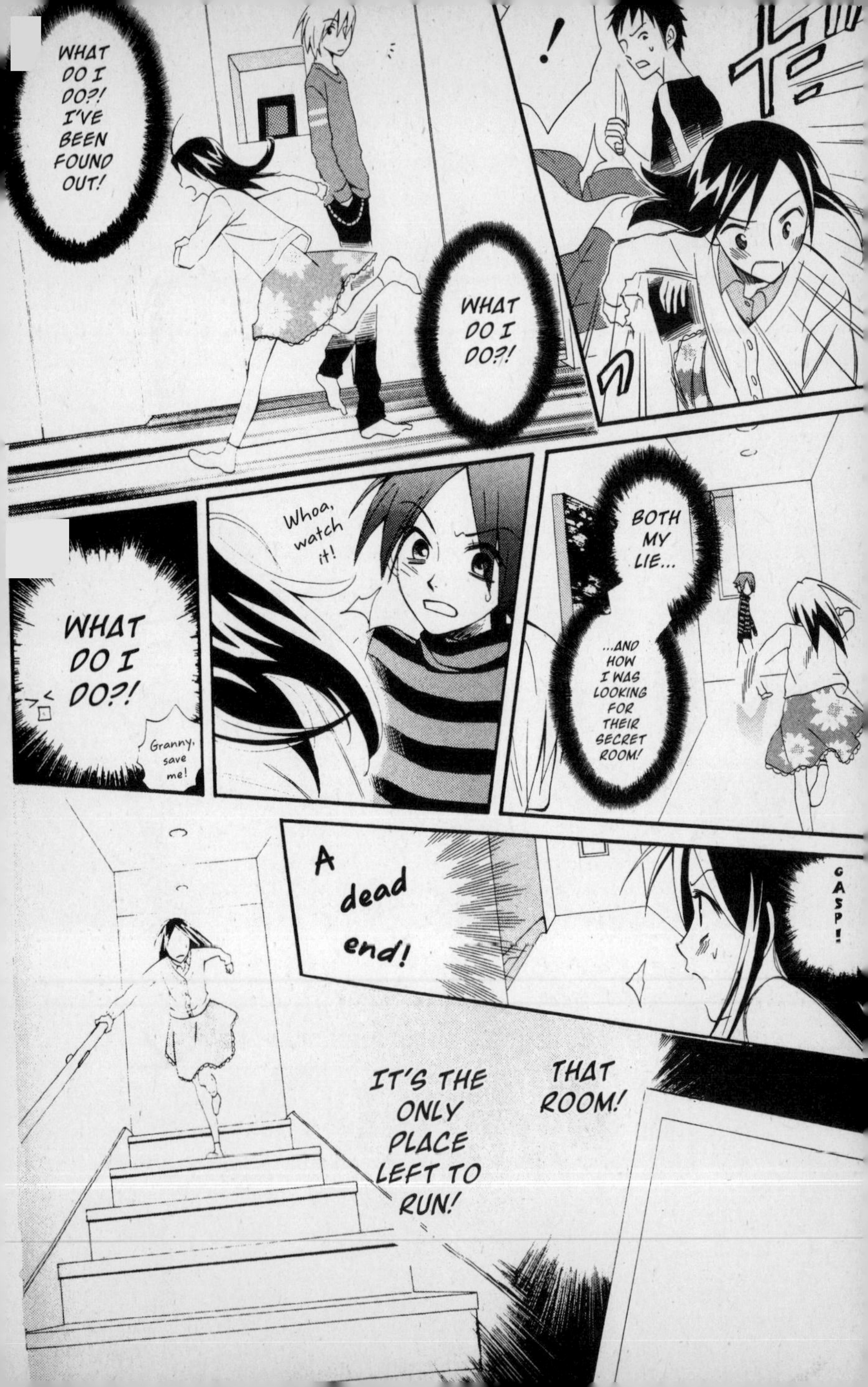
!
WHAT DO I DO?!
WHAT DO I DO?! I'VE BEEN FOUND OUT!
BOTH MY LIE...
...AND HOW I WAS LOOKING FOR THEIR SECRET ROOM!
Whoa, watch it!
WHAT DO I DO?!
Granny, save me!
GASP!
A dead end!
THAT ROOM!
IT'S THE ONLY PLACE LEFT TO RUN!

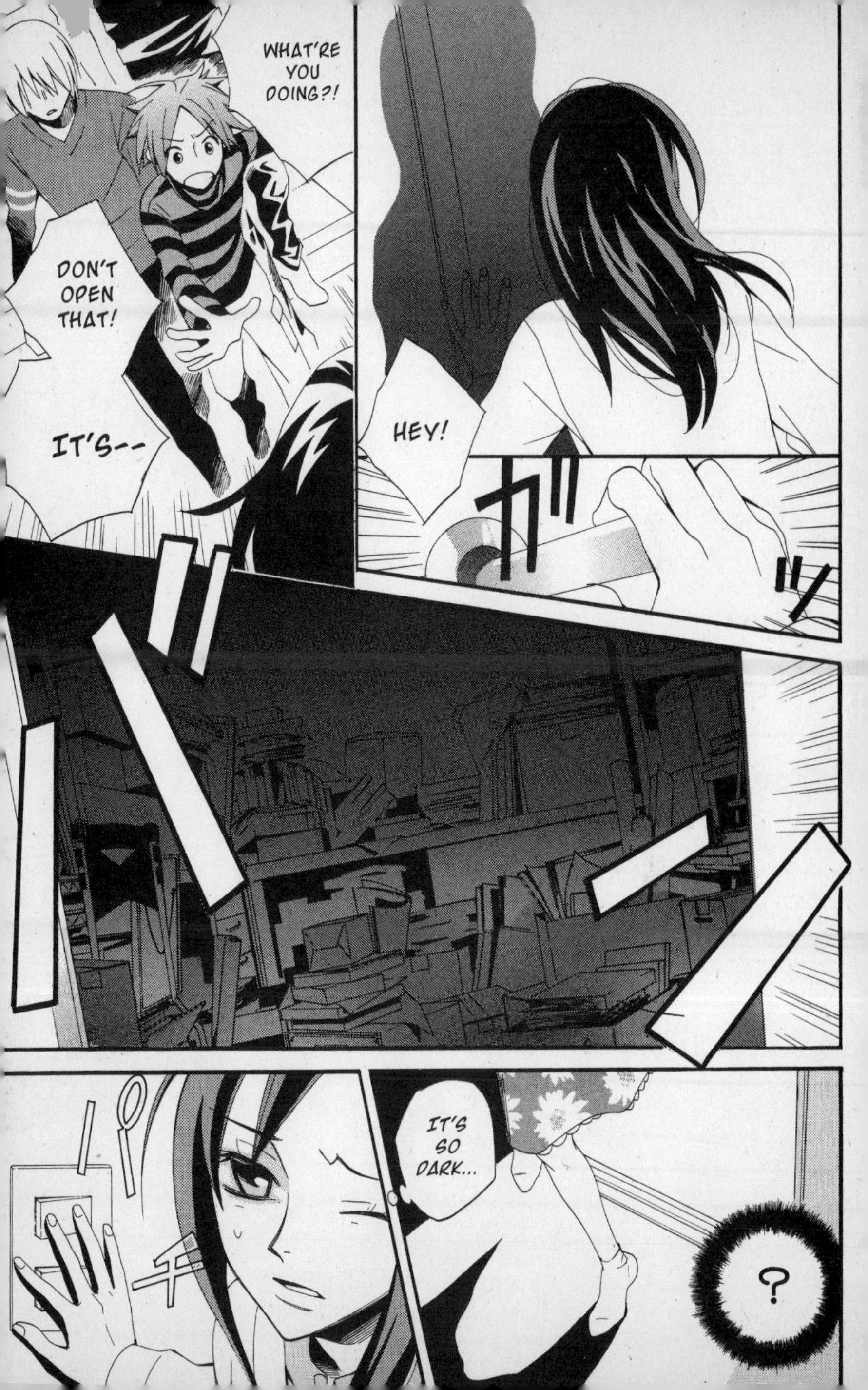
HEY!
ガッ
WHAT'RE YOU DOING?!
DON'T OPEN THAT!
IT'S--
?
IT'S SO DARK...

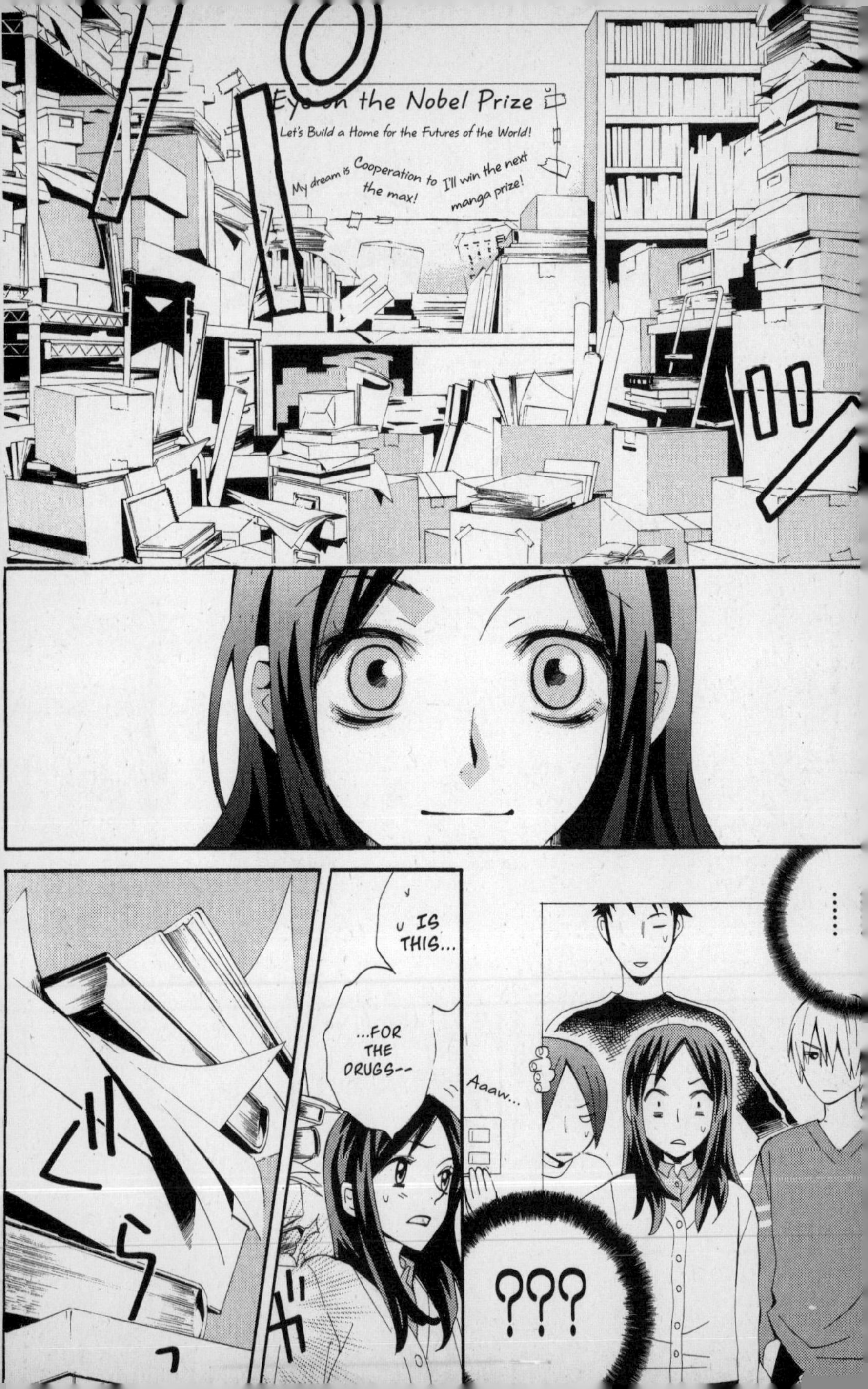

on the Nobel Prize
Let's Build a Home for the Futures of the World!
I'll win the next manga prize!
Cooperation to the max!
My dream is
......
IS THIS...
...FOR THE DRUGS--
Aaaw...
???

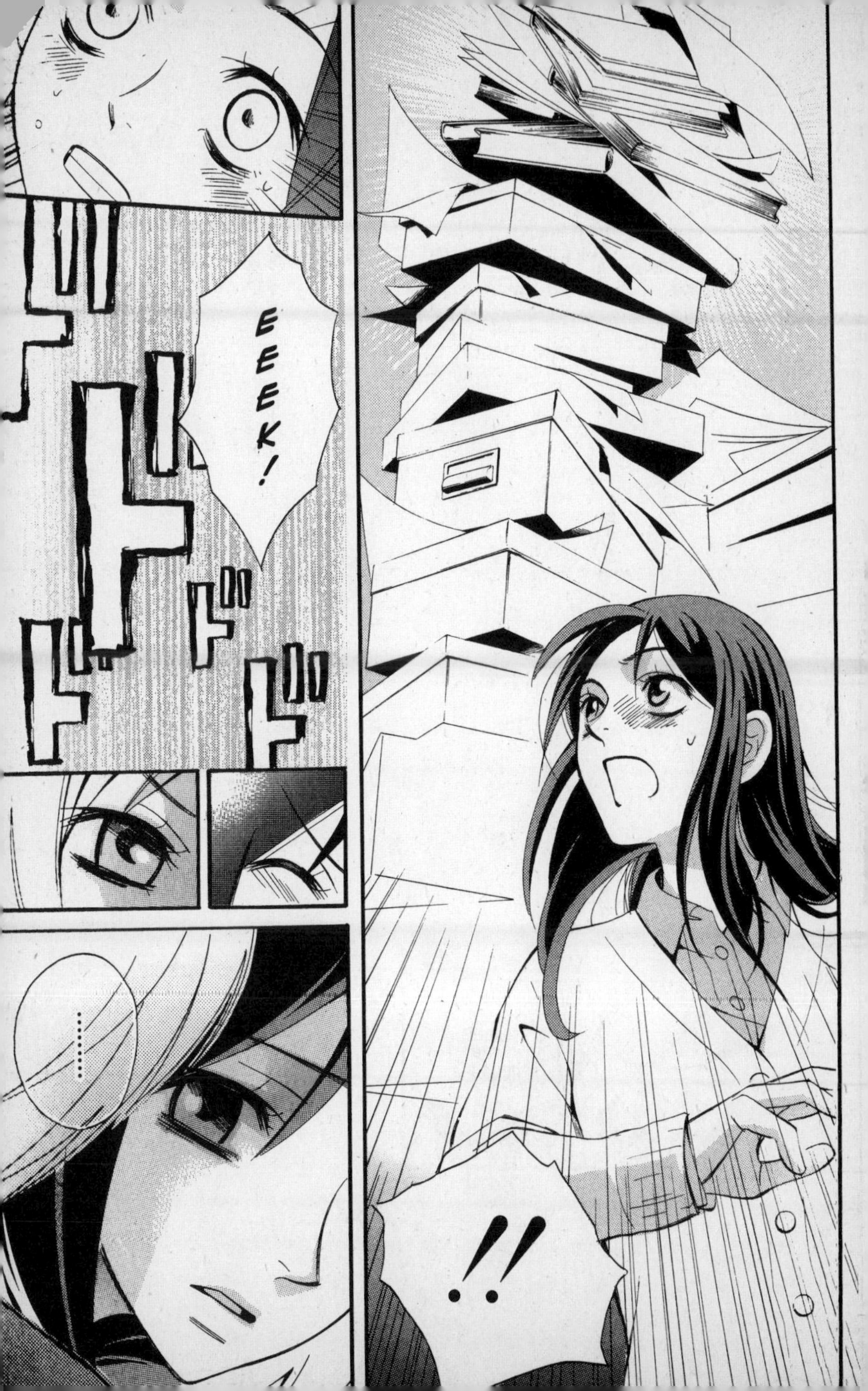
!!
EEEK!
ドドドドド
......

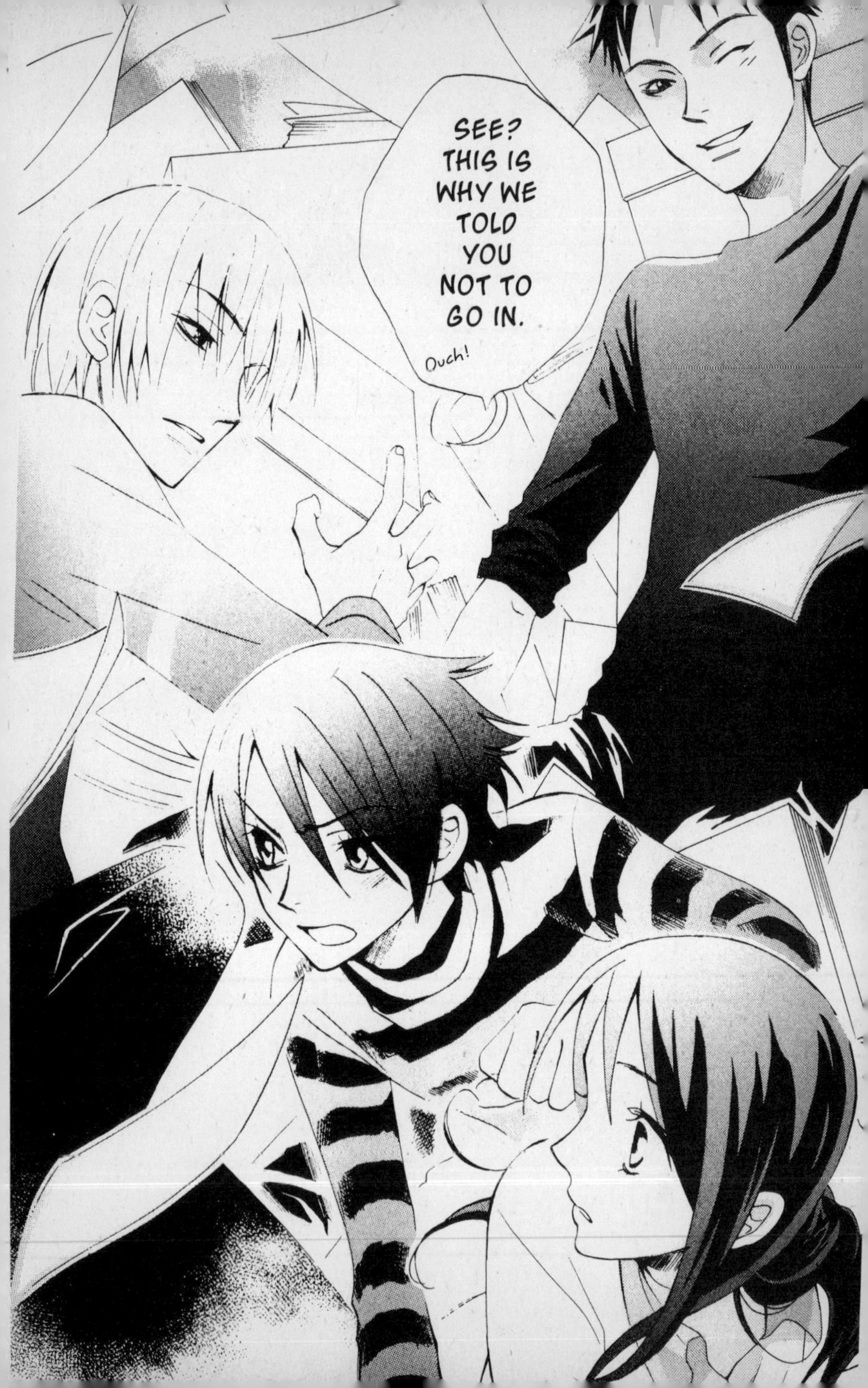
SEE? THIS IS WHY WE TOLD YOU NOT TO GO IN.
Ouch!

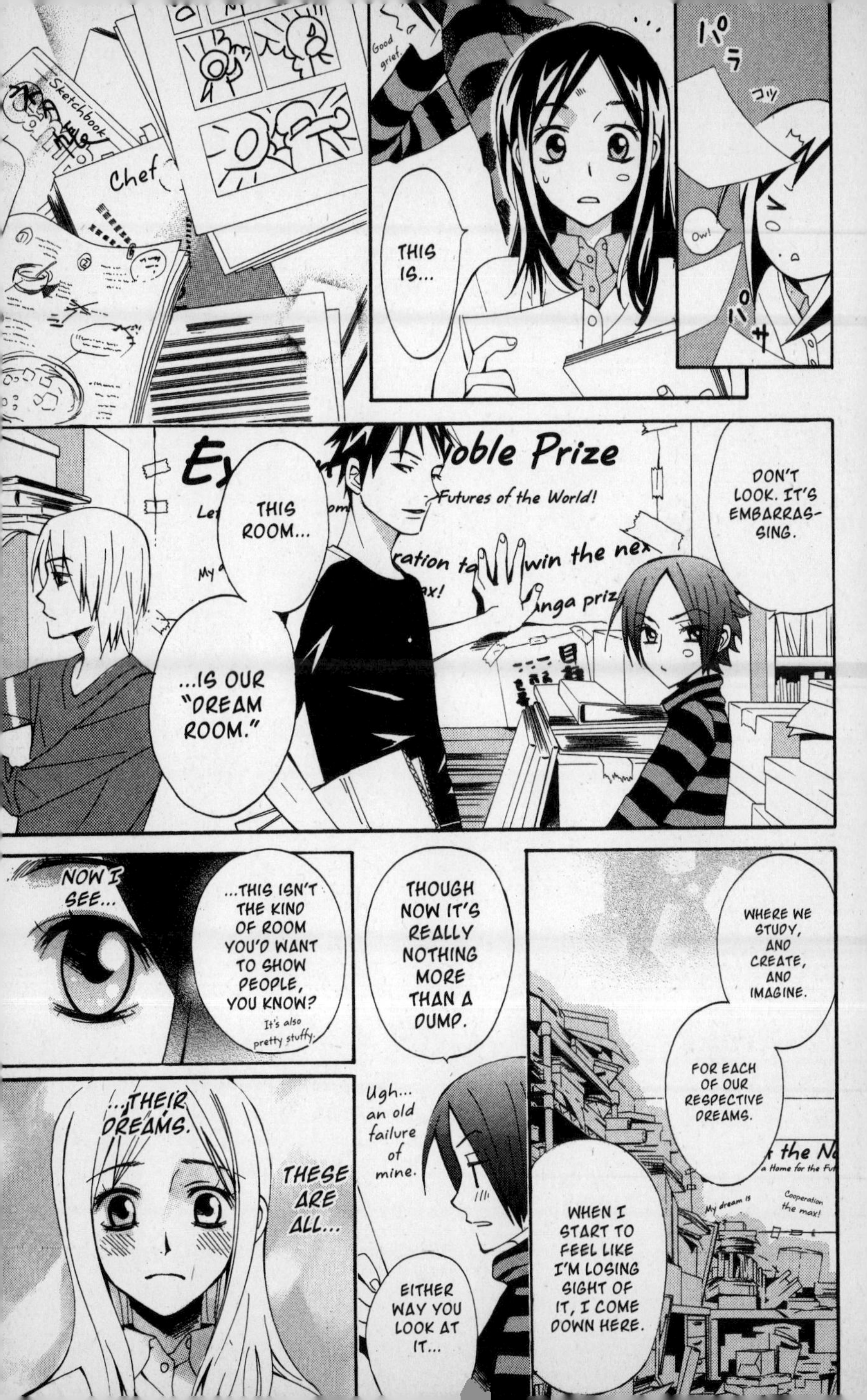
パラ
コツ
Ow!
パサ
Good grief.
THIS IS...
Sketchbook
Chef
DON'T LOOK. IT'S EMBARRASSING.
Futures of the World!
THIS ROOM...
...IS OUR "DREAM ROOM."
WHERE WE STUDY, AND CREATE, AND IMAGINE.
FOR EACH OF OUR RESPECTIVE DREAMS.
My dream is
Cooperation the max!
WHEN I START TO FEEL LIKE I'M LOSING SIGHT OF IT, I COME DOWN HERE.
THOUGH NOW IT'S REALLY NOTHING MORE THAN A DUMP.
Ugh... an old failure of mine.
EITHER WAY YOU LOOK AT IT...
...THIS ISN'T THE KIND OF ROOM YOU'D WANT TO SHOW PEOPLE, YOU KNOW?
It's also pretty stuffy.
NOW I SEE...
THESE ARE ALL...
...THEIR DREAMS.

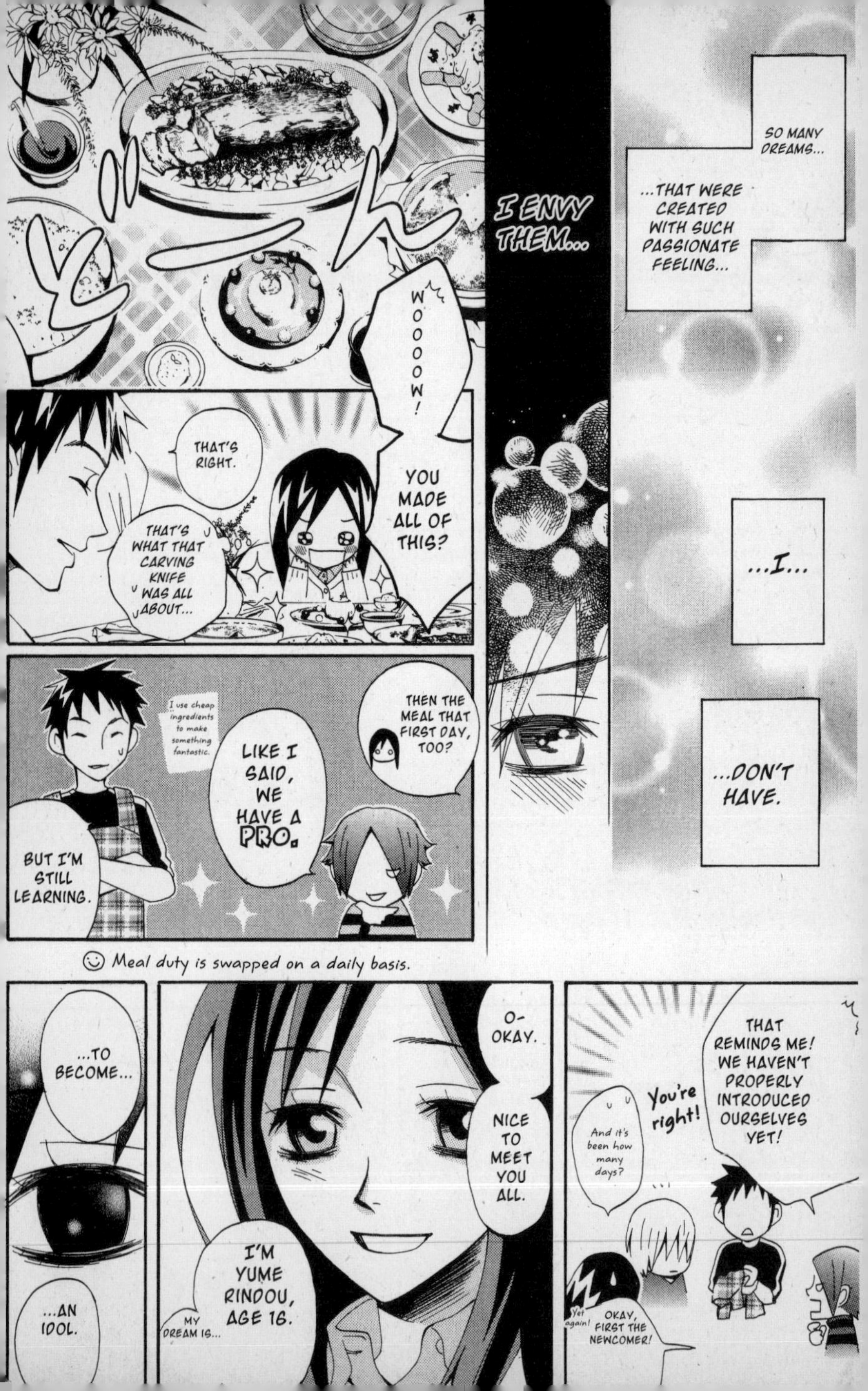
SO MANY DREAMS...
...THAT WERE CREATED WITH SUCH PASSIONATE FEELING...
I ENVY THEM...
...I...
...DON'T HAVE.
WOOOOOW!
YOU MADE ALL OF THIS?
THAT'S RIGHT.
THAT'S WHAT THAT CARVING KNIFE WAS ALL ABOUT...
THEN THE MEAL THAT FIRST DAY, TOO?
LIKE I SAID, WE HAVE A PRO.
I use cheap ingredients to make something fantastic.
BUT I'M STILL LEARNING.
Meal duty is swapped on a daily basis.
THAT REMINDS ME! WE HAVEN'T PROPERLY INTRODUCED OURSELVES YET!
You're right!
And it's been how many days?
OKAY, FIRST THE NEWCOMER!
Yet again!
O-OKAY.
NICE TO MEET YOU ALL.
I'M YUME RINDOU, AGE 16.
MY DREAM IS...
...TO BECOME...
...AN IDOL.

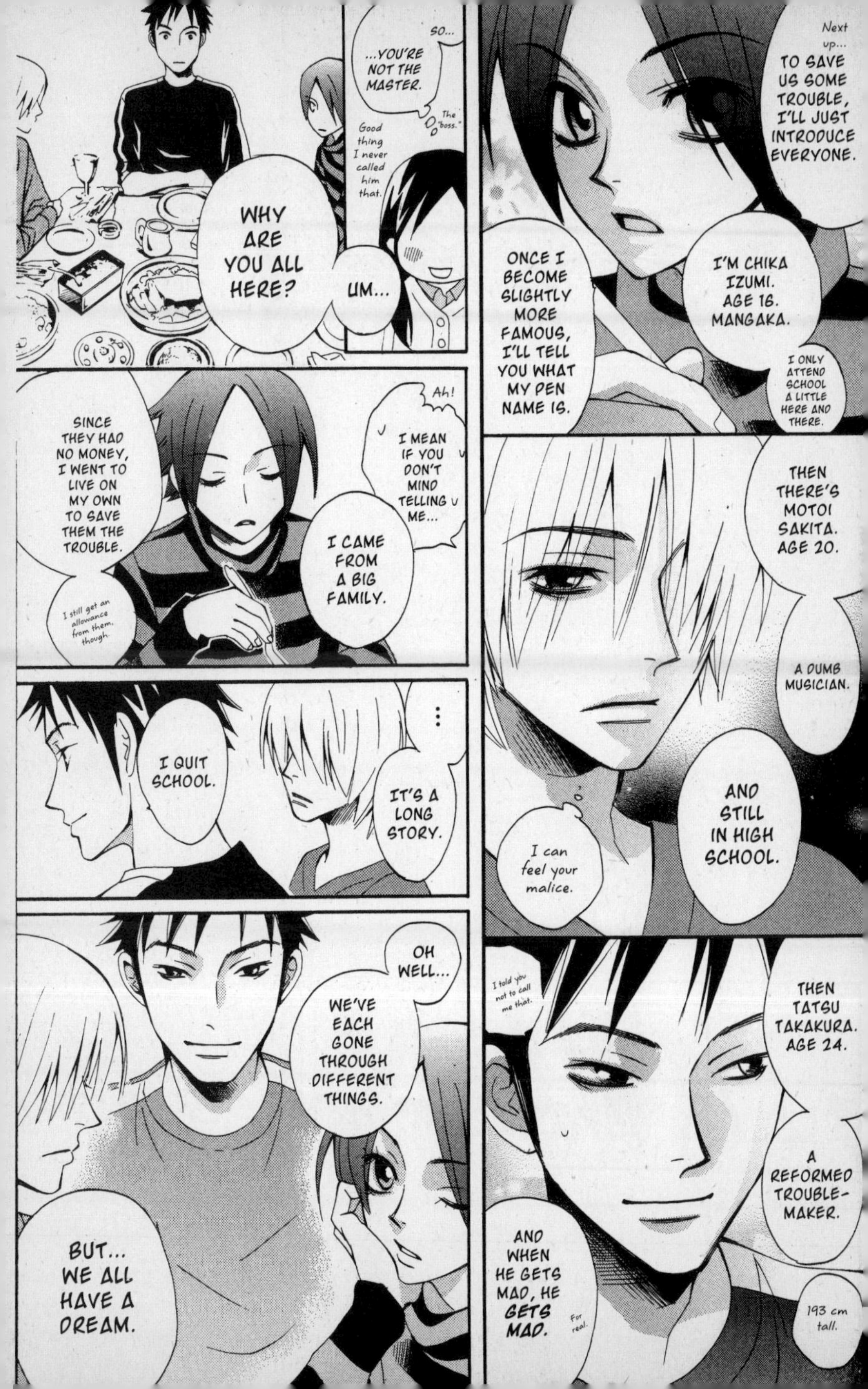
SO...
...YOU'RE NOT THE MASTER.
The "boss."
Good thing I never called him that.
UM...
WHY ARE YOU ALL HERE?
Ah!
I MEAN IF YOU DON'T MIND TELLING ME...
I CAME FROM A BIG FAMILY.
SINCE THEY HAD NO MONEY, I WENT TO LIVE ON MY OWN TO SAVE THEM THE TROUBLE.
I still get an allowance from them, though.
...
I QUIT SCHOOL.
IT'S A LONG STORY.
OH WELL...
WE'VE EACH GONE THROUGH DIFFERENT THINGS.
BUT... WE ALL HAVE A DREAM.
Next up...
TO SAVE US SOME TROUBLE, I'LL JUST INTRODUCE EVERYONE.
I'M CHIKA IZUMI. AGE 16. MANGAKA.
I ONLY ATTEND SCHOOL A LITTLE HERE AND THERE.
ONCE I BECOME SLIGHTLY MORE FAMOUS, I'LL TELL YOU WHAT MY PEN NAME IS.
THEN THERE'S MOTOI SAKITA. AGE 20.
A DUMB MUSICIAN.
AND STILL IN HIGH SCHOOL.
I can feel your malice.
THEN TATSU TAKAKURA. AGE 24.
I told you not to call me that.
A REFORMED TROUBLE-MAKER.
193 cm tall.
AND WHEN HE GETS MAD, HE GETS MAD.
For real.

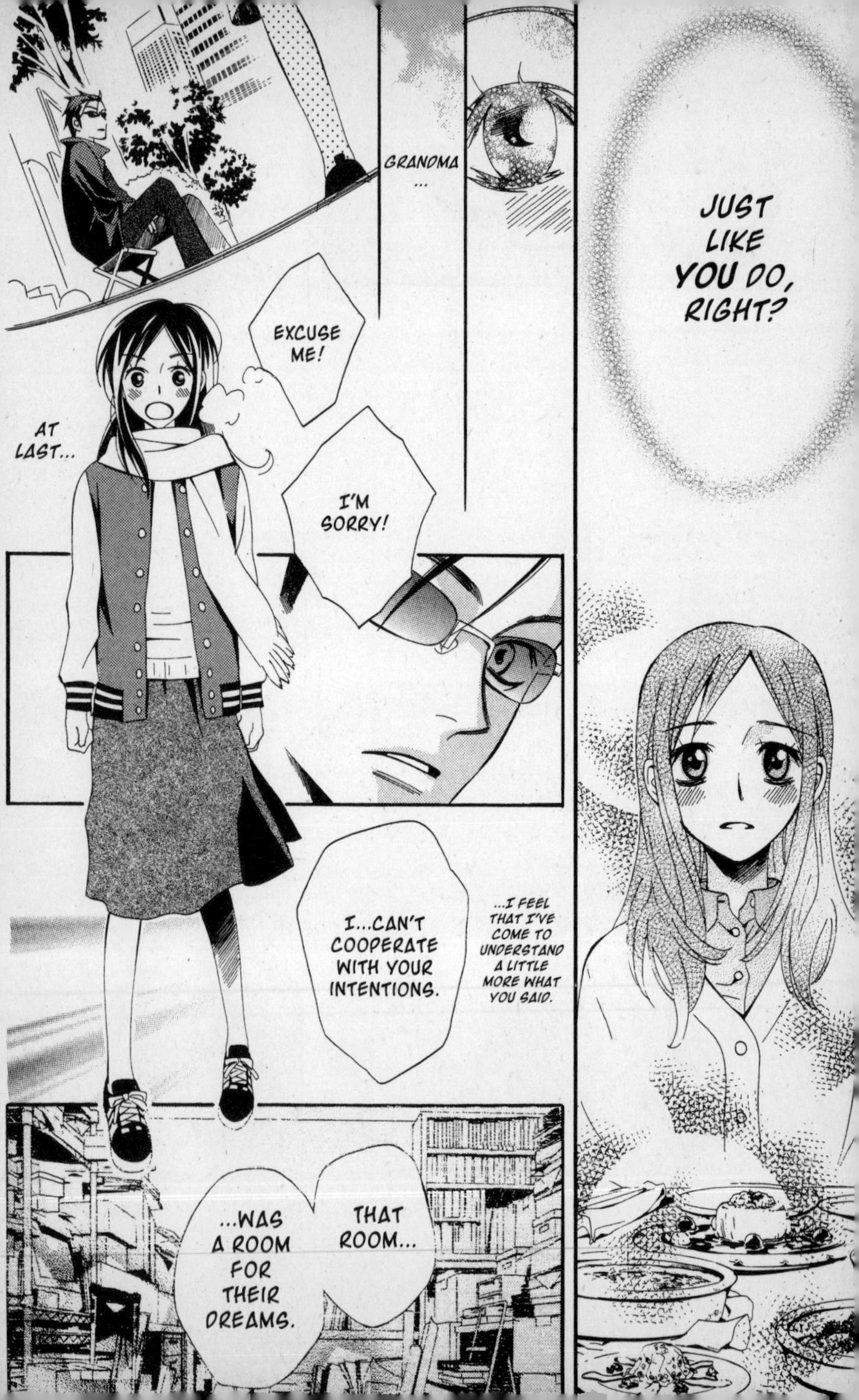
JUST LIKE YOU DO, RIGHT?
GRANDMA...
EXCUSE ME!
I'M SORRY!
AT LAST...
...I FEEL THAT I'VE COME TO UNDERSTAND A LITTLE MORE WHAT YOU SAID.
I...CAN'T COOPERATE WITH YOUR INTENTIONS.
THAT ROOM...
...WAS A ROOM FOR THEIR DREAMS.

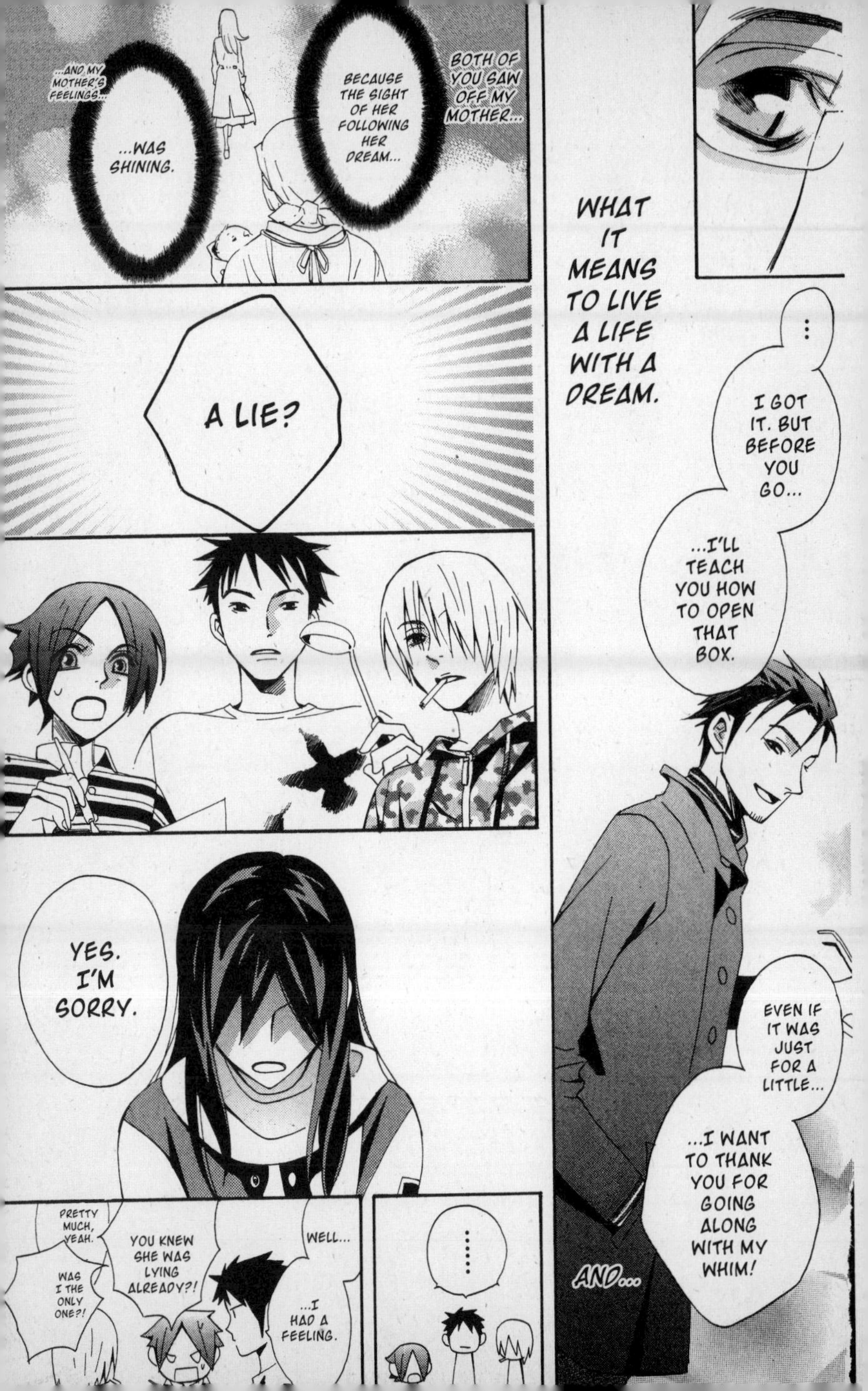
BOTH OF YOU SAW OFF MY MOTHER...
BECAUSE THE SIGHT OF HER FOLLOWING HER DREAM...
...WAS SHINING.
...AND MY MOTHER'S FEELINGS...
WHAT IT MEANS TO LIVE A LIFE WITH A DREAM.
...
I GOT IT. BUT BEFORE YOU GO...
...I'LL TEACH YOU HOW TO OPEN THAT BOX.
EVEN IF IT WAS JUST FOR A LITTLE...
...I WANT TO THANK YOU FOR GOING ALONG WITH MY WHIM!
AND...
A LIE?
YES. I'M SORRY.
......
WELL...
...I HAD A FEELING.
YOU KNEW SHE WAS LYING ALREADY?!
PRETTY MUCH, YEAH.
WAS I THE ONLY ONE?!

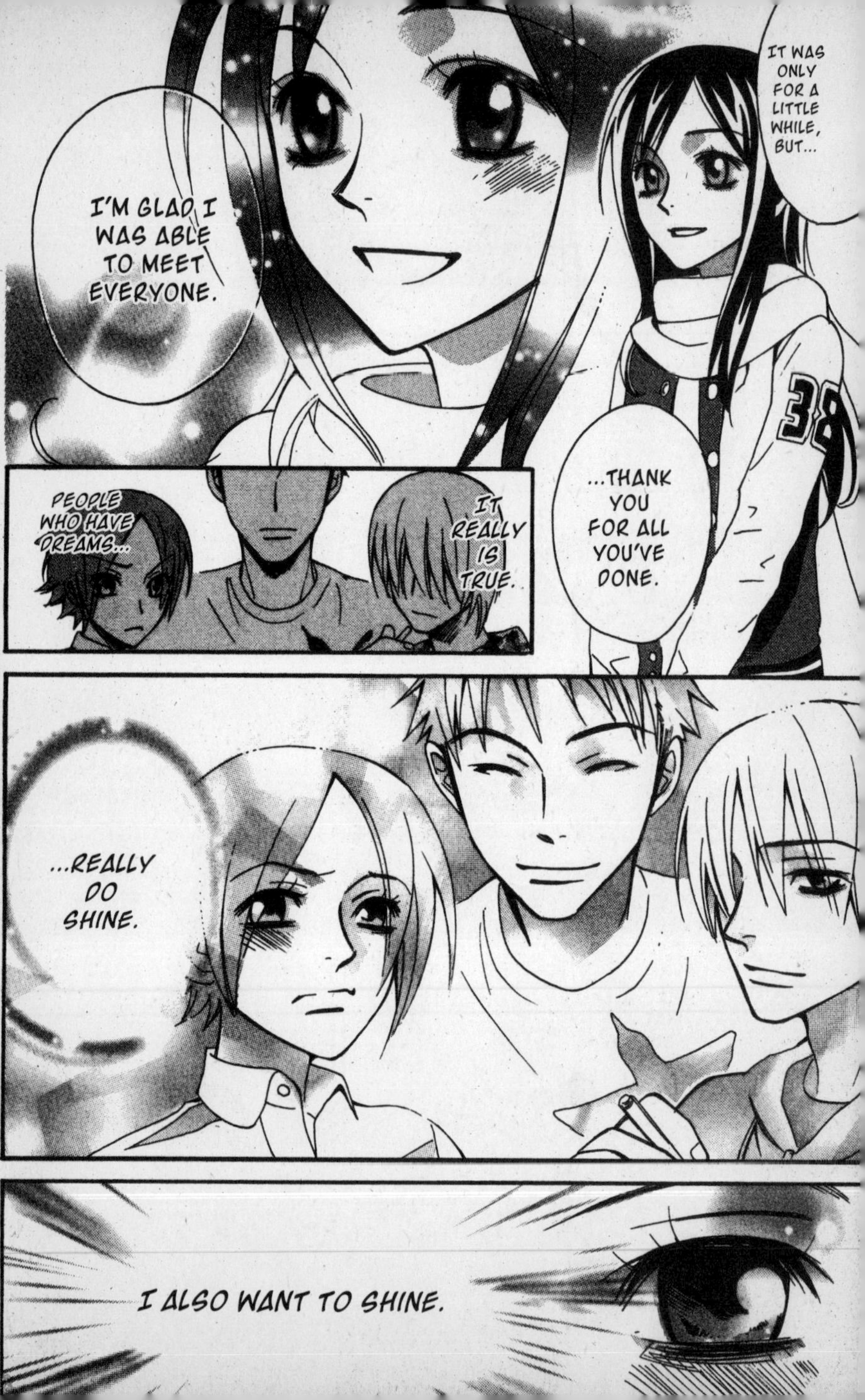
IT WAS ONLY FOR A LITTLE WHILE, BUT...
...THANK YOU FOR ALL YOU'VE DONE.
I'M GLAD I WAS ABLE TO MEET EVERYONE.
IT REALLY IS TRUE.
PEOPLE WHO HAVE DREAMS...
...REALLY DO SHINE.
I ALSO WANT TO SHINE.

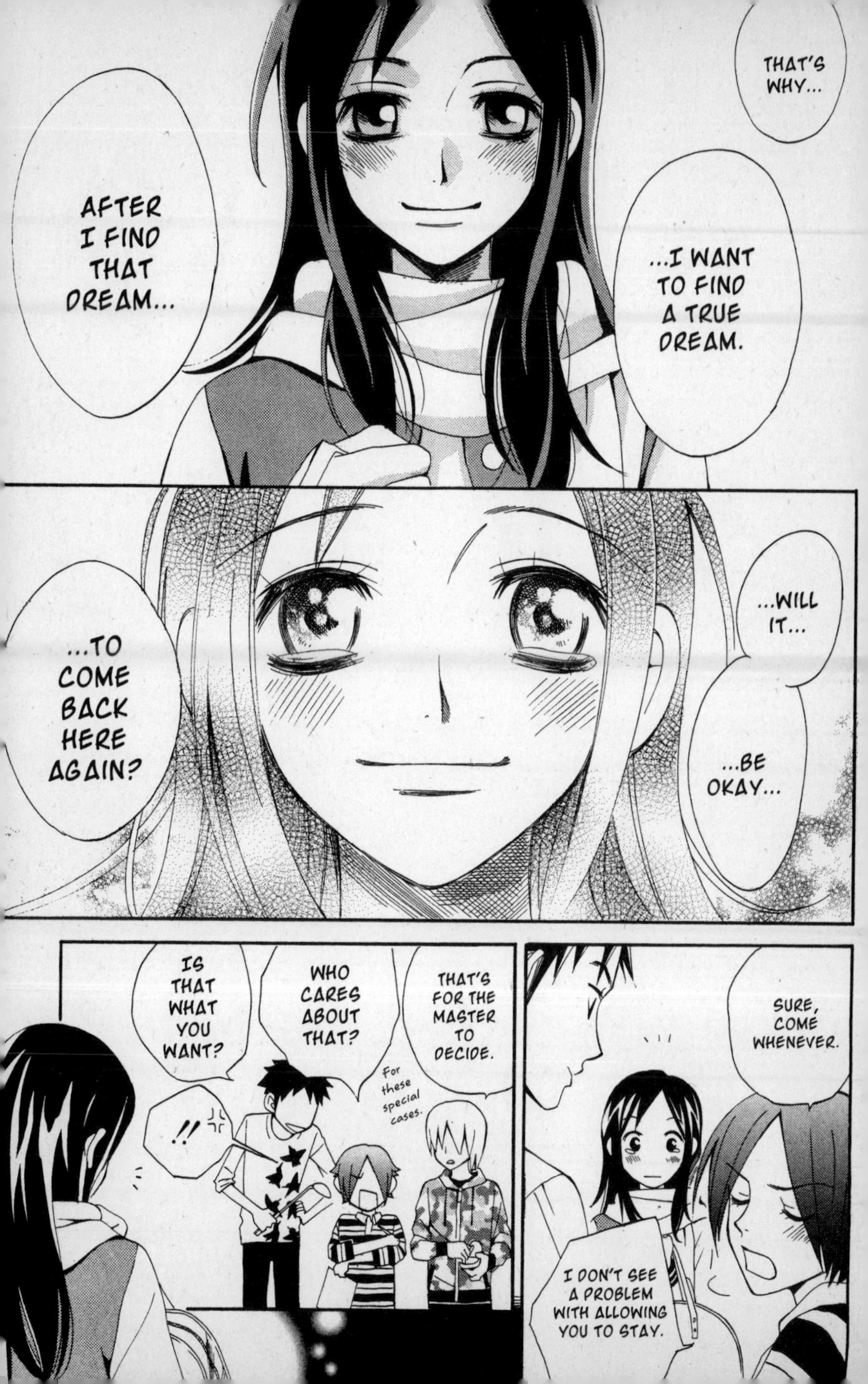
THAT'S WHY...
...I WANT TO FIND A TRUE DREAM.
AFTER I FIND THAT DREAM...
...WILL IT...
...BE OKAY...
...TO COME BACK HERE AGAIN?
SURE, COME WHENEVER.
I DON'T SEE A PROBLEM WITH ALLOWING YOU TO STAY.
THAT'S FOR THE MASTER TO DECIDE.
For these special cases.
WHO CARES ABOUT THAT?
IS THAT WHAT YOU WANT?
!!

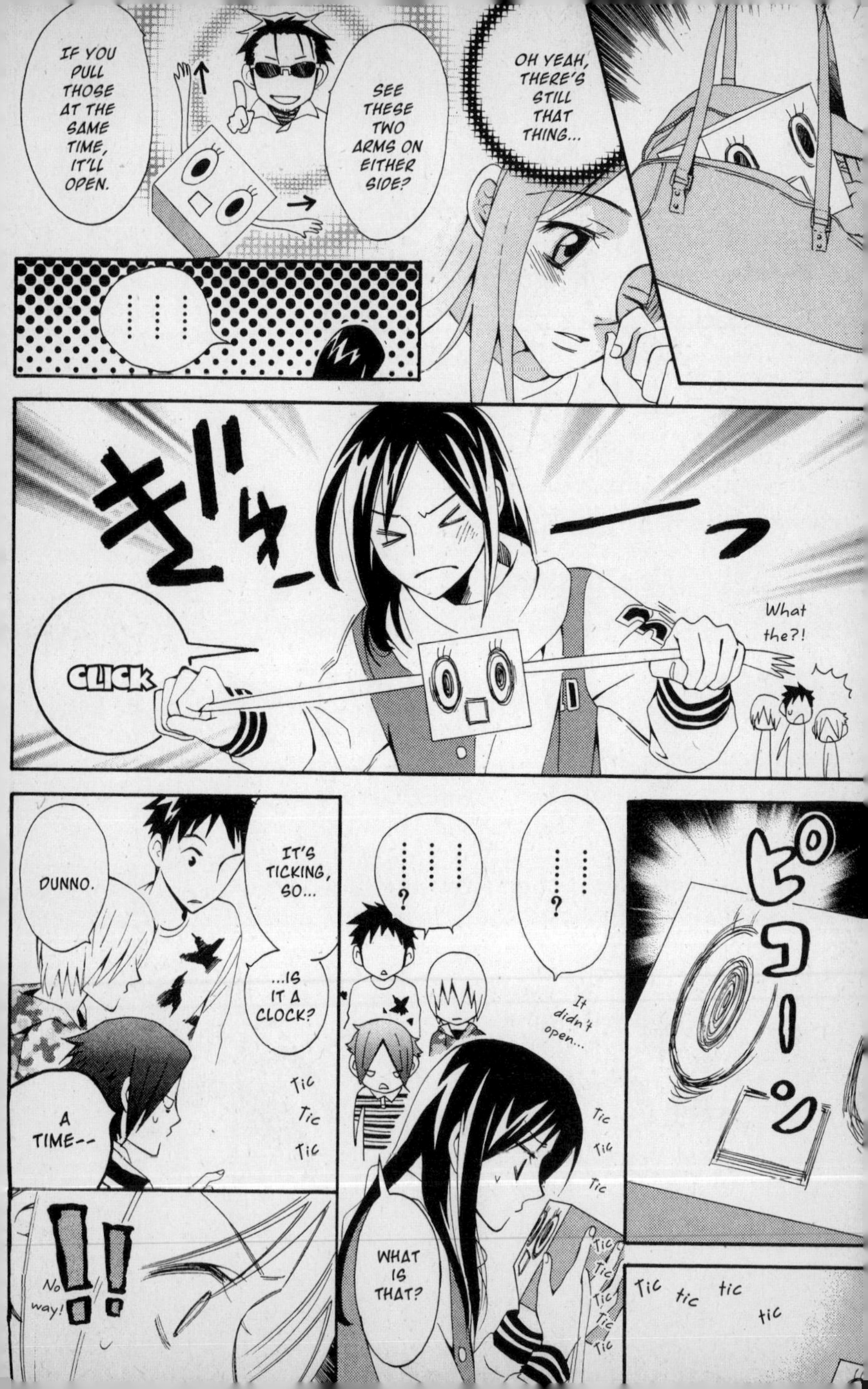
OH YEAH, THERE'S STILL THAT THING...
SEE THESE TWO ARMS ON EITHER SIDE?
IF YOU PULL THOSE AT THE SAME TIME, IT'LL OPEN.
......
ぎゅーっ
What the?!
CLICK
ピコーン
......?
......?
It didn't open...
Tic
Tic
Tic
IT'S TICKING, SO...
DUNNO.
...IS IT A CLOCK?
A TIME--
Tic
Tic
Tic
Tic tic tic tic
WHAT IS THAT?
Tic
Tic
Tic
Tic
Tic
Tic
!!
No way!

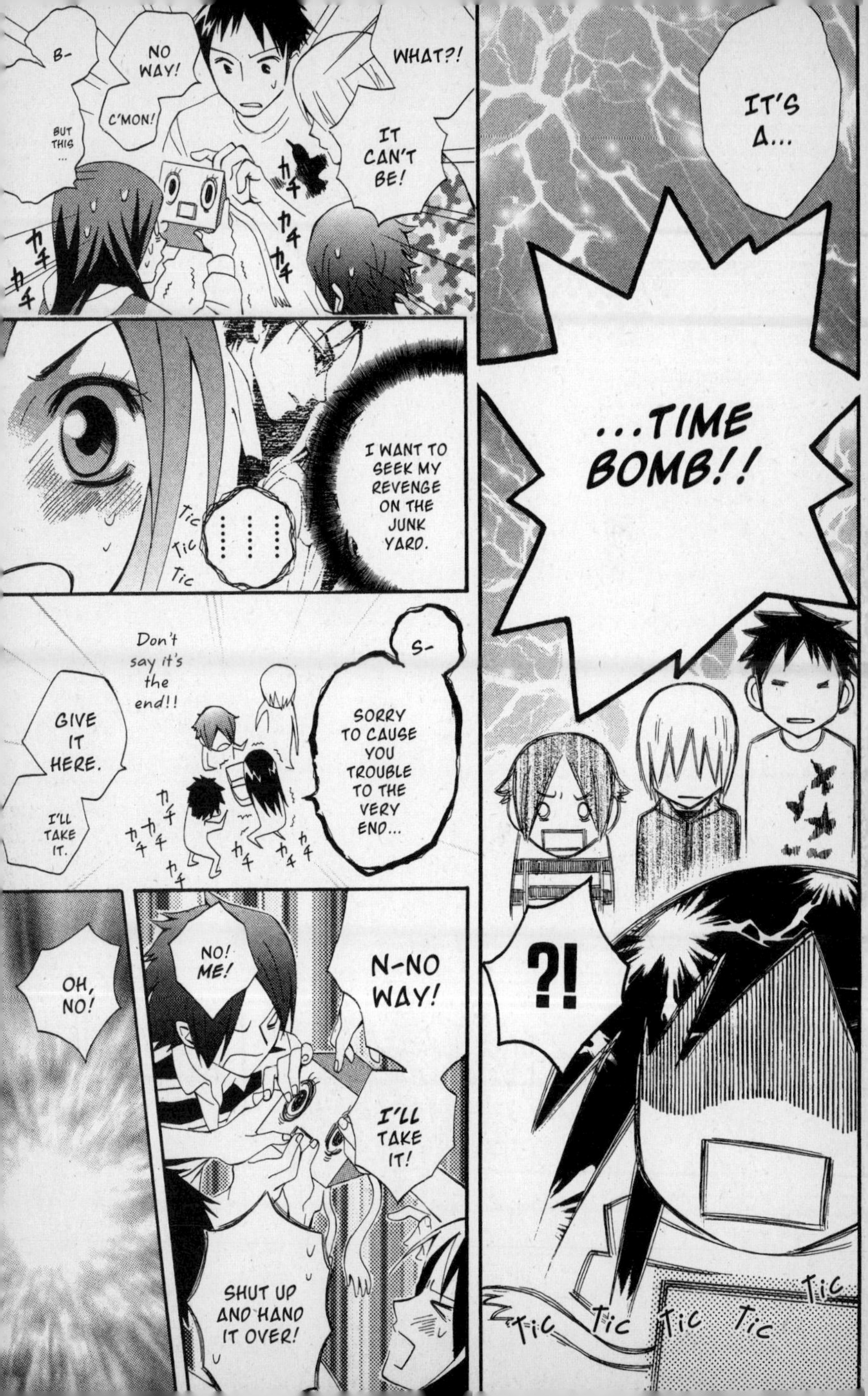
IT'S A...
...TIME BOMB!!
?!
Tic Tic Tic Tic Tic
WHAT?!
NO WAY!
B-
C'MON!
BUT THIS...
IT CAN'T BE!
カチ カチ カチ カチ カチ
I WANT TO SEEK MY REVENGE ON THE JUNK YARD.
......
Tic Tic Tic
S-
SORRY TO CAUSE YOU TROUBLE TO THE VERY END...
Don't say it's the end!!
GIVE IT HERE.
I'LL TAKE IT.
カチ カチ カチ カチ カチ カチ
N-NO WAY!
NO! ME!
I'LL TAKE IT!
SHUT UP AND HAND IT OVER!
OH, NO!

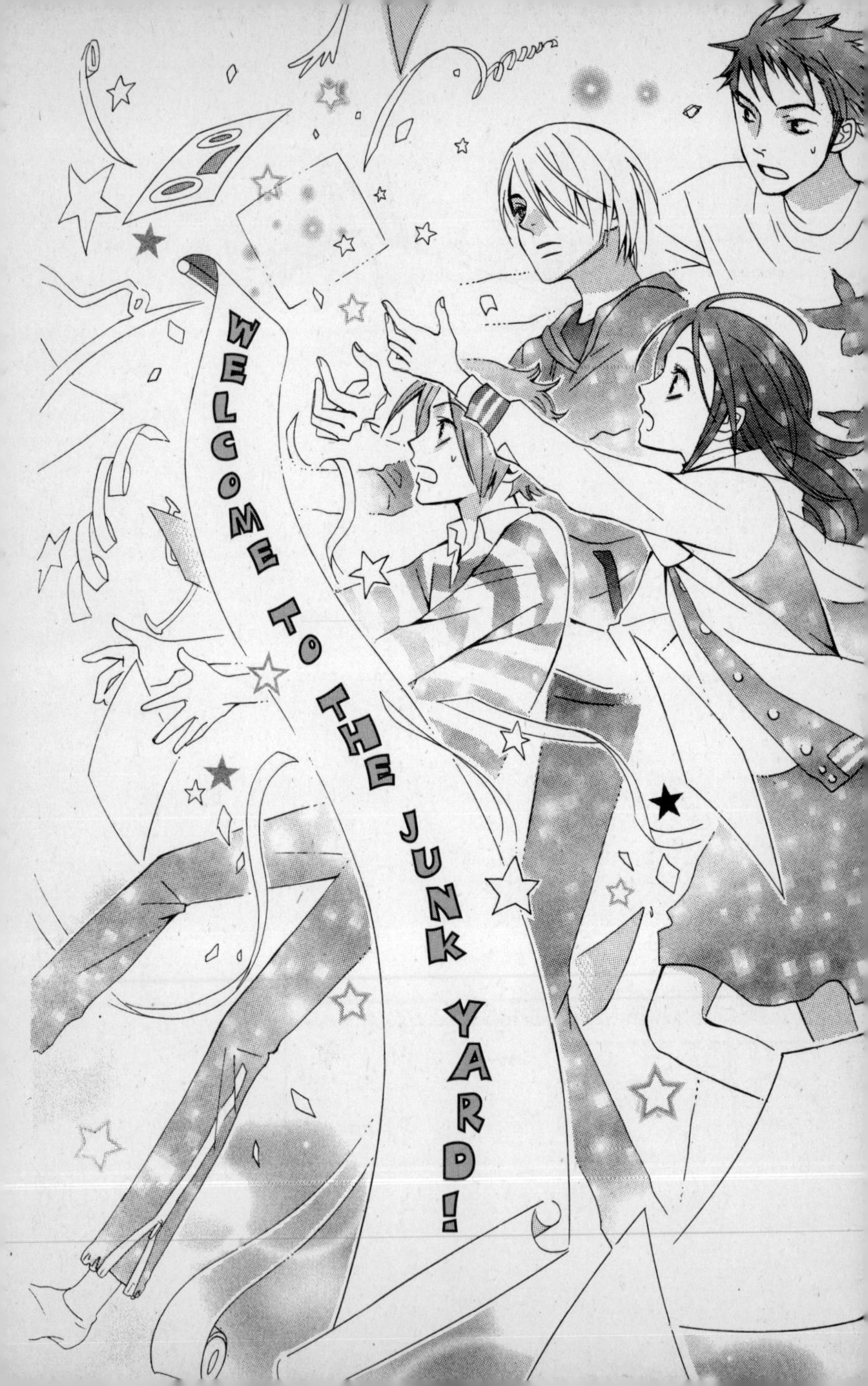
WELCOME TO THE JUNK YARD!

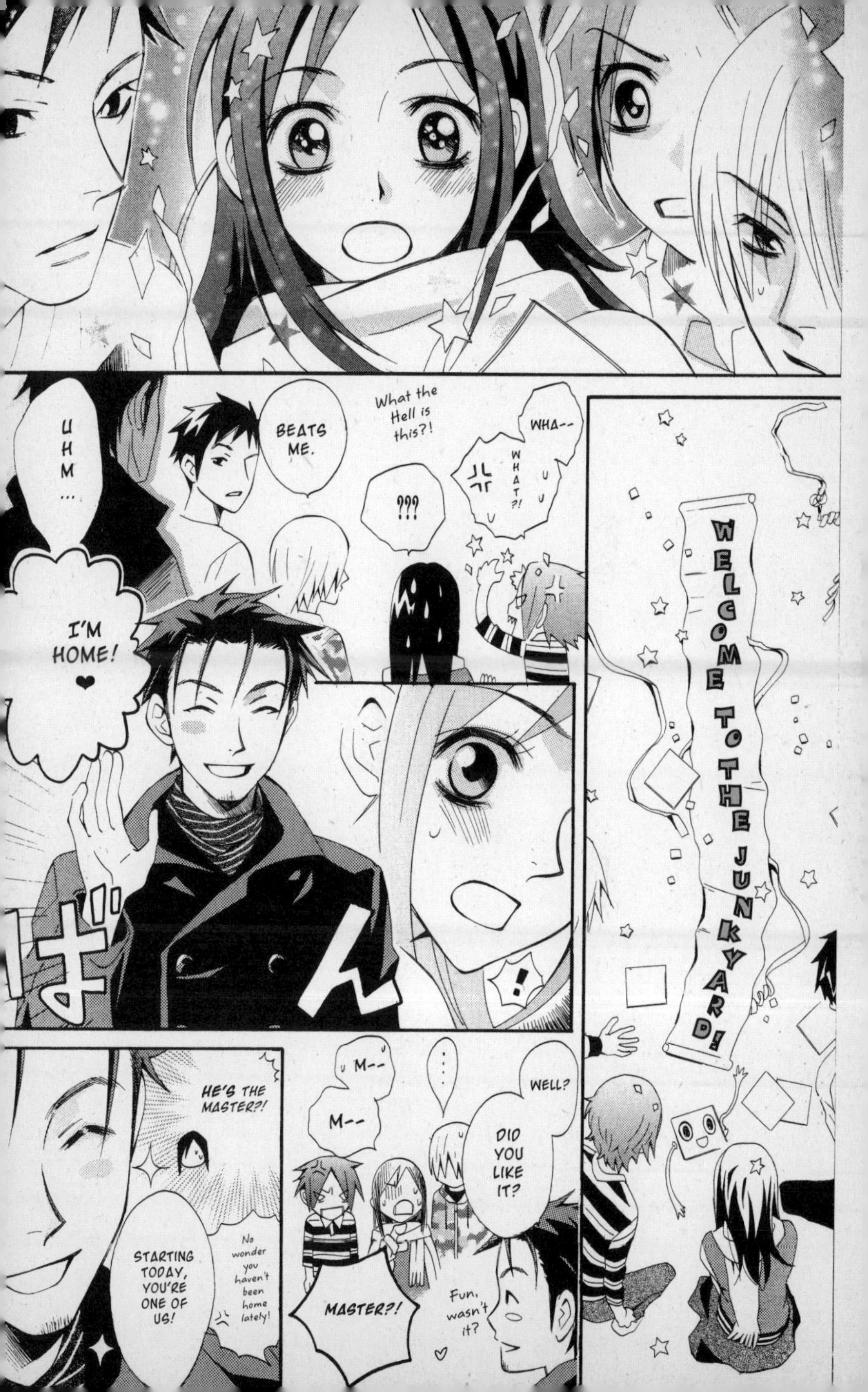
WELCOME TO THE JUNKYARD!
WHA--
WHAT?!
What the Hell is this?!
???
BEATS ME.
UHM...
!
I'M HOME! ❤
ぱん
WELL?
DID YOU LIKE IT?
...
M--
M--
Fun, wasn't it?
MASTER?!
HE'S THE MASTER?!
STARTING TODAY, YOU'RE ONE OF US!
No wonder you haven't been home lately!

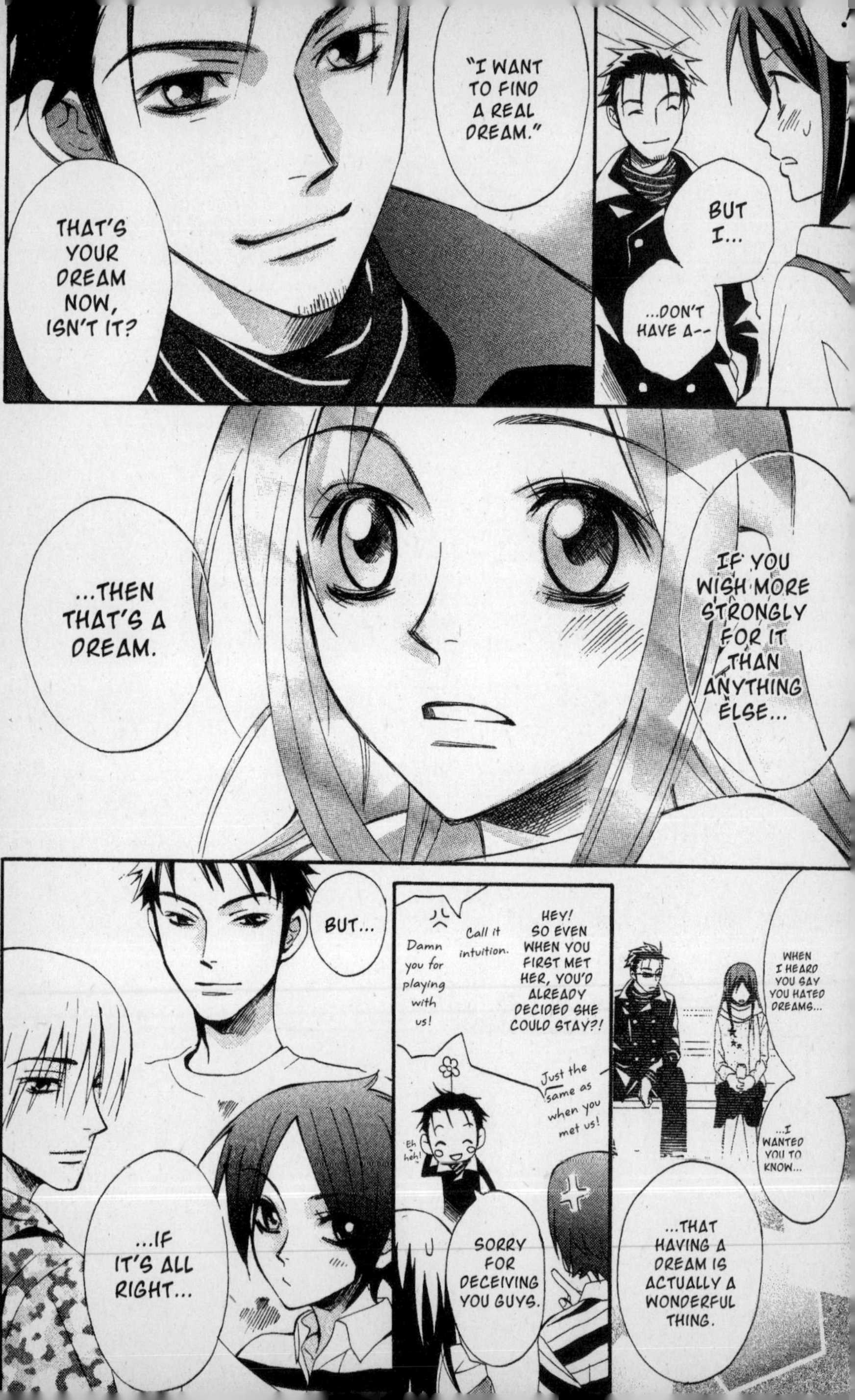
BUT I...
...DON'T HAVE A--
"I WANT TO FIND A REAL DREAM."
THAT'S YOUR DREAM NOW, ISN'T IT?
IF YOU WISH MORE STRONGLY FOR IT THAN ANYTHING ELSE...
...THEN THAT'S A DREAM.
WHEN I HEARD YOU SAY YOU HATED DREAMS...
...I WANTED YOU TO KNOW...
...THAT HAVING A DREAM IS ACTUALLY A WONDERFUL THING.
HEY! SO EVEN WHEN YOU FIRST MET HER, YOU'D ALREADY DECIDED SHE COULD STAY?!
Call it intuition.
Damn you for playing with us!
Just the same as when you met us!
Eh heh!
SORRY FOR DECEIVING YOU GUYS.
BUT...
...IF IT'S ALL RIGHT...

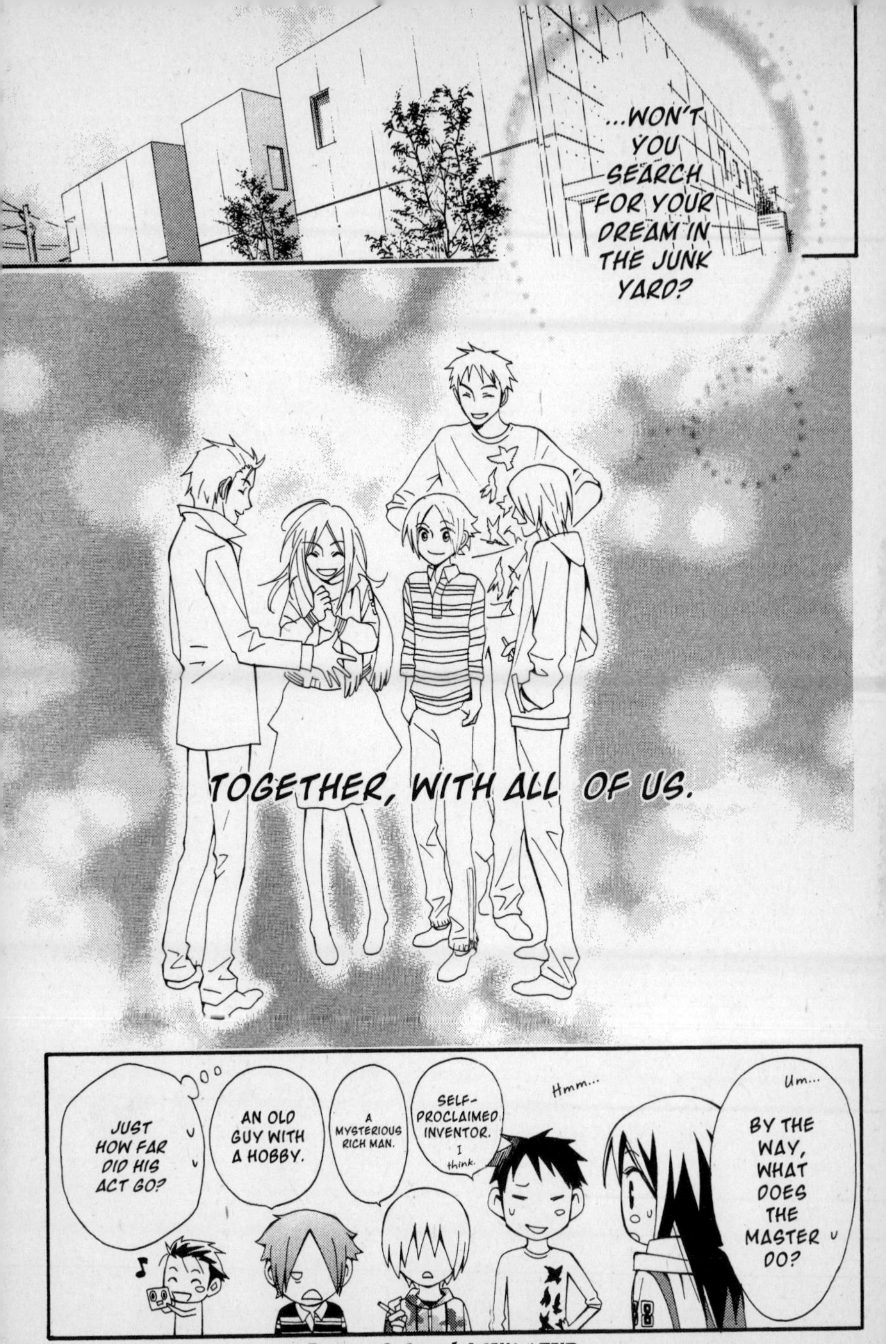
...WON'T YOU SEARCH FOR YOUR DREAM IN THE JUNK YARD?
TOGETHER, WITH ALL OF US.
Um...
BY THE WAY, WHAT DOES THE MASTER DO?
Hmm...
SELF-PROCLAIMED INVENTOR. I think.
A MYSTERIOUS RICH MAN.
AN OLD GUY WITH A HOBBY.
JUST HOW FAR DID HIS ACT GO?

Dream Colored JUNK / END

THANK YOU FOR READING! I HOPE TO SEE YOU AGAIN!

SPECIAL THANKS!!

→ NECCHII, SAYAKA-SAN, YUUKI-SEMPAI, UME, ABE-SAN, INOUE-SAN, SHIMADA-SAN, EJI, FUJIWARA-SAN, YANEYAN, IZUMI-SAN, MY FAMILY, AND ALL THE OTHERS TO WHOM I OWE SO MUCH! REALLY A MILLION THANK YOU'S TO EVERYONE! I'D NEVER BE ABLE TO DO IT ON MY OWN.

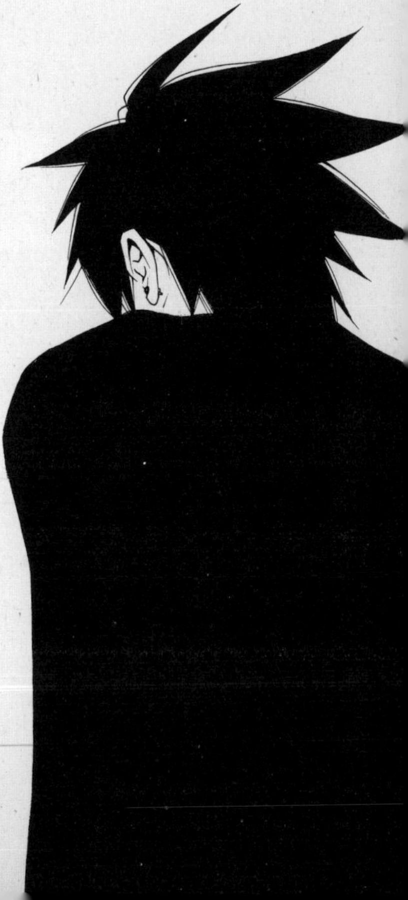

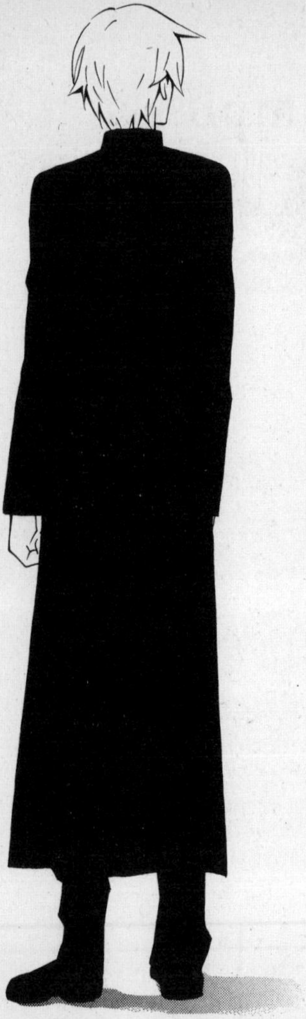

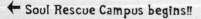

← Soul Rescue Campus begins!!

I keep deliberating between thinking it was a good idea or not to throw in a Soul Rescue Campus story after all this.

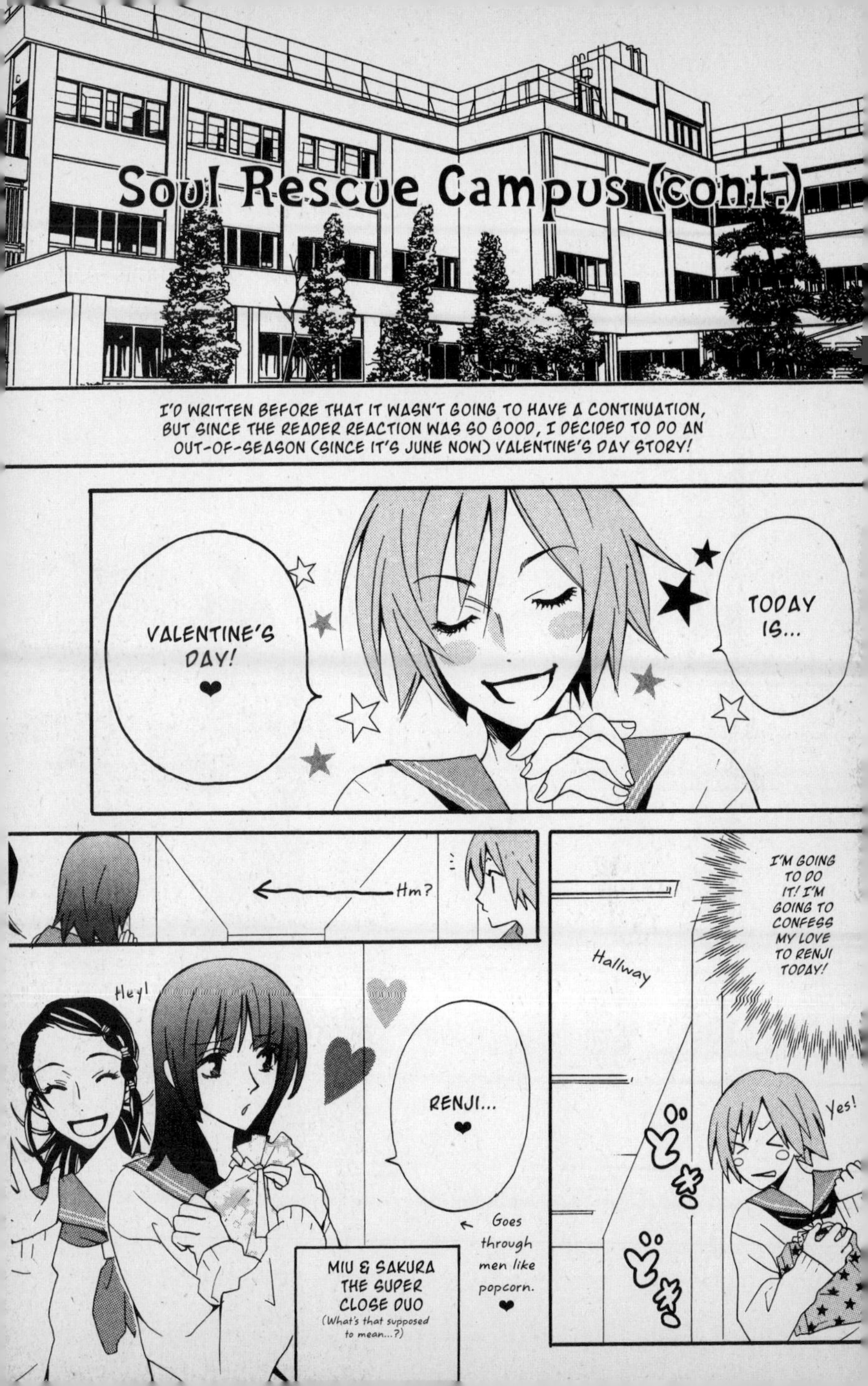
Soul Rescue Campus (cont.)
I'D WRITTEN BEFORE THAT IT WASN'T GOING TO HAVE A CONTINUATION, BUT SINCE THE READER REACTION WAS SO GOOD, I DECIDED TO DO AN OUT-OF-SEASON (SINCE IT'S JUNE NOW) VALENTINE'S DAY STORY!
TODAY IS...
VALENTINE'S DAY! ❤
I'M GOING TO DO IT! I'M GOING TO CONFESS MY LOVE TO RENJI TODAY!
Hallway
Yes!
Hm?
RENJI... ❤
Goes through men like popcorn. ❤
Hey!
MIU & SAKURA THE SUPER CLOSE DUO
(What's that supposed to mean...?)

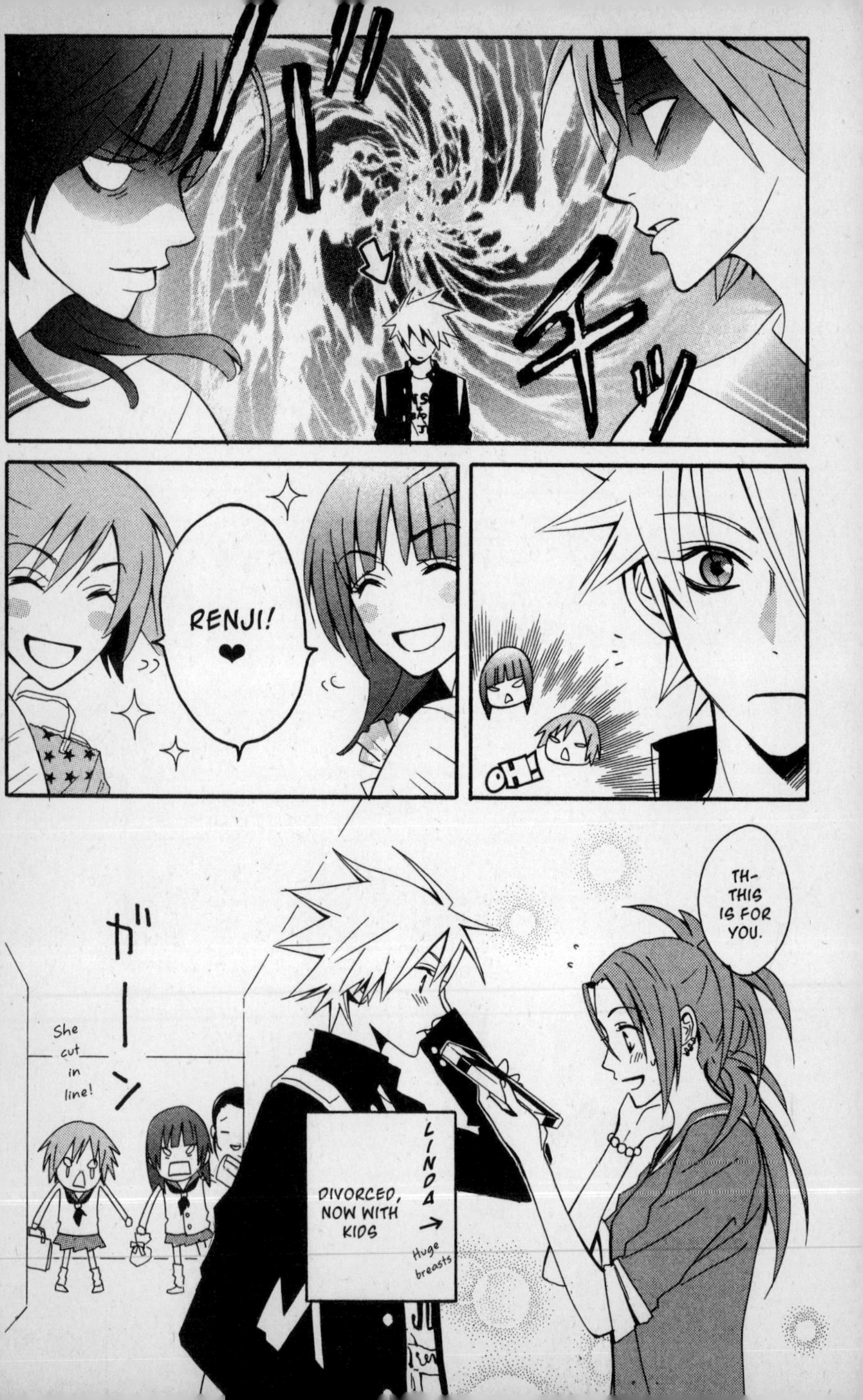
OH!
RENJI! ❤
TH- THIS IS FOR YOU.
ガーン
LINDA
DIVORCED, NOW WITH KIDS
Huge breasts
She cut in line!

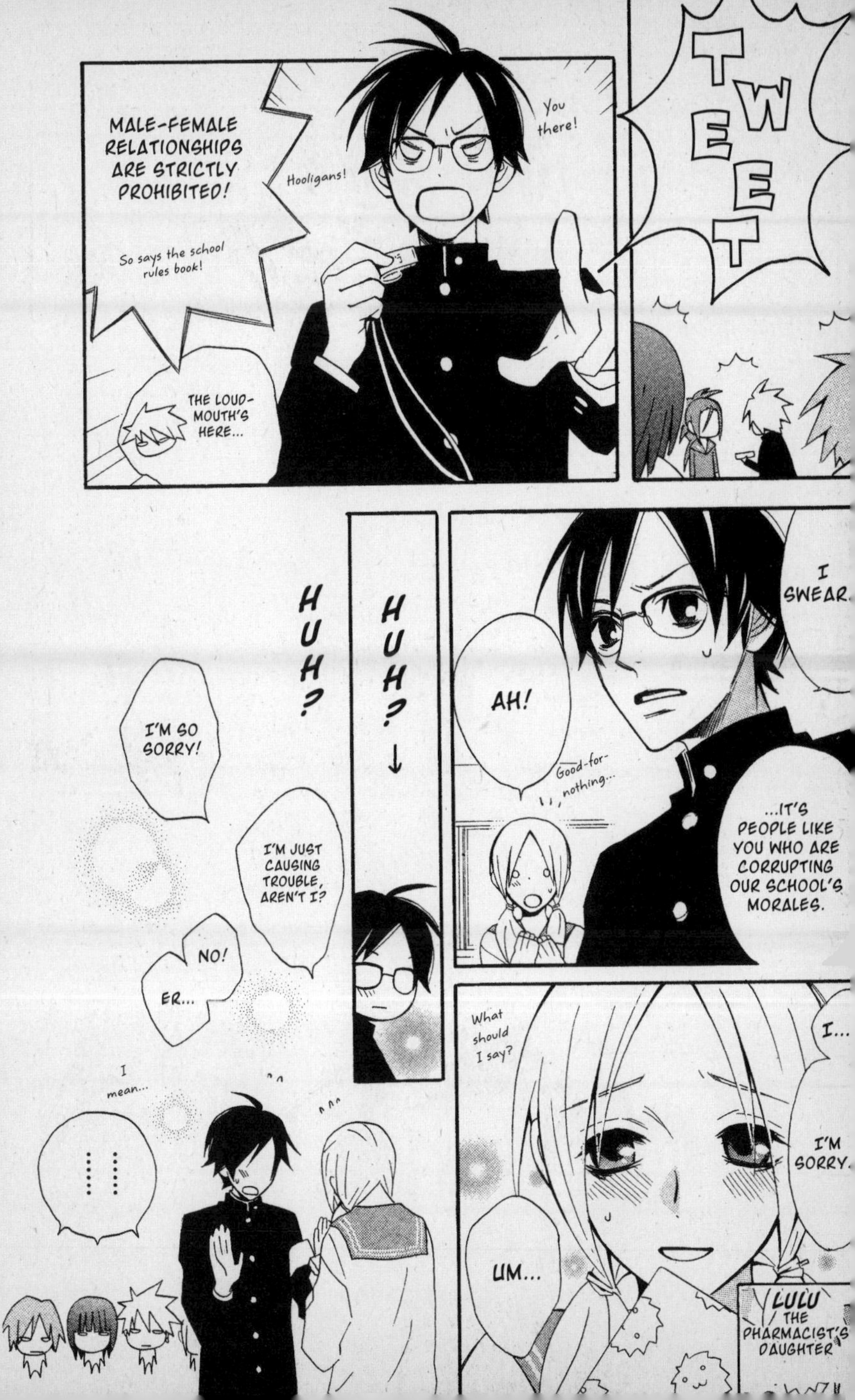
TWEET
You there!
Hooligans!
MALE-FEMALE RELATIONSHIPS ARE STRICTLY PROHIBITED!
So says the school rules book!
THE LOUD-MOUTH'S HERE...
I SWEAR.
AH!
Good-for-nothing...
...IT'S PEOPLE LIKE YOU WHO ARE CORRUPTING OUR SCHOOL'S MORALES.
I...
What should I say?
I'M SORRY.
UM...
LULU THE PHARMACIST'S DAUGHTER
HUH?
HUH? ↓
I'M SO SORRY!
I'M JUST CAUSING TROUBLE, AREN'T I?
NO!
ER...
I mean...
......

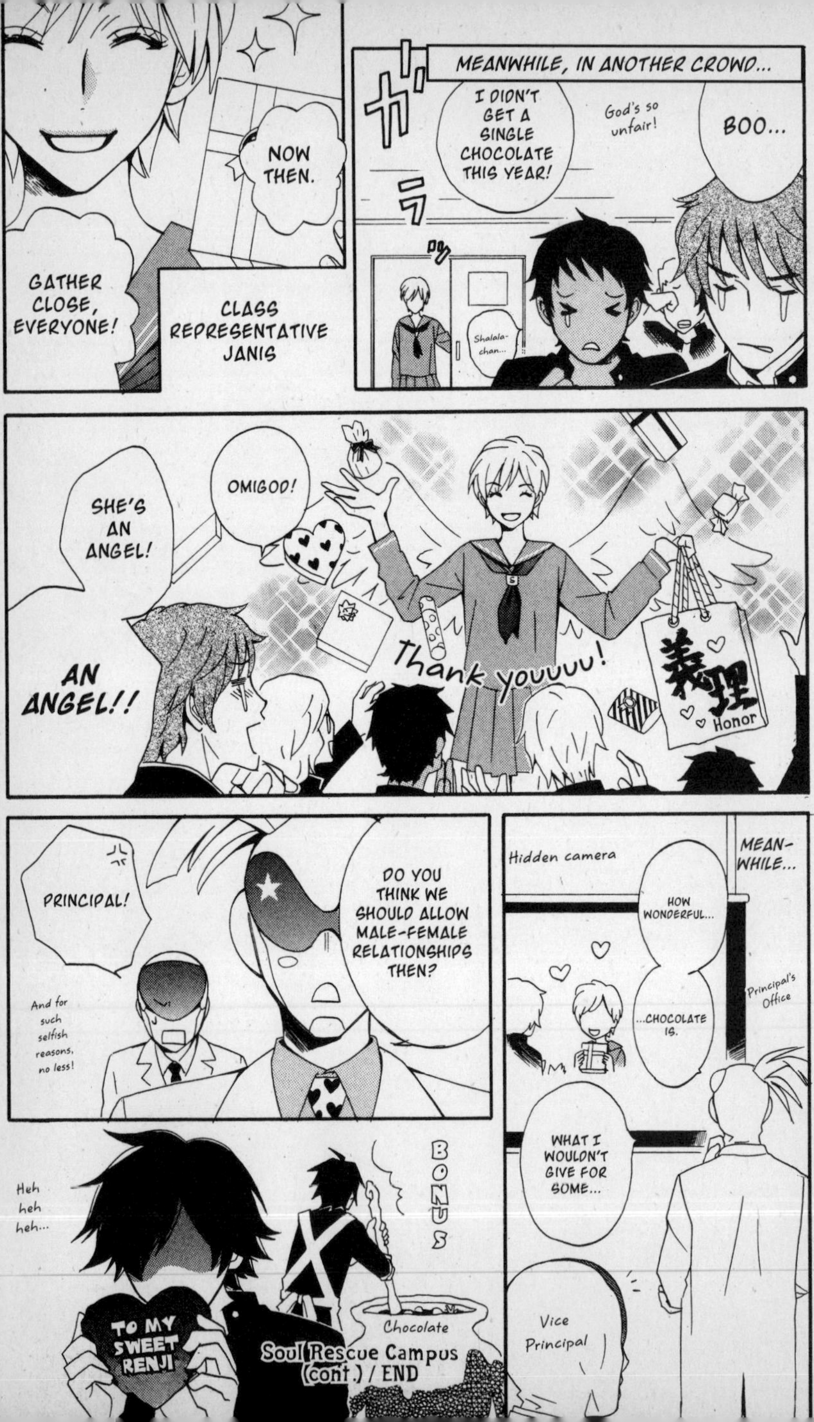
MEANWHILE, IN ANOTHER CROWD...
BOO...
God's so unfair!
I DIDN'T GET A SINGLE CHOCOLATE THIS YEAR!
ガラッ
Shalala-chan...
NOW THEN.
CLASS REPRESENTATIVE JANIS
GATHER CLOSE, EVERYONE!
義理
Honor
OMIGOD!
SHE'S AN ANGEL!
Thank youuuu!
AN ANGEL!!
MEAN-WHILE...
Hidden camera
HOW WONDERFUL...
...CHOCOLATE IS.
Principal's Office
WHAT I WOULDN'T GIVE FOR SOME...
Vice Principal
DO YOU THINK WE SHOULD ALLOW MALE-FEMALE RELATIONSHIPS THEN?
PRINCIPAL!
And for such selfish reasons, no less!
BONUS
Chocolate
Heh heh heh...
TO MY SWEET RENJI
Soul Rescue Campus (cont.) / END

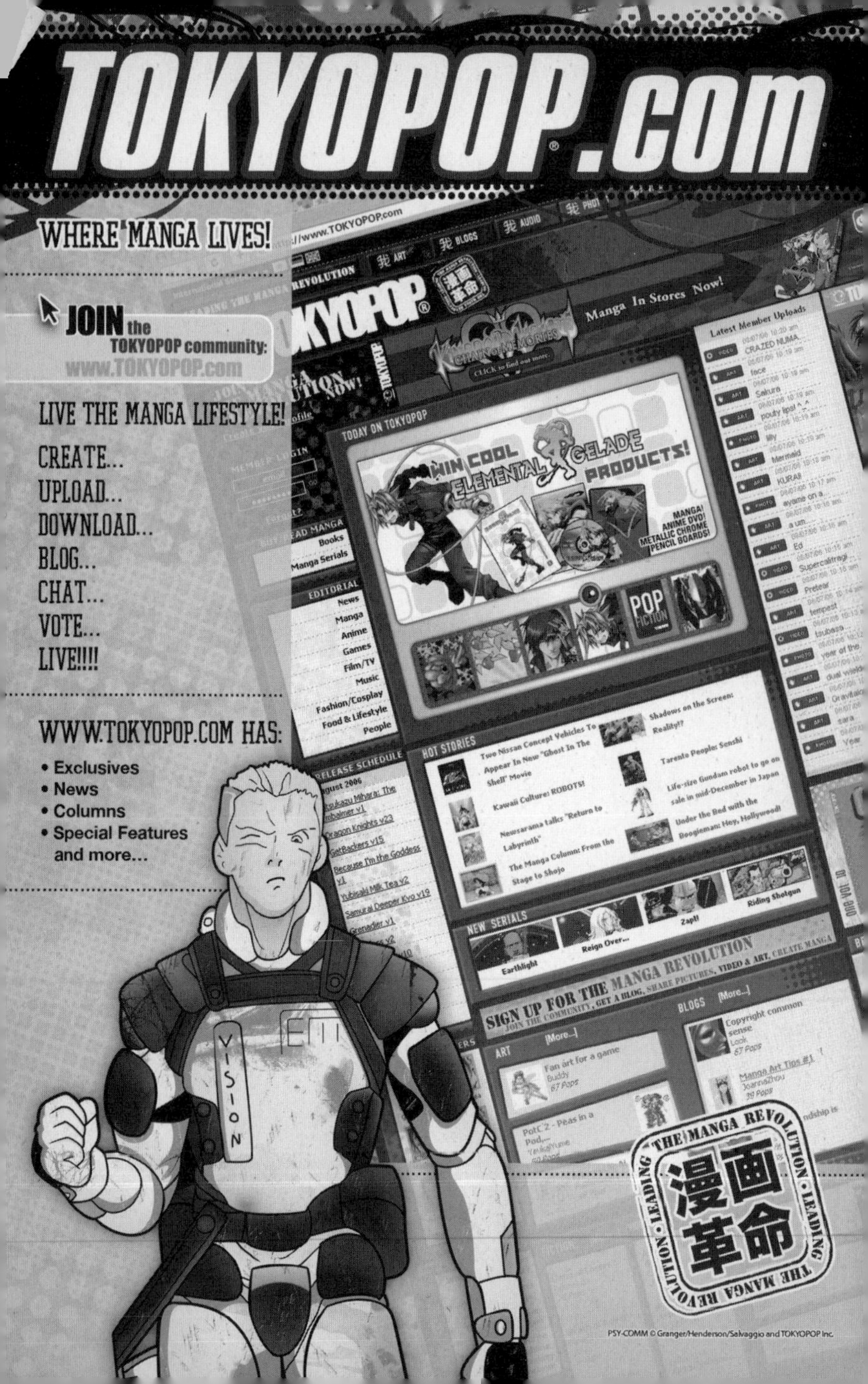
TOKYOPOP®.com
WHERE MANGA LIVES!
JOIN the TOKYOPOP community:
www.TOKYOPOP.com
LIVE THE MANGA LIFESTYLE!
CREATE...
UPLOAD...
DOWNLOAD...
BLOG...
CHAT...
VOTE...
LIVE!!!!
WWW.TOKYOPOP.COM HAS:
• Exclusives
• News
• Columns
• Special Features and more...
THE MANGA REVOLUTION · LEADING · 漫画革命
PSY-COMM © Granger/Henderson/Salvaggio and TOKYOPOP Inc.